THE DAILY
GOAL
SLAYERS
PLANNER

AS A PASTOR'S WIFE, MOTHER TO FOUR ACTIVE CHILDREN (ALL UNDER SIX YEARS OLD, MAY I ADD) AND THE BRAINS BEHIND TWO THRIVING BUSINESSES, MY NON-STOP DAYS MAKE HAVING A PLAN IN PLACE DAILY *A LIFESTYLE*. **WHILE I KNOW MANY OF YOU HAVE VARIOUS FAMILY DYNAMICS, PLANNING YOUR WEEKS AND DAYS ARE VITAL TO LIVING A SUCCESSFUL AND WELL-BALANCED LIFE.**

SCRIPTURE

Choose a scripture to meditate on for the entire day.

MOTIVATIONAL QUOTE

Do you need to be motivated in a certain area of your life? Search for a quote that will keep you going throughout the day.

ONE GOAL

Focus on one thing you want to accomplish today.

ONE FUN THING

All work and no play is no fun. Plan to do something exciting each day!

HEALTH + FITNESS

Move! Get your blood flowing with at least 30 minutes of exercise.

WATER INTAKE

The eight glasses of water each day rule is out. You should be drinking one-half of your body weight in ounces each day.

ONE POSITIVE

At the end of the day, document one positive thing that happened. Count your blessings!

TODAY I GAVE

Doesn't it feel good to be a cheerful giver? Record it here.

SIX THINGS TO DO EACH DAY

1. Make time as soon as you wake up each morning for prayer and meditation.

2. Take five minutes to plan your day and leave room for the unexpected.

3. Set aside time for self-care. Remember, your body is your temple.

4. Move! Get your blood flowing with at least 30 minutes of exercise.

5. Read for 30-60 minutes.

6. With your 'ideal life' at the forefront, create space and time for personal development.

DAILY
GOAL SLAYERS
PLANNER

SETTING YOURSELF UP FOR SUCCESS DAILY!

DATE

____ / ____ / ____

SCRIPTURE

MOTIVATIONAL QUOTE

ONE GOAL

ONE FUN THING

✱	IMPORTANT TIME	SCHEDULE	SLAYED?
	5:00AM		☐Y ☐N
	5:30AM		☐Y ☐N
	6:00AM		☐Y ☐N
	6:30AM		☐Y ☐N
	7:00AM		☐Y ☐N
	7:30AM		☐Y ☐N
	8:00AM		☐Y ☐N
	8:30AM		☐Y ☐N
	9:00AM		☐Y ☐N
	9:30AM		☐Y ☐N
	10:00AM		☐Y ☐N
	10:30AM		☐Y ☐N
	11:00AM		☐Y ☐N
	11:30AM		☐Y ☐N
	12:00PM		☐Y ☐N
	12:30PM		☐Y ☐N
	1:00PM		☐Y ☐N
	1:30PM		☐Y ☐N
	2:00PM		☐Y ☐N
	2:30PM		☐Y ☐N
	3:00PM		☐Y ☐N
	3:30PM		☐Y ☐N
	4:00PM		☐Y ☐N
	4:30PM		☐Y ☐N
	5:00PM		☐Y ☐N
	5:30PM		☐Y ☐N
	6:00PM		☐Y ☐N
	6:30PM		☐Y ☐N
	7:00PM		☐Y ☐N
	7:30PM		☐Y ☐N
	8:00PM		☐Y ☐N
	8:30PM		☐Y ☐N
	9:00PM		☐Y ☐N
	9:30PM		☐Y ☐N

HEALTH • FITNESS

WATER INTAKE

OZ OZ OZ OZ OZ

OZ OZ OZ OZ OZ

TAKE 5 MINUTES EACH MORNING TO PLAN YOUR DAY.

GET EIGHT HOURS OF SLEEP!

NOTE HIGH PRIORITY TASKS WITH A ✱

ANALYZE WHY A TASK WAS NOT COMPLETED, THEN MOVE TO NEXT DAY.

ONE POSITIVE

TODAY I GAVE

DAILY
GOAL SLAYERS
PLANNER

SETTING YOURSELF UP FOR SUCCESS DAILY!

DATE

_____/_____/_____

SCRIPTURE

MOTIVATIONAL QUOTE

ONE GOAL

ONE FUN THING

HEALTH • FITNESS

WATER INTAKE

OZ OZ OZ OZ OZ
OZ OZ OZ OZ OZ

✱	IMPORTANT TIME	SCHEDULE	SLAYED?
	5:00AM		☐Y ☐N
	5:30AM		☐Y ☐N
	6:00AM		☐Y ☐N
	6:30AM		☐Y ☐N
	7:00AM		☐Y ☐N
	7:30AM		☐Y ☐N
	8:00AM		☐Y ☐N
	8:30AM		☐Y ☐N
	9:00AM		☐Y ☐N
	9:30AM		☐Y ☐N
	10:00AM		☐Y ☐N
	10:30AM		☐Y ☐N
	11:00AM		☐Y ☐N
	11:30AM		☐Y ☐N
	12:00PM		☐Y ☐N
	12:30PM		☐Y ☐N
	1:00PM		☐Y ☐N
	1:30PM		☐Y ☐N
	2:00PM		☐Y ☐N
	2:30PM		☐Y ☐N
	3:00PM		☐Y ☐N
	3:30PM		☐Y ☐N
	4:00PM		☐Y ☐N
	4:30PM		☐Y ☐N
	5:00PM		☐Y ☐N
	5:30PM		☐Y ☐N
	6:00PM		☐Y ☐N
	6:30PM		☐Y ☐N
	7:00PM		☐Y ☐N
	7:30PM		☐Y ☐N
	8:00PM		☐Y ☐N
	8:30PM		☐Y ☐N
	9:00PM		☐Y ☐N
	9:30PM		☐Y ☐N

TAKE 5 MINUTES EACH MORNING TO PLAN YOUR DAY.

GET EIGHT HOURS OF SLEEP!

NOTE HIGH PRIORITY TASKS WITH A ✱

ANALYZE WHY A TASK WAS NOT COMPLETED, THEN MOVE TO NEXT DAY.

ONE POSITIVE

TODAY I GAVE

DAILY
GOAL SLAYERS
PLANNER

SETTING YOURSELF UP FOR SUCCESS DAILY!

DATE

_____ / _____ / _____

SCRIPTURE

MOTIVATIONAL QUOTE

ONE GOAL

ONE FUN THING

*	IMPORTANT TIME	SCHEDULE	SLAYED?
	5:00AM		☐Y ☐N
	5:30AM		☐Y ☐N
	6:00AM		☐Y ☐N
	6:30AM		☐Y ☐N
	7:00AM		☐Y ☐N
	7:30AM		☐Y ☐N
	8:00AM		☐Y ☐N
	8:30AM		☐Y ☐N
	9:00AM		☐Y ☐N
	9:30AM		☐Y ☐N
	10:00AM		☐Y ☐N
	10:30AM		☐Y ☐N
	11:00AM		☐Y ☐N
	11:30AM		☐Y ☐N
	12:00PM		☐Y ☐N
	12:30PM		☐Y ☐N
	1:00PM		☐Y ☐N
	1:30PM		☐Y ☐N
	2:00PM		☐Y ☐N
	2:30PM		☐Y ☐N
	3:00PM		☐Y ☐N
	3:30PM		☐Y ☐N
	4:00PM		☐Y ☐N
	4:30PM		☐Y ☐N
	5:00PM		☐Y ☐N
	5:30PM		☐Y ☐N
	6:00PM		☐Y ☐N
	6:30PM		☐Y ☐N
	7:00PM		☐Y ☐N
	7:30PM		☐Y ☐N
	8:00PM		☐Y ☐N
	8:30PM		☐Y ☐N
	9:00PM		☐Y ☐N
	9:30PM		☐Y ☐N

HEALTH · FITNESS

WATER INTAKE

OZ. OZ. OZ. OZ. OZ.
OZ. OZ. OZ. OZ. OZ.

TAKE 5 MINUTES EACH MORNING TO PLAN YOUR DAY.

GET EIGHT HOURS OF SLEEP!

NOTE HIGH PRIORITY TASKS WITH A *

ANALYZE WHY A TASK WAS NOT COMPLETED, THEN MOVE TO NEXT DAY.

ONE POSITIVE

TODAY I GAVE

DAILY
GOAL SLAYERS
PLANNER

SETTING YOURSELF UP FOR SUCCESS DAILY!

DATE
____ / ____ / ____

SCRIPTURE

MOTIVATIONAL QUOTE

ONE GOAL

ONE FUN THING

HEALTH · FITNESS

WATER INTAKE

OZ. OZ. OZ. OZ. OZ.
OZ. OZ. OZ. OZ. OZ.

*	IMPORTANT TIME	SCHEDULE	SLAYED?
	5:00AM		☐Y ☐N
	5:30AM		☐Y ☐N
	6:00AM		☐Y ☐N
	6:30AM		☐Y ☐N
	7:00AM		☐Y ☐N
	7:30AM		☐Y ☐N
	8:00AM		☐Y ☐N
	8:30AM		☐Y ☐N
	9:00AM		☐Y ☐N
	9:30AM		☐Y ☐N
	10:00AM		☐Y ☐N
	10:30AM		☐Y ☐N
	11:00AM		☐Y ☐N
	11:30AM		☐Y ☐N
	12:00PM		☐Y ☐N
	12:30PM		☐Y ☐N
	1:00PM		☐Y ☐N
	1:30PM		☐Y ☐N
	2:00PM		☐Y ☐N
	2:30PM		☐Y ☐N
	3:00PM		☐Y ☐N
	3:30PM		☐Y ☐N
	4:00PM		☐Y ☐N
	4:30PM		☐Y ☐N
	5:00PM		☐Y ☐N
	5:30PM		☐Y ☐N
	6:00PM		☐Y ☐N
	6:30PM		☐Y ☐N
	7:00PM		☐Y ☐N
	7:30PM		☐Y ☐N
	8:00PM		☐Y ☐N
	8:30PM		☐Y ☐N
	9:00PM		☐Y ☐N
	9:30PM		☐Y ☐N

TAKE 5 MINUTES EACH MORNING TO PLAN YOUR DAY.

GET EIGHT HOURS OF SLEEP!

NOTE HIGH PRIORITY TASKS WITH A *

ANALYZE WHY A TASK WAS NOT COMPLETED, THEN MOVE TO NEXT DAY.

ONE POSITIVE

TODAY I GAVE

DAILY
GOAL SLAYERS
PLANNER

SETTING YOURSELF UP FOR SUCCESS DAILY!

DATE

____ / ____ / ____

SCRIPTURE

MOTIVATIONAL QUOTE

ONE GOAL

ONE FUN THING

HEALTH + FITNESS

WATER INTAKE

OZ. OZ. OZ. OZ. OZ.

OZ. OZ. OZ. OZ. OZ.

*	IMPORTANT TIME	SCHEDULE	SLAYED?
	5:00AM		☐Y ☐N
	5:30AM		☐Y ☐N
	6:00AM		☐Y ☐N
	6:30AM		☐Y ☐N
	7:00AM		☐Y ☐N
	7:30AM		☐Y ☐N
	8:00AM		☐Y ☐N
	8:30AM		☐Y ☐N
	9:00AM		☐Y ☐N
	9:30AM		☐Y ☐N
	10:00AM		☐Y ☐N
	10:30AM		☐Y ☐N
	11:00AM		☐Y ☐N
	11:30AM		☐Y ☐N
	12:00PM		☐Y ☐N
	12:30PM		☐Y ☐N
	1:00PM		☐Y ☐N
	1:30PM		☐Y ☐N
	2:00PM		☐Y ☐N
	2:30PM		☐Y ☐N
	3:00PM		☐Y ☐N
	3:30PM		☐Y ☐N
	4:00PM		☐Y ☐N
	4:30PM		☐Y ☐N
	5:00PM		☐Y ☐N
	5:30PM		☐Y ☐N
	6:00PM		☐Y ☐N
	6:30PM		☐Y ☐N
	7:00PM		☐Y ☐N
	7:30PM		☐Y ☐N
	8:00PM		☐Y ☐N
	8:30PM		☐Y ☐N
	9:00PM		☐Y ☐N
	9:30PM		☐Y ☐N

TAKE 5 MINUTES EACH MORNING TO PLAN YOUR DAY.

GET EIGHT HOURS OF SLEEP!

NOTE HIGH PRIORITY TASKS WITH A *

ANALYZE WHY A TASK WAS NOT COMPLETED, THEN MOVE TO NEXT DAY.

ONE POSITIVE

TODAY I GAVE

DAILY
GOAL SLAYERS
PLANNER

SETTING YOURSELF UP FOR SUCCESS DAILY!

DATE

____ / ____ / ____

SCRIPTURE

MOTIVATIONAL QUOTE

ONE GOAL

ONE FUN THING

HEALTH • FITNESS

WATER INTAKE

*	IMPORTANT TIME	SCHEDULE	SLAYED?
	5:00AM		☐Y ☐N
	5:30AM		☐Y ☐N
	6:00AM		☐Y ☐N
	6:30AM		☐Y ☐N
	7:00AM		☐Y ☐N
	7:30AM		☐Y ☐N
	8:00AM		☐Y ☐N
	8:30AM		☐Y ☐N
	9:00AM		☐Y ☐N
	9:30AM		☐Y ☐N
	10:00AM		☐Y ☐N
	10:30AM		☐Y ☐N
	11:00AM		☐Y ☐N
	11:30AM		☐Y ☐N
	12:00PM		☐Y ☐N
	12:30PM		☐Y ☐N
	1:00PM		☐Y ☐N
	1:30PM		☐Y ☐N
	2:00PM		☐Y ☐N
	2:30PM		☐Y ☐N
	3:00PM		☐Y ☐N
	3:30PM		☐Y ☐N
	4:00PM		☐Y ☐N
	4:30PM		☐Y ☐N
	5:00PM		☐Y ☐N
	5:30PM		☐Y ☐N
	6:00PM		☐Y ☐N
	6:30PM		☐Y ☐N
	7:00PM		☐Y ☐N
	7:30PM		☐Y ☐N
	8:00PM		☐Y ☐N
	8:30PM		☐Y ☐N
	9:00PM		☐Y ☐N
	9:30PM		☐Y ☐N

TAKE 5 MINUTES EACH MORNING TO PLAN YOUR DAY.

GET EIGHT HOURS OF SLEEP!

NOTE HIGH PRIORITY TASKS WITH A *

ANALYZE WHY A TASK WAS NOT COMPLETED, THEN MOVE TO NEXT DAY.

ONE POSITIVE

TODAY I GAVE

DAILY
GOAL SLAYERS
PLANNER

SETTING YOURSELF UP FOR SUCCESS DAILY!

DATE

____ / ____ / ____

SCRIPTURE

MOTIVATIONAL QUOTE

ONE GOAL

ONE FUN THING

*	IMPORTANT TIME	SCHEDULE	SLAYED?
	5:00AM		☐Y ☐N
	5:30AM		☐Y ☐N
	6:00AM		☐Y ☐N
	6:30AM		☐Y ☐N
	7:00AM		☐Y ☐N
	7:30AM		☐Y ☐N
	8:00AM		☐Y ☐N
	8:30AM		☐Y ☐N
	9:00AM		☐Y ☐N
	9:30AM		☐Y ☐N
	10:00AM		☐Y ☐N
	10:30AM		☐Y ☐N
	11:00AM		☐Y ☐N
	11:30AM		☐Y ☐N
	12:00PM		☐Y ☐N
	12:30PM		☐Y ☐N
	1:00PM		☐Y ☐N
	1:30PM		☐Y ☐N
	2:00PM		☐Y ☐N
	2:30PM		☐Y ☐N
	3:00PM		☐Y ☐N
	3:30PM		☐Y ☐N
	4:00PM		☐Y ☐N
	4:30PM		☐Y ☐N
	5:00PM		☐Y ☐N
	5:30PM		☐Y ☐N
	6:00PM		☐Y ☐N
	6:30PM		☐Y ☐N
	7:00PM		☐Y ☐N
	7:30PM		☐Y ☐N
	8:00PM		☐Y ☐N
	8:30PM		☐Y ☐N
	9:00PM		☐Y ☐N
	9:30PM		☐Y ☐N

HEALTH • FITNESS

WATER INTAKE

OZ. OZ. OZ. OZ. OZ.

OZ. OZ. OZ. OZ. OZ.

TAKE 5 MINUTES EACH MORNING TO PLAN YOUR DAY.

GET EIGHT HOURS OF SLEEP!

NOTE HIGH PRIORITY TASKS WITH A *

ANALYZE WHY A TASK WAS NOT COMPLETED. THEN MOVE TO NEXT DAY.

ONE POSITIVE

TODAY I GAVE

DAILY
GOAL SLAYERS
PLANNER

SETTING YOURSELF UP FOR SUCCESS DAILY!

DATE

_____ / _____ / _____

SCRIPTURE

MOTIVATIONAL QUOTE

ONE GOAL

ONE FUN THING

HEALTH + FITNESS

WATER INTAKE

OZ OZ OZ OZ OZ

OZ OZ OZ OZ OZ

*	IMPORTANT TIME	SCHEDULE	SLAYED?
	5:00AM		☐Y ☐N
	5:30AM		☐Y ☐N
	6:00AM		☐Y ☐N
	6:30AM		☐Y ☐N
	7:00AM		☐Y ☐N
	7:30AM		☐Y ☐N
	8:00AM		☐Y ☐N
	8:30AM		☐Y ☐N
	9:00AM		☐Y ☐N
	9:30AM		☐Y ☐N
	10:00AM		☐Y ☐N
	10:30AM		☐Y ☐N
	11:00AM		☐Y ☐N
	11:30AM		☐Y ☐N
	12:00PM		☐Y ☐N
	12:30PM		☐Y ☐N
	1:00PM		☐Y ☐N
	1:30PM		☐Y ☐N
	2:00PM		☐Y ☐N
	2:30PM		☐Y ☐N
	3:00PM		☐Y ☐N
	3:30PM		☐Y ☐N
	4:00PM		☐Y ☐N
	4:30PM		☐Y ☐N
	5:00PM		☐Y ☐N
	5:30PM		☐Y ☐N
	6:00PM		☐Y ☐N
	6:30PM		☐Y ☐N
	7:00PM		☐Y ☐N
	7:30PM		☐Y ☐N
	8:00PM		☐Y ☐N
	8:30PM		☐Y ☐N
	9:00PM		☐Y ☐N
	9:30PM		☐Y ☐N

TAKE 5 MINUTES EACH MORNING TO PLAN YOUR DAY.

GET EIGHT HOURS OF SLEEP!

NOTE HIGH PRIORITY TASKS WITH A *

ANALYZE WHY A TASK WAS NOT COMPLETED, THEN MOVE TO NEXT DAY.

ONE POSITIVE

TODAY I GAVE

DAILY
GOAL SLAYERS
PLANNER

SETTING YOURSELF UP FOR SUCCESS DAILY!

DATE

____ / ____ / ____

SCRIPTURE

MOTIVATIONAL QUOTE

ONE GOAL

ONE FUN THING

HEALTH • FITNESS

WATER INTAKE

✱	IMPORTANT TIME	SCHEDULE	SLAYED?
	5:00AM		☐Y ☐N
	5:30AM		☐Y ☐N
	6:00AM		☐Y ☐N
	6:30AM		☐Y ☐N
	7:00AM		☐Y ☐N
	7:30AM		☐Y ☐N
	8:00AM		☐Y ☐N
	8:30AM		☐Y ☐N
	9:00AM		☐Y ☐N
	9:30AM		☐Y ☐N
	10:00AM		☐Y ☐N
	10:30AM		☐Y ☐N
	11:00AM		☐Y ☐N
	11:30AM		☐Y ☐N
	12:00PM		☐Y ☐N
	12:30PM		☐Y ☐N
	1:00PM		☐Y ☐N
	1:30PM		☐Y ☐N
	2:00PM		☐Y ☐N
	2:30PM		☐Y ☐N
	3:00PM		☐Y ☐N
	3:30PM		☐Y ☐N
	4:00PM		☐Y ☐N
	4:30PM		☐Y ☐N
	5:00PM		☐Y ☐N
	5:30PM		☐Y ☐N
	6:00PM		☐Y ☐N
	6:30PM		☐Y ☐N
	7:00PM		☐Y ☐N
	7:30PM		☐Y ☐N
	8:00PM		☐Y ☐N
	8:30PM		☐Y ☐N
	9:00PM		☐Y ☐N
	9:30PM		☐Y ☐N

TAKE 5 MINUTES EACH MORNING TO PLAN YOUR DAY.

GET EIGHT HOURS OF SLEEP!

NOTE HIGH PRIORITY TASKS WITH A ✱

ANALYZE WHY A TASK WAS NOT COMPLETED, THEN MOVE TO NEXT DAY.

ONE POSITIVE

TODAY I GAVE

DAILY
GOAL SLAYERS
PLANNER

SETTING YOURSELF UP FOR SUCCESS DAILY!

DATE

_____ / _____ / _____

SCRIPTURE

MOTIVATIONAL QUOTE

ONE GOAL

ONE FUN THING

HEALTH • FITNESS

WATER INTAKE

*	IMPORTANT TIME	SCHEDULE	SLAYED?
	5:00AM		☐Y ☐N
	5:30AM		☐Y ☐N
	6:00AM		☐Y ☐N
	6:30AM		☐Y ☐N
	7:00AM		☐Y ☐N
	7:30AM		☐Y ☐N
	8:00AM		☐Y ☐N
	8:30AM		☐Y ☐N
	9:00AM		☐Y ☐N
	9:30AM		☐Y ☐N
	10:00AM		☐Y ☐N
	10:30AM		☐Y ☐N
	11:00AM		☐Y ☐N
	11:30AM		☐Y ☐N
	12:00PM		☐Y ☐N
	12:30PM		☐Y ☐N
	1:00PM		☐Y ☐N
	1:30PM		☐Y ☐N
	2:00PM		☐Y ☐N
	2:30PM		☐Y ☐N
	3:00PM		☐Y ☐N
	3:30PM		☐Y ☐N
	4:00PM		☐Y ☐N
	4:30PM		☐Y ☐N
	5:00PM		☐Y ☐N
	5:30PM		☐Y ☐N
	6:00PM		☐Y ☐N
	6:30PM		☐Y ☐N
	7:00PM		☐Y ☐N
	7:30PM		☐Y ☐N
	8:00PM		☐Y ☐N
	8:30PM		☐Y ☐N
	9:00PM		☐Y ☐N
	9:30PM		☐Y ☐N

TAKE 5 MINUTES EACH MORNING TO PLAN YOUR DAY.

GET EIGHT HOURS OF SLEEP!

NOTE HIGH PRIORITY TASKS WITH A *

ANALYZE WHY A TASK WAS NOT COMPLETED, THEN MOVE TO NEXT DAY.

ONE POSITIVE

TODAY I GAVE

DAILY
GOAL SLAYERS
PLANNER

SETTING YOURSELF UP FOR SUCCESS DAILY!

DATE

_____ / _____ / _____

SCRIPTURE

MOTIVATIONAL QUOTE

ONE GOAL

ONE FUN THING

✱	IMPORTANT TIME	SCHEDULE	SLAYED?
	5:00AM		☐Y ☐N
	5:30AM		☐Y ☐N
	6:00AM		☐Y ☐N
	6:30AM		☐Y ☐N
	7:00AM		☐Y ☐N
	7:30AM		☐Y ☐N
	8:00AM		☐Y ☐N
	8:30AM		☐Y ☐N
	9:00AM		☐Y ☐N
	9:30AM		☐Y ☐N
	10:00AM		☐Y ☐N
	10:30AM		☐Y ☐N
	11:00AM		☐Y ☐N
	11:30AM		☐Y ☐N
	12:00PM		☐Y ☐N
	12:30PM		☐Y ☐N
	1:00PM		☐Y ☐N
	1:30PM		☐Y ☐N
	2:00PM		☐Y ☐N
	2:30PM		☐Y ☐N
	3:00PM		☐Y ☐N
	3:30PM		☐Y ☐N
	4:00PM		☐Y ☐N
	4:30PM		☐Y ☐N
	5:00PM		☐Y ☐N
	5:30PM		☐Y ☐N
	6:00PM		☐Y ☐N
	6:30PM		☐Y ☐N
	7:00PM		☐Y ☐N
	7:30PM		☐Y ☐N
	8:00PM		☐Y ☐N
	8:30PM		☐Y ☐N
	9:00PM		☐Y ☐N
	9:30PM		☐Y ☐N

HEALTH • FITNESS

WATER INTAKE

OZ. OZ. OZ. OZ. OZ.
OZ. OZ. OZ. OZ. OZ.

TAKE 5 MINUTES EACH MORNING TO PLAN YOUR DAY.

GET EIGHT HOURS OF SLEEP!

NOTE HIGH PRIORITY TASKS WITH A ✱

ANALYZE WHY A TASK WAS NOT COMPLETED, THEN MOVE TO NEXT DAY.

ONE POSITIVE

TODAY I GAVE

DAILY
GOAL SLAYERS
PLANNER

SETTING YOURSELF UP FOR SUCCESS DAILY!

DATE

_____ / _____ / _____

SCRIPTURE

MOTIVATIONAL QUOTE

ONE GOAL

ONE FUN THING

*	IMPORTANT TIME	SCHEDULE	SLAYED?
	5:00AM		☐Y ☐N
	5:30AM		☐Y ☐N
	6:00AM		☐Y ☐N
	6:30AM		☐Y ☐N
	7:00AM		☐Y ☐N
	7:30AM		☐Y ☐N
	8:00AM		☐Y ☐N
	8:30AM		☐Y ☐N
	9:00AM		☐Y ☐N
	9:30AM		☐Y ☐N
	10:00AM		☐Y ☐N
	10:30AM		☐Y ☐N
	11:00AM		☐Y ☐N
	11:30AM		☐Y ☐N
	12:00PM		☐Y ☐N
	12:30PM		☐Y ☐N
	1:00PM		☐Y ☐N
	1:30PM		☐Y ☐N
	2:00PM		☐Y ☐N
	2:30PM		☐Y ☐N
	3:00PM		☐Y ☐N
	3:30PM		☐Y ☐N
	4:00PM		☐Y ☐N
	4:30PM		☐Y ☐N
	5:00PM		☐Y ☐N
	5:30PM		☐Y ☐N
	6:00PM		☐Y ☐N
	6:30PM		☐Y ☐N
	7:00PM		☐Y ☐N
	7:30PM		☐Y ☐N
	8:00PM		☐Y ☐N
	8:30PM		☐Y ☐N
	9:00PM		☐Y ☐N
	9:30PM		☐Y ☐N

HEALTH + FITNESS

WATER INTAKE

OZ. OZ. OZ. OZ. OZ.

OZ. OZ. OZ. OZ. OZ.

TAKE 5 MINUTES EACH MORNING TO PLAN YOUR DAY.

GET EIGHT HOURS OF SLEEP!

NOTE HIGH PRIORITY TASKS WITH A *

ANALYZE WHY A TASK WAS NOT COMPLETED, THEN MOVE TO NEXT DAY.

ONE POSITIVE

TODAY I GAVE

DAILY
GOAL SLAYERS
PLANNER

SETTING YOURSELF UP FOR SUCCESS DAILY!

DATE
_____ / _____ / _____

SCRIPTURE

MOTIVATIONAL QUOTE

ONE GOAL

ONE FUN THING

HEALTH • FITNESS

WATER INTAKE

✱	IMPORTANT TIME	SCHEDULE	SLAYED?
	5:00AM		☐Y ☐N
	5:30AM		☐Y ☐N
	6:00AM		☐Y ☐N
	6:30AM		☐Y ☐N
	7:00AM		☐Y ☐N
	7:30AM		☐Y ☐N
	8:00AM		☐Y ☐N
	8:30AM		☐Y ☐N
	9:00AM		☐Y ☐N
	9:30AM		☐Y ☐N
	10:00AM		☐Y ☐N
	10:30AM		☐Y ☐N
	11:00AM		☐Y ☐N
	11:30AM		☐Y ☐N
	12:00PM		☐Y ☐N
	12:30PM		☐Y ☐N
	1:00PM		☐Y ☐N
	1:30PM		☐Y ☐N
	2:00PM		☐Y ☐N
	2:30PM		☐Y ☐N
	3:00PM		☐Y ☐N
	3:30PM		☐Y ☐N
	4:00PM		☐Y ☐N
	4:30PM		☐Y ☐N
	5:00PM		☐Y ☐N
	5:30PM		☐Y ☐N
	6:00PM		☐Y ☐N
	6:30PM		☐Y ☐N
	7:00PM		☐Y ☐N
	7:30PM		☐Y ☐N
	8:00PM		☐Y ☐N
	8:30PM		☐Y ☐N
	9:00PM		☐Y ☐N
	9:30PM		☐Y ☐N

TAKE 5 MINUTES EACH MORNING TO PLAN YOUR DAY.

GET EIGHT HOURS OF SLEEP!

NOTE HIGH PRIORITY TASKS WITH A ✱

ANALYZE WHY A TASK WAS NOT COMPLETED, THEN MOVE TO NEXT DAY.

ONE POSITIVE

TODAY I GAVE

DAILY
GOAL SLAYERS
PLANNER

SETTING YOURSELF UP FOR SUCCESS DAILY!

DATE

____/____/____

SCRIPTURE

MOTIVATIONAL QUOTE

ONE GOAL

ONE FUN THING

HEALTH • FITNESS

WATER INTAKE

*	IMPORTANT TIME	SCHEDULE	SLAYED?
	5:00AM		☐Y ☐N
	5:30AM		☐Y ☐N
	6:00AM		☐Y ☐N
	6:30AM		☐Y ☐N
	7:00AM		☐Y ☐N
	7:30AM		☐Y ☐N
	8:00AM		☐Y ☐N
	8:30AM		☐Y ☐N
	9:00AM		☐Y ☐N
	9:30AM		☐Y ☐N
	10:00AM		☐Y ☐N
	10:30AM		☐Y ☐N
	11:00AM		☐Y ☐N
	11:30AM		☐Y ☐N
	12:00PM		☐Y ☐N
	12:30PM		☐Y ☐N
	1:00PM		☐Y ☐N
	1:30PM		☐Y ☐N
	2:00PM		☐Y ☐N
	2:30PM		☐Y ☐N
	3:00PM		☐Y ☐N
	3:30PM		☐Y ☐N
	4:00PM		☐Y ☐N
	4:30PM		☐Y ☐N
	5:00PM		☐Y ☐N
	5:30PM		☐Y ☐N
	6:00PM		☐Y ☐N
	6:30PM		☐Y ☐N
	7:00PM		☐Y ☐N
	7:30PM		☐Y ☐N
	8:00PM		☐Y ☐N
	8:30PM		☐Y ☐N
	9:00PM		☐Y ☐N
	9:30PM		☐Y ☐N

TAKE 5 MINUTES EACH MORNING TO PLAN YOUR DAY.

GET EIGHT HOURS OF SLEEP!

NOTE HIGH PRIORITY TASKS WITH A *

ANALYZE WHY A TASK WAS NOT COMPLETED, THEN MOVE TO NEXT DAY.

ONE POSITIVE

TODAY I GAVE

DAILY
GOAL SLAYERS
PLANNER

SETTING YOURSELF UP FOR SUCCESS DAILY!

DATE

____ / ____ / _____

SCRIPTURE

MOTIVATIONAL QUOTE

ONE GOAL

ONE FUN THING

∗	IMPORTANT TIME	SCHEDULE	SLAYED?
	5:00AM		☐Y ☐N
	5:30AM		☐Y ☐N
	6:00AM		☐Y ☐N
	6:30AM		☐Y ☐N
	7:00AM		☐Y ☐N
	7:30AM		☐Y ☐N
	8:00AM		☐Y ☐N
	8:30AM		☐Y ☐N
	9:00AM		☐Y ☐N
	9:30AM		☐Y ☐N
	10:00AM		☐Y ☐N
	10:30AM		☐Y ☐N
	11:00AM		☐Y ☐N
	11:30AM		☐Y ☐N
	12:00PM		☐Y ☐N
	12:30PM		☐Y ☐N
	1:00PM		☐Y ☐N
	1:30PM		☐Y ☐N
	2:00PM		☐Y ☐N
	2:30PM		☐Y ☐N
	3:00PM		☐Y ☐N
	3:30PM		☐Y ☐N
	4:00PM		☐Y ☐N
	4:30PM		☐Y ☐N
	5:00PM		☐Y ☐N
	5:30PM		☐Y ☐N
	6:00PM		☐Y ☐N
	6:30PM		☐Y ☐N
	7:00PM		☐Y ☐N
	7:30PM		☐Y ☐N
	8:00PM		☐Y ☐N
	8:30PM		☐Y ☐N
	9:00PM		☐Y ☐N
	9:30PM		☐Y ☐N

HEALTH ∗ FITNESS

WATER INTAKE

OZ. OZ. OZ. OZ. OZ.

OZ. OZ. OZ. OZ. OZ.

TAKE 5 MINUTES EACH MORNING TO PLAN YOUR DAY.

GET EIGHT HOURS OF SLEEP!

NOTE HIGH PRIORITY TASKS WITH A ∗

ANALYZE WHY A TASK WAS NOT COMPLETED. THEN MOVE TO NEXT DAY.

ONE POSITIVE

TODAY I GAVE

DAILY
GOAL SLAYERS
PLANNER

SETTING YOURSELF UP FOR SUCCESS DAILY!

DATE

_____ / _____ / _____

SCRIPTURE

MOTIVATIONAL QUOTE

ONE GOAL

ONE FUN THING

HEALTH • FITNESS

WATER INTAKE

OZ. OZ. OZ. OZ. OZ.

OZ. OZ. OZ. OZ. OZ.

✱	IMPORTANT TIME	SCHEDULE	SLAYED?
	5:00AM		☐Y ☐N
	5:30AM		☐Y ☐N
	6:00AM		☐Y ☐N
	6:30AM		☐Y ☐N
	7:00AM		☐Y ☐N
	7:30AM		☐Y ☐N
	8:00AM		☐Y ☐N
	8:30AM		☐Y ☐N
	9:00AM		☐Y ☐N
	9:30AM		☐Y ☐N
	10:00AM		☐Y ☐N
	10:30AM		☐Y ☐N
	11:00AM		☐Y ☐N
	11:30AM		☐Y ☐N
	12:00PM		☐Y ☐N
	12:30PM		☐Y ☐N
	1:00PM		☐Y ☐N
	1:30PM		☐Y ☐N
	2:00PM		☐Y ☐N
	2:30PM		☐Y ☐N
	3:00PM		☐Y ☐N
	3:30PM		☐Y ☐N
	4:00PM		☐Y ☐N
	4:30PM		☐Y ☐N
	5:00PM		☐Y ☐N
	5:30PM		☐Y ☐N
	6:00PM		☐Y ☐N
	6:30PM		☐Y ☐N
	7:00PM		☐Y ☐N
	7:30PM		☐Y ☐N
	8:00PM		☐Y ☐N
	8:30PM		☐Y ☐N
	9:00PM		☐Y ☐N
	9:30PM		☐Y ☐N

TAKE 5 MINUTES EACH MORNING TO PLAN YOUR DAY.

GET EIGHT HOURS OF SLEEP!

NOTE HIGH PRIORITY TASKS WITH A ✱

ANALYZE WHY A TASK WAS NOT COMPLETED, THEN MOVE TO NEXT DAY.

ONE POSITIVE

TODAY I GAVE

DAILY
GOAL SLAYERS
PLANNER

SETTING YOURSELF UP FOR SUCCESS DAILY!

DATE

____ / ____ / ____

SCRIPTURE

MOTIVATIONAL QUOTE

ONE GOAL

ONE FUN THING

HEALTH • FITNESS

✱	IMPORTANT TIME	SCHEDULE	SLAYED?
	5:00AM		☐Y ☐N
	5:30AM		☐Y ☐N
	6:00AM		☐Y ☐N
	6:30AM		☐Y ☐N
	7:00AM		☐Y ☐N
	7:30AM		☐Y ☐N
	8:00AM		☐Y ☐N
	8:30AM		☐Y ☐N
	9:00AM		☐Y ☐N
	9:30AM		☐Y ☐N
	10:00AM		☐Y ☐N
	10:30AM		☐Y ☐N
	11:00AM		☐Y ☐N
	11:30AM		☐Y ☐N
	12:00PM		☐Y ☐N
	12:30PM		☐Y ☐N
	1:00PM		☐Y ☐N
	1:30PM		☐Y ☐N
	2:00PM		☐Y ☐N
	2:30PM		☐Y ☐N
	3:00PM		☐Y ☐N
	3:30PM		☐Y ☐N
	4:00PM		☐Y ☐N
	4:30PM		☐Y ☐N
	5:00PM		☐Y ☐N
	5:30PM		☐Y ☐N
	6:00PM		☐Y ☐N
	6:30PM		☐Y ☐N
	7:00PM		☐Y ☐N
	7:30PM		☐Y ☐N
	8:00PM		☐Y ☐N
	8:30PM		☐Y ☐N
	9:00PM		☐Y ☐N
	9:30PM		☐Y ☐N

WATER INTAKE

OZ OZ OZ OZ OZ

OZ OZ OZ OZ OZ

TAKE 5 MINUTES EACH MORNING TO PLAN YOUR DAY.

GET EIGHT HOURS OF SLEEP!

NOTE HIGH PRIORITY TASKS WITH A ✱

ANALYZE WHY A TASK WAS NOT COMPLETED, THEN MOVE TO NEXT DAY.

ONE POSITIVE

TODAY I GAVE

DAILY
GOAL SLAYERS
PLANNER

SETTING YOURSELF UP FOR SUCCESS DAILY!

DATE

_____ / _____ / _____

SCRIPTURE

MOTIVATIONAL QUOTE

ONE GOAL

ONE FUN THING

HEALTH + FITNESS

WATER INTAKE

OZ OZ OZ OZ OZ

OZ OZ OZ OZ OZ

*	IMPORTANT TIME	SCHEDULE	SLAYED?
	5:00AM		☐Y ☐N
	5:30AM		☐Y ☐N
	6:00AM		☐Y ☐N
	6:30AM		☐Y ☐N
	7:00AM		☐Y ☐N
	7:30AM		☐Y ☐N
	8:00AM		☐Y ☐N
	8:30AM		☐Y ☐N
	9:00AM		☐Y ☐N
	9:30AM		☐Y ☐N
	10:00AM		☐Y ☐N
	10:30AM		☐Y ☐N
	11:00AM		☐Y ☐N
	11:30AM		☐Y ☐N
	12:00PM		☐Y ☐N
	12:30PM		☐Y ☐N
	1:00PM		☐Y ☐N
	1:30PM		☐Y ☐N
	2:00PM		☐Y ☐N
	2:30PM		☐Y ☐N
	3:00PM		☐Y ☐N
	3:30PM		☐Y ☐N
	4:00PM		☐Y ☐N
	4:30PM		☐Y ☐N
	5:00PM		☐Y ☐N
	5:30PM		☐Y ☐N
	6:00PM		☐Y ☐N
	6:30PM		☐Y ☐N
	7:00PM		☐Y ☐N
	7:30PM		☐Y ☐N
	8:00PM		☐Y ☐N
	8:30PM		☐Y ☐N
	9:00PM		☐Y ☐N
	9:30PM		☐Y ☐N

TAKE 5 MINUTES EACH MORNING TO PLAN YOUR DAY.

GET EIGHT HOURS OF SLEEP!

NOTE HIGH PRIORITY TASKS WITH A *

ANALYZE WHY A TASK WAS NOT COMPLETED, THEN MOVE TO NEXT DAY.

ONE POSITIVE

TODAY I GAVE

DAILY
GOAL SLAYERS
PLANNER

SETTING YOURSELF UP FOR SUCCESS DAILY!

DATE

_____ / _____ / _____

SCRIPTURE

MOTIVATIONAL QUOTE

ONE GOAL

ONE FUN THING

HEALTH + FITNESS

WATER INTAKE

*	IMPORTANT TIME	SCHEDULE	SLAYED?
	5:00AM		☐Y ☐N
	5:30AM		☐Y ☐N
	6:00AM		☐Y ☐N
	6:30AM		☐Y ☐N
	7:00AM		☐Y ☐N
	7:30AM		☐Y ☐N
	8:00AM		☐Y ☐N
	8:30AM		☐Y ☐N
	9:00AM		☐Y ☐N
	9:30AM		☐Y ☐N
	10:00AM		☐Y ☐N
	10:30AM		☐Y ☐N
	11:00AM		☐Y ☐N
	11:30AM		☐Y ☐N
	12:00PM		☐Y ☐N
	12:30PM		☐Y ☐N
	1:00PM		☐Y ☐N
	1:30PM		☐Y ☐N
	2:00PM		☐Y ☐N
	2:30PM		☐Y ☐N
	3:00PM		☐Y ☐N
	3:30PM		☐Y ☐N
	4:00PM		☐Y ☐N
	4:30PM		☐Y ☐N
	5:00PM		☐Y ☐N
	5:30PM		☐Y ☐N
	6:00PM		☐Y ☐N
	6:30PM		☐Y ☐N
	7:00PM		☐Y ☐N
	7:30PM		☐Y ☐N
	8:00PM		☐Y ☐N
	8:30PM		☐Y ☐N
	9:00PM		☐Y ☐N
	9:30PM		☐Y ☐N

TAKE 5 MINUTES EACH MORNING TO PLAN YOUR DAY.

GET EIGHT HOURS OF SLEEP!

NOTE HIGH PRIORITY TASKS WITH A *

ANALYZE WHY A TASK WAS NOT COMPLETED, THEN MOVE TO NEXT DAY.

ONE POSITIVE

TODAY I GAVE

DAILY
GOAL SLAYERS
PLANNER

SETTING YOURSELF UP FOR SUCCESS DAILY!

DATE
_____ / _____ / _____

SCRIPTURE

MOTIVATIONAL QUOTE

ONE GOAL

ONE FUN THING

HEALTH • FITNESS

WATER INTAKE

✱	IMPORTANT TIME	SCHEDULE	SLAYED?
	5:00AM		☐Y ☐N
	5:30AM		☐Y ☐N
	6:00AM		☐Y ☐N
	6:30AM		☐Y ☐N
	7:00AM		☐Y ☐N
	7:30AM		☐Y ☐N
	8:00AM		☐Y ☐N
	8:30AM		☐Y ☐N
	9:00AM		☐Y ☐N
	9:30AM		☐Y ☐N
	10:00AM		☐Y ☐N
	10:30AM		☐Y ☐N
	11:00AM		☐Y ☐N
	11:30AM		☐Y ☐N
	12:00PM		☐Y ☐N
	12:30PM		☐Y ☐N
	1:00PM		☐Y ☐N
	1:30PM		☐Y ☐N
	2:00PM		☐Y ☐N
	2:30PM		☐Y ☐N
	3:00PM		☐Y ☐N
	3:30PM		☐Y ☐N
	4:00PM		☐Y ☐N
	4:30PM		☐Y ☐N
	5:00PM		☐Y ☐N
	5:30PM		☐Y ☐N
	6:00PM		☐Y ☐N
	6:30PM		☐Y ☐N
	7:00PM		☐Y ☐N
	7:30PM		☐Y ☐N
	8:00PM		☐Y ☐N
	8:30PM		☐Y ☐N
	9:00PM		☐Y ☐N
	9:30PM		☐Y ☐N

TAKE 5 MINUTES EACH MORNING TO PLAN YOUR DAY.

GET EIGHT HOURS OF SLEEP!

NOTE HIGH PRIORITY TASKS WITH A ✱

ANALYZE WHY A TASK WAS NOT COMPLETED, THEN MOVE TO NEXT DAY.

ONE POSITIVE

TODAY I GAVE

DAILY
GOAL SLAYERS
PLANNER

SETTING YOURSELF UP FOR SUCCESS DAILY!

DATE

_____ / _____ / _____

SCRIPTURE

MOTIVATIONAL QUOTE

ONE GOAL

ONE FUN THING

HEALTH + FITNESS

WATER INTAKE

OZ. OZ. OZ. OZ. OZ.

OZ. OZ. OZ. OZ. OZ.

✳	IMPORTANT TIME	SCHEDULE	SLAYED?
	5:00AM		☐Y ☐N
	5:30AM		☐Y ☐N
	6:00AM		☐Y ☐N
	6:30AM		☐Y ☐N
	7:00AM		☐Y ☐N
	7:30AM		☐Y ☐N
	8:00AM		☐Y ☐N
	8:30AM		☐Y ☐N
	9:00AM		☐Y ☐N
	9:30AM		☐Y ☐N
	10:00AM		☐Y ☐N
	10:30AM		☐Y ☐N
	11:00AM		☐Y ☐N
	11:30AM		☐Y ☐N
	12:00PM		☐Y ☐N
	12:30PM		☐Y ☐N
	1:00PM		☐Y ☐N
	1:30PM		☐Y ☐N
	2:00PM		☐Y ☐N
	2:30PM		☐Y ☐N
	3:00PM		☐Y ☐N
	3:30PM		☐Y ☐N
	4:00PM		☐Y ☐N
	4:30PM		☐Y ☐N
	5:00PM		☐Y ☐N
	5:30PM		☐Y ☐N
	6:00PM		☐Y ☐N
	6:30PM		☐Y ☐N
	7:00PM		☐Y ☐N
	7:30PM		☐Y ☐N
	8:00PM		☐Y ☐N
	8:30PM		☐Y ☐N
	9:00PM		☐Y ☐N
	9:30PM		☐Y ☐N

TAKE 5 MINUTES EACH MORNING TO PLAN YOUR DAY.

GET EIGHT HOURS OF SLEEP!

NOTE HIGH PRIORITY TASKS WITH A ✳

ANALYZE WHY A TASK WAS NOT COMPLETED, THEN MOVE TO NEXT DAY.

ONE POSITIVE

TODAY I GAVE

DAILY
GOAL SLAYERS
PLANNER

SETTING YOURSELF UP FOR SUCCESS DAILY!

DATE
_____ / _____ / _____

SCRIPTURE

MOTIVATIONAL QUOTE

ONE GOAL

ONE FUN THING

HEALTH • FITNESS

WATER INTAKE

OZ OZ OZ OZ OZ
OZ OZ OZ OZ OZ

✱	IMPORTANT TIME	SCHEDULE	SLAYED?
	5:00AM		☐Y ☐N
	5:30AM		☐Y ☐N
	6:00AM		☐Y ☐N
	6:30AM		☐Y ☐N
	7:00AM		☐Y ☐N
	7:30AM		☐Y ☐N
	8:00AM		☐Y ☐N
	8:30AM		☐Y ☐N
	9:00AM		☐Y ☐N
	9:30AM		☐Y ☐N
	10:00AM		☐Y ☐N
	10:30AM		☐Y ☐N
	11:00AM		☐Y ☐N
	11:30AM		☐Y ☐N
	12:00PM		☐Y ☐N
	12:30PM		☐Y ☐N
	1:00PM		☐Y ☐N
	1:30PM		☐Y ☐N
	2:00PM		☐Y ☐N
	2:30PM		☐Y ☐N
	3:00PM		☐Y ☐N
	3:30PM		☐Y ☐N
	4:00PM		☐Y ☐N
	4:30PM		☐Y ☐N
	5:00PM		☐Y ☐N
	5:30PM		☐Y ☐N
	6:00PM		☐Y ☐N
	6:30PM		☐Y ☐N
	7:00PM		☐Y ☐N
	7:30PM		☐Y ☐N
	8:00PM		☐Y ☐N
	8:30PM		☐Y ☐N
	9:00PM		☐Y ☐N
	9:30PM		☐Y ☐N

TAKE 5 MINUTES EACH MORNING TO PLAN YOUR DAY.

GET EIGHT HOURS OF SLEEP!

NOTE HIGH PRIORITY TASKS WITH A ✱

ANALYZE WHY A TASK WAS NOT COMPLETED, THEN MOVE TO NEXT DAY.

ONE POSITIVE

TODAY I GAVE

DAILY GOAL SLAYERS PLANNER

SETTING YOURSELF UP FOR SUCCESS DAILY!

DATE

____/____/____

SCRIPTURE

MOTIVATIONAL QUOTE

ONE GOAL

ONE FUN THING

HEALTH • FITNESS

WATER INTAKE

OZ. OZ. OZ. OZ. OZ.

OZ. OZ. OZ. OZ. OZ.

*	IMPORTANT TIME	SCHEDULE	SLAYED?
	5:00AM		☐Y ☐N
	5:30AM		☐Y ☐N
	6:00AM		☐Y ☐N
	6:30AM		☐Y ☐N
	7:00AM		☐Y ☐N
	7:30AM		☐Y ☐N
	8.00AM		☐Y ☐N
	8:30AM		☐Y ☐N
	9:00AM		☐Y ☐N
	9:30AM		☐Y ☐N
	10:00AM		☐Y ☐N
	10:30AM		☐Y ☐N
	11:00AM		☐Y ☐N
	11:30AM		☐Y ☐N
	12:00PM		☐Y ☐N
	12:30PM		☐Y ☐N
	1:00PM		☐Y ☐N
	1:30PM		☐Y ☐N
	2:00PM		☐Y ☐N
	2:30PM		☐Y ☐N
	3:00PM		☐Y ☐N
	3:30PM		☐Y ☐N
	4:00PM		☐Y ☐N
	4:30PM		☐Y ☐N
	5:00PM		☐Y ☐N
	5:30PM		☐Y ☐N
	6:00PM		☐Y ☐N
	6:30PM		☐Y ☐N
	7:00PM		☐Y ☐N
	7:30PM		☐Y ☐N
	8:00PM		☐Y ☐N
	8:30PM		☐Y ☐N
	9:00PM		☐Y ☐N
	9:30PM		☐Y ☐N

TAKE 5 MINUTES EACH MORNING TO PLAN YOUR DAY.

GET EIGHT HOURS OF SLEEP!

NOTE HIGH PRIORITY TASKS WITH A *

ANALYZE WHY A TASK WAS NOT COMPLETED, THEN MOVE TO NEXT DAY.

ONE POSITIVE

TODAY I GAVE

DAILY
GOAL SLAYERS
PLANNER

SETTING YOURSELF UP FOR SUCCESS DAILY!

DATE

____ / ____ / ____

SCRIPTURE

MOTIVATIONAL QUOTE

ONE GOAL

ONE FUN THING

HEALTH • FITNESS

WATER INTAKE

OZ. OZ. OZ. OZ. OZ.

OZ. OZ. OZ. OZ. OZ.

✱	IMPORTANT TIME	SCHEDULE	SLAYED?
	5:00AM		☐Y ☐N
	5:30AM		☐Y ☐N
	6:00AM		☐Y ☐N
	6:30AM		☐Y ☐N
	7:00AM		☐Y ☐N
	7:30AM		☐Y ☐N
	8:00AM		☐Y ☐N
	8:30AM		☐Y ☐N
	9:00AM		☐Y ☐N
	9:30AM		☐Y ☐N
	10:00AM		☐Y ☐N
	10:30AM		☐Y ☐N
	11:00AM		☐Y ☐N
	11:30AM		☐Y ☐N
	12:00PM		☐Y ☐N
	12:30PM		☐Y ☐N
	1:00PM		☐Y ☐N
	1:30PM		☐Y ☐N
	2:00PM		☐Y ☐N
	2:30PM		☐Y ☐N
	3:00PM		☐Y ☐N
	3:30PM		☐Y ☐N
	4:00PM		☐Y ☐N
	4:30PM		☐Y ☐N
	5:00PM		☐Y ☐N
	5:30PM		☐Y ☐N
	6:00PM		☐Y ☐N
	6:30PM		☐Y ☐N
	7:00PM		☐Y ☐N
	7:30PM		☐Y ☐N
	8:00PM		☐Y ☐N
	8:30PM		☐Y ☐N
	9:00PM		☐Y ☐N
	9:30PM		☐Y ☐N

TAKE 5 MINUTES EACH MORNING TO PLAN YOUR DAY.

GET EIGHT HOURS OF SLEEP!

NOTE HIGH PRIORITY TASKS WITH A ✱

ANALYZE WHY A TASK WAS NOT COMPLETED, THEN MOVE TO NEXT DAY.

ONE POSITIVE

TODAY I GAVE

DAILY
GOAL SLAYERS
PLANNER

SETTING YOURSELF UP FOR SUCCESS DAILY!

DATE
____ / ____ / ____

SCRIPTURE

MOTIVATIONAL QUOTE

ONE GOAL

ONE FUN THING

*	IMPORTANT TIME	SCHEDULE	SLAYED?
	5:00AM		☐Y ☐N
	5:30AM		☐Y ☐N
	6:00AM		☐Y ☐N
	6:30AM		☐Y ☐N
	7:00AM		☐Y ☐N
	7:30AM		☐Y ☐N
	8:00AM		☐Y ☐N
	8:30AM		☐Y ☐N
	9:00AM		☐Y ☐N
	9:30AM		☐Y ☐N
	10:00AM		☐Y ☐N
	10:30AM		☐Y ☐N
	11:00AM		☐Y ☐N
	11:30AM		☐Y ☐N
	12:00PM		☐Y ☐N
	12:30PM		☐Y ☐N
	1:00PM		☐Y ☐N
	1:30PM		☐Y ☐N
	2:00PM		☐Y ☐N
	2:30PM		☐Y ☐N
	3:00PM		☐Y ☐N
	3:30PM		☐Y ☐N
	4:00PM		☐Y ☐N
	4:30PM		☐Y ☐N
	5:00PM		☐Y ☐N
	5:30PM		☐Y ☐N
	6:00PM		☐Y ☐N
	6:30PM		☐Y ☐N
	7:00PM		☐Y ☐N
	7:30PM		☐Y ☐N
	8:00PM		☐Y ☐N
	8:30PM		☐Y ☐N
	9:00PM		☐Y ☐N
	9:30PM		☐Y ☐N

HEALTH + FITNESS

WATER INTAKE

OZ. OZ. OZ. OZ. OZ.
OZ. OZ. OZ. OZ. OZ.

TAKE 5 MINUTES EACH MORNING TO PLAN YOUR DAY.

GET EIGHT HOURS OF SLEEP!

NOTE HIGH PRIORITY TASKS WITH A *

ANALYZE WHY A TASK WAS NOT COMPLETED. THEN MOVE TO NEXT DAY.

ONE POSITIVE

TODAY I GAVE

DAILY
GOAL SLAYERS
PLANNER

SETTING YOURSELF UP FOR SUCCESS DAILY!

DATE

_____ / _____ / _____

SCRIPTURE

MOTIVATIONAL QUOTE

ONE GOAL

ONE FUN THING

HEALTH • FITNESS

WATER INTAKE

*	IMPORTANT TIME	SCHEDULE	SLAYED?
	5:00AM		☐Y ☐N
	5:30AM		☐Y ☐N
	6:00AM		☐Y ☐N
	6:30AM		☐Y ☐N
	7:00AM		☐Y ☐N
	7:30AM		☐Y ☐N
	8:00AM		☐Y ☐N
	8:30AM		☐Y ☐N
	9:00AM		☐Y ☐N
	9:30AM		☐Y ☐N
	10:00AM		☐Y ☐N
	10:30AM		☐Y ☐N
	11:00AM		☐Y ☐N
	11:30AM		☐Y ☐N
	12:00PM		☐Y ☐N
	12:30PM		☐Y ☐N
	1:00PM		☐Y ☐N
	1:30PM		☐Y ☐N
	2:00PM		☐Y ☐N
	2:30PM		☐Y ☐N
	3:00PM		☐Y ☐N
	3:30PM		☐Y ☐N
	4:00PM		☐Y ☐N
	4:30PM		☐Y ☐N
	5:00PM		☐Y ☐N
	5:30PM		☐Y ☐N
	6:00PM		☐Y ☐N
	6:30PM		☐Y ☐N
	7:00PM		☐Y ☐N
	7:30PM		☐Y ☐N
	8:00PM		☐Y ☐N
	8:30PM		☐Y ☐N
	9:00PM		☐Y ☐N
	9:30PM		☐Y ☐N

TAKE 5 MINUTES EACH MORNING TO PLAN YOUR DAY.

GET EIGHT HOURS OF SLEEP!

NOTE HIGH PRIORITY TASKS WITH A *

ANALYZE WHY A TASK WAS NOT COMPLETED, THEN MOVE TO NEXT DAY.

ONE POSITIVE

TODAY I GAVE

DAILY
GOAL SLAYERS
PLANNER

SETTING YOURSELF UP FOR SUCCESS DAILY!

DATE

_____ / _____ / _____

SCRIPTURE

MOTIVATIONAL QUOTE

ONE GOAL

ONE FUN THING

HEALTH • FITNESS

WATER INTAKE

*	IMPORTANT TIME	SCHEDULE	SLAYED?
	5:00AM		☐Y ☐N
	5:30AM		☐Y ☐N
	6:00AM		☐Y ☐N
	6:30AM		☐Y ☐N
	7:00AM		☐Y ☐N
	7:30AM		☐Y ☐N
	8:00AM		☐Y ☐N
	8:30AM		☐Y ☐N
	9:00AM		☐Y ☐N
	9:30AM		☐Y ☐N
	10:00AM		☐Y ☐N
	10:30AM		☐Y ☐N
	11:00AM		☐Y ☐N
	11:30AM		☐Y ☐N
	12:00PM		☐Y ☐N
	12:30PM		☐Y ☐N
	1:00PM		☐Y ☐N
	1:30PM		☐Y ☐N
	2:00PM		☐Y ☐N
	2:30PM		☐Y ☐N
	3:00PM		☐Y ☐N
	3:30PM		☐Y ☐N
	4:00PM		☐Y ☐N
	4:30PM		☐Y ☐N
	5:00PM		☐Y ☐N
	5:30PM		☐Y ☐N
	6:00PM		☐Y ☐N
	6:30PM		☐Y ☐N
	7:00PM		☐Y ☐N
	7:30PM		☐Y ☐N
	8:00PM		☐Y ☐N
	8:30PM		☐Y ☐N
	9:00PM		☐Y ☐N
	9:30PM		☐Y ☐N

TAKE 5 MINUTES EACH MORNING TO PLAN YOUR DAY.

GET EIGHT HOURS OF SLEEP!

NOTE HIGH PRIORITY TASKS WITH A *

ANALYZE WHY A TASK WAS NOT COMPLETED, THEN MOVE TO NEXT DAY.

ONE POSITIVE

TODAY I GAVE

DAILY
GOAL SLAYERS
PLANNER

SETTING YOURSELF UP FOR SUCCESS DAILY!

DATE

_____ / _____ / _____

SCRIPTURE

MOTIVATIONAL QUOTE

ONE GOAL

ONE FUN THING

HEALTH • FITNESS

WATER INTAKE

✱	IMPORTANT TIME	SCHEDULE	SLAYED?
	5:00AM		☐Y ☐N
	5:30AM		☐Y ☐N
	6:00AM		☐Y ☐N
	6:30AM		☐Y ☐N
	7:00AM		☐Y ☐N
	7:30AM		☐Y ☐N
	8:00AM		☐Y ☐N
	8:30AM		☐Y ☐N
	9:00AM		☐Y ☐N
	9:30AM		☐Y ☐N
	10:00AM		☐Y ☐N
	10:30AM		☐Y ☐N
	11:00AM		☐Y ☐N
	11:30AM		☐Y ☐N
	12:00PM		☐Y ☐N
	12:30PM		☐Y ☐N
	1:00PM		☐Y ☐N
	1:30PM		☐Y ☐N
	2:00PM		☐Y ☐N
	2:30PM		☐Y ☐N
	3:00PM		☐Y ☐N
	3:30PM		☐Y ☐N
	4:00PM		☐Y ☐N
	4:30PM		☐Y ☐N
	5:00PM		☐Y ☐N
	5:30PM		☐Y ☐N
	6:00PM		☐Y ☐N
	6:30PM		☐Y ☐N
	7:00PM		☐Y ☐N
	7:30PM		☐Y ☐N
	8:00PM		☐Y ☐N
	8:30PM		☐Y ☐N
	9:00PM		☐Y ☐N
	9:30PM		☐Y ☐N

TAKE 5 MINUTES EACH MORNING TO PLAN YOUR DAY.

GET EIGHT HOURS OF SLEEP!

NOTE HIGH PRIORITY TASKS WITH A ✱

ANALYZE WHY A TASK WAS NOT COMPLETED, THEN MOVE TO NEXT DAY.

ONE POSITIVE

TODAY I GAVE

DAILY
GOAL SLAYERS
PLANNER

SETTING YOURSELF UP FOR SUCCESS DAILY!

DATE

____ / ____ / ____

SCRIPTURE

MOTIVATIONAL QUOTE

ONE GOAL

ONE FUN THING

HEALTH + FITNESS

WATER INTAKE

OZ. OZ. OZ. OZ. OZ.

OZ. OZ. OZ. OZ. OZ.

✳	IMPORTANT TIME	SCHEDULE	SLAYED?
	5:00AM		☐Y ☐N
	5:30AM		☐Y ☐N
	6:00AM		☐Y ☐N
	6:30AM		☐Y ☐N
	7:00AM		☐Y ☐N
	7:30AM		☐Y ☐N
	8:00AM		☐Y ☐N
	8:30AM		☐Y ☐N
	9:00AM		☐Y ☐N
	9:30AM		☐Y ☐N
	10:00AM		☐Y ☐N
	10:30AM		☐Y ☐N
	11:00AM		☐Y ☐N
	11:30AM		☐Y ☐N
	12:00PM		☐Y ☐N
	12:30PM		☐Y ☐N
	1:00PM		☐Y ☐N
	1:30PM		☐Y ☐N
	2:00PM		☐Y ☐N
	2:30PM		☐Y ☐N
	3:00PM		☐Y ☐N
	3:30PM		☐Y ☐N
	4:00PM		☐Y ☐N
	4:30PM		☐Y ☐N
	5:00PM		☐Y ☐N
	5:30PM		☐Y ☐N
	6:00PM		☐Y ☐N
	6:30PM		☐Y ☐N
	7:00PM		☐Y ☐N
	7:30PM		☐Y ☐N
	8:00PM		☐Y ☐N
	8:30PM		☐Y ☐N
	9:00PM		☐Y ☐N
	9:30PM		☐Y ☐N

TAKE 5 MINUTES EACH MORNING TO PLAN YOUR DAY.

GET EIGHT HOURS OF SLEEP!

NOTE HIGH PRIORITY TASKS WITH A ✳

ANALYZE WHY A TASK WAS NOT COMPLETED. THEN MOVE TO NEXT DAY.

ONE POSITIVE

TODAY I GAVE

DAILY
GOAL SLAYERS
PLANNER

SETTING YOURSELF UP FOR SUCCESS DAILY!

DATE
_____ / _____ / _____

SCRIPTURE

MOTIVATIONAL QUOTE

ONE GOAL

ONE FUN THING

HEALTH + FITNESS

WATER INTAKE

*	IMPORTANT TIME	SCHEDULE	SLAYED?
	5:00AM		☐Y ☐N
	5:30AM		☐Y ☐N
	6:00AM		☐Y ☐N
	6:30AM		☐Y ☐N
	7:00AM		☐Y ☐N
	7:30AM		☐Y ☐N
	8:00AM		☐Y ☐N
	8:30AM		☐Y ☐N
	9:00AM		☐Y ☐N
	9:30AM		☐Y ☐N
	10:00AM		☐Y ☐N
	10:30AM		☐Y ☐N
	11:00AM		☐Y ☐N
	11:30AM		☐Y ☐N
	12:00PM		☐Y ☐N
	12:30PM		☐Y ☐N
	1:00PM		☐Y ☐N
	1:30PM		☐Y ☐N
	2:00PM		☐Y ☐N
	2:30PM		☐Y ☐N
	3:00PM		☐Y ☐N
	3:30PM		☐Y ☐N
	4:00PM		☐Y ☐N
	4:30PM		☐Y ☐N
	5:00PM		☐Y ☐N
	5:30PM		☐Y ☐N
	6:00PM		☐Y ☐N
	6:30PM		☐Y ☐N
	7:00PM		☐Y ☐N
	7:30PM		☐Y ☐N
	8:00PM		☐Y ☐N
	8:30PM		☐Y ☐N
	9:00PM		☐Y ☐N
	9:30PM		☐Y ☐N

TAKE 5 MINUTES EACH MORNING TO PLAN YOUR DAY.

GET EIGHT HOURS OF SLEEP!

NOTE HIGH PRIORITY TASKS WITH A *

ANALYZE WHY A TASK WAS NOT COMPLETED, THEN MOVE TO NEXT DAY.

ONE POSITIVE

TODAY I GAVE

DAILY
GOAL SLAYERS
PLANNER

SETTING YOURSELF UP FOR SUCCESS DAILY!

DATE

____ / ____ / ____

SCRIPTURE

MOTIVATIONAL QUOTE

ONE GOAL

ONE FUN THING

HEALTH + FITNESS

WATER INTAKE

OZ. OZ. OZ. OZ. OZ.

OZ. OZ. OZ. OZ. OZ.

*	IMPORTANT TIME	SCHEDULE	SLAYED?	
	5:00AM		☐Y	☐N
	5:30AM		☐Y	☐N
	6:00AM		☐Y	☐N
	6:30AM		☐Y	☐N
	7:00AM		☐Y	☐N
	7:30AM		☐Y	☐N
	8:00AM		☐Y	☐N
	8:30AM		☐Y	☐N
	9:00AM		☐Y	☐N
	9:30AM		☐Y	☐N
	10:00AM		☐Y	☐N
	10:30AM		☐Y	☐N
	11:00AM		☐Y	☐N
	11:30AM		☐Y	☐N
	12:00PM		☐Y	☐N
	12:30PM		☐Y	☐N
	1:00PM		☐Y	☐N
	1:30PM		☐Y	☐N
	2:00PM		☐Y	☐N
	2:30PM		☐Y	☐N
	3:00PM		☐Y	☐N
	3:30PM		☐Y	☐N
	4:00PM		☐Y	☐N
	4:30PM		☐Y	☐N
	5:00PM		☐Y	☐N
	5:30PM		☐Y	☐N
	6:00PM		☐Y	☐N
	6:30PM		☐Y	☐N
	7:00PM		☐Y	☐N
	7:30PM		☐Y	☐N
	8:00PM		☐Y	☐N
	8:30PM		☐Y	☐N
	9:00PM		☐Y	☐N
	9:30PM		☐Y	☐N

TAKE 5 MINUTES EACH MORNING TO PLAN YOUR DAY.

GET EIGHT HOURS OF SLEEP!

NOTE HIGH PRIORITY TASKS WITH A *

ANALYZE WHY A TASK WAS NOT COMPLETED. THEN MOVE TO NEXT DAY.

ONE POSITIVE

TODAY I GAVE

DAILY
GOAL SLAYERS
PLANNER

SETTING YOURSELF UP FOR SUCCESS DAILY!

DATE

___/___/___

SCRIPTURE

MOTIVATIONAL QUOTE

ONE GOAL

ONE FUN THING

HEALTH • FITNESS

WATER INTAKE

OZ. OZ. OZ. OZ. OZ.

OZ. OZ. OZ. OZ. OZ.

✳	IMPORTANT TIME	SCHEDULE	SLAYED?
	5:00AM		☐Y ☐N
	5:30AM		☐Y ☐N
	6:00AM		☐Y ☐N
	6:30AM		☐Y ☐N
	7:00AM		☐Y ☐N
	7:30AM		☐Y ☐N
	8:00AM		☐Y ☐N
	8:30AM		☐Y ☐N
	9:00AM		☐Y ☐N
	9:30AM		☐Y ☐N
	10:00AM		☐Y ☐N
	10:30AM		☐Y ☐N
	11:00AM		☐Y ☐N
	11:30AM		☐Y ☐N
	12:00PM		☐Y ☐N
	12:30PM		☐Y ☐N
	1:00PM		☐Y ☐N
	1:30PM		☐Y ☐N
	2:00PM		☐Y ☐N
	2:30PM		☐Y ☐N
	3:00PM		☐Y ☐N
	3:30PM		☐Y ☐N
	4:00PM		☐Y ☐N
	4:30PM		☐Y ☐N
	5:00PM		☐Y ☐N
	5:30PM		☐Y ☐N
	6:00PM		☐Y ☐N
	6:30PM		☐Y ☐N
	7:00PM		☐Y ☐N
	7:30PM		☐Y ☐N
	8:00PM		☐Y ☐N
	8:30PM		☐Y ☐N
	9:00PM		☐Y ☐N
	9:30PM		☐Y ☐N

TAKE 5 MINUTES EACH MORNING TO PLAN YOUR DAY.

GET EIGHT HOURS OF SLEEP!

NOTE HIGH PRIORITY TASKS WITH A ✳

ANALYZE WHY A TASK WAS NOT COMPLETED, THEN MOVE TO NEXT DAY.

ONE POSITIVE

TODAY I GAVE

DAILY
GOAL SLAYERS
PLANNER

SETTING YOURSELF UP FOR SUCCESS DAILY!

DATE
_____/_____/_____

SCRIPTURE

MOTIVATIONAL QUOTE

ONE GOAL

ONE FUN THING

*	IMPORTANT TIME	SCHEDULE	SLAYED?
	5:00AM		☐Y ☐N
	5:30AM		☐Y ☐N
	6:00AM		☐Y ☐N
	6:30AM		☐Y ☐N
	7:00AM		☐Y ☐N
	7:30AM		☐Y ☐N
	8:00AM		☐Y ☐N
	8:30AM		☐Y ☐N
	9:00AM		☐Y ☐N
	9:30AM		☐Y ☐N
	10:00AM		☐Y ☐N
	10:30AM		☐Y ☐N
	11:00AM		☐Y ☐N
	11:30AM		☐Y ☐N
	12:00PM		☐Y ☐N
	12:30PM		☐Y ☐N
	1:00PM		☐Y ☐N
	1:30PM		☐Y ☐N
	2:00PM		☐Y ☐N
	2:30PM		☐Y ☐N
	3:00PM		☐Y ☐N
	3:30PM		☐Y ☐N
	4:00PM		☐Y ☐N
	4:30PM		☐Y ☐N
	5:00PM		☐Y ☐N
	5:30PM		☐Y ☐N
	6:00PM		☐Y ☐N
	6:30PM		☐Y ☐N
	7:00PM		☐Y ☐N
	7:30PM		☐Y ☐N
	8:00PM		☐Y ☐N
	8:30PM		☐Y ☐N
	9:00PM		☐Y ☐N
	9:30PM		☐Y ☐N

HEALTH · FITNESS

WATER INTAKE

OZ. OZ. OZ. OZ. OZ.
OZ. OZ. OZ. OZ. OZ.

TAKE 5 MINUTES EACH MORNING TO PLAN YOUR DAY.

GET EIGHT HOURS OF SLEEP!

NOTE HIGH PRIORITY TASKS WITH A *

ANALYZE WHY A TASK WAS NOT COMPLETED, THEN MOVE TO NEXT DAY.

ONE POSITIVE

TODAY I GAVE

DAILY
GOAL SLAYERS
PLANNER

SETTING YOURSELF UP FOR SUCCESS DAILY!

DATE

_____ / _____ / _____

SCRIPTURE

MOTIVATIONAL QUOTE

ONE GOAL

ONE FUN THING

HEALTH • FITNESS

WATER INTAKE

OZ. OZ. OZ. OZ. OZ.
OZ. OZ. OZ. OZ. OZ.

*	IMPORTANT TIME	SCHEDULE	SLAYED?
	5:00AM		☐Y ☐N
	5:30AM		☐Y ☐N
	6:00AM		☐Y ☐N
	6:30AM		☐Y ☐N
	7:00AM		☐Y ☐N
	7:30AM		☐Y ☐N
	8:00AM		☐Y ☐N
	8:30AM		☐Y ☐N
	9:00AM		☐Y ☐N
	9:30AM		☐Y ☐N
	10:00AM		☐Y ☐N
	10:30AM		☐Y ☐N
	11:00AM		☐Y ☐N
	11:30AM		☐Y ☐N
	12:00PM		☐Y ☐N
	12:30PM		☐Y ☐N
	1:00PM		☐Y ☐N
	1:30PM		☐Y ☐N
	2:00PM		☐Y ☐N
	2:30PM		☐Y ☐N
	3:00PM		☐Y ☐N
	3:30PM		☐Y ☐N
	4:00PM		☐Y ☐N
	4:30PM		☐Y ☐N
	5:00PM		☐Y ☐N
	5:30PM		☐Y ☐N
	6:00PM		☐Y ☐N
	6:30PM		☐Y ☐N
	7:00PM		☐Y ☐N
	7:30PM		☐Y ☐N
	8:00PM		☐Y ☐N
	8:30PM		☐Y ☐N
	9:00PM		☐Y ☐N
	9:30PM		☐Y ☐N

TAKE 5 MINUTES EACH MORNING TO PLAN YOUR DAY.

GET EIGHT HOURS OF SLEEP!

NOTE HIGH PRIORITY TASKS WITH A *

ANALYZE WHY A TASK WAS NOT COMPLETED, THEN MOVE TO NEXT DAY.

ONE POSITIVE

TODAY I GAVE

DAILY
GOAL SLAYERS
PLANNER

SETTING YOURSELF UP FOR SUCCESS DAILY!

DATE

____ / ____ / _____

SCRIPTURE

MOTIVATIONAL QUOTE

ONE GOAL

ONE FUN THING

HEALTH + FITNESS

*	IMPORTANT TIME	SCHEDULE	SLAYED?
	5:00AM		☐Y ☐N
	5:30AM		☐Y ☐N
	6:00AM		☐Y ☐N
	6:30AM		☐Y ☐N
	7:00AM		☐Y ☐N
	7:30AM		☐Y ☐N
	8:00AM		☐Y ☐N
	8:30AM		☐Y ☐N
	9:00AM		☐Y ☐N
	9:30AM		☐Y ☐N
	10:00AM		☐Y ☐N
	10:30AM		☐Y ☐N
	11:00AM		☐Y ☐N
	11:30AM		☐Y ☐N
	12:00PM		☐Y ☐N
	12:30PM		☐Y ☐N
	1:00PM		☐Y ☐N
	1:30PM		☐Y ☐N
	2:00PM		☐Y ☐N
	2:30PM		☐Y ☐N
	3:00PM		☐Y ☐N
	3:30PM		☐Y ☐N
	4:00PM		☐Y ☐N
	4:30PM		☐Y ☐N
	5:00PM		☐Y ☐N
	5:30PM		☐Y ☐N
	6:00PM		☐Y ☐N
	6:30PM		☐Y ☐N
	7:00PM		☐Y ☐N
	7:30PM		☐Y ☐N
	8:00PM		☐Y ☐N
	8:30PM		☐Y ☐N
	9:00PM		☐Y ☐N
	9:30PM		☐Y ☐N

WATER INTAKE

OZ. OZ. OZ. OZ. OZ.
OZ. OZ. OZ. OZ. OZ.

TAKE 5 MINUTES EACH MORNING TO PLAN YOUR DAY.

GET EIGHT HOURS OF SLEEP!

NOTE HIGH PRIORITY TASKS WITH A *

ANALYZE WHY A TASK WAS NOT COMPLETED, THEN MOVE TO NEXT DAY.

ONE POSITIVE

TODAY I GAVE

DAILY
GOAL SLAYERS
PLANNER

SETTING YOURSELF UP FOR SUCCESS DAILY!

DATE

_____ / _____ / _____

SCRIPTURE

MOTIVATIONAL QUOTE

ONE GOAL

ONE FUN THING

HEALTH · FITNESS

WATER INTAKE

✱	IMPORTANT TIME	SCHEDULE	SLAYED?
	5:00AM		☐Y ☐N
	5:30AM		☐Y ☐N
	6:00AM		☐Y ☐N
	6:30AM		☐Y ☐N
	7:00AM		☐Y ☐N
	7:30AM		☐Y ☐N
	8:00AM		☐Y ☐N
	8:30AM		☐Y ☐N
	9:00AM		☐Y ☐N
	9:30AM		☐Y ☐N
	10:00AM		☐Y ☐N
	10:30AM		☐Y ☐N
	11:00AM		☐Y ☐N
	11:30AM		☐Y ☐N
	12:00PM		☐Y ☐N
	12:30PM		☐Y ☐N
	1:00PM		☐Y ☐N
	1:30PM		☐Y ☐N
	2:00PM		☐Y ☐N
	2:30PM		☐Y ☐N
	3:00PM		☐Y ☐N
	3:30PM		☐Y ☐N
	4:00PM		☐Y ☐N
	4:30PM		☐Y ☐N
	5:00PM		☐Y ☐N
	5:30PM		☐Y ☐N
	6:00PM		☐Y ☐N
	6:30PM		☐Y ☐N
	7:00PM		☐Y ☐N
	7:30PM		☐Y ☐N
	8:00PM		☐Y ☐N
	8:30PM		☐Y ☐N
	9:00PM		☐Y ☐N
	9:30PM		☐Y ☐N

TAKE 5 MINUTES EACH MORNING TO PLAN YOUR DAY.

GET EIGHT HOURS OF SLEEP!

NOTE HIGH PRIORITY TASKS WITH A ✱

ANALYZE WHY A TASK WAS NOT COMPLETED, THEN MOVE TO NEXT DAY.

ONE POSITIVE

TODAY I GAVE

DAILY
GOAL SLAYERS
PLANNER

SETTING YOURSELF UP FOR SUCCESS DAILY!

DATE

_____ / _____ / _____

SCRIPTURE

MOTIVATIONAL QUOTE

ONE GOAL

ONE FUN THING

*	IMPORTANT TIME	SCHEDULE	SLAYED?
	5:00AM		☐Y ☐N
	5:30AM		☐Y ☐N
	6:00AM		☐Y ☐N
	6:30AM		☐Y ☐N
	7:00AM		☐Y ☐N
	7:30AM		☐Y ☐N
	8:00AM		☐Y ☐N
	8:30AM		☐Y ☐N
	9:00AM		☐Y ☐N
	9:30AM		☐Y ☐N
	10:00AM		☐Y ☐N
	10:30AM		☐Y ☐N
	11:00AM		☐Y ☐N
	11:30AM		☐Y ☐N
	12:00PM		☐Y ☐N
	12:30PM		☐Y ☐N
	1:00PM		☐Y ☐N
	1:30PM		☐Y ☐N
	2:00PM		☐Y ☐N
	2:30PM		☐Y ☐N
	3:00PM		☐Y ☐N
	3:30PM		☐Y ☐N
	4:00PM		☐Y ☐N
	4:30PM		☐Y ☐N
	5:00PM		☐Y ☐N
	5:30PM		☐Y ☐N
	6:00PM		☐Y ☐N
	6:30PM		☐Y ☐N
	7:00PM		☐Y ☐N
	7:30PM		☐Y ☐N
	8:00PM		☐Y ☐N
	8:30PM		☐Y ☐N
	9:00PM		☐Y ☐N
	9:30PM		☐Y ☐N

HEALTH • FITNESS

WATER INTAKE

OZ. OZ. OZ. OZ. OZ.
OZ. OZ. OZ. OZ. OZ.

TAKE 5 MINUTES EACH MORNING TO PLAN YOUR DAY.

GET EIGHT HOURS OF SLEEP!

NOTE HIGH PRIORITY TASKS WITH A *

ANALYZE WHY A TASK WAS NOT COMPLETED, THEN MOVE TO NEXT DAY.

ONE POSITIVE

TODAY I GAVE

DAILY GOAL SLAYERS PLANNER

SETTING YOURSELF UP FOR SUCCESS DAILY!

DATE
_____ / _____ / _____

SCRIPTURE

MOTIVATIONAL QUOTE

ONE GOAL

ONE FUN THING

HEALTH • FITNESS

WATER INTAKE
OZ OZ OZ OZ OZ
OZ OZ OZ OZ OZ

*	IMPORTANT TIME	SCHEDULE	SLAYED?
	5:00AM		☐Y ☐N
	5:30AM		☐Y ☐N
	6:00AM		☐Y ☐N
	6:30AM		☐Y ☐N
	7:00AM		☐Y ☐N
	7:30AM		☐Y ☐N
	8:00AM		☐Y ☐N
	8:30AM		☐Y ☐N
	9:00AM		☐Y ☐N
	9:30AM		☐Y ☐N
	10:00AM		☐Y ☐N
	10:30AM		☐Y ☐N
	11:00AM		☐Y ☐N
	11:30AM		☐Y ☐N
	12:00PM		☐Y ☐N
	12:30PM		☐Y ☐N
	1:00PM		☐Y ☐N
	1:30PM		☐Y ☐N
	2:00PM		☐Y ☐N
	2:30PM		☐Y ☐N
	3:00PM		☐Y ☐N
	3:30PM		☐Y ☐N
	4:00PM		☐Y ☐N
	4:30PM		☐Y ☐N
	5:00PM		☐Y ☐N
	5:30PM		☐Y ☐N
	6:00PM		☐Y ☐N
	6:30PM		☐Y ☐N
	7:00PM		☐Y ☐N
	7:30PM		☐Y ☐N
	8:00PM		☐Y ☐N
	8:30PM		☐Y ☐N
	9:00PM		☐Y ☐N
	9:30PM		☐Y ☐N

TAKE 5 MINUTES EACH MORNING TO PLAN YOUR DAY.

GET EIGHT HOURS OF SLEEP!

NOTE HIGH PRIORITY TASKS WITH A *

ANALYZE WHY A TASK WAS NOT COMPLETED, THEN MOVE TO NEXT DAY.

ONE POSITIVE

TODAY I GAVE

DAILY
GOAL SLAYERS
PLANNER

SETTING YOURSELF UP FOR SUCCESS DAILY!

DATE

_____ / _____ / _____

SCRIPTURE

MOTIVATIONAL QUOTE

ONE GOAL

ONE FUN THING

HEALTH • FITNESS

WATER INTAKE

OZ. OZ. OZ. OZ. OZ.

OZ. OZ. OZ. OZ. OZ.

*	IMPORTANT TIME	SCHEDULE	SLAYED?
	5:00AM		☐Y ☐N
	5:30AM		☐Y ☐N
	6:00AM		☐Y ☐N
	6:30AM		☐Y ☐N
	7:00AM		☐Y ☐N
	7:30AM		☐Y ☐N
	8:00AM		☐Y ☐N
	8:30AM		☐Y ☐N
	9:00AM		☐Y ☐N
	9:30AM		☐Y ☐N
	10:00AM		☐Y ☐N
	10:30AM		☐Y ☐N
	11:00AM		☐Y ☐N
	11:30AM		☐Y ☐N
	12:00PM		☐Y ☐N
	12:30PM		☐Y ☐N
	1:00PM		☐Y ☐N
	1:30PM		☐Y ☐N
	2:00PM		☐Y ☐N
	2:30PM		☐Y ☐N
	3:00PM		☐Y ☐N
	3:30PM		☐Y ☐N
	4:00PM		☐Y ☐N
	4:30PM		☐Y ☐N
	5:00PM		☐Y ☐N
	5:30PM		☐Y ☐N
	6:00PM		☐Y ☐N
	6:30PM		☐Y ☐N
	7:00PM		☐Y ☐N
	7:30PM		☐Y ☐N
	8:00PM		☐Y ☐N
	8:30PM		☐Y ☐N
	9:00PM		☐Y ☐N
	9:30PM		☐Y ☐N

TAKE 5 MINUTES EACH MORNING TO PLAN YOUR DAY.

GET EIGHT HOURS OF SLEEP!

NOTE HIGH PRIORITY TASKS WITH A *

ANALYZE WHY A TASK WAS NOT COMPLETED, THEN MOVE TO NEXT DAY.

ONE POSITIVE

TODAY I GAVE

DAILY
GOAL SLAYERS
PLANNER

SETTING YOURSELF UP FOR SUCCESS DAILY!

DATE

_____/_____/_____

SCRIPTURE

MOTIVATIONAL QUOTE

ONE GOAL

ONE FUN THING

*	IMPORTANT TIME	SCHEDULE	SLAYED?
	5:00AM		☐Y ☐N
	5:30AM		☐Y ☐N
	6:00AM		☐Y ☐N
	6:30AM		☐Y ☐N
	7:00AM		☐Y ☐N
	7:30AM		☐Y ☐N
	8:00AM		☐Y ☐N
	8:30AM		☐Y ☐N
	9:00AM		☐Y ☐N
	9:30AM		☐Y ☐N
	10:00AM		☐Y ☐N
	10:30AM		☐Y ☐N
	11:00AM		☐Y ☐N
	11:30AM		☐Y ☐N
	12:00PM		☐Y ☐N
	12:30PM		☐Y ☐N
	1:00PM		☐Y ☐N
	1:30PM		☐Y ☐N
	2:00PM		☐Y ☐N
	2:30PM		☐Y ☐N
	3:00PM		☐Y ☐N
	3:30PM		☐Y ☐N
	4:00PM		☐Y ☐N
	4:30PM		☐Y ☐N
	5:00PM		☐Y ☐N
	5:30PM		☐Y ☐N
	6:00PM		☐Y ☐N
	6:30PM		☐Y ☐N
	7:00PM		☐Y ☐N
	7:30PM		☐Y ☐N
	8:00PM		☐Y ☐N
	8:30PM		☐Y ☐N
	9:00PM		☐Y ☐N
	9:30PM		☐Y ☐N

HEALTH • FITNESS

WATER INTAKE

OZ. OZ. OZ. OZ. OZ.

OZ. OZ. OZ. OZ. OZ.

TAKE 5 MINUTES EACH MORNING TO PLAN YOUR DAY.

GET EIGHT HOURS OF SLEEP!

NOTE HIGH PRIORITY TASKS WITH A *

ANALYZE WHY A TASK WAS NOT COMPLETED, THEN MOVE TO NEXT DAY.

ONE POSITIVE

TODAY I GAVE

DAILY
GOAL SLAYERS
PLANNER

SETTING YOURSELF UP FOR SUCCESS DAILY!

DATE

_____ / _____ / _____

SCRIPTURE

MOTIVATIONAL QUOTE

ONE GOAL

ONE FUN THING

*	IMPORTANT TIME	SCHEDULE	SLAYED?
	5:00AM		☐Y ☐N
	5:30AM		☐Y ☐N
	6:00AM		☐Y ☐N
	6:30AM		☐Y ☐N
	7:00AM		☐Y ☐N
	7:30AM		☐Y ☐N
	8:00AM		☐Y ☐N
	8:30AM		☐Y ☐N
	9:00AM		☐Y ☐N
	9:30AM		☐Y ☐N
	10:00AM		☐Y ☐N
	10:30AM		☐Y ☐N
	11:00AM		☐Y ☐N
	11:30AM		☐Y ☐N
	12:00PM		☐Y ☐N
	12:30PM		☐Y ☐N
	1:00PM		☐Y ☐N
	1:30PM		☐Y ☐N
	2:00PM		☐Y ☐N
	2:30PM		☐Y ☐N
	3:00PM		☐Y ☐N
	3:30PM		☐Y ☐N
	4:00PM		☐Y ☐N
	4:30PM		☐Y ☐N
	5:00PM		☐Y ☐N
	5:30PM		☐Y ☐N
	6:00PM		☐Y ☐N
	6:30PM		☐Y ☐N
	7:00PM		☐Y ☐N
	7:30PM		☐Y ☐N
	8:00PM		☐Y ☐N
	8:30PM		☐Y ☐N
	9:00PM		☐Y ☐N
	9:30PM		☐Y ☐N

HEALTH • FITNESS

WATER INTAKE

OZ. OZ. OZ. OZ. OZ.
OZ. OZ. OZ. OZ. OZ.

TAKE 5 MINUTES EACH MORNING TO PLAN YOUR DAY.

GET EIGHT HOURS OF SLEEP!

NOTE HIGH PRIORITY TASKS WITH A *

ANALYZE WHY A TASK WAS NOT COMPLETED, THEN MOVE TO NEXT DAY.

ONE POSITIVE

TODAY I GAVE

DAILY
GOAL SLAYERS
PLANNER

SETTING YOURSELF UP FOR SUCCESS DAILY!

DATE

_____ / _____ / _____

SCRIPTURE

MOTIVATIONAL QUOTE

ONE GOAL

ONE FUN THING

HEALTH • FITNESS

WATER INTAKE

*	IMPORTANT TIME	SCHEDULE	SLAYED?
	5:00AM		☐Y ☐N
	5:30AM		☐Y ☐N
	6:00AM		☐Y ☐N
	6:30AM		☐Y ☐N
	7:00AM		☐Y ☐N
	7:30AM		☐Y ☐N
	8:00AM		☐Y ☐N
	8:30AM		☐Y ☐N
	9:00AM		☐Y ☐N
	9:30AM		☐Y ☐N
	10:00AM		☐Y ☐N
	10:30AM		☐Y ☐N
	11:00AM		☐Y ☐N
	11:30AM		☐Y ☐N
	12:00PM		☐Y ☐N
	12:30PM		☐Y ☐N
	1:00PM		☐Y ☐N
	1:30PM		☐Y ☐N
	2:00PM		☐Y ☐N
	2:30PM		☐Y ☐N
	3:00PM		☐Y ☐N
	3:30PM		☐Y ☐N
	4:00PM		☐Y ☐N
	4:30PM		☐Y ☐N
	5:00PM		☐Y ☐N
	5:30PM		☐Y ☐N
	6:00PM		☐Y ☐N
	6:30PM		☐Y ☐N
	7:00PM		☐Y ☐N
	7:30PM		☐Y ☐N
	8:00PM		☐Y ☐N
	8:30PM		☐Y ☐N
	9:00PM		☐Y ☐N
	9:30PM		☐Y ☐N

TAKE 5 MINUTES EACH MORNING TO PLAN YOUR DAY.

GET EIGHT HOURS OF SLEEP!

NOTE HIGH PRIORITY TASKS WITH A *

ANALYZE WHY A TASK WAS NOT COMPLETED, THEN MOVE TO NEXT DAY.

ONE POSITIVE

TODAY I GAVE

DAILY
GOAL SLAYERS
PLANNER

SETTING YOURSELF UP FOR SUCCESS DAILY!

DATE

_____ / _____ / _____

SCRIPTURE

MOTIVATIONAL QUOTE

ONE GOAL

ONE FUN THING

*	IMPORTANT TIME	SCHEDULE	SLAYED?
	5:00AM		☐Y ☐N
	5:30AM		☐Y ☐N
	6:00AM		☐Y ☐N
	6:30AM		☐Y ☐N
	7:00AM		☐Y ☐N
	7:30AM		☐Y ☐N
	8:00AM		☐Y ☐N
	8:30AM		☐Y ☐N
	9:00AM		☐Y ☐N
	9:30AM		☐Y ☐N
	10:00AM		☐Y ☐N
	10:30AM		☐Y ☐N
	11:00AM		☐Y ☐N
	11:30AM		☐Y ☐N
	12:00PM		☐Y ☐N
	12:30PM		☐Y ☐N
	1:00PM		☐Y ☐N
	1:30PM		☐Y ☐N
	2:00PM		☐Y ☐N
	2:30PM		☐Y ☐N
	3:00PM		☐Y ☐N
	3:30PM		☐Y ☐N
	4:00PM		☐Y ☐N
	4:30PM		☐Y ☐N
	5:00PM		☐Y ☐N
	5:30PM		☐Y ☐N
	6:00PM		☐Y ☐N
	6:30PM		☐Y ☐N
	7:00PM		☐Y ☐N
	7:30PM		☐Y ☐N
	8:00PM		☐Y ☐N
	8:30PM		☐Y ☐N
	9:00PM		☐Y ☐N
	9:30PM		☐Y ☐N

HEALTH + FITNESS

WATER INTAKE

OZ. OZ. OZ. OZ. OZ.

OZ. OZ. OZ. OZ. OZ.

TAKE 5 MINUTES EACH MORNING TO PLAN YOUR DAY.

GET EIGHT HOURS OF SLEEP!

NOTE HIGH PRIORITY TASKS WITH A *

ANALYZE WHY A TASK WAS NOT COMPLETED, THEN MOVE TO NEXT DAY.

ONE POSITIVE

TODAY I GAVE

DAILY
GOAL SLAYERS
PLANNER

SETTING YOURSELF UP FOR SUCCESS DAILY!

DATE

_____ / _____ / _____

SCRIPTURE

MOTIVATIONAL QUOTE

ONE GOAL

ONE FUN THING

✱	IMPORTANT TIME	SCHEDULE	SLAYED?
	5:00AM		☐Y ☐N
	5:30AM		☐Y ☐N
	6:00AM		☐Y ☐N
	6:30AM		☐Y ☐N
	7:00AM		☐Y ☐N
	7:30AM		☐Y ☐N
	8:00AM		☐Y ☐N
	8:30AM		☐Y ☐N
	9:00AM		☐Y ☐N
	9:30AM		☐Y ☐N
	10:00AM		☐Y ☐N
	10:30AM		☐Y ☐N
	11:00AM		☐Y ☐N
	11:30AM		☐Y ☐N
	12:00PM		☐Y ☐N
	12:30PM		☐Y ☐N
	1:00PM		☐Y ☐N
	1:30PM		☐Y ☐N
	2:00PM		☐Y ☐N
	2:30PM		☐Y ☐N
	3:00PM		☐Y ☐N
	3:30PM		☐Y ☐N
	4:00PM		☐Y ☐N
	4:30PM		☐Y ☐N
	5:00PM		☐Y ☐N
	5:30PM		☐Y ☐N
	6:00PM		☐Y ☐N
	6:30PM		☐Y ☐N
	7:00PM		☐Y ☐N
	7:30PM		☐Y ☐N
	8:00PM		☐Y ☐N
	8:30PM		☐Y ☐N
	9:00PM		☐Y ☐N
	9:30PM		☐Y ☐N

HEALTH • FITNESS

WATER INTAKE

OZ. OZ. OZ. OZ. OZ.
OZ. OZ. OZ. OZ. OZ.

TAKE 5 MINUTES EACH MORNING TO PLAN YOUR DAY.

GET EIGHT HOURS OF SLEEP!

NOTE HIGH PRIORITY TASKS WITH A ✱

ANALYZE WHY A TASK WAS NOT COMPLETED, THEN MOVE TO NEXT DAY.

ONE POSITIVE

TODAY I GAVE

DAILY
GOAL SLAYERS
PLANNER

SETTING YOURSELF UP FOR SUCCESS DAILY!

DATE

____ / ____ / ____

SCRIPTURE

MOTIVATIONAL QUOTE

ONE GOAL

ONE FUN THING

✳	IMPORTANT TIME	SCHEDULE	SLAYED?
	5:00AM		☐Y ☐N
	5:30AM		☐Y ☐N
	6:00AM		☐Y ☐N
	6:30AM		☐Y ☐N
	7:00AM		☐Y ☐N
	7:30AM		☐Y ☐N
	8:00AM		☐Y ☐N
	8:30AM		☐Y ☐N
	9:00AM		☐Y ☐N
	9:30AM		☐Y ☐N
	10:00AM		☐Y ☐N
	10:30AM		☐Y ☐N
	11:00AM		☐Y ☐N
	11:30AM		☐Y ☐N
	12:00PM		☐Y ☐N
	12:30PM		☐Y ☐N
	1:00PM		☐Y ☐N
	1:30PM		☐Y ☐N
	2:00PM		☐Y ☐N
	2:30PM		☐Y ☐N
	3:00PM		☐Y ☐N
	3:30PM		☐Y ☐N
	4:00PM		☐Y ☐N
	4:30PM		☐Y ☐N
	5:00PM		☐Y ☐N
	5:30PM		☐Y ☐N
	6:00PM		☐Y ☐N
	6:30PM		☐Y ☐N
	7:00PM		☐Y ☐N
	7:30PM		☐Y ☐N
	8:00PM		☐Y ☐N
	8:30PM		☐Y ☐N
	9:00PM		☐Y ☐N
	9:30PM		☐Y ☐N

HEALTH • FITNESS

WATER INTAKE

OZ. OZ. OZ. OZ. OZ.

OZ. OZ. OZ. OZ. OZ.

TAKE 5 MINUTES EACH MORNING TO PLAN YOUR DAY.

GET EIGHT HOURS OF SLEEP!

NOTE HIGH PRIORITY TASKS WITH A ✳

ANALYZE WHY A TASK WAS NOT COMPLETED, THEN MOVE TO NEXT DAY.

ONE POSITIVE

TODAY I GAVE

DAILY
GOAL SLAYERS
PLANNER

SETTING YOURSELF UP FOR SUCCESS DAILY!

DATE

_____ / _____ / _____

SCRIPTURE

MOTIVATIONAL QUOTE

ONE GOAL

ONE FUN THING

HEALTH • FITNESS

WATER INTAKE

*	IMPORTANT TIME	SCHEDULE	SLAYED?
	5:00AM		☐Y ☐N
	5:30AM		☐Y ☐N
	6:00AM		☐Y ☐N
	6:30AM		☐Y ☐N
	7:00AM		☐Y ☐N
	7:30AM		☐Y ☐N
	8:00AM		☐Y ☐N
	8:30AM		☐Y ☐N
	9:00AM		☐Y ☐N
	9:30AM		☐Y ☐N
	10:00AM		☐Y ☐N
	10:30AM		☐Y ☐N
	11:00AM		☐Y ☐N
	11:30AM		☐Y ☐N
	12:00PM		☐Y ☐N
	12:30PM		☐Y ☐N
	1:00PM		☐Y ☐N
	1:30PM		☐Y ☐N
	2:00PM		☐Y ☐N
	2:30PM		☐Y ☐N
	3:00PM		☐Y ☐N
	3:30PM		☐Y ☐N
	4:00PM		☐Y ☐N
	4:30PM		☐Y ☐N
	5:00PM		☐Y ☐N
	5:30PM		☐Y ☐N
	6:00PM		☐Y ☐N
	6:30PM		☐Y ☐N
	7:00PM		☐Y ☐N
	7:30PM		☐Y ☐N
	8:00PM		☐Y ☐N
	8:30PM		☐Y ☐N
	9:00PM		☐Y ☐N
	9:30PM		☐Y ☐N

TAKE 5 MINUTES EACH MORNING TO PLAN YOUR DAY.

GET EIGHT HOURS OF SLEEP!

NOTE HIGH PRIORITY TASKS WITH A *

ANALYZE WHY A TASK WAS NOT COMPLETED, THEN MOVE TO NEXT DAY.

ONE POSITIVE

TODAY I GAVE

DAILY
GOAL SLAYERS
PLANNER

SETTING YOURSELF UP FOR SUCCESS DAILY!

DATE

_____ / _____ / _____

SCRIPTURE

MOTIVATIONAL QUOTE

ONE GOAL

ONE FUN THING

*	IMPORTANT TIME	SCHEDULE	SLAYED?
	5:00AM		□Y □N
	5:30AM		□Y □N
	6:00AM		□Y □N
	6:30AM		□Y □N
	7:00AM		□Y □N
	7:30AM		□Y □N
	8:00AM		□Y □N
	8:30AM		□Y □N
	9:00AM		□Y □N
	9:30AM		□Y □N
	10:00AM		□Y □N
	10:30AM		□Y □N
	11:00AM		□Y □N
	11:30AM		□Y □N
	12:00PM		□Y □N
	12:30PM		□Y □N
	1:00PM		□Y □N
	1:30PM		□Y □N
	2:00PM		□Y □N
	2:30PM		□Y □N
	3:00PM		□Y □N
	3:30PM		□Y □N
	4:00PM		□Y □N
	4:30PM		□Y □N
	5:00PM		□Y □N
	5:30PM		□Y □N
	6:00PM		□Y □N
	6:30PM		□Y □N
	7:00PM		□Y □N
	7:30PM		□Y □N
	8:00PM		□Y □N
	8:30PM		□Y □N
	9:00PM		□Y □N
	9:30PM		□Y □N

HEALTH · FITNESS

WATER INTAKE

OZ. OZ. OZ. OZ. OZ.

OZ. OZ. OZ. OZ. OZ.

TAKE 5 MINUTES EACH MORNING TO PLAN YOUR DAY.

GET EIGHT HOURS OF SLEEP!

NOTE HIGH PRIORITY TASKS WITH A *

ANALYZE WHY A TASK WAS NOT COMPLETED, THEN MOVE TO NEXT DAY.

ONE POSITIVE

TODAY I GAVE

DAILY
GOAL SLAYERS
PLANNER

SETTING YOURSELF UP FOR SUCCESS DAILY!

DATE

____ / ____ / ____

SCRIPTURE

MOTIVATIONAL QUOTE

ONE GOAL

ONE FUN THING

HEALTH · FITNESS

WATER INTAKE

*	IMPORTANT TIME	SCHEDULE	SLAYED?
	5:00AM		☐Y ☐N
	5:30AM		☐Y ☐N
	6:00AM		☐Y ☐N
	6:30AM		☐Y ☐N
	7:00AM		☐Y ☐N
	7:30AM		☐Y ☐N
	8:00AM		☐Y ☐N
	8:30AM		☐Y ☐N
	9:00AM		☐Y ☐N
	9:30AM		☐Y ☐N
	10:00AM		☐Y ☐N
	10:30AM		☐Y ☐N
	11:00AM		☐Y ☐N
	11:30AM		☐Y ☐N
	12:00PM		☐Y ☐N
	12:30PM		☐Y ☐N
	1:00PM		☐Y ☐N
	1:30PM		☐Y ☐N
	2:00PM		☐Y ☐N
	2:30PM		☐Y ☐N
	3:00PM		☐Y ☐N
	3:30PM		☐Y ☐N
	4:00PM		☐Y ☐N
	4:30PM		☐Y ☐N
	5:00PM		☐Y ☐N
	5:30PM		☐Y ☐N
	6:00PM		☐Y ☐N
	6:30PM		☐Y ☐N
	7:00PM		☐Y ☐N
	7:30PM		☐Y ☐N
	8:00PM		☐Y ☐N
	8:30PM		☐Y ☐N
	9:00PM		☐Y ☐N
	9:30PM		☐Y ☐N

TAKE 5 MINUTES EACH MORNING TO PLAN YOUR DAY.

GET EIGHT HOURS OF SLEEP!

NOTE HIGH PRIORITY TASKS WITH A *

ANALYZE WHY A TASK WAS NOT COMPLETED, THEN MOVE TO NEXT DAY.

ONE POSITIVE

TODAY I GAVE

DAILY
GOAL SLAYERS
PLANNER

SETTING YOURSELF UP FOR SUCCESS DAILY!

DATE

_____ / _____ / _____

SCRIPTURE

MOTIVATIONAL QUOTE

ONE GOAL

ONE FUN THING

HEALTH • FITNESS

*	IMPORTANT TIME	SCHEDULE	SLAYED?
	5:00AM		☐Y ☐N
	5:30AM		☐Y ☐N
	6:00AM		☐Y ☐N
	6:30AM		☐Y ☐N
	7:00AM		☐Y ☐N
	7:30AM		☐Y ☐N
	8:00AM		☐Y ☐N
	8:30AM		☐Y ☐N
	9:00AM		☐Y ☐N
	9:30AM		☐Y ☐N
	10:00AM		☐Y ☐N
	10:30AM		☐Y ☐N
	11:00AM		☐Y ☐N
	11:30AM		☐Y ☐N
	12:00PM		☐Y ☐N
	12:30PM		☐Y ☐N
	1:00PM		☐Y ☐N
	1:30PM		☐Y ☐N
	2:00PM		☐Y ☐N
	2:30PM		☐Y ☐N
	3:00PM		☐Y ☐N
	3:30PM		☐Y ☐N
	4:00PM		☐Y ☐N
	4:30PM		☐Y ☐N
	5:00PM		☐Y ☐N
	5:30PM		☐Y ☐N
	6:00PM		☐Y ☐N
	6:30PM		☐Y ☐N
	7:00PM		☐Y ☐N
	7:30PM		☐Y ☐N
	8:00PM		☐Y ☐N
	8:30PM		☐Y ☐N
	9:00PM		☐Y ☐N
	9:30PM		☐Y ☐N

WATER INTAKE

OZ. OZ. OZ. OZ. OZ.
OZ. OZ. OZ. OZ. OZ.

TAKE 5 MINUTES EACH MORNING TO PLAN YOUR DAY.

GET EIGHT HOURS OF SLEEP!

NOTE HIGH PRIORITY TASKS WITH A *

ANALYZE WHY A TASK WAS NOT COMPLETED, THEN MOVE TO NEXT DAY.

ONE POSITIVE

TODAY I GAVE

DAILY
GOAL SLAYERS
PLANNER

SETTING YOURSELF UP FOR SUCCESS DAILY!

DATE

_____ / _____ / _____

SCRIPTURE

MOTIVATIONAL QUOTE

ONE GOAL

ONE FUN THING

HEALTH · FITNESS

*	IMPORTANT TIME	SCHEDULE	SLAYED?
	5:00AM		☐Y ☐N
	5:30AM		☐Y ☐N
	6:00AM		☐Y ☐N
	6:30AM		☐Y ☐N
	7:00AM		☐Y ☐N
	7:30AM		☐Y ☐N
	8:00AM		☐Y ☐N
	8:30AM		☐Y ☐N
	9:00AM		☐Y ☐N
	9:30AM		☐Y ☐N
	10:00AM		☐Y ☐N
	10:30AM		☐Y ☐N
	11:00AM		☐Y ☐N
	11:30AM		☐Y ☐N
	12:00PM		☐Y ☐N
	12:30PM		☐Y ☐N
	1:00PM		☐Y ☐N
	1:30PM		☐Y ☐N
	2:00PM		☐Y ☐N
	2:30PM		☐Y ☐N
	3:00PM		☐Y ☐N
	3:30PM		☐Y ☐N
	4:00PM		☐Y ☐N
	4:30PM		☐Y ☐N
	5:00PM		☐Y ☐N
	5:30PM		☐Y ☐N
	6:00PM		☐Y ☐N
	6:30PM		☐Y ☐N
	7:00PM		☐Y ☐N
	7:30PM		☐Y ☐N
	8:00PM		☐Y ☐N
	8:30PM		☐Y ☐N
	9:00PM		☐Y ☐N
	9:30PM		☐Y ☐N

WATER INTAKE

OZ OZ OZ OZ OZ
OZ OZ OZ OZ OZ

TAKE 5 MINUTES EACH MORNING TO PLAN YOUR DAY.

GET EIGHT HOURS OF SLEEP!

NOTE HIGH PRIORITY TASKS WITH A *

ANALYZE WHY A TASK WAS NOT COMPLETED, THEN MOVE TO NEXT DAY.

ONE POSITIVE

TODAY I GAVE

DAILY
GOAL SLAYERS
PLANNER

SETTING YOURSELF UP FOR SUCCESS DAILY!

DATE

_____ / _____ / _____

SCRIPTURE

MOTIVATIONAL QUOTE

ONE GOAL

ONE FUN THING

HEALTH + FITNESS

WATER INTAKE

OZ. OZ. OZ. OZ. OZ.

OZ. OZ. OZ. OZ. OZ.

*	IMPORTANT TIME	SCHEDULE	SLAYED?
	5:00AM		☐Y ☐N
	5:30AM		☐Y ☐N
	6:00AM		☐Y ☐N
	6:30AM		☐Y ☐N
	7:00AM		☐Y ☐N
	7:30AM		☐Y ☐N
	8:00AM		☐Y ☐N
	8:30AM		☐Y ☐N
	9:00AM		☐Y ☐N
	9:30AM		☐Y ☐N
	10:00AM		☐Y ☐N
	10:30AM		☐Y ☐N
	11:00AM		☐Y ☐N
	11:30AM		☐Y ☐N
	12:00PM		☐Y ☐N
	12:30PM		☐Y ☐N
	1:00PM		☐Y ☐N
	1:30PM		☐Y ☐N
	2:00PM		☐Y ☐N
	2:30PM		☐Y ☐N
	3:00PM		☐Y ☐N
	3:30PM		☐Y ☐N
	4:00PM		☐Y ☐N
	4:30PM		☐Y ☐N
	5:00PM		☐Y ☐N
	5:30PM		☐Y ☐N
	6:00PM		☐Y ☐N
	6:30PM		☐Y ☐N
	7:00PM		☐Y ☐N
	7:30PM		☐Y ☐N
	8:00PM		☐Y ☐N
	8:30PM		☐Y ☐N
	9:00PM		☐Y ☐N
	9:30PM		☐Y ☐N

TAKE 5 MINUTES EACH MORNING TO PLAN YOUR DAY.

GET EIGHT HOURS OF SLEEP!

NOTE HIGH PRIORITY TASKS WITH A *

ANALYZE WHY A TASK WAS NOT COMPLETED, THEN MOVE TO NEXT DAY.

ONE POSITIVE

TODAY I GAVE

DAILY
GOAL SLAYERS
PLANNER

SETTING YOURSELF UP FOR SUCCESS DAILY!

DATE

_____ / _____ / _____

SCRIPTURE

MOTIVATIONAL QUOTE

ONE GOAL

ONE FUN THING

*	IMPORTANT TIME	SCHEDULE	SLAYED?
	5:00AM		☐Y ☐N
	5:30AM		☐Y ☐N
	6:00AM		☐Y ☐N
	6:30AM		☐Y ☐N
	7:00AM		☐Y ☐N
	7:30AM		☐Y ☐N
	8:00AM		☐Y ☐N
	8:30AM		☐Y ☐N
	9:00AM		☐Y ☐N
	9:30AM		☐Y ☐N
	10:00AM		☐Y ☐N
	10:30AM		☐Y ☐N
	11:00AM		☐Y ☐N
	11:30AM		☐Y ☐N
	12:00PM		☐Y ☐N
	12:30PM		☐Y ☐N
	1:00PM		☐Y ☐N
	1:30PM		☐Y ☐N
	2:00PM		☐Y ☐N
	2:30PM		☐Y ☐N
	3:00PM		☐Y ☐N
	3:30PM		☐Y ☐N
	4:00PM		☐Y ☐N
	4:30PM		☐Y ☐N
	5:00PM		☐Y ☐N
	5:30PM		☐Y ☐N
	6:00PM		☐Y ☐N
	6:30PM		☐Y ☐N
	7:00PM		☐Y ☐N
	7:30PM		☐Y ☐N
	8:00PM		☐Y ☐N
	8:30PM		☐Y ☐N
	9:00PM		☐Y ☐N
	9:30PM		☐Y ☐N

HEALTH • FITNESS

WATER INTAKE

OZ OZ OZ OZ OZ
OZ OZ OZ OZ OZ

TAKE 5 MINUTES EACH MORNING TO PLAN YOUR DAY.

GET EIGHT HOURS OF SLEEP!

NOTE HIGH PRIORITY TASKS WITH A *

ANALYZE WHY A TASK WAS NOT COMPLETED, THEN MOVE TO NEXT DAY.

ONE POSITIVE

TODAY I GAVE

DAILY
GOAL SLAYERS
PLANNER

SETTING YOURSELF UP FOR SUCCESS DAILY!

DATE

____ / ____ / ____

SCRIPTURE

MOTIVATIONAL QUOTE

ONE GOAL

ONE FUN THING

HEALTH + FITNESS

WATER INTAKE

OZ OZ OZ OZ OZ

OZ OZ OZ OZ OZ

*	IMPORTANT TIME	SCHEDULE	SLAYED?
	5:00AM		☐Y ☐N
	5:30AM		☐Y ☐N
	6:00AM		☐Y ☐N
	6:30AM		☐Y ☐N
	7:00AM		☐Y ☐N
	7:30AM		☐Y ☐N
	8:00AM		☐Y ☐N
	8:30AM		☐Y ☐N
	9:00AM		☐Y ☐N
	9:30AM		☐Y ☐N
	10:00AM		☐Y ☐N
	10:30AM		☐Y ☐N
	11:00AM		☐Y ☐N
	11:30AM		☐Y ☐N
	12:00PM		☐Y ☐N
	12:30PM		☐Y ☐N
	1:00PM		☐Y ☐N
	1:30PM		☐Y ☐N
	2:00PM		☐Y ☐N
	2:30PM		☐Y ☐N
	3:00PM		☐Y ☐N
	3:30PM		☐Y ☐N
	4:00PM		☐Y ☐N
	4:30PM		☐Y ☐N
	5:00PM		☐Y ☐N
	5:30PM		☐Y ☐N
	6:00PM		☐Y ☐N
	6:30PM		☐Y ☐N
	7:00PM		☐Y ☐N
	7:30PM		☐Y ☐N
	8:00PM		☐Y ☐N
	8:30PM		☐Y ☐N
	9:00PM		☐Y ☐N
	9:30PM		☐Y ☐N

TAKE 5 MINUTES EACH MORNING TO PLAN YOUR DAY.

GET EIGHT HOURS OF SLEEP!

NOTE HIGH PRIORITY TASKS WITH A *

ANALYZE WHY A TASK WAS NOT COMPLETED, THEN MOVE TO NEXT DAY.

ONE POSITIVE

TODAY I GAVE

DAILY
GOAL SLAYERS
PLANNER

SETTING YOURSELF UP FOR SUCCESS DAILY!

DATE

_____ / _____ / _____

SCRIPTURE

MOTIVATIONAL QUOTE

ONE GOAL

ONE FUN THING

HEALTH + FITNESS

WATER INTAKE

OZ OZ OZ OZ OZ
OZ OZ OZ OZ OZ

*	IMPORTANT TIME	SCHEDULE	SLAYED?
	5:00AM		☐Y ☐N
	5:30AM		☐Y ☐N
	6:00AM		☐Y ☐N
	6:30AM		☐Y ☐N
	7:00AM		☐Y ☐N
	7:30AM		☐Y ☐N
	8:00AM		☐Y ☐N
	8:30AM		☐Y ☐N
	9:00AM		☐Y ☐N
	9:30AM		☐Y ☐N
	10:00AM		☐Y ☐N
	10:30AM		☐Y ☐N
	11:00AM		☐Y ☐N
	11:30AM		☐Y ☐N
	12:00PM		☐Y ☐N
	12:30PM		☐Y ☐N
	1:00PM		☐Y ☐N
	1:30PM		☐Y ☐N
	2:00PM		☐Y ☐N
	2:30PM		☐Y ☐N
	3:00PM		☐Y ☐N
	3:30PM		☐Y ☐N
	4:00PM		☐Y ☐N
	4:30PM		☐Y ☐N
	5:00PM		☐Y ☐N
	5:30PM		☐Y ☐N
	6:00PM		☐Y ☐N
	6:30PM		☐Y ☐N
	7:00PM		☐Y ☐N
	7:30PM		☐Y ☐N
	8:00PM		☐Y ☐N
	8:30PM		☐Y ☐N
	9:00PM		☐Y ☐N
	9:30PM		☐Y ☐N

TAKE 5 MINUTES EACH MORNING TO PLAN YOUR DAY.

GET EIGHT HOURS OF SLEEP!

NOTE HIGH PRIORITY TASKS WITH A *

ANALYZE WHY A TASK WAS NOT COMPLETED, THEN MOVE TO NEXT DAY.

ONE POSITIVE

TODAY I GAVE

DAILY
GOAL SLAYERS
PLANNER

SETTING YOURSELF UP FOR SUCCESS DAILY!

DATE

_____/_____/_____

SCRIPTURE

MOTIVATIONAL QUOTE

ONE GOAL

ONE FUN THING

*	IMPORTANT TIME	SCHEDULE	SLAYED?
	5:00AM		☐Y ☐N
	5:30AM		☐Y ☐N
	6:00AM		☐Y ☐N
	6:30AM		☐Y ☐N
	7:00AM		☐Y ☐N
	7:30AM		☐Y ☐N
	8:00AM		☐Y ☐N
	8:30AM		☐Y ☐N
	9:00AM		☐Y ☐N
	9:30AM		☐Y ☐N
	10:00AM		☐Y ☐N
	10:30AM		☐Y ☐N
	11:00AM		☐Y ☐N
	11:30AM		☐Y ☐N
	12:00PM		☐Y ☐N
	12:30PM		☐Y ☐N
	1:00PM		☐Y ☐N
	1:30PM		☐Y ☐N
	2:00PM		☐Y ☐N
	2:30PM		☐Y ☐N
	3:00PM		☐Y ☐N
	3:30PM		☐Y ☐N
	4:00PM		☐Y ☐N
	4:30PM		☐Y ☐N
	5:00PM		☐Y ☐N
	5:30PM		☐Y ☐N
	6:00PM		☐Y ☐N
	6:30PM		☐Y ☐N
	7:00PM		☐Y ☐N
	7:30PM		☐Y ☐N
	8:00PM		☐Y ☐N
	8:30PM		☐Y ☐N
	9:00PM		☐Y ☐N
	9:30PM		☐Y ☐N

HEALTH + FITNESS

WATER INTAKE

OZ. OZ. OZ. OZ. OZ.
OZ. OZ. OZ. OZ. OZ.

TAKE 5 MINUTES EACH MORNING TO PLAN YOUR DAY.

GET EIGHT HOURS OF SLEEP!

NOTE HIGH PRIORITY TASKS WITH A *

ANALYZE WHY A TASK WAS NOT COMPLETED, THEN MOVE TO NEXT DAY.

ONE POSITIVE

TODAY I GAVE

DAILY
GOAL SLAYERS
PLANNER

SETTING YOURSELF UP FOR SUCCESS DAILY!

DATE

____ / ____ / ____

SCRIPTURE

MOTIVATIONAL QUOTE

ONE GOAL

ONE FUN THING

HEALTH • FITNESS

WATER INTAKE

OZ. OZ. OZ. OZ. OZ.

OZ. OZ. OZ. OZ. OZ.

*	IMPORTANT TIME	SCHEDULE	SLAYED?
	5:00AM		☐Y ☐N
	5:30AM		☐Y ☐N
	6:00AM		☐Y ☐N
	6:30AM		☐Y ☐N
	7:00AM		☐Y ☐N
	7:30AM		☐Y ☐N
	8:00AM		☐Y ☐N
	8:30AM		☐Y ☐N
	9:00AM		☐Y ☐N
	9:30AM		☐Y ☐N
	10:00AM		☐Y ☐N
	10:30AM		☐Y ☐N
	11:00AM		☐Y ☐N
	11:30AM		☐Y ☐N
	12:00PM		☐Y ☐N
	12:30PM		☐Y ☐N
	1:00PM		☐Y ☐N
	1:30PM		☐Y ☐N
	2:00PM		☐Y ☐N
	2:30PM		☐Y ☐N
	3:00PM		☐Y ☐N
	3:30PM		☐Y ☐N
	4:00PM		☐Y ☐N
	4:30PM		☐Y ☐N
	5:00PM		☐Y ☐N
	5:30PM		☐Y ☐N
	6:00PM		☐Y ☐N
	6:30PM		☐Y ☐N
	7:00PM		☐Y ☐N
	7:30PM		☐Y ☐N
	8:00PM		☐Y ☐N
	8:30PM		☐Y ☐N
	9:00PM		☐Y ☐N
	9:30PM		☐Y ☐N

TAKE 5 MINUTES EACH MORNING TO PLAN YOUR DAY.

GET EIGHT HOURS OF SLEEP!

NOTE HIGH PRIORITY TASKS WITH A *

ANALYZE WHY A TASK WAS NOT COMPLETED, THEN MOVE TO NEXT DAY.

ONE POSITIVE

TODAY I GAVE

DAILY
GOAL SLAYERS
PLANNER

SETTING YOURSELF UP FOR SUCCESS DAILY!

DATE

____ / ____ / ____

SCRIPTURE

MOTIVATIONAL QUOTE

ONE GOAL

ONE FUN THING

*	IMPORTANT TIME	SCHEDULE	SLAYED?
	5:00AM		☐Y ☐N
	5:30AM		☐Y ☐N
	6:00AM		☐Y ☐N
	6:30AM		☐Y ☐N
	7:00AM		☐Y ☐N
	7:30AM		☐Y ☐N
	8:00AM		☐Y ☐N
	8:30AM		☐Y ☐N
	9:00AM		☐Y ☐N
	9:30AM		☐Y ☐N
	10:00AM		☐Y ☐N
	10:30AM		☐Y ☐N
	11:00AM		☐Y ☐N
	11:30AM		☐Y ☐N
	12:00PM		☐Y ☐N
	12:30PM		☐Y ☐N
	1:00PM		☐Y ☐N
	1:30PM		☐Y ☐N
	2:00PM		☐Y ☐N
	2:30PM		☐Y ☐N
	3:00PM		☐Y ☐N
	3:30PM		☐Y ☐N
	4:00PM		☐Y ☐N
	4:30PM		☐Y ☐N
	5:00PM		☐Y ☐N
	5:30PM		☐Y ☐N
	6:00PM		☐Y ☐N
	6:30PM		☐Y ☐N
	7:00PM		☐Y ☐N
	7:30PM		☐Y ☐N
	8:00PM		☐Y ☐N
	8:30PM		☐Y ☐N
	9:00PM		☐Y ☐N
	9:30PM		☐Y ☐N

HEALTH • FITNESS

WATER INTAKE

OZ. OZ. OZ. OZ. OZ.
OZ. OZ. OZ. OZ. OZ.

TAKE 5 MINUTES EACH MORNING TO PLAN YOUR DAY.

GET EIGHT HOURS OF SLEEP!

NOTE HIGH PRIORITY TASKS WITH A *

ANALYZE WHY A TASK WAS NOT COMPLETED, THEN MOVE TO NEXT DAY.

ONE POSITIVE

TODAY I GAVE

DAILY GOAL SLAYERS PLANNER

SETTING YOURSELF UP FOR SUCCESS DAILY!

DATE

____/____/____

SCRIPTURE

MOTIVATIONAL QUOTE

ONE GOAL

ONE FUN THING

*	IMPORTANT TIME	SCHEDULE	SLAYED?
	5:00AM		☐Y ☐N
	5:30AM		☐Y ☐N
	6:00AM		☐Y ☐N
	6:30AM		☐Y ☐N
	7:00AM		☐Y ☐N
	7:30AM		☐Y ☐N
	8:00AM		☐Y ☐N
	8:30AM		☐Y ☐N
	9:00AM		☐Y ☐N
	9:30AM		☐Y ☐N
	10:00AM		☐Y ☐N
	10:30AM		☐Y ☐N
	11:00AM		☐Y ☐N
	11:30AM		☐Y ☐N
	12:00PM		☐Y ☐N
	12:30PM		☐Y ☐N
	1:00PM		☐Y ☐N
	1:30PM		☐Y ☐N
	2:00PM		☐Y ☐N
	2:30PM		☐Y ☐N
	3:00PM		☐Y ☐N
	3:30PM		☐Y ☐N
	4:00PM		☐Y ☐N
	4:30PM		☐Y ☐N
	5:00PM		☐Y ☐N
	5:30PM		☐Y ☐N
	6:00PM		☐Y ☐N
	6:30PM		☐Y ☐N
	7:00PM		☐Y ☐N
	7:30PM		☐Y ☐N
	8:00PM		☐Y ☐N
	8:30PM		☐Y ☐N
	9:00PM		☐Y ☐N
	9:30PM		☐Y ☐N

HEALTH • FITNESS

WATER INTAKE

OZ OZ OZ OZ OZ
OZ OZ OZ OZ OZ

TAKE 5 MINUTES EACH MORNING TO PLAN YOUR DAY.

GET EIGHT HOURS OF SLEEP!

NOTE HIGH PRIORITY TASKS WITH A *

ANALYZE WHY A TASK WAS NOT COMPLETED, THEN MOVE TO NEXT DAY.

ONE POSITIVE

TODAY I GAVE

DAILY
GOAL SLAYERS
PLANNER

SETTING YOURSELF UP FOR SUCCESS DAILY!

DATE

_____ / _____ / _____

SCRIPTURE

MOTIVATIONAL QUOTE

ONE GOAL

ONE FUN THING

*	IMPORTANT TIME	SCHEDULE	SLAYED?
	5:00AM		☐Y ☐N
	5:30AM		☐Y ☐N
	6:00AM		☐Y ☐N
	6:30AM		☐Y ☐N
	7:00AM		☐Y ☐N
	7:30AM		☐Y ☐N
	8:00AM		☐Y ☐N
	8:30AM		☐Y ☐N
	9:00AM		☐Y ☐N
	9:30AM		☐Y ☐N
	10:00AM		☐Y ☐N
	10:30AM		☐Y ☐N
	11:00AM		☐Y ☐N
	11:30AM		☐Y ☐N
	12:00PM		☐Y ☐N
	12:30PM		☐Y ☐N
	1:00PM		☐Y ☐N
	1:30PM		☐Y ☐N
	2:00PM		☐Y ☐N
	2:30PM		☐Y ☐N
	3:00PM		☐Y ☐N
	3:30PM		☐Y ☐N
	4:00PM		☐Y ☐N
	4:30PM		☐Y ☐N
	5:00PM		☐Y ☐N
	5:30PM		☐Y ☐N
	6:00PM		☐Y ☐N
	6:30PM		☐Y ☐N
	7:00PM		☐Y ☐N
	7:30PM		☐Y ☐N
	8:00PM		☐Y ☐N
	8:30PM		☐Y ☐N
	9:00PM		☐Y ☐N
	9:30PM		☐Y ☐N

HEALTH + FITNESS

WATER INTAKE

OZ. OZ. OZ. OZ. OZ.

OZ. OZ. OZ. OZ. OZ.

TAKE 5 MINUTES EACH MORNING TO PLAN YOUR DAY.

GET EIGHT HOURS OF SLEEP!

NOTE HIGH PRIORITY TASKS WITH A *

ANALYZE WHY A TASK WAS NOT COMPLETED, THEN MOVE TO NEXT DAY.

ONE POSITIVE

TODAY I GAVE

DAILY
GOAL SLAYERS
PLANNER

SETTING YOURSELF UP FOR SUCCESS DAILY!

DATE

____/____/____

SCRIPTURE

MOTIVATIONAL QUOTE

ONE GOAL

ONE FUN THING

HEALTH + FITNESS

WATER INTAKE

*	IMPORTANT TIME	SCHEDULE	SLAYED?
	5:00AM		☐Y ☐N
	5:30AM		☐Y ☐N
	6:00AM		☐Y ☐N
	6:30AM		☐Y ☐N
	7:00AM		☐Y ☐N
	7:30AM		☐Y ☐N
	8:00AM		☐Y ☐N
	8:30AM		☐Y ☐N
	9:00AM		☐Y ☐N
	9:30AM		☐Y ☐N
	10:00AM		☐Y ☐N
	10:30AM		☐Y ☐N
	11:00AM		☐Y ☐N
	11:30AM		☐Y ☐N
	12:00PM		☐Y ☐N
	12:30PM		☐Y ☐N
	1:00PM		☐Y ☐N
	1:30PM		☐Y ☐N
	2:00PM		☐Y ☐N
	2:30PM		☐Y ☐N
	3:00PM		☐Y ☐N
	3:30PM		☐Y ☐N
	4:00PM		☐Y ☐N
	4:30PM		☐Y ☐N
	5:00PM		☐Y ☐N
	5:30PM		☐Y ☐N
	6:00PM		☐Y ☐N
	6:30PM		☐Y ☐N
	7:00PM		☐Y ☐N
	7:30PM		☐Y ☐N
	8:00PM		☐Y ☐N
	8:30PM		☐Y ☐N
	9:00PM		☐Y ☐N
	9:30PM		☐Y ☐N

TAKE 5 MINUTES EACH MORNING TO PLAN YOUR DAY.

GET EIGHT HOURS OF SLEEP!

NOTE HIGH PRIORITY TASKS WITH A *

ANALYZE WHY A TASK WAS NOT COMPLETED, THEN MOVE TO NEXT DAY.

ONE POSITIVE

TODAY I GAVE

DAILY
GOAL SLAYERS
PLANNER

SETTING YOURSELF UP FOR SUCCESS DAILY!

DATE

____ / ____ / ____

SCRIPTURE

MOTIVATIONAL QUOTE

ONE GOAL

ONE FUN THING

✱	IMPORTANT TIME	SCHEDULE	SLAYED?
	5:00AM		☐Y ☐N
	5:30AM		☐Y ☐N
	6:00AM		☐Y ☐N
	6:30AM		☐Y ☐N
	7:00AM		☐Y ☐N
	7:30AM		☐Y ☐N
	8:00AM		☐Y ☐N
	8:30AM		☐Y ☐N
	9:00AM		☐Y ☐N
	9:30AM		☐Y ☐N
	10:00AM		☐Y ☐N
	10:30AM		☐Y ☐N
	11:00AM		☐Y ☐N
	11:30AM		☐Y ☐N
	12:00PM		☐Y ☐N
	12:30PM		☐Y ☐N
	1:00PM		☐Y ☐N
	1:30PM		☐Y ☐N
	2:00PM		☐Y ☐N
	2:30PM		☐Y ☐N
	3:00PM		☐Y ☐N
	3:30PM		☐Y ☐N
	4:00PM		☐Y ☐N
	4:30PM		☐Y ☐N
	5:00PM		☐Y ☐N
	5:30PM		☐Y ☐N
	6:00PM		☐Y ☐N
	6:30PM		☐Y ☐N
	7:00PM		☐Y ☐N
	7:30PM		☐Y ☐N
	8:00PM		☐Y ☐N
	8:30PM		☐Y ☐N
	9:00PM		☐Y ☐N
	9:30PM		☐Y ☐N

HEALTH • FITNESS

WATER INTAKE

OZ. OZ. OZ. OZ. OZ.
OZ. OZ. OZ. OZ. OZ.

TAKE 5 MINUTES EACH MORNING TO PLAN YOUR DAY.

GET EIGHT HOURS OF SLEEP!

NOTE HIGH PRIORITY TASKS WITH A ✱

ANALYZE WHY A TASK WAS NOT COMPLETED, THEN MOVE TO NEXT DAY.

ONE POSITIVE

TODAY I GAVE

DAILY
GOAL SLAYERS
PLANNER

SETTING YOURSELF UP FOR SUCCESS DAILY!

DATE

____ / ____ / ____

SCRIPTURE

MOTIVATIONAL QUOTE

ONE GOAL

ONE FUN THING

*	IMPORTANT TIME	SCHEDULE	SLAYED?
	5:00AM		☐Y ☐N
	5:30AM		☐Y ☐N
	6:00AM		☐Y ☐N
	6:30AM		☐Y ☐N
	7:00AM		☐Y ☐N
	7:30AM		☐Y ☐N
	8:00AM		☐Y ☐N
	8:30AM		☐Y ☐N
	9:00AM		☐Y ☐N
	9:30AM		☐Y ☐N
	10:00AM		☐Y ☐N
	10:30AM		☐Y ☐N
	11:00AM		☐Y ☐N
	11:30AM		☐Y ☐N
	12:00PM		☐Y ☐N
	12:30PM		☐Y ☐N
	1:00PM		☐Y ☐N
	1:30PM		☐Y ☐N
	2:00PM		☐Y ☐N
	2:30PM		☐Y ☐N
	3:00PM		☐Y ☐N
	3:30PM		☐Y ☐N
	4:00PM		☐Y ☐N
	4:30PM		☐Y ☐N
	5:00PM		☐Y ☐N
	5:30PM		☐Y ☐N
	6:00PM		☐Y ☐N
	6:30PM		☐Y ☐N
	7:00PM		☐Y ☐N
	7:30PM		☐Y ☐N
	8:00PM		☐Y ☐N
	8:30PM		☐Y ☐N
	9:00PM		☐Y ☐N
	9:30PM		☐Y ☐N

HEALTH • FITNESS

WATER INTAKE

OZ. OZ. OZ. OZ. OZ.
OZ. OZ. OZ. OZ. OZ.

TAKE 5 MINUTES EACH MORNING TO PLAN YOUR DAY.

GET EIGHT HOURS OF SLEEP!

NOTE HIGH PRIORITY TASKS WITH A *

ANALYZE WHY A TASK WAS NOT COMPLETED, THEN MOVE TO NEXT DAY.

ONE POSITIVE

TODAY I GAVE

DAILY
GOAL SLAYERS
PLANNER

SETTING YOURSELF UP FOR SUCCESS DAILY!

DATE

_____ / _____ / _____

SCRIPTURE

MOTIVATIONAL QUOTE

ONE GOAL

ONE FUN THING

HEALTH + FITNESS

*	IMPORTANT TIME	SCHEDULE	SLAYED?
	5:00AM		☐Y ☐N
	5:30AM		☐Y ☐N
	6:00AM		☐Y ☐N
	6:30AM		☐Y ☐N
	7:00AM		☐Y ☐N
	7:30AM		☐Y ☐N
	8:00AM		☐Y ☐N
	8:30AM		☐Y ☐N
	9:00AM		☐Y ☐N
	9:30AM		☐Y ☐N
	10:00AM		☐Y ☐N
	10:30AM		☐Y ☐N
	11:00AM		☐Y ☐N
	11:30AM		☐Y ☐N
	12:00PM		☐Y ☐N
	12:30PM		☐Y ☐N
	1:00PM		☐Y ☐N
	1:30PM		☐Y ☐N
	2:00PM		☐Y ☐N
	2:30PM		☐Y ☐N
	3:00PM		☐Y ☐N
	3:30PM		☐Y ☐N
	4:00PM		☐Y ☐N
	4:30PM		☐Y ☐N
	5:00PM		☐Y ☐N
	5:30PM		☐Y ☐N
	6:00PM		☐Y ☐N
	6:30PM		☐Y ☐N
	7:00PM		☐Y ☐N
	7:30PM		☐Y ☐N
	8:00PM		☐Y ☐N
	8:30PM		☐Y ☐N
	9:00PM		☐Y ☐N
	9:30PM		☐Y ☐N

WATER INTAKE

OZ. OZ. OZ. OZ. OZ.
OZ. OZ. OZ. OZ. OZ.

TAKE 5 MINUTES EACH MORNING TO PLAN YOUR DAY.

GET EIGHT HOURS OF SLEEP!

NOTE HIGH PRIORITY TASKS WITH A *

ANALYZE WHY A TASK WAS NOT COMPLETED, THEN MOVE TO NEXT DAY.

ONE POSITIVE

TODAY I GAVE

DAILY
GOAL SLAYERS
PLANNER

SETTING YOURSELF UP FOR SUCCESS DAILY!

DATE

_____ / _____ / _____

SCRIPTURE

MOTIVATIONAL QUOTE

ONE GOAL

ONE FUN THING

HEALTH • FITNESS

WATER INTAKE

OZ OZ OZ OZ OZ

OZ OZ OZ OZ OZ

✱	IMPORTANT TIME	SCHEDULE	SLAYED?
	5:00AM		☐Y ☐N
	5:30AM		☐Y ☐N
	6:00AM		☐Y ☐N
	6:30AM		☐Y ☐N
	7:00AM		☐Y ☐N
	7:30AM		☐Y ☐N
	8:00AM		☐Y ☐N
	8:30AM		☐Y ☐N
	9:00AM		☐Y ☐N
	9:30AM		☐Y ☐N
	10:00AM		☐Y ☐N
	10:30AM		☐Y ☐N
	11:00AM		☐Y ☐N
	11:30AM		☐Y ☐N
	12:00PM		☐Y ☐N
	12:30PM		☐Y ☐N
	1:00PM		☐Y ☐N
	1:30PM		☐Y ☐N
	2:00PM		☐Y ☐N
	2:30PM		☐Y ☐N
	3:00PM		☐Y ☐N
	3:30PM		☐Y ☐N
	4:00PM		☐Y ☐N
	4:30PM		☐Y ☐N
	5:00PM		☐Y ☐N
	5:30PM		☐Y ☐N
	6:00PM		☐Y ☐N
	6:30PM		☐Y ☐N
	7:00PM		☐Y ☐N
	7:30PM		☐Y ☐N
	8:00PM		☐Y ☐N
	8:30PM		☐Y ☐N
	9:00PM		☐Y ☐N
	9:30PM		☐Y ☐N

TAKE 5 MINUTES EACH MORNING TO PLAN YOUR DAY.

GET EIGHT HOURS OF SLEEP!

NOTE HIGH PRIORITY TASKS WITH A ✱

ANALYZE WHY A TASK WAS NOT COMPLETED, THEN MOVE TO NEXT DAY.

ONE POSITIVE

TODAY I GAVE

DAILY
GOAL SLAYERS
PLANNER

SETTING YOURSELF UP FOR SUCCESS DAILY!

DATE
_____ / _____ / _____

SCRIPTURE

MOTIVATIONAL QUOTE

ONE GOAL

ONE FUN THING

HEALTH • FITNESS

WATER INTAKE

OZ. OZ. OZ. OZ. OZ.

OZ. OZ. OZ. OZ. OZ.

✱	IMPORTANT TIME	SCHEDULE	SLAYED?
	5:00AM		☐Y ☐N
	5:30AM		☐Y ☐N
	6:00AM		☐Y ☐N
	6:30AM		☐Y ☐N
	7:00AM		☐Y ☐N
	7:30AM		☐Y ☐N
	8:00AM		☐Y ☐N
	8:30AM		☐Y ☐N
	9:00AM		☐Y ☐N
	9:30AM		☐Y ☐N
	10:00AM		☐Y ☐N
	10:30AM		☐Y ☐N
	11:00AM		☐Y ☐N
	11:30AM		☐Y ☐N
	12:00PM		☐Y ☐N
	12:30PM		☐Y ☐N
	1:00PM		☐Y ☐N
	1:30PM		☐Y ☐N
	2:00PM		☐Y ☐N
	2:30PM		☐Y ☐N
	3:00PM		☐Y ☐N
	3:30PM		☐Y ☐N
	4:00PM		☐Y ☐N
	4:30PM		☐Y ☐N
	5:00PM		☐Y ☐N
	5:30PM		☐Y ☐N
	6:00PM		☐Y ☐N
	6:30PM		☐Y ☐N
	7:00PM		☐Y ☐N
	7:30PM		☐Y ☐N
	8:00PM		☐Y ☐N
	8:30PM		☐Y ☐N
	9:00PM		☐Y ☐N
	9:30PM		☐Y ☐N

TAKE 5 MINUTES EACH MORNING TO PLAN YOUR DAY.

GET EIGHT HOURS OF SLEEP!

NOTE HIGH PRIORITY TASKS WITH A ✱

ANALYZE WHY A TASK WAS NOT COMPLETED, THEN MOVE TO NEXT DAY.

ONE POSITIVE

TODAY I GAVE

DAILY
GOAL SLAYERS
PLANNER

SETTING YOURSELF UP FOR SUCCESS DAILY!

DATE
_____ / _____ / _____

SCRIPTURE

MOTIVATIONAL QUOTE

ONE GOAL

ONE FUN THING

HEALTH • FITNESS

WATER INTAKE

| OZ. | OZ. | OZ. | OZ. | OZ. |

*	IMPORTANT TIME	SCHEDULE	SLAYED?
	5:00AM		☐Y ☐N
	5:30AM		☐Y ☐N
	6:00AM		☐Y ☐N
	6:30AM		☐Y ☐N
	7:00AM		☐Y ☐N
	7:30AM		☐Y ☐N
	8:00AM		☐Y ☐N
	8:30AM		☐Y ☐N
	9:00AM		☐Y ☐N
	9:30AM		☐Y ☐N
	10:00AM		☐Y ☐N
	10:30AM		☐Y ☐N
	11:00AM		☐Y ☐N
	11:30AM		☐Y ☐N
	12:00PM		☐Y ☐N
	12:30PM		☐Y ☐N
	1:00PM		☐Y ☐N
	1:30PM		☐Y ☐N
	2:00PM		☐Y ☐N
	2:30PM		☐Y ☐N
	3:00PM		☐Y ☐N
	3:30PM		☐Y ☐N
	4:00PM		☐Y ☐N
	4:30PM		☐Y ☐N
	5:00PM		☐Y ☐N
	5:30PM		☐Y ☐N
	6:00PM		☐Y ☐N
	6:30PM		☐Y ☐N
	7:00PM		☐Y ☐N
	7:30PM		☐Y ☐N
	8:00PM		☐Y ☐N
	8:30PM		☐Y ☐N
	9:00PM		☐Y ☐N
	9:30PM		☐Y ☐N

TAKE 5 MINUTES EACH MORNING TO PLAN YOUR DAY.

GET EIGHT HOURS OF SLEEP!

NOTE HIGH PRIORITY TASKS WITH A *

ANALYZE WHY A TASK WAS NOT COMPLETED, THEN MOVE TO NEXT DAY.

ONE POSITIVE

TODAY I GAVE

DAILY
GOAL SLAYERS
PLANNER

SETTING YOURSELF UP FOR SUCCESS DAILY!

DATE

____/____/____

SCRIPTURE

MOTIVATIONAL QUOTE

ONE GOAL

ONE FUN THING

HEALTH + FITNESS

WATER INTAKE

OZ. OZ. OZ. OZ. OZ.

OZ. OZ. OZ. OZ. OZ.

*	IMPORTANT TIME	SCHEDULE	SLAYED?	
	5:00AM		☐Y	☐N
	5:30AM		☐Y	☐N
	6:00AM		☐Y	☐N
	6:30AM		☐Y	☐N
	7:00AM		☐Y	☐N
	7:30AM		☐Y	☐N
	8:00AM		☐Y	☐N
	8:30AM		☐Y	☐N
	9:00AM		☐Y	☐N
	9:30AM		☐Y	☐N
	10:00AM		☐Y	☐N
	10:30AM		☐Y	☐N
	11:00AM		☐Y	☐N
	11:30AM		☐Y	☐N
	12:00PM		☐Y	☐N
	12:30PM		☐Y	☐N
	1:00PM		☐Y	☐N
	1:30PM		☐Y	☐N
	2:00PM		☐Y	☐N
	2:30PM		☐Y	☐N
	3:00PM		☐Y	☐N
	3:30PM		☐Y	☐N
	4:00PM		☐Y	☐N
	4:30PM		☐Y	☐N
	5:00PM		☐Y	☐N
	5:30PM		☐Y	☐N
	6:00PM		☐Y	☐N
	6:30PM		☐Y	☐N
	7:00PM		☐Y	☐N
	7:30PM		☐Y	☐N
	8:00PM		☐Y	☐N
	8:30PM		☐Y	☐N
	9:00PM		☐Y	☐N
	9:30PM		☐Y	☐N

TAKE 5 MINUTES EACH MORNING TO PLAN YOUR DAY.

GET EIGHT HOURS OF SLEEP!

NOTE HIGH PRIORITY TASKS WITH A *

ANALYZE WHY A TASK WAS NOT COMPLETED, THEN MOVE TO NEXT DAY.

ONE POSITIVE

TODAY I GAVE

DAILY
GOAL SLAYERS
PLANNER

SETTING YOURSELF UP FOR SUCCESS DAILY!

DATE

____ / ____ / ____

SCRIPTURE

MOTIVATIONAL QUOTE

ONE GOAL

ONE FUN THING

HEALTH + FITNESS

WATER INTAKE

*	IMPORTANT TIME	SCHEDULE	SLAYED?
	5:00AM		☐Y ☐N
	5:30AM		☐Y ☐N
	6:00AM		☐Y ☐N
	6:30AM		☐Y ☐N
	7:00AM		☐Y ☐N
	7:30AM		☐Y ☐N
	8:00AM		☐Y ☐N
	8:30AM		☐Y ☐N
	9:00AM		☐Y ☐N
	9:30AM		☐Y ☐N
	10:00AM		☐Y ☐N
	10:30AM		☐Y ☐N
	11:00AM		☐Y ☐N
	11:30AM		☐Y ☐N
	12:00PM		☐Y ☐N
	12:30PM		☐Y ☐N
	1:00PM		☐Y ☐N
	1:30PM		☐Y ☐N
	2:00PM		☐Y ☐N
	2:30PM		☐Y ☐N
	3:00PM		☐Y ☐N
	3:30PM		☐Y ☐N
	4:00PM		☐Y ☐N
	4:30PM		☐Y ☐N
	5:00PM		☐Y ☐N
	5:30PM		☐Y ☐N
	6:00PM		☐Y ☐N
	6:30PM		☐Y ☐N
	7:00PM		☐Y ☐N
	7:30PM		☐Y ☐N
	8:00PM		☐Y ☐N
	8:30PM		☐Y ☐N
	9:00PM		☐Y ☐N
	9:30PM		☐Y ☐N

TAKE 5 MINUTES EACH MORNING TO PLAN YOUR DAY.

GET EIGHT HOURS OF SLEEP!

NOTE HIGH PRIORITY TASKS WITH A ✱

ANALYZE WHY A TASK WAS NOT COMPLETED, THEN MOVE TO NEXT DAY.

ONE POSITIVE

TODAY I GAVE

DAILY
GOAL SLAYERS
PLANNER

SETTING YOURSELF UP FOR SUCCESS DAILY!

DATE

_____ / _____ / _____

SCRIPTURE

MOTIVATIONAL QUOTE

ONE GOAL

ONE FUN THING

HEALTH · FITNESS

WATER INTAKE

OZ. OZ. OZ. OZ. OZ.

OZ. OZ. OZ. OZ. OZ.

✱	IMPORTANT TIME	SCHEDULE	SLAYED?
	5:00AM		☐Y ☐N
	5:30AM		☐Y ☐N
	6:00AM		☐Y ☐N
	6:30AM		☐Y ☐N
	7:00AM		☐Y ☐N
	7:30AM		☐Y ☐N
	8:00AM		☐Y ☐N
	8:30AM		☐Y ☐N
	9:00AM		☐Y ☐N
	9:30AM		☐Y ☐N
	10:00AM		☐Y ☐N
	10:30AM		☐Y ☐N
	11:00AM		☐Y ☐N
	11:30AM		☐Y ☐N
	12:00PM		☐Y ☐N
	12:30PM		☐Y ☐N
	1:00PM		☐Y ☐N
	1:30PM		☐Y ☐N
	2:00PM		☐Y ☐N
	2:30PM		☐Y ☐N
	3:00PM		☐Y ☐N
	3:30PM		☐Y ☐N
	4:00PM		☐Y ☐N
	4:30PM		☐Y ☐N
	5:00PM		☐Y ☐N
	5:30PM		☐Y ☐N
	6:00PM		☐Y ☐N
	6:30PM		☐Y ☐N
	7:00PM		☐Y ☐N
	7:30PM		☐Y ☐N
	8:00PM		☐Y ☐N
	8:30PM		☐Y ☐N
	9:00PM		☐Y ☐N
	9:30PM		☐Y ☐N

TAKE 5 MINUTES EACH MORNING TO PLAN YOUR DAY.

GET EIGHT HOURS OF SLEEP!

NOTE HIGH PRIORITY TASKS WITH A ✱

ANALYZE WHY A TASK WAS NOT COMPLETED, THEN MOVE TO NEXT DAY.

ONE POSITIVE

TODAY I GAVE

DAILY
GOAL SLAYERS
PLANNER

SETTING YOURSELF UP FOR SUCCESS DAILY!

DATE

_____ / _____ / _____

SCRIPTURE

MOTIVATIONAL QUOTE

ONE GOAL

ONE FUN THING

HEALTH + FITNESS

WATER INTAKE

OZ. OZ. OZ. OZ. OZ.

OZ. OZ. OZ. OZ. OZ.

*	IMPORTANT TIME	SCHEDULE	SLAYED?
	5:00AM		☐Y ☐N
	5:30AM		☐Y ☐N
	6:00AM		☐Y ☐N
	6:30AM		☐Y ☐N
	7:00AM		☐Y ☐N
	7:30AM		☐Y ☐N
	8:00AM		☐Y ☐N
	8:30AM		☐Y ☐N
	9:00AM		☐Y ☐N
	9:30AM		☐Y ☐N
	10:00AM		☐Y ☐N
	10:30AM		☐Y ☐N
	11:00AM		☐Y ☐N
	11:30AM		☐Y ☐N
	12:00PM		☐Y ☐N
	12:30PM		☐Y ☐N
	1:00PM		☐Y ☐N
	1:30PM		☐Y ☐N
	2:00PM		☐Y ☐N
	2:30PM		☐Y ☐N
	3:00PM		☐Y ☐N
	3:30PM		☐Y ☐N
	4:00PM		☐Y ☐N
	4:30PM		☐Y ☐N
	5:00PM		☐Y ☐N
	5:30PM		☐Y ☐N
	6:00PM		☐Y ☐N
	6:30PM		☐Y ☐N
	7:00PM		☐Y ☐N
	7:30PM		☐Y ☐N
	8:00PM		☐Y ☐N
	8:30PM		☐Y ☐N
	9:00PM		☐Y ☐N
	9:30PM		☐Y ☐N

TAKE 5 MINUTES EACH MORNING TO PLAN YOUR DAY.

GET EIGHT HOURS OF SLEEP!

NOTE HIGH PRIORITY TASKS WITH A *

ANALYZE WHY A TASK WAS NOT COMPLETED, THEN MOVE TO NEXT DAY.

ONE POSITIVE

TODAY I GAVE

DAILY GOAL SLAYERS PLANNER

SETTING YOURSELF UP FOR SUCCESS DAILY!

DATE

_____ / _____ / _____

SCRIPTURE

MOTIVATIONAL QUOTE

ONE GOAL

ONE FUN THING

*	IMPORTANT TIME	SCHEDULE	SLAYED?
	5:00AM		☐Y ☐N
	5:30AM		☐Y ☐N
	6:00AM		☐Y ☐N
	6:30AM		☐Y ☐N
	7:00AM		☐Y ☐N
	7:30AM		☐Y ☐N
	8:00AM		☐Y ☐N
	8:30AM		☐Y ☐N
	9:00AM		☐Y ☐N
	9:30AM		☐Y ☐N
	10:00AM		☐Y ☐N
	10:30AM		☐Y ☐N
	11:00AM		☐Y ☐N
	11:30AM		☐Y ☐N
	12:00PM		☐Y ☐N
	12:30PM		☐Y ☐N
	1:00PM		☐Y ☐N
	1:30PM		☐Y ☐N
	2:00PM		☐Y ☐N
	2:30PM		☐Y ☐N
	3:00PM		☐Y ☐N
	3:30PM		☐Y ☐N
	4:00PM		☐Y ☐N
	4:30PM		☐Y ☐N
	5:00PM		☐Y ☐N
	5:30PM		☐Y ☐N
	6:00PM		☐Y ☐N
	6:30PM		☐Y ☐N
	7:00PM		☐Y ☐N
	7:30PM		☐Y ☐N
	8:00PM		☐Y ☐N
	8:30PM		☐Y ☐N
	9:00PM		☐Y ☐N
	9:30PM		☐Y ☐N

HEALTH + FITNESS

WATER INTAKE

OZ. OZ. OZ. OZ. OZ.
OZ. OZ. OZ. OZ. OZ.

TAKE 5 MINUTES EACH MORNING TO PLAN YOUR DAY.

GET EIGHT HOURS OF SLEEP!

NOTE HIGH PRIORITY TASKS WITH A *

ANALYZE WHY A TASK WAS NOT COMPLETED, THEN MOVE TO NEXT DAY.

ONE POSITIVE

TODAY I GAVE

DAILY
GOAL SLAYERS
PLANNER

SETTING YOURSELF UP FOR SUCCESS DAILY!

DATE

____ / ____ / ____

SCRIPTURE

MOTIVATIONAL QUOTE

ONE GOAL

ONE FUN THING

HEALTH • FITNESS

WATER INTAKE

OZ. OZ. OZ. OZ. OZ.
OZ. OZ. OZ. OZ. OZ.

*	IMPORTANT TIME	SCHEDULE	SLAYED?
	5:00AM		☐Y ☐N
	5:30AM		☐Y ☐N
	6:00AM		☐Y ☐N
	6:30AM		☐Y ☐N
	7:00AM		☐Y ☐N
	7:30AM		☐Y ☐N
	8:00AM		☐Y ☐N
	8:30AM		☐Y ☐N
	9:00AM		☐Y ☐N
	9:30AM		☐Y ☐N
	10:00AM		☐Y ☐N
	10:30AM		☐Y ☐N
	11:00AM		☐Y ☐N
	11:30AM		☐Y ☐N
	12:00PM		☐Y ☐N
	12:30PM		☐Y ☐N
	1:00PM		☐Y ☐N
	1:30PM		☐Y ☐N
	2:00PM		☐Y ☐N
	2:30PM		☐Y ☐N
	3:00PM		☐Y ☐N
	3:30PM		☐Y ☐N
	4:00PM		☐Y ☐N
	4:30PM		☐Y ☐N
	5:00PM		☐Y ☐N
	5:30PM		☐Y ☐N
	6:00PM		☐Y ☐N
	6:30PM		☐Y ☐N
	7:00PM		☐Y ☐N
	7:30PM		☐Y ☐N
	8:00PM		☐Y ☐N
	8:30PM		☐Y ☐N
	9:00PM		☐Y ☐N
	9:30PM		☐Y ☐N

TAKE 5 MINUTES EACH MORNING TO PLAN YOUR DAY.

GET EIGHT HOURS OF SLEEP!

NOTE HIGH PRIORITY TASKS WITH A *

ANALYZE WHY A TASK WAS NOT COMPLETED, THEN MOVE TO NEXT DAY.

ONE POSITIVE

TODAY I GAVE

DAILY
GOAL SLAYERS
PLANNER

SETTING YOURSELF UP FOR SUCCESS DAILY!

DATE

____ / ____ / ____

SCRIPTURE

MOTIVATIONAL QUOTE

ONE GOAL

ONE FUN THING

HEALTH + FITNESS

WATER INTAKE

*	IMPORTANT TIME	SCHEDULE	SLAYED?
	5:00AM		☐Y ☐N
	5:30AM		☐Y ☐N
	6:00AM		☐Y ☐N
	6:30AM		☐Y ☐N
	7:00AM		☐Y ☐N
	7:30AM		☐Y ☐N
	8:00AM		☐Y ☐N
	8:30AM		☐Y ☐N
	9:00AM		☐Y ☐N
	9:30AM		☐Y ☐N
	10:00AM		☐Y ☐N
	10:30AM		☐Y ☐N
	11:00AM		☐Y ☐N
	11:30AM		☐Y ☐N
	12:00PM		☐Y ☐N
	12:30PM		☐Y ☐N
	1:00PM		☐Y ☐N
	1:30PM		☐Y ☐N
	2:00PM		☐Y ☐N
	2:30PM		☐Y ☐N
	3:00PM		☐Y ☐N
	3:30PM		☐Y ☐N
	4:00PM		☐Y ☐N
	4:30PM		☐Y ☐N
	5:00PM		☐Y ☐N
	5:30PM		☐Y ☐N
	6:00PM		☐Y ☐N
	6:30PM		☐Y ☐N
	7:00PM		☐Y ☐N
	7:30PM		☐Y ☐N
	8:00PM		☐Y ☐N
	8:30PM		☐Y ☐N
	9:00PM		☐Y ☐N
	9:30PM		☐Y ☐N

TAKE 5 MINUTES EACH MORNING TO PLAN YOUR DAY.

GET EIGHT HOURS OF SLEEP!

NOTE HIGH PRIORITY TASKS WITH A *

ANALYZE WHY A TASK WAS NOT COMPLETED, THEN MOVE TO NEXT DAY.

ONE POSITIVE

TODAY I GAVE

DAILY
GOAL SLAYERS
PLANNER

SETTING YOURSELF UP FOR SUCCESS DAILY!

DATE

____ / ____ / ____

SCRIPTURE

MOTIVATIONAL QUOTE

ONE GOAL

ONE FUN THING

*	IMPORTANT TIME	SCHEDULE	SLAYED?
	5:00AM		☐Y ☐N
	5:30AM		☐Y ☐N
	6:00AM		☐Y ☐N
	6:30AM		☐Y ☐N
	7:00AM		☐Y ☐N
	7:30AM		☐Y ☐N
	8:00AM		☐Y ☐N
	8:30AM		☐Y ☐N
	9:00AM		☐Y ☐N
	9:30AM		☐Y ☐N
	10:00AM		☐Y ☐N
	10:30AM		☐Y ☐N
	11:00AM		☐Y ☐N
	11:30AM		☐Y ☐N
	12:00PM		☐Y ☐N
	12:30PM		☐Y ☐N
	1:00PM		☐Y ☐N
	1:30PM		☐Y ☐N
	2:00PM		☐Y ☐N
	2:30PM		☐Y ☐N
	3:00PM		☐Y ☐N
	3:30PM		☐Y ☐N
	4:00PM		☐Y ☐N
	4:30PM		☐Y ☐N
	5:00PM		☐Y ☐N
	5:30PM		☐Y ☐N
	6:00PM		☐Y ☐N
	6:30PM		☐Y ☐N
	7:00PM		☐Y ☐N
	7:30PM		☐Y ☐N
	8:00PM		☐Y ☐N
	8:30PM		☐Y ☐N
	9:00PM		☐Y ☐N
	9:30PM		☐Y ☐N

HEALTH + FITNESS

WATER INTAKE

OZ. OZ. OZ. OZ. OZ.
OZ. OZ. OZ. OZ. OZ.

TAKE 5 MINUTES EACH MORNING TO PLAN YOUR DAY.

GET EIGHT HOURS OF SLEEP!

NOTE HIGH PRIORITY TASKS WITH A *

ANALYZE WHY A TASK WAS NOT COMPLETED, THEN MOVE TO NEXT DAY.

ONE POSITIVE

TODAY I GAVE

DAILY
GOAL SLAYERS
PLANNER

SETTING YOURSELF UP FOR SUCCESS DAILY!

DATE

_____/_____/_____

SCRIPTURE

MOTIVATIONAL QUOTE

ONE GOAL

ONE FUN THING

*	IMPORTANT TIME	SCHEDULE	SLAYED?
	5:00AM		☐Y ☐N
	5:30AM		☐Y ☐N
	6:00AM		☐Y ☐N
	6:30AM		☐Y ☐N
	7:00AM		☐Y ☐N
	7:30AM		☐Y ☐N
	8:00AM		☐Y ☐N
	8:30AM		☐Y ☐N
	9:00AM		☐Y ☐N
	9:30AM		☐Y ☐N
	10:00AM		☐Y ☐N
	10:30AM		☐Y ☐N
	11:00AM		☐Y ☐N
	11:30AM		☐Y ☐N
	12:00PM		☐Y ☐N
	12:30PM		☐Y ☐N
	1:00PM		☐Y ☐N
	1:30PM		☐Y ☐N
	2:00PM		☐Y ☐N
	2:30PM		☐Y ☐N
	3:00PM		☐Y ☐N
	3:30PM		☐Y ☐N
	4:00PM		☐Y ☐N
	4:30PM		☐Y ☐N
	5:00PM		☐Y ☐N
	5:30PM		☐Y ☐N
	6:00PM		☐Y ☐N
	6:30PM		☐Y ☐N
	7:00PM		☐Y ☐N
	7:30PM		☐Y ☐N
	8:00PM		☐Y ☐N
	8:30PM		☐Y ☐N
	9:00PM		☐Y ☐N
	9:30PM		☐Y ☐N

HEALTH + FITNESS

WATER INTAKE

OZ. OZ. OZ. OZ. OZ.
OZ. OZ. OZ. OZ. OZ.

TAKE 5 MINUTES EACH MORNING TO PLAN YOUR DAY.

GET EIGHT HOURS OF SLEEP!

NOTE HIGH PRIORITY TASKS WITH A *

ANALYZE WHY A TASK WAS NOT COMPLETED, THEN MOVE TO NEXT DAY.

ONE POSITIVE

TODAY I GAVE

DAILY
GOAL SLAYERS
PLANNER

SETTING YOURSELF UP FOR SUCCESS DAILY!

DATE

_____ / _____ / _____

SCRIPTURE

MOTIVATIONAL QUOTE

ONE GOAL

ONE FUN THING

HEALTH • FITNESS

WATER INTAKE

OZ OZ OZ OZ OZ

OZ OZ OZ OZ OZ

✱	IMPORTANT TIME	SCHEDULE	SLAYED?
	5:00AM		☐Y ☐N
	5:30AM		☐Y ☐N
	6:00AM		☐Y ☐N
	6:30AM		☐Y ☐N
	7:00AM		☐Y ☐N
	7:30AM		☐Y ☐N
	8:00AM		☐Y ☐N
	8:30AM		☐Y ☐N
	9:00AM		☐Y ☐N
	9:30AM		☐Y ☐N
	10:00AM		☐Y ☐N
	10:30AM		☐Y ☐N
	11:00AM		☐Y ☐N
	11:30AM		☐Y ☐N
	12:00PM		☐Y ☐N
	12:30PM		☐Y ☐N
	1:00PM		☐Y ☐N
	1:30PM		☐Y ☐N
	2:00PM		☐Y ☐N
	2:30PM		☐Y ☐N
	3:00PM		☐Y ☐N
	3:30PM		☐Y ☐N
	4:00PM		☐Y ☐N
	4:30PM		☐Y ☐N
	5:00PM		☐Y ☐N
	5:30PM		☐Y ☐N
	6:00PM		☐Y ☐N
	6:30PM		☐Y ☐N
	7:00PM		☐Y ☐N
	7:30PM		☐Y ☐N
	8:00PM		☐Y ☐N
	8:30PM		☐Y ☐N
	9:00PM		☐Y ☐N
	9:30PM		☐Y ☐N

TAKE 5 MINUTES EACH MORNING TO PLAN YOUR DAY.

GET EIGHT HOURS OF SLEEP!

NOTE HIGH PRIORITY TASKS WITH A ✱

ANALYZE WHY A TASK WAS NOT COMPLETED, THEN MOVE TO NEXT DAY.

ONE POSITIVE

TODAY I GAVE

DAILY
GOAL SLAYERS
PLANNER

SETTING YOURSELF UP FOR SUCCESS DAILY!

DATE

_____ / _____ / _____

SCRIPTURE

MOTIVATIONAL QUOTE

ONE GOAL

ONE FUN THING

HEALTH • FITNESS

WATER INTAKE

OZ OZ OZ OZ OZ

OZ OZ OZ OZ OZ

*	IMPORTANT TIME	SCHEDULE	SLAYED?
	5:00AM		☐Y ☐N
	5:30AM		☐Y ☐N
	6:00AM		☐Y ☐N
	6:30AM		☐Y ☐N
	7:00AM		☐Y ☐N
	7:30AM		☐Y ☐N
	8:00AM		☐Y ☐N
	8:30AM		☐Y ☐N
	9:00AM		☐Y ☐N
	9:30AM		☐Y ☐N
	10:00AM		☐Y ☐N
	10:30AM		☐Y ☐N
	11:00AM		☐Y ☐N
	11:30AM		☐Y ☐N
	12:00PM		☐Y ☐N
	12:30PM		☐Y ☐N
	1:00PM		☐Y ☐N
	1:30PM		☐Y ☐N
	2:00PM		☐Y ☐N
	2:30PM		☐Y ☐N
	3:00PM		☐Y ☐N
	3:30PM		☐Y ☐N
	4:00PM		☐Y ☐N
	4:30PM		☐Y ☐N
	5:00PM		☐Y ☐N
	5:30PM		☐Y ☐N
	6:00PM		☐Y ☐N
	6:30PM		☐Y ☐N
	7:00PM		☐Y ☐N
	7:30PM		☐Y ☐N
	8:00PM		☐Y ☐N
	8:30PM		☐Y ☐N
	9:00PM		☐Y ☐N
	9:30PM		☐Y ☐N

TAKE 5 MINUTES EACH MORNING TO PLAN YOUR DAY.

GET EIGHT HOURS OF SLEEP!

NOTE HIGH PRIORITY TASKS WITH A *

ANALYZE WHY A TASK WAS NOT COMPLETED, THEN MOVE TO NEXT DAY.

ONE POSITIVE

TODAY I GAVE

DAILY
GOAL SLAYERS
PLANNER

SETTING YOURSELF UP FOR SUCCESS DAILY!

DATE

____ / ____ / ____

SCRIPTURE

MOTIVATIONAL QUOTE

ONE GOAL

ONE FUN THING

✱	IMPORTANT TIME	SCHEDULE	SLAYED?
	5:00AM		☐Y ☐N
	5:30AM		☐Y ☐N
	6:00AM		☐Y ☐N
	6:30AM		☐Y ☐N
	7:00AM		☐Y ☐N
	7:30AM		☐Y ☐N
	8:00AM		☐Y ☐N
	8:30AM		☐Y ☐N
	9:00AM		☐Y ☐N
	9:30AM		☐Y ☐N
	10:00AM		☐Y ☐N
	10:30AM		☐Y ☐N
	11:00AM		☐Y ☐N
	11:30AM		☐Y ☐N
	12:00PM		☐Y ☐N
	12:30PM		☐Y ☐N
	1:00PM		☐Y ☐N
	1:30PM		☐Y ☐N
	2:00PM		☐Y ☐N
	2:30PM		☐Y ☐N
	3:00PM		☐Y ☐N
	3:30PM		☐Y ☐N
	4:00PM		☐Y ☐N
	4:30PM		☐Y ☐N
	5:00PM		☐Y ☐N
	5:30PM		☐Y ☐N
	6:00PM		☐Y ☐N
	6:30PM		☐Y ☐N
	7:00PM		☐Y ☐N
	7:30PM		☐Y ☐N
	8:00PM		☐Y ☐N
	8:30PM		☐Y ☐N
	9:00PM		☐Y ☐N
	9:30PM		☐Y ☐N

HEALTH • FITNESS

WATER INTAKE

OZ OZ OZ OZ OZ
OZ OZ OZ OZ OZ

TAKE 5 MINUTES EACH MORNING TO PLAN YOUR DAY.

GET EIGHT HOURS OF SLEEP!

NOTE HIGH PRIORITY TASKS WITH A ✱

ANALYZE WHY A TASK WAS NOT COMPLETED, THEN MOVE TO NEXT DAY.

ONE POSITIVE

TODAY I GAVE

DAILY
GOAL SLAYERS
PLANNER

SETTING YOURSELF UP FOR SUCCESS DAILY!

DATE

_____ / _____ / _____

SCRIPTURE

MOTIVATIONAL QUOTE

ONE GOAL

ONE FUN THING

HEALTH + FITNESS

WATER INTAKE

| OZ. | OZ. | OZ. | OZ. | OZ. |
| OZ. | OZ. | OZ. | OZ. | OZ. |

*	IMPORTANT TIME	SCHEDULE	SLAYED?
	5:00AM		☐Y ☐N
	5:30AM		☐Y ☐N
	6:00AM		☐Y ☐N
	6:30AM		☐Y ☐N
	7:00AM		☐Y ☐N
	7:30AM		☐Y ☐N
	8:00AM		☐Y ☐N
	8:30AM		☐Y ☐N
	9:00AM		☐Y ☐N
	9:30AM		☐Y ☐N
	10:00AM		☐Y ☐N
	10:30AM		☐Y ☐N
	11:00AM		☐Y ☐N
	11:30AM		☐Y ☐N
	12:00PM		☐Y ☐N
	12:30PM		☐Y ☐N
	1:00PM		☐Y ☐N
	1:30PM		☐Y ☐N
	2:00PM		☐Y ☐N
	2:30PM		☐Y ☐N
	3:00PM		☐Y ☐N
	3:30PM		☐Y ☐N
	4:00PM		☐Y ☐N
	4:30PM		☐Y ☐N
	5:00PM		☐Y ☐N
	5:30PM		☐Y ☐N
	6:00PM		☐Y ☐N
	6:30PM		☐Y ☐N
	7:00PM		☐Y ☐N
	7:30PM		☐Y ☐N
	8:00PM		☐Y ☐N
	8:30PM		☐Y ☐N
	9:00PM		☐Y ☐N
	9:30PM		☐Y ☐N

TAKE 5 MINUTES EACH MORNING TO PLAN YOUR DAY.

GET EIGHT HOURS OF SLEEP!

NOTE HIGH PRIORITY TASKS WITH A *

ANALYZE WHY A TASK WAS NOT COMPLETED, THEN MOVE TO NEXT DAY.

ONE POSITIVE

TODAY I GAVE

DAILY
GOAL SLAYERS
PLANNER

SETTING YOURSELF UP FOR SUCCESS DAILY!

DATE

_____ / _____ / _____

SCRIPTURE

MOTIVATIONAL QUOTE

ONE GOAL

ONE FUN THING

✱	IMPORTANT TIME	SCHEDULE	SLAYED?
	5:00AM		☐Y ☐N
	5:30AM		☐Y ☐N
	6:00AM		☐Y ☐N
	6:30AM		☐Y ☐N
	7:00AM		☐Y ☐N
	7:30AM		☐Y ☐N
	8:00AM		☐Y ☐N
	8:30AM		☐Y ☐N
	9:00AM		☐Y ☐N
	9:30AM		☐Y ☐N
	10:00AM		☐Y ☐N
	10:30AM		☐Y ☐N
	11:00AM		☐Y ☐N
	11:30AM		☐Y ☐N
	12:00PM		☐Y ☐N
	12:30PM		☐Y ☐N
	1:00PM		☐Y ☐N
	1:30PM		☐Y ☐N
	2:00PM		☐Y ☐N
	2:30PM		☐Y ☐N
	3:00PM		☐Y ☐N
	3:30PM		☐Y ☐N
	4:00PM		☐Y ☐N
	4:30PM		☐Y ☐N
	5:00PM		☐Y ☐N
	5:30PM		☐Y ☐N
	6:00PM		☐Y ☐N
	6:30PM		☐Y ☐N
	7:00PM		☐Y ☐N
	7:30PM		☐Y ☐N
	8:00PM		☐Y ☐N
	8:30PM		☐Y ☐N
	9:00PM		☐Y ☐N
	9:30PM		☐Y ☐N

HEALTH + FITNESS

WATER INTAKE

OZ. OZ. OZ. OZ. OZ.
OZ. OZ. OZ. OZ. OZ.

TAKE 5 MINUTES EACH MORNING TO PLAN YOUR DAY.

GET EIGHT HOURS OF SLEEP!

NOTE HIGH PRIORITY TASKS WITH A ✱

ANALYZE WHY A TASK WAS NOT COMPLETED, THEN MOVE TO NEXT DAY.

ONE POSITIVE

TODAY I GAVE

DAILY
GOAL SLAYERS
PLANNER

SETTING YOURSELF UP FOR SUCCESS DAILY!

DATE

_____ / _____ / _____

SCRIPTURE

MOTIVATIONAL QUOTE

ONE GOAL

ONE FUN THING

HEALTH + FITNESS

WATER INTAKE

OZ OZ OZ OZ OZ

OZ OZ OZ OZ OZ

*	IMPORTANT TIME	SCHEDULE	SLAYED?
	5:00AM		☐Y ☐N
	5:30AM		☐Y ☐N
	6:00AM		☐Y ☐N
	6:30AM		☐Y ☐N
	7:00AM		☐Y ☐N
	7:30AM		☐Y ☐N
	8:00AM		☐Y ☐N
	8:30AM		☐Y ☐N
	9:00AM		☐Y ☐N
	9:30AM		☐Y ☐N
	10:00AM		☐Y ☐N
	10:30AM		☐Y ☐N
	11:00AM		☐Y ☐N
	11:30AM		☐Y ☐N
	12:00PM		☐Y ☐N
	12:30PM		☐Y ☐N
	1:00PM		☐Y ☐N
	1:30PM		☐Y ☐N
	2:00PM		☐Y ☐N
	2:30PM		☐Y ☐N
	3:00PM		☐Y ☐N
	3:30PM		☐Y ☐N
	4:00PM		☐Y ☐N
	4:30PM		☐Y ☐N
	5:00PM		☐Y ☐N
	5:30PM		☐Y ☐N
	6:00PM		☐Y ☐N
	6:30PM		☐Y ☐N
	7:00PM		☐Y ☐N
	7:30PM		☐Y ☐N
	8:00PM		☐Y ☐N
	8:30PM		☐Y ☐N
	9:00PM		☐Y ☐N
	9:30PM		☐Y ☐N

TAKE 5 MINUTES EACH MORNING TO PLAN YOUR DAY.

GET EIGHT HOURS OF SLEEP!

NOTE HIGH PRIORITY TASKS WITH A *

ANALYZE WHY A TASK WAS NOT COMPLETED, THEN MOVE TO NEXT DAY.

ONE POSITIVE

TODAY I GAVE

DAILY
GOAL SLAYERS
PLANNER

SETTING YOURSELF UP FOR SUCCESS DAILY!

DATE
_____ / _____ / _____

SCRIPTURE

MOTIVATIONAL QUOTE

ONE GOAL

ONE FUN THING

HEALTH • FITNESS

WATER INTAKE

OZ. OZ. OZ. OZ. OZ.

OZ. OZ. OZ. OZ. OZ.

✱	IMPORTANT TIME	SCHEDULE	SLAYED?
	5:00AM		☐Y ☐N
	5:30AM		☐Y ☐N
	6:00AM		☐Y ☐N
	6:30AM		☐Y ☐N
	7:00AM		☐Y ☐N
	7:30AM		☐Y ☐N
	8:00AM		☐Y ☐N
	8:30AM		☐Y ☐N
	9:00AM		☐Y ☐N
	9:30AM		☐Y ☐N
	10:00AM		☐Y ☐N
	10:30AM		☐Y ☐N
	11:00AM		☐Y ☐N
	11:30AM		☐Y ☐N
	12:00PM		☐Y ☐N
	12:30PM		☐Y ☐N
	1:00PM		☐Y ☐N
	1:30PM		☐Y ☐N
	2:00PM		☐Y ☐N
	2:30PM		☐Y ☐N
	3:00PM		☐Y ☐N
	3:30PM		☐Y ☐N
	4:00PM		☐Y ☐N
	4:30PM		☐Y ☐N
	5:00PM		☐Y ☐N
	5:30PM		☐Y ☐N
	6:00PM		☐Y ☐N
	6:30PM		☐Y ☐N
	7:00PM		☐Y ☐N
	7:30PM		☐Y ☐N
	8:00PM		☐Y ☐N
	8:30PM		☐Y ☐N
	9:00PM		☐Y ☐N
	9:30PM		☐Y ☐N

TAKE 5 MINUTES EACH MORNING TO PLAN YOUR DAY.

GET EIGHT HOURS OF SLEEP!

NOTE HIGH PRIORITY TASKS WITH A ✱

ANALYZE WHY A TASK WAS NOT COMPLETED, THEN MOVE TO NEXT DAY.

ONE POSITIVE

TODAY I GAVE

DAILY
GOAL SLAYERS
PLANNER

SETTING YOURSELF UP FOR SUCCESS DAILY!

DATE

_____ / _____ / _____

SCRIPTURE

MOTIVATIONAL QUOTE

ONE GOAL

ONE FUN THING

HEALTH • FITNESS

✱	IMPORTANT TIME	SCHEDULE	SLAYED?
	5:00AM		☐Y ☐N
	5:30AM		☐Y ☐N
	6:00AM		☐Y ☐N
	6:30AM		☐Y ☐N
	7:00AM		☐Y ☐N
	7:30AM		☐Y ☐N
	8:00AM		☐Y ☐N
	8:30AM		☐Y ☐N
	9:00AM		☐Y ☐N
	9:30AM		☐Y ☐N
	10:00AM		☐Y ☐N
	10:30AM		☐Y ☐N
	11:00AM		☐Y ☐N
	11:30AM		☐Y ☐N
	12:00PM		☐Y ☐N
	12:30PM		☐Y ☐N
	1:00PM		☐Y ☐N
	1:30PM		☐Y ☐N
	2:00PM		☐Y ☐N
	2:30PM		☐Y ☐N
	3:00PM		☐Y ☐N
	3:30PM		☐Y ☐N
	4:00PM		☐Y ☐N
	4:30PM		☐Y ☐N
	5:00PM		☐Y ☐N
	5:30PM		☐Y ☐N
	6:00PM		☐Y ☐N
	6:30PM		☐Y ☐N
	7:00PM		☐Y ☐N
	7:30PM		☐Y ☐N
	8:00PM		☐Y ☐N
	8:30PM		☐Y ☐N
	9:00PM		☐Y ☐N
	9:30PM		☐Y ☐N

WATER INTAKE

OZ. OZ. OZ. OZ. OZ.
OZ. OZ. OZ. OZ. OZ.

TAKE 5 MINUTES EACH MORNING TO PLAN YOUR DAY.

GET EIGHT HOURS OF SLEEP!

NOTE HIGH PRIORITY TASKS WITH A ✱

ANALYZE WHY A TASK WAS NOT COMPLETED, THEN MOVE TO NEXT DAY.

ONE POSITIVE

TODAY I GAVE

DAILY
GOAL SLAYERS
PLANNER

SETTING YOURSELF UP FOR SUCCESS DAILY!

DATE

_____ / _____ / _____

SCRIPTURE

MOTIVATIONAL QUOTE

ONE GOAL

ONE FUN THING

HEALTH • FITNESS

WATER INTAKE

*	IMPORTANT TIME	SCHEDULE	SLAYED?
	5:00AM		☐Y ☐N
	5:30AM		☐Y ☐N
	6:00AM		☐Y ☐N
	6:30AM		☐Y ☐N
	7:00AM		☐Y ☐N
	7:30AM		☐Y ☐N
	8:00AM		☐Y ☐N
	8:30AM		☐Y ☐N
	9:00AM		☐Y ☐N
	9:30AM		☐Y ☐N
	10:00AM		☐Y ☐N
	10:30AM		☐Y ☐N
	11:00AM		☐Y ☐N
	11:30AM		☐Y ☐N
	12:00PM		☐Y ☐N
	12:30PM		☐Y ☐N
	1:00PM		☐Y ☐N
	1:30PM		☐Y ☐N
	2:00PM		☐Y ☐N
	2:30PM		☐Y ☐N
	3:00PM		☐Y ☐N
	3:30PM		☐Y ☐N
	4:00PM		☐Y ☐N
	4:30PM		☐Y ☐N
	5:00PM		☐Y ☐N
	5:30PM		☐Y ☐N
	6:00PM		☐Y ☐N
	6:30PM		☐Y ☐N
	7:00PM		☐Y ☐N
	7:30PM		☐Y ☐N
	8:00PM		☐Y ☐N
	8:30PM		☐Y ☐N
	9:00PM		☐Y ☐N
	9:30PM		☐Y ☐N

TAKE 5 MINUTES EACH MORNING TO PLAN YOUR DAY.

GET EIGHT HOURS OF SLEEP!

NOTE HIGH PRIORITY TASKS WITH A *

ANALYZE WHY A TASK WAS NOT COMPLETED, THEN MOVE TO NEXT DAY.

ONE POSITIVE

TODAY I GAVE

DAILY
GOAL SLAYERS
PLANNER

SETTING YOURSELF UP FOR SUCCESS DAILY!

DATE

_____ / _____ / _____

SCRIPTURE

MOTIVATIONAL QUOTE

ONE GOAL

ONE FUN THING

*	IMPORTANT TIME	SCHEDULE	SLAYED?
	5:00AM		☐Y ☐N
	5:30AM		☐Y ☐N
	6:00AM		☐Y ☐N
	6:30AM		☐Y ☐N
	7:00AM		☐Y ☐N
	7:30AM		☐Y ☐N
	8:00AM		☐Y ☐N
	8:30AM		☐Y ☐N
	9:00AM		☐Y ☐N
	9:30AM		☐Y ☐N
	10:00AM		☐Y ☐N
	10:30AM		☐Y ☐N
	11:00AM		☐Y ☐N
	11:30AM		☐Y ☐N
	12:00PM		☐Y ☐N
	12:30PM		☐Y ☐N
	1:00PM		☐Y ☐N
	1:30PM		☐Y ☐N
	2:00PM		☐Y ☐N
	2:30PM		☐Y ☐N
	3:00PM		☐Y ☐N
	3:30PM		☐Y ☐N
	4:00PM		☐Y ☐N
	4:30PM		☐Y ☐N
	5:00PM		☐Y ☐N
	5:30PM		☐Y ☐N
	6:00PM		☐Y ☐N
	6:30PM		☐Y ☐N
	7:00PM		☐Y ☐N
	7:30PM		☐Y ☐N
	8:00PM		☐Y ☐N
	8:30PM		☐Y ☐N
	9:00PM		☐Y ☐N
	9:30PM		☐Y ☐N

HEALTH • FITNESS

WATER INTAKE

OZ. OZ. OZ. OZ. OZ.
OZ. OZ. OZ. OZ. OZ.

TAKE 5 MINUTES EACH MORNING TO PLAN YOUR DAY.

GET EIGHT HOURS OF SLEEP!

NOTE HIGH PRIORITY TASKS WITH A *

ANALYZE WHY A TASK WAS NOT COMPLETED, THEN MOVE TO NEXT DAY.

ONE POSITIVE

TODAY I GAVE

DAILY
GOAL SLAYERS
PLANNER

SETTING YOURSELF UP FOR SUCCESS DAILY!

DATE

____ / ____ / ____

SCRIPTURE

MOTIVATIONAL QUOTE

ONE GOAL

ONE FUN THING

HEALTH • FITNESS

WATER INTAKE

OZ. OZ. OZ. OZ. OZ.

OZ. OZ. OZ. OZ. OZ.

✱	IMPORTANT TIME	SCHEDULE	SLAYED?
	5:00AM		☐Y ☐N
	5:30AM		☐Y ☐N
	6:00AM		☐Y ☐N
	6:30AM		☐Y ☐N
	7:00AM		☐Y ☐N
	7:30AM		☐Y ☐N
	8:00AM		☐Y ☐N
	8:30AM		☐Y ☐N
	9:00AM		☐Y ☐N
	9:30AM		☐Y ☐N
	10:00AM		☐Y ☐N
	10:30AM		☐Y ☐N
	11:00AM		☐Y ☐N
	11:30AM		☐Y ☐N
	12:00PM		☐Y ☐N
	12:30PM		☐Y ☐N
	1:00PM		☐Y ☐N
	1:30PM		☐Y ☐N
	2:00PM		☐Y ☐N
	2:30PM		☐Y ☐N
	3:00PM		☐Y ☐N
	3:30PM		☐Y ☐N
	4:00PM		☐Y ☐N
	4:30PM		☐Y ☐N
	5:00PM		☐Y ☐N
	5:30PM		☐Y ☐N
	6:00PM		☐Y ☐N
	6:30PM		☐Y ☐N
	7:00PM		☐Y ☐N
	7:30PM		☐Y ☐N
	8:00PM		☐Y ☐N
	8:30PM		☐Y ☐N
	9:00PM		☐Y ☐N
	9:30PM		☐Y ☐N

TAKE 5 MINUTES EACH MORNING TO PLAN YOUR DAY.

GET EIGHT HOURS OF SLEEP!

NOTE HIGH PRIORITY TASKS WITH A ✱

ANALYZE WHY A TASK WAS NOT COMPLETED, THEN MOVE TO NEXT DAY.

ONE POSITIVE

TODAY I GAVE

DAILY
GOAL SLAYERS
PLANNER

SETTING YOURSELF UP FOR SUCCESS DAILY!

DATE

_____ / _____ / _____

SCRIPTURE

MOTIVATIONAL QUOTE

ONE GOAL

ONE FUN THING

*	IMPORTANT TIME	SCHEDULE	SLAYED?
	5:00AM		☐Y ☐N
	5:30AM		☐Y ☐N
	6:00AM		☐Y ☐N
	6:30AM		☐Y ☐N
	7:00AM		☐Y ☐N
	7:30AM		☐Y ☐N
	8:00AM		☐Y ☐N
	8:30AM		☐Y ☐N
	9:00AM		☐Y ☐N
	9:30AM		☐Y ☐N
	10:00AM		☐Y ☐N
	10:30AM		☐Y ☐N
	11:00AM		☐Y ☐N
	11:30AM		☐Y ☐N
	12:00PM		☐Y ☐N
	12:30PM		☐Y ☐N
	1:00PM		☐Y ☐N
	1:30PM		☐Y ☐N
	2:00PM		☐Y ☐N
	2:30PM		☐Y ☐N
	3:00PM		☐Y ☐N
	3:30PM		☐Y ☐N
	4:00PM		☐Y ☐N
	4:30PM		☐Y ☐N
	5:00PM		☐Y ☐N
	5:30PM		☐Y ☐N
	6:00PM		☐Y ☐N
	6:30PM		☐Y ☐N
	7:00PM		☐Y ☐N
	7:30PM		☐Y ☐N
	8:00PM		☐Y ☐N
	8:30PM		☐Y ☐N
	9:00PM		☐Y ☐N
	9:30PM		☐Y ☐N

HEALTH + FITNESS

WATER INTAKE

OZ. OZ. OZ. OZ. OZ.

OZ. OZ. OZ. OZ. OZ.

TAKE 5 MINUTES EACH MORNING TO PLAN YOUR DAY.

GET EIGHT HOURS OF SLEEP!

NOTE HIGH PRIORITY TASKS WITH A *

ANALYZE WHY A TASK WAS NOT COMPLETED, THEN MOVE TO NEXT DAY.

ONE POSITIVE

TODAY I GAVE

DAILY
GOAL SLAYERS
PLANNER

SETTING YOURSELF UP FOR SUCCESS DAILY!

DATE

_____ / _____ / _____

SCRIPTURE

MOTIVATIONAL QUOTE

ONE GOAL

ONE FUN THING

✱	IMPORTANT TIME	SCHEDULE	SLAYED?
	5:00AM		☐Y ☐N
	5:30AM		☐Y ☐N
	6:00AM		☐Y ☐N
	6:30AM		☐Y ☐N
	7:00AM		☐Y ☐N
	7:30AM		☐Y ☐N
	8:00AM		☐Y ☐N
	8:30AM		☐Y ☐N
	9:00AM		☐Y ☐N
	9:30AM		☐Y ☐N
	10:00AM		☐Y ☐N
	10:30AM		☐Y ☐N
	11:00AM		☐Y ☐N
	11:30AM		☐Y ☐N
	12:00PM		☐Y ☐N
	12:30PM		☐Y ☐N
	1:00PM		☐Y ☐N
	1:30PM		☐Y ☐N
	2:00PM		☐Y ☐N
	2:30PM		☐Y ☐N
	3:00PM		☐Y ☐N
	3:30PM		☐Y ☐N
	4:00PM		☐Y ☐N
	4:30PM		☐Y ☐N
	5:00PM		☐Y ☐N
	5:30PM		☐Y ☐N
	6:00PM		☐Y ☐N
	6:30PM		☐Y ☐N
	7:00PM		☐Y ☐N
	7:30PM		☐Y ☐N
	8:00PM		☐Y ☐N
	8:30PM		☐Y ☐N
	9:00PM		☐Y ☐N
	9:30PM		☐Y ☐N

HEALTH · FITNESS

WATER INTAKE

OZ. OZ. OZ. OZ. OZ.
OZ. OZ. OZ. OZ. OZ.

TAKE 5 MINUTES EACH MORNING TO PLAN YOUR DAY.

GET EIGHT HOURS OF SLEEP!

NOTE HIGH PRIORITY TASKS WITH A ✱

ANALYZE WHY A TASK WAS NOT COMPLETED, THEN MOVE TO NEXT DAY.

ONE POSITIVE

TODAY I GAVE

DAILY
GOAL SLAYERS
PLANNER

SETTING YOURSELF UP FOR SUCCESS DAILY!

DATE

_____ / _____ / _____

SCRIPTURE

MOTIVATIONAL QUOTE

ONE GOAL

ONE FUN THING

HEALTH • FITNESS

WATER INTAKE

OZ. OZ. OZ. OZ. OZ.

OZ. OZ. OZ. OZ. OZ.

✱	IMPORTANT TIME	SCHEDULE	SLAYED?
	5:00AM		☐Y ☐N
	5:30AM		☐Y ☐N
	6:00AM		☐Y ☐N
	6:30AM		☐Y ☐N
	7:00AM		☐Y ☐N
	7:30AM		☐Y ☐N
	8:00AM		☐Y ☐N
	8:30AM		☐Y ☐N
	9:00AM		☐Y ☐N
	9:30AM		☐Y ☐N
	10:00AM		☐Y ☐N
	10:30AM		☐Y ☐N
	11:00AM		☐Y ☐N
	11:30AM		☐Y ☐N
	12:00PM		☐Y ☐N
	12:30PM		☐Y ☐N
	1:00PM		☐Y ☐N
	1:30PM		☐Y ☐N
	2:00PM		☐Y ☐N
	2:30PM		☐Y ☐N
	3:00PM		☐Y ☐N
	3:30PM		☐Y ☐N
	4:00PM		☐Y ☐N
	4:30PM		☐Y ☐N
	5:00PM		☐Y ☐N
	5:30PM		☐Y ☐N
	6:00PM		☐Y ☐N
	6:30PM		☐Y ☐N
	7:00PM		☐Y ☐N
	7:30PM		☐Y ☐N
	8:00PM		☐Y ☐N
	8:30PM		☐Y ☐N
	9:00PM		☐Y ☐N
	9:30PM		☐Y ☐N

TAKE 5 MINUTES EACH MORNING TO PLAN YOUR DAY.

GET EIGHT HOURS OF SLEEP!

NOTE HIGH PRIORITY TASKS WITH A ✱

ANALYZE WHY A TASK WAS NOT COMPLETED, THEN MOVE TO NEXT DAY.

ONE POSITIVE

TODAY I GAVE

DAILY
GOAL SLAYERS
PLANNER

SETTING YOURSELF UP FOR SUCCESS DAILY!

DATE

___ / ___ / ___

SCRIPTURE

MOTIVATIONAL QUOTE

ONE GOAL

ONE FUN THING

HEALTH + FITNESS

WATER INTAKE

✱	IMPORTANT TIME	SCHEDULE	SLAYED?
	5:00AM		☐Y ☐N
	5:30AM		☐Y ☐N
	6:00AM		☐Y ☐N
	6:30AM		☐Y ☐N
	7:00AM		☐Y ☐N
	7:30AM		☐Y ☐N
	8:00AM		☐Y ☐N
	8:30AM		☐Y ☐N
	9:00AM		☐Y ☐N
	9:30AM		☐Y ☐N
	10:00AM		☐Y ☐N
	10:30AM		☐Y ☐N
	11:00AM		☐Y ☐N
	11:30AM		☐Y ☐N
	12:00PM		☐Y ☐N
	12:30PM		☐Y ☐N
	1:00PM		☐Y ☐N
	1:30PM		☐Y ☐N
	2:00PM		☐Y ☐N
	2:30PM		☐Y ☐N
	3:00PM		☐Y ☐N
	3:30PM		☐Y ☐N
	4:00PM		☐Y ☐N
	4:30PM		☐Y ☐N
	5:00PM		☐Y ☐N
	5:30PM		☐Y ☐N
	6:00PM		☐Y ☐N
	6:30PM		☐Y ☐N
	7:00PM		☐Y ☐N
	7:30PM		☐Y ☐N
	8:00PM		☐Y ☐N
	8:30PM		☐Y ☐N
	9:00PM		☐Y ☐N
	9:30PM		☐Y ☐N

TAKE 5 MINUTES EACH MORNING TO PLAN YOUR DAY.

GET EIGHT HOURS OF SLEEP!

NOTE HIGH PRIORITY TASKS WITH A ✱

ANALYZE WHY A TASK WAS NOT COMPLETED, THEN MOVE TO NEXT DAY.

ONE POSITIVE

TODAY I GAVE

DAILY
GOAL SLAYERS
PLANNER

SETTING YOURSELF UP FOR SUCCESS DAILY!

DATE

_____ / _____ / _____

SCRIPTURE

MOTIVATIONAL QUOTE

ONE GOAL

ONE FUN THING

*	IMPORTANT TIME	SCHEDULE	SLAYED?
	5:00AM		☐Y ☐N
	5:30AM		☐Y ☐N
	6:00AM		☐Y ☐N
	6:30AM		☐Y ☐N
	7:00AM		☐Y ☐N
	7:30AM		☐Y ☐N
	8:00AM		☐Y ☐N
	8:30AM		☐Y ☐N
	9:00AM		☐Y ☐N
	9:30AM		☐Y ☐N
	10:00AM		☐Y ☐N
	10:30AM		☐Y ☐N
	11:00AM		☐Y ☐N
	11:30AM		☐Y ☐N
	12:00PM		☐Y ☐N
	12:30PM		☐Y ☐N
	1:00PM		☐Y ☐N
	1:30PM		☐Y ☐N
	2:00PM		☐Y ☐N
	2:30PM		☐Y ☐N
	3:00PM		☐Y ☐N
	3:30PM		☐Y ☐N
	4:00PM		☐Y ☐N
	4:30PM		☐Y ☐N
	5:00PM		☐Y ☐N
	5:30PM		☐Y ☐N
	6:00PM		☐Y ☐N
	6:30PM		☐Y ☐N
	7:00PM		☐Y ☐N
	7:30PM		☐Y ☐N
	8:00PM		☐Y ☐N
	8:30PM		☐Y ☐N
	9:00PM		☐Y ☐N
	9:30PM		☐Y ☐N

HEALTH • FITNESS

WATER INTAKE

OZ. OZ. OZ. OZ. OZ.
OZ. OZ. OZ. OZ. OZ.

TAKE 5 MINUTES EACH MORNING TO PLAN YOUR DAY.

GET EIGHT HOURS OF SLEEP!

NOTE HIGH PRIORITY TASKS WITH A *

ANALYZE WHY A TASK WAS NOT COMPLETED, THEN MOVE TO NEXT DAY.

ONE POSITIVE

TODAY I GAVE

DAILY
GOAL SLAYERS
PLANNER

SETTING YOURSELF UP FOR SUCCESS DAILY!

DATE

_____ / _____ / _____

SCRIPTURE

MOTIVATIONAL QUOTE

ONE GOAL

ONE FUN THING

HEALTH + FITNESS

*	IMPORTANT TIME	SCHEDULE	SLAYED?
	5:00AM		☐Y ☐N
	5:30AM		☐Y ☐N
	6:00AM		☐Y ☐N
	6:30AM		☐Y ☐N
	7:00AM		☐Y ☐N
	7:30AM		☐Y ☐N
	8:00AM		☐Y ☐N
	8:30AM		☐Y ☐N
	9:00AM		☐Y ☐N
	9:30AM		☐Y ☐N
	10:00AM		☐Y ☐N
	10:30AM		☐Y ☐N
	11:00AM		☐Y ☐N
	11:30AM		☐Y ☐N
	12:00PM		☐Y ☐N
	12:30PM		☐Y ☐N
	1:00PM		☐Y ☐N
	1:30PM		☐Y ☐N
	2:00PM		☐Y ☐N
	2:30PM		☐Y ☐N
	3:00PM		☐Y ☐N
	3:30PM		☐Y ☐N
	4:00PM		☐Y ☐N
	4:30PM		☐Y ☐N
	5:00PM		☐Y ☐N
	5:30PM		☐Y ☐N
	6:00PM		☐Y ☐N
	6:30PM		☐Y ☐N
	7:00PM		☐Y ☐N
	7:30PM		☐Y ☐N
	8:00PM		☐Y ☐N
	8:30PM		☐Y ☐N
	9:00PM		☐Y ☐N
	9:30PM		☐Y ☐N

WATER INTAKE

OZ. OZ. OZ. OZ. OZ.
OZ. OZ. OZ. OZ. OZ.

TAKE 5 MINUTES EACH MORNING TO PLAN YOUR DAY.

GET EIGHT HOURS OF SLEEP!

NOTE HIGH PRIORITY TASKS WITH A *

ANALYZE WHY A TASK WAS NOT COMPLETED, THEN MOVE TO NEXT DAY.

ONE POSITIVE

TODAY I GAVE

DAILY
GOAL SLAYERS
PLANNER

SETTING YOURSELF UP FOR SUCCESS DAILY!

DATE

_____ / _____ / _____

SCRIPTURE

MOTIVATIONAL QUOTE

ONE GOAL

ONE FUN THING

HEALTH • FITNESS

WATER INTAKE

OZ. OZ. OZ. OZ. OZ.

OZ. OZ. OZ. OZ. OZ.

✱	IMPORTANT TIME	SCHEDULE	SLAYED?
	5:00AM		☐Y ☐N
	5:30AM		☐Y ☐N
	6:00AM		☐Y ☐N
	6:30AM		☐Y ☐N
	7:00AM		☐Y ☐N
	7:30AM		☐Y ☐N
	8:00AM		☐Y ☐N
	8:30AM		☐Y ☐N
	9:00AM		☐Y ☐N
	9:30AM		☐Y ☐N
	10:00AM		☐Y ☐N
	10:30AM		☐Y ☐N
	11:00AM		☐Y ☐N
	11:30AM		☐Y ☐N
	12:00PM		☐Y ☐N
	12:30PM		☐Y ☐N
	1:00PM		☐Y ☐N
	1:30PM		☐Y ☐N
	2:00PM		☐Y ☐N
	2:30PM		☐Y ☐N
	3:00PM		☐Y ☐N
	3:30PM		☐Y ☐N
	4:00PM		☐Y ☐N
	4:30PM		☐Y ☐N
	5:00PM		☐Y ☐N
	5:30PM		☐Y ☐N
	6:00PM		☐Y ☐N
	6:30PM		☐Y ☐N
	7:00PM		☐Y ☐N
	7:30PM		☐Y ☐N
	8:00PM		☐Y ☐N
	8:30PM		☐Y ☐N
	9:00PM		☐Y ☐N
	9:30PM		☐Y ☐N

TAKE 5 MINUTES EACH MORNING TO PLAN YOUR DAY.

GET EIGHT HOURS OF SLEEP!

NOTE HIGH PRIORITY TASKS WITH A ✱

ANALYZE WHY A TASK WAS NOT COMPLETED, THEN MOVE TO NEXT DAY.

ONE POSITIVE

TODAY I GAVE

DAILY
GOAL SLAYERS
PLANNER

SETTING YOURSELF UP FOR SUCCESS DAILY!

DATE

_____ / _____ / _____

SCRIPTURE

MOTIVATIONAL QUOTE

ONE GOAL

ONE FUN THING

HEALTH • FITNESS

WATER INTAKE

OZ OZ OZ OZ OZ

OZ OZ OZ OZ OZ

*	IMPORTANT TIME	SCHEDULE	SLAYED?
	5:00AM		☐Y ☐N
	5:30AM		☐Y ☐N
	6:00AM		☐Y ☐N
	6:30AM		☐Y ☐N
	7:00AM		☐Y ☐N
	7:30AM		☐Y ☐N
	8:00AM		☐Y ☐N
	8:30AM		☐Y ☐N
	9:00AM		☐Y ☐N
	9:30AM		☐Y ☐N
	10:00AM		☐Y ☐N
	10:30AM		☐Y ☐N
	11:00AM		☐Y ☐N
	11:30AM		☐Y ☐N
	12:00PM		☐Y ☐N
	12:30PM		☐Y ☐N
	1:00PM		☐Y ☐N
	1:30PM		☐Y ☐N
	2:00PM		☐Y ☐N
	2:30PM		☐Y ☐N
	3:00PM		☐Y ☐N
	3:30PM		☐Y ☐N
	4:00PM		☐Y ☐N
	4:30PM		☐Y ☐N
	5:00PM		☐Y ☐N
	5:30PM		☐Y ☐N
	6:00PM		☐Y ☐N
	6:30PM		☐Y ☐N
	7:00PM		☐Y ☐N
	7:30PM		☐Y ☐N
	8:00PM		☐Y ☐N
	8:30PM		☐Y ☐N
	9:00PM		☐Y ☐N
	9:30PM		☐Y ☐N

TAKE 5 MINUTES EACH MORNING TO PLAN YOUR DAY.

GET EIGHT HOURS OF SLEEP!

NOTE HIGH PRIORITY TASKS WITH A *

ANALYZE WHY A TASK WAS NOT COMPLETED, THEN MOVE TO NEXT DAY.

ONE POSITIVE

TODAY I GAVE

DAILY
GOAL SLAYERS
PLANNER

SETTING YOURSELF UP FOR SUCCESS DAILY!

DATE

_____ / _____ / _____

SCRIPTURE

MOTIVATIONAL QUOTE

ONE GOAL

ONE FUN THING

*	IMPORTANT TIME	SCHEDULE	SLAYED?
	5:00AM		☐Y ☐N
	5:30AM		☐Y ☐N
	6:00AM		☐Y ☐N
	6:30AM		☐Y ☐N
	7:00AM		☐Y ☐N
	7:30AM		☐Y ☐N
	8:00AM		☐Y ☐N
	8:30AM		☐Y ☐N
	9:00AM		☐Y ☐N
	9:30AM		☐Y ☐N
	10:00AM		☐Y ☐N
	10:30AM		☐Y ☐N
	11:00AM		☐Y ☐N
	11:30AM		☐Y ☐N
	12:00PM		☐Y ☐N
	12:30PM		☐Y ☐N
	1:00PM		☐Y ☐N
	1:30PM		☐Y ☐N
	2:00PM		☐Y ☐N
	2:30PM		☐Y ☐N
	3:00PM		☐Y ☐N
	3:30PM		☐Y ☐N
	4:00PM		☐Y ☐N
	4:30PM		☐Y ☐N
	5:00PM		☐Y ☐N
	5:30PM		☐Y ☐N
	6:00PM		☐Y ☐N
	6:30PM		☐Y ☐N
	7:00PM		☐Y ☐N
	7:30PM		☐Y ☐N
	8:00PM		☐Y ☐N
	8:30PM		☐Y ☐N
	9:00PM		☐Y ☐N
	9:30PM		☐Y ☐N

HEALTH • FITNESS

WATER INTAKE

OZ. OZ. OZ. OZ. OZ.
OZ. OZ. OZ. OZ. OZ.

TAKE 5 MINUTES EACH MORNING TO PLAN YOUR DAY.

GET EIGHT HOURS OF SLEEP!

NOTE HIGH PRIORITY TASKS WITH A *

ANALYZE WHY A TASK WAS NOT COMPLETED, THEN MOVE TO NEXT DAY.

ONE POSITIVE

TODAY I GAVE

DAILY
GOAL SLAYERS
PLANNER

SETTING YOURSELF UP FOR SUCCESS DAILY!

DATE

____ / ____ / ____

SCRIPTURE

MOTIVATIONAL QUOTE

ONE GOAL

ONE FUN THING

HEALTH • FITNESS

WATER INTAKE

*	IMPORTANT TIME	SCHEDULE	SLAYED?
	5:00AM		☐Y ☐N
	5:30AM		☐Y ☐N
	6:00AM		☐Y ☐N
	6:30AM		☐Y ☐N
	7:00AM		☐Y ☐N
	7:30AM		☐Y ☐N
	8:00AM		☐Y ☐N
	8:30AM		☐Y ☐N
	9:00AM		☐Y ☐N
	9:30AM		☐Y ☐N
	10:00AM		☐Y ☐N
	10:30AM		☐Y ☐N
	11:00AM		☐Y ☐N
	11:30AM		☐Y ☐N
	12:00PM		☐Y ☐N
	12:30PM		☐Y ☐N
	1:00PM		☐Y ☐N
	1:30PM		☐Y ☐N
	2:00PM		☐Y ☐N
	2:30PM		☐Y ☐N
	3:00PM		☐Y ☐N
	3:30PM		☐Y ☐N
	4:00PM		☐Y ☐N
	4:30PM		☐Y ☐N
	5:00PM		☐Y ☐N
	5:30PM		☐Y ☐N
	6:00PM		☐Y ☐N
	6:30PM		☐Y ☐N
	7:00PM		☐Y ☐N
	7:30PM		☐Y ☐N
	8:00PM		☐Y ☐N
	8:30PM		☐Y ☐N
	9:00PM		☐Y ☐N
	9:30PM		☐Y ☐N

TAKE 5 MINUTES EACH MORNING TO PLAN YOUR DAY.

GET EIGHT HOURS OF SLEEP!

NOTE HIGH PRIORITY TASKS WITH A *

ANALYZE WHY A TASK WAS NOT COMPLETED, THEN MOVE TO NEXT DAY.

ONE POSITIVE

TODAY I GAVE

DAILY
GOAL SLAYERS
PLANNER

SETTING YOURSELF UP FOR SUCCESS DAILY!

DATE

_____ / _____ / _____

SCRIPTURE

MOTIVATIONAL QUOTE

ONE GOAL

ONE FUN THING

HEALTH • FITNESS

WATER INTAKE

OZ OZ OZ OZ OZ

OZ OZ OZ OZ OZ

*	IMPORTANT TIME	SCHEDULE	SLAYED?
	5:00AM		☐Y ☐N
	5:30AM		☐Y ☐N
	6:00AM		☐Y ☐N
	6:30AM		☐Y ☐N
	7:00AM		☐Y ☐N
	7:30AM		☐Y ☐N
	8:00AM		☐Y ☐N
	8:30AM		☐Y ☐N
	9:00AM		☐Y ☐N
	9:30AM		☐Y ☐N
	10:00AM		☐Y ☐N
	10:30AM		☐Y ☐N
	11:00AM		☐Y ☐N
	11:30AM		☐Y ☐N
	12:00PM		☐Y ☐N
	12:30PM		☐Y ☐N
	1:00PM		☐Y ☐N
	1:30PM		☐Y ☐N
	2:00PM		☐Y ☐N
	2:30PM		☐Y ☐N
	3:00PM		☐Y ☐N
	3:30PM		☐Y ☐N
	4:00PM		☐Y ☐N
	4:30PM		☐Y ☐N
	5:00PM		☐Y ☐N
	5:30PM		☐Y ☐N
	6:00PM		☐Y ☐N
	6:30PM		☐Y ☐N
	7:00PM		☐Y ☐N
	7:30PM		☐Y ☐N
	8:00PM		☐Y ☐N
	8:30PM		☐Y ☐N
	9:00PM		☐Y ☐N
	9:30PM		☐Y ☐N

TAKE 5 MINUTES EACH MORNING TO PLAN YOUR DAY.

GET EIGHT HOURS OF SLEEP!

NOTE HIGH PRIORITY TASKS WITH A *

ANALYZE WHY A TASK WAS NOT COMPLETED, THEN MOVE TO NEXT DAY.

ONE POSITIVE

TODAY I GAVE

DAILY
GOAL SLAYERS
PLANNER

SETTING YOURSELF UP FOR SUCCESS DAILY!

DATE

_____ / _____ / _____

SCRIPTURE

MOTIVATIONAL QUOTE

ONE GOAL

ONE FUN THING

HEALTH • FITNESS

WATER INTAKE

✱	IMPORTANT TIME	SCHEDULE	SLAYED?
	5:00AM		☐Y ☐N
	5:30AM		☐Y ☐N
	6:00AM		☐Y ☐N
	6:30AM		☐Y ☐N
	7:00AM		☐Y ☐N
	7:30AM		☐Y ☐N
	8:00AM		☐Y ☐N
	8:30AM		☐Y ☐N
	9:00AM		☐Y ☐N
	9:30AM		☐Y ☐N
	10:00AM		☐Y ☐N
	10:30AM		☐Y ☐N
	11:00AM		☐Y ☐N
	11:30AM		☐Y ☐N
	12:00PM		☐Y ☐N
	12:30PM		☐Y ☐N
	1:00PM		☐Y ☐N
	1:30PM		☐Y ☐N
	2:00PM		☐Y ☐N
	2:30PM		☐Y ☐N
	3:00PM		☐Y ☐N
	3:30PM		☐Y ☐N
	4:00PM		☐Y ☐N
	4:30PM		☐Y ☐N
	5:00PM		☐Y ☐N
	5:30PM		☐Y ☐N
	6:00PM		☐Y ☐N
	6:30PM		☐Y ☐N
	7:00PM		☐Y ☐N
	7:30PM		☐Y ☐N
	8:00PM		☐Y ☐N
	8:30PM		☐Y ☐N
	9:00PM		☐Y ☐N
	9:30PM		☐Y ☐N

TAKE 5 MINUTES EACH MORNING TO PLAN YOUR DAY.

GET EIGHT HOURS OF SLEEP!

NOTE HIGH PRIORITY TASKS WITH A ✱

ANALYZE WHY A TASK WAS NOT COMPLETED, THEN MOVE TO NEXT DAY.

ONE POSITIVE

TODAY I GAVE

DAILY
GOAL SLAYERS
PLANNER

SETTING YOURSELF UP FOR SUCCESS DAILY!

DATE

_____ / _____ / _____

SCRIPTURE

MOTIVATIONAL QUOTE

ONE GOAL

ONE FUN THING

HEALTH • FITNESS

WATER INTAKE

*	IMPORTANT TIME	SCHEDULE	SLAYED?
	5:00AM		☐Y ☐N
	5:30AM		☐Y ☐N
	6:00AM		☐Y ☐N
	6:30AM		☐Y ☐N
	7:00AM		☐Y ☐N
	7:30AM		☐Y ☐N
	8:00AM		☐Y ☐N
	8:30AM		☐Y ☐N
	9:00AM		☐Y ☐N
	9:30AM		☐Y ☐N
	10:00AM		☐Y ☐N
	10:30AM		☐Y ☐N
	11:00AM		☐Y ☐N
	11:30AM		☐Y ☐N
	12:00PM		☐Y ☐N
	12:30PM		☐Y ☐N
	1:00PM		☐Y ☐N
	1:30PM		☐Y ☐N
	2:00PM		☐Y ☐N
	2:30PM		☐Y ☐N
	3:00PM		☐Y ☐N
	3:30PM		☐Y ☐N
	4:00PM		☐Y ☐N
	4:30PM		☐Y ☐N
	5:00PM		☐Y ☐N
	5:30PM		☐Y ☐N
	6:00PM		☐Y ☐N
	6:30PM		☐Y ☐N
	7:00PM		☐Y ☐N
	7:30PM		☐Y ☐N
	8:00PM		☐Y ☐N
	8:30PM		☐Y ☐N
	9:00PM		☐Y ☐N
	9:30PM		☐Y ☐N

TAKE 5 MINUTES EACH MORNING TO PLAN YOUR DAY.

GET EIGHT HOURS OF SLEEP!

NOTE HIGH PRIORITY TASKS WITH A *

ANALYZE WHY A TASK WAS NOT COMPLETED, THEN MOVE TO NEXT DAY.

ONE POSITIVE

TODAY I GAVE

DAILY
GOAL SLAYERS
PLANNER

SETTING YOURSELF UP FOR SUCCESS DAILY!

DATE

____ / ____ / ____

SCRIPTURE

MOTIVATIONAL QUOTE

ONE GOAL

ONE FUN THING

HEALTH • FITNESS

✱	IMPORTANT TIME	SCHEDULE	SLAYED?
	5:00AM		☐Y ☐N
	5:30AM		☐Y ☐N
	6:00AM		☐Y ☐N
	6:30AM		☐Y ☐N
	7:00AM		☐Y ☐N
	7:30AM		☐Y ☐N
	8:00AM		☐Y ☐N
	8:30AM		☐Y ☐N
	9:00AM		☐Y ☐N
	9:30AM		☐Y ☐N
	10:00AM		☐Y ☐N
	10:30AM		☐Y ☐N
	11:00AM		☐Y ☐N
	11:30AM		☐Y ☐N
	12:00PM		☐Y ☐N
	12:30PM		☐Y ☐N
	1:00PM		☐Y ☐N
	1:30PM		☐Y ☐N
	2:00PM		☐Y ☐N
	2:30PM		☐Y ☐N
	3:00PM		☐Y ☐N
	3:30PM		☐Y ☐N
	4:00PM		☐Y ☐N
	4:30PM		☐Y ☐N
	5:00PM		☐Y ☐N
	5:30PM		☐Y ☐N
	6:00PM		☐Y ☐N
	6:30PM		☐Y ☐N
	7:00PM		☐Y ☐N
	7:30PM		☐Y ☐N
	8:00PM		☐Y ☐N
	8:30PM		☐Y ☐N
	9:00PM		☐Y ☐N
	9:30PM		☐Y ☐N

WATER INTAKE

OZ. OZ. OZ. OZ. OZ.
OZ. OZ. OZ. OZ. OZ.

TAKE 5 MINUTES EACH MORNING TO PLAN YOUR DAY.

GET EIGHT HOURS OF SLEEP!

NOTE HIGH PRIORITY TASKS WITH A ✱

ANALYZE WHY A TASK WAS NOT COMPLETED, THEN MOVE TO NEXT DAY.

ONE POSITIVE

TODAY I GAVE

DAILY
GOAL SLAYERS
PLANNER

SETTING YOURSELF UP FOR SUCCESS DAILY!

DATE

_____ / _____ / _____

SCRIPTURE

MOTIVATIONAL QUOTE

ONE GOAL

ONE FUN THING

*	IMPORTANT TIME	SCHEDULE	SLAYED?
	5:00AM		☐Y ☐N
	5:30AM		☐Y ☐N
	6:00AM		☐Y ☐N
	6:30AM		☐Y ☐N
	7:00AM		☐Y ☐N
	7:30AM		☐Y ☐N
	8.00AM		☐Y ☐N
	8:30AM		☐Y ☐N
	9:00AM		☐Y ☐N
	9:30AM		☐Y ☐N
	10:00AM		☐Y ☐N
	10:30AM		☐Y ☐N
	11:00AM		☐Y ☐N
	11:30AM		☐Y ☐N
	12:00PM		☐Y ☐N
	12:30PM		☐Y ☐N
	1:00PM		☐Y ☐N
	1:30PM		☐Y ☐N
	2:00PM		☐Y ☐N
	2:30PM		☐Y ☐N
	3:00PM		☐Y ☐N
	3:30PM		☐Y ☐N
	4:00PM		☐Y ☐N
	4:30PM		☐Y ☐N
	5:00PM		☐Y ☐N
	5:30PM		☐Y ☐N
	6:00PM		☐Y ☐N
	6:30PM		☐Y ☐N
	7:00PM		☐Y ☐N
	7:30PM		☐Y ☐N
	8:00PM		☐Y ☐N
	8:30PM		☐Y ☐N
	9:00PM		☐Y ☐N
	9:30PM		☐Y ☐N

HEALTH + FITNESS

WATER INTAKE

OZ OZ OZ OZ OZ
OZ OZ OZ OZ OZ

TAKE 5 MINUTES EACH MORNING TO PLAN YOUR DAY.

GET EIGHT HOURS OF SLEEP!

NOTE HIGH PRIORITY TASKS WITH A *

ANALYZE WHY A TASK WAS NOT COMPLETED, THEN MOVE TO NEXT DAY.

ONE POSITIVE

TODAY I GAVE

DAILY
GOAL SLAYERS
PLANNER

SETTING YOURSELF UP FOR SUCCESS DAILY!

DATE

_____ / _____ / _____

SCRIPTURE

MOTIVATIONAL QUOTE

ONE GOAL

ONE FUN THING

*	IMPORTANT TIME	SCHEDULE	SLAYED?
	5:00AM		☐Y ☐N
	5:30AM		☐Y ☐N
	6:00AM		☐Y ☐N
	6:30AM		☐Y ☐N
	7:00AM		☐Y ☐N
	7:30AM		☐Y ☐N
	8:00AM		☐Y ☐N
	8:30AM		☐Y ☐N
	9:00AM		☐Y ☐N
	9:30AM		☐Y ☐N
	10:00AM		☐Y ☐N
	10:30AM		☐Y ☐N
	11:00AM		☐Y ☐N
	11:30AM		☐Y ☐N
	12:00PM		☐Y ☐N
	12:30PM		☐Y ☐N
	1:00PM		☐Y ☐N
	1:30PM		☐Y ☐N
	2:00PM		☐Y ☐N
	2:30PM		☐Y ☐N
	3:00PM		☐Y ☐N
	3:30PM		☐Y ☐N
	4:00PM		☐Y ☐N
	4:30PM		☐Y ☐N
	5:00PM		☐Y ☐N
	5:30PM		☐Y ☐N
	6:00PM		☐Y ☐N
	6:30PM		☐Y ☐N
	7:00PM		☐Y ☐N
	7:30PM		☐Y ☐N
	8:00PM		☐Y ☐N
	8:30PM		☐Y ☐N
	9:00PM		☐Y ☐N
	9:30PM		☐Y ☐N

HEALTH • FITNESS

WATER INTAKE

OZ OZ OZ OZ OZ
OZ OZ OZ OZ OZ

TAKE 5 MINUTES EACH MORNING TO PLAN YOUR DAY.

GET EIGHT HOURS OF SLEEP!

NOTE HIGH PRIORITY TASKS WITH A *

ANALYZE WHY A TASK WAS NOT COMPLETED, THEN MOVE TO NEXT DAY.

ONE POSITIVE

TODAY I GAVE

DAILY
GOAL SLAYERS
PLANNER

SETTING YOURSELF UP FOR SUCCESS DAILY!

DATE
_____ / _____ / _____

SCRIPTURE

MOTIVATIONAL QUOTE

ONE GOAL

ONE FUN THING

*	IMPORTANT TIME	SCHEDULE	SLAYED?
	5:00AM		☐Y ☐N
	5:30AM		☐Y ☐N
	6:00AM		☐Y ☐N
	6:30AM		☐Y ☐N
	7:00AM		☐Y ☐N
	7:30AM		☐Y ☐N
	8:00AM		☐Y ☐N
	8:30AM		☐Y ☐N
	9:00AM		☐Y ☐N
	9:30AM		☐Y ☐N
	10:00AM		☐Y ☐N
	10:30AM		☐Y ☐N
	11:00AM		☐Y ☐N
	11:30AM		☐Y ☐N
	12:00PM		☐Y ☐N
	12:30PM		☐Y ☐N
	1:00PM		☐Y ☐N
	1:30PM		☐Y ☐N
	2:00PM		☐Y ☐N
	2:30PM		☐Y ☐N
	3:00PM		☐Y ☐N
	3:30PM		☐Y ☐N
	4:00PM		☐Y ☐N
	4:30PM		☐Y ☐N
	5:00PM		☐Y ☐N
	5:30PM		☐Y ☐N
	6:00PM		☐Y ☐N
	6:30PM		☐Y ☐N
	7:00PM		☐Y ☐N
	7:30PM		☐Y ☐N
	8:00PM		☐Y ☐N
	8:30PM		☐Y ☐N
	9:00PM		☐Y ☐N
	9:30PM		☐Y ☐N

HEALTH + FITNESS

WATER INTAKE

OZ. OZ. OZ. OZ. OZ.
OZ. OZ. OZ. OZ. OZ.

TAKE 5 MINUTES EACH MORNING TO PLAN YOUR DAY.

GET EIGHT HOURS OF SLEEP!

NOTE HIGH PRIORITY TASKS WITH A *

ANALYZE WHY A TASK WAS NOT COMPLETED, THEN MOVE TO NEXT DAY.

ONE POSITIVE

TODAY I GAVE

DAILY
GOAL SLAYERS
PLANNER

SETTING YOURSELF UP FOR SUCCESS DAILY!

DATE

_____ / _____ / _____

SCRIPTURE

MOTIVATIONAL QUOTE

ONE GOAL

ONE FUN THING

*	IMPORTANT TIME	SCHEDULE	SLAYED?
	5:00AM		☐Y ☐N
	5:30AM		☐Y ☐N
	6:00AM		☐Y ☐N
	6:30AM		☐Y ☐N
	7:00AM		☐Y ☐N
	7:30AM		☐Y ☐N
	8:00AM		☐Y ☐N
	8:30AM		☐Y ☐N
	9:00AM		☐Y ☐N
	9:30AM		☐Y ☐N
	10:00AM		☐Y ☐N
	10:30AM		☐Y ☐N
	11:00AM		☐Y ☐N
	11:30AM		☐Y ☐N
	12:00PM		☐Y ☐N
	12:30PM		☐Y ☐N
	1:00PM		☐Y ☐N
	1:30PM		☐Y ☐N
	2:00PM		☐Y ☐N
	2:30PM		☐Y ☐N
	3:00PM		☐Y ☐N
	3:30PM		☐Y ☐N
	4:00PM		☐Y ☐N
	4:30PM		☐Y ☐N
	5:00PM		☐Y ☐N
	5:30PM		☐Y ☐N
	6:00PM		☐Y ☐N
	6:30PM		☐Y ☐N
	7:00PM		☐Y ☐N
	7:30PM		☐Y ☐N
	8:00PM		☐Y ☐N
	8:30PM		☐Y ☐N
	9:00PM		☐Y ☐N
	9:30PM		☐Y ☐N

HEALTH • FITNESS

WATER INTAKE

OZ. OZ. OZ. OZ. OZ.
OZ. OZ. OZ. OZ. OZ.

TAKE 5 MINUTES EACH MORNING TO PLAN YOUR DAY.

GET EIGHT HOURS OF SLEEP!

NOTE HIGH PRIORITY TASKS WITH A *

ANALYZE WHY A TASK WAS NOT COMPLETED, THEN MOVE TO NEXT DAY.

ONE POSITIVE

TODAY I GAVE

DAILY
GOAL SLAYERS
PLANNER

SETTING YOURSELF UP FOR SUCCESS DAILY!

DATE

_____ / _____ / _____

SCRIPTURE

MOTIVATIONAL QUOTE

ONE GOAL

ONE FUN THING

*	IMPORTANT TIME	SCHEDULE	SLAYED?
	5:00AM		☐Y ☐N
	5:30AM		☐Y ☐N
	6:00AM		☐Y ☐N
	6:30AM		☐Y ☐N
	7:00AM		☐Y ☐N
	7:30AM		☐Y ☐N
	8:00AM		☐Y ☐N
	8:30AM		☐Y ☐N
	9:00AM		☐Y ☐N
	9:30AM		☐Y ☐N
	10:00AM		☐Y ☐N
	10:30AM		☐Y ☐N
	11:00AM		☐Y ☐N
	11:30AM		☐Y ☐N
	12:00PM		☐Y ☐N
	12:30PM		☐Y ☐N
	1:00PM		☐Y ☐N
	1:30PM		☐Y ☐N
	2:00PM		☐Y ☐N
	2:30PM		☐Y ☐N
	3:00PM		☐Y ☐N
	3:30PM		☐Y ☐N
	4:00PM		☐Y ☐N
	4:30PM		☐Y ☐N
	5:00PM		☐Y ☐N
	5:30PM		☐Y ☐N
	6:00PM		☐Y ☐N
	6:30PM		☐Y ☐N
	7:00PM		☐Y ☐N
	7:30PM		☐Y ☐N
	8:00PM		☐Y ☐N
	8:30PM		☐Y ☐N
	9:00PM		☐Y ☐N
	9:30PM		☐Y ☐N

HEALTH • FITNESS

WATER INTAKE

OZ OZ OZ OZ OZ
OZ OZ OZ OZ OZ

TAKE 5 MINUTES EACH MORNING TO PLAN YOUR DAY.

GET EIGHT HOURS OF SLEEP!

NOTE HIGH PRIORITY TASKS WITH A *

ANALYZE WHY A TASK WAS NOT COMPLETED, THEN MOVE TO NEXT DAY.

ONE POSITIVE

TODAY I GAVE

DAILY
GOAL SLAYERS
PLANNER

SETTING YOURSELF UP FOR SUCCESS DAILY!

DATE

_____ / _____ / _____

SCRIPTURE

MOTIVATIONAL QUOTE

ONE GOAL

ONE FUN THING

*	IMPORTANT TIME	SCHEDULE	SLAYED?
	5:00AM		☐Y ☐N
	5:30AM		☐Y ☐N
	6:00AM		☐Y ☐N
	6:30AM		☐Y ☐N
	7:00AM		☐Y ☐N
	7:30AM		☐Y ☐N
	8:00AM		☐Y ☐N
	8:30AM		☐Y ☐N
	9:00AM		☐Y ☐N
	9:30AM		☐Y ☐N
	10:00AM		☐Y ☐N
	10:30AM		☐Y ☐N
	11:00AM		☐Y ☐N
	11:30AM		☐Y ☐N
	12:00PM		☐Y ☐N
	12:30PM		☐Y ☐N
	1:00PM		☐Y ☐N
	1:30PM		☐Y ☐N
	2:00PM		☐Y ☐N
	2:30PM		☐Y ☐N
	3:00PM		☐Y ☐N
	3:30PM		☐Y ☐N
	4:00PM		☐Y ☐N
	4:30PM		☐Y ☐N
	5:00PM		☐Y ☐N
	5:30PM		☐Y ☐N
	6:00PM		☐Y ☐N
	6:30PM		☐Y ☐N
	7:00PM		☐Y ☐N
	7:30PM		☐Y ☐N
	8:00PM		☐Y ☐N
	8:30PM		☐Y ☐N
	9:00PM		☐Y ☐N
	9:30PM		☐Y ☐N

HEALTH + FITNESS

WATER INTAKE

OZ OZ OZ OZ OZ
OZ OZ OZ OZ OZ

TAKE 5 MINUTES EACH MORNING TO PLAN YOUR DAY.

GET EIGHT HOURS OF SLEEP!

NOTE HIGH PRIORITY TASKS WITH A *

ANALYZE WHY A TASK WAS NOT COMPLETED, THEN MOVE TO NEXT DAY.

ONE POSITIVE

TODAY I GAVE

DAILY
GOAL SLAYERS
PLANNER

SETTING YOURSELF UP FOR SUCCESS DAILY!

DATE

_____ / _____ / _____

SCRIPTURE

MOTIVATIONAL QUOTE

ONE GOAL

ONE FUN THING

*	IMPORTANT TIME	SCHEDULE	SLAYED?
	5:00AM		☐Y ☐N
	5:30AM		☐Y ☐N
	6:00AM		☐Y ☐N
	6:30AM		☐Y ☐N
	7:00AM		☐Y ☐N
	7:30AM		☐Y ☐N
	8:00AM		☐Y ☐N
	8:30AM		☐Y ☐N
	9:00AM		☐Y ☐N
	9:30AM		☐Y ☐N
	10:00AM		☐Y ☐N
	10:30AM		☐Y ☐N
	11:00AM		☐Y ☐N
	11:30AM		☐Y ☐N
	12:00PM		☐Y ☐N
	12:30PM		☐Y ☐N
	1:00PM		☐Y ☐N
	1:30PM		☐Y ☐N
	2:00PM		☐Y ☐N
	2:30PM		☐Y ☐N
	3:00PM		☐Y ☐N
	3:30PM		☐Y ☐N
	4:00PM		☐Y ☐N
	4:30PM		☐Y ☐N
	5:00PM		☐Y ☐N
	5:30PM		☐Y ☐N
	6:00PM		☐Y ☐N
	6:30PM		☐Y ☐N
	7:00PM		☐Y ☐N
	7:30PM		☐Y ☐N
	8:00PM		☐Y ☐N
	8:30PM		☐Y ☐N
	9:00PM		☐Y ☐N
	9:30PM		☐Y ☐N

HEALTH • FITNESS

WATER INTAKE

OZ. OZ. OZ. OZ. OZ.

OZ. OZ. OZ. OZ. OZ.

TAKE 5 MINUTES EACH MORNING TO PLAN YOUR DAY.

GET EIGHT HOURS OF SLEEP!

NOTE HIGH PRIORITY TASKS WITH A *

ANALYZE WHY A TASK WAS NOT COMPLETED, THEN MOVE TO NEXT DAY.

ONE POSITIVE

TODAY I GAVE

DAILY
GOAL SLAYERS
PLANNER

SETTING YOURSELF UP FOR SUCCESS DAILY!

DATE

_____ / _____ / _____

SCRIPTURE

MOTIVATIONAL QUOTE

ONE GOAL

ONE FUN THING

HEALTH · FITNESS

WATER INTAKE

*	IMPORTANT TIME	SCHEDULE	SLAYED?
	5:00AM		☐Y ☐N
	5:30AM		☐Y ☐N
	6:00AM		☐Y ☐N
	6:30AM		☐Y ☐N
	7:00AM		☐Y ☐N
	7:30AM		☐Y ☐N
	8:00AM		☐Y ☐N
	8:30AM		☐Y ☐N
	9:00AM		☐Y ☐N
	9:30AM		☐Y ☐N
	10:00AM		☐Y ☐N
	10:30AM		☐Y ☐N
	11:00AM		☐Y ☐N
	11:30AM		☐Y ☐N
	12:00PM		☐Y ☐N
	12:30PM		☐Y ☐N
	1:00PM		☐Y ☐N
	1:30PM		☐Y ☐N
	2:00PM		☐Y ☐N
	2:30PM		☐Y ☐N
	3:00PM		☐Y ☐N
	3:30PM		☐Y ☐N
	4:00PM		☐Y ☐N
	4:30PM		☐Y ☐N
	5:00PM		☐Y ☐N
	5:30PM		☐Y ☐N
	6:00PM		☐Y ☐N
	6:30PM		☐Y ☐N
	7:00PM		☐Y ☐N
	7:30PM		☐Y ☐N
	8:00PM		☐Y ☐N
	8:30PM		☐Y ☐N
	9:00PM		☐Y ☐N
	9:30PM		☐Y ☐N

TAKE 5 MINUTES EACH MORNING TO PLAN YOUR DAY.

GET EIGHT HOURS OF SLEEP!

NOTE HIGH PRIORITY TASKS WITH A *

ANALYZE WHY A TASK WAS NOT COMPLETED, THEN MOVE TO NEXT DAY.

ONE POSITIVE

TODAY I GAVE

DATE

___/___/___

SCRIPTURE

MOTIVATIONAL QUOTE

ONE GOAL

ONE FUN THING

✱	IMPORTANT TIME	SCHEDULE	SLAYED?
	5:00AM		☐Y ☐N
	5:30AM		☐Y ☐N
	6:00AM		☐Y ☐N
	6:30AM		☐Y ☐N
	7:00AM		☐Y ☐N
	7:30AM		☐Y ☐N
	8:00AM		☐Y ☐N
	8:30AM		☐Y ☐N
	9:00AM		☐Y ☐N
	9:30AM		☐Y ☐N
	10:00AM		☐Y ☐N
	10:30AM		☐Y ☐N
	11:00AM		☐Y ☐N
	11:30AM		☐Y ☐N
	12:00PM		☐Y ☐N
	12:30PM		☐Y ☐N
	1:00PM		☐Y ☐N
	1:30PM		☐Y ☐N
	2:00PM		☐Y ☐N
	2:30PM		☐Y ☐N
	3:00PM		☐Y ☐N
	3:30PM		☐Y ☐N
	4:00PM		☐Y ☐N
	4:30PM		☐Y ☐N
	5:00PM		☐Y ☐N
	5:30PM		☐Y ☐N
	6:00PM		☐Y ☐N
	6:30PM		☐Y ☐N
	7:00PM		☐Y ☐N
	7:30PM		☐Y ☐N
	8:00PM		☐Y ☐N
	8:30PM		☐Y ☐N
	9:00PM		☐Y ☐N
	9:30PM		☐Y ☐N

HEALTH • FITNESS

WATER INTAKE

OZ. OZ. OZ. OZ. OZ.

OZ. OZ. OZ. OZ. OZ.

TAKE 5 MINUTES EACH MORNING TO PLAN YOUR DAY.

GET EIGHT HOURS OF SLEEP!

NOTE HIGH PRIORITY TASKS WITH A ✱

ANALYZE WHY A TASK WAS NOT COMPLETED. THEN MOVE TO NEXT DAY.

ONE POSITIVE

TODAY I GAVE

DAILY
GOAL SLAYERS
PLANNER

SETTING YOURSELF UP FOR SUCCESS DAILY!

DATE

____ / ____ / ____

SCRIPTURE

MOTIVATIONAL QUOTE

ONE GOAL

ONE FUN THING

HEALTH + FITNESS

✱	IMPORTANT TIME	SCHEDULE	SLAYED?
	5:00AM		☐Y ☐N
	5:30AM		☐Y ☐N
	6:00AM		☐Y ☐N
	6:30AM		☐Y ☐N
	7:00AM		☐Y ☐N
	7:30AM		☐Y ☐N
	8:00AM		☐Y ☐N
	8:30AM		☐Y ☐N
	9:00AM		☐Y ☐N
	9:30AM		☐Y ☐N
	10:00AM		☐Y ☐N
	10:30AM		☐Y ☐N
	11:00AM		☐Y ☐N
	11:30AM		☐Y ☐N
	12:00PM		☐Y ☐N
	12:30PM		☐Y ☐N
	1:00PM		☐Y ☐N
	1:30PM		☐Y ☐N
	2:00PM		☐Y ☐N
	2:30PM		☐Y ☐N
	3:00PM		☐Y ☐N
	3:30PM		☐Y ☐N
	4:00PM		☐Y ☐N
	4:30PM		☐Y ☐N
	5:00PM		☐Y ☐N
	5:30PM		☐Y ☐N
	6:00PM		☐Y ☐N
	6:30PM		☐Y ☐N
	7:00PM		☐Y ☐N
	7:30PM		☐Y ☐N
	8:00PM		☐Y ☐N
	8:30PM		☐Y ☐N
	9:00PM		☐Y ☐N
	9:30PM		☐Y ☐N

WATER INTAKE

OZ. OZ. OZ. OZ. OZ.

OZ. OZ. OZ. OZ. OZ.

TAKE 5 MINUTES EACH MORNING TO PLAN YOUR DAY.

GET EIGHT HOURS OF SLEEP!

NOTE HIGH PRIORITY TASKS WITH A ✱

ANALYZE WHY A TASK WAS NOT COMPLETED, THEN MOVE TO NEXT DAY.

ONE POSITIVE

TODAY I GAVE

DAILY
GOAL SLAYERS
PLANNER

SETTING YOURSELF UP FOR SUCCESS DAILY!

DATE

_____ / _____ / _____

SCRIPTURE

MOTIVATIONAL QUOTE

ONE GOAL

ONE FUN THING

HEALTH • FITNESS

WATER INTAKE

*	IMPORTANT TIME	SCHEDULE	SLAYED?
	5:00AM		☐Y ☐N
	5:30AM		☐Y ☐N
	6:00AM		☐Y ☐N
	6:30AM		☐Y ☐N
	7:00AM		☐Y ☐N
	7:30AM		☐Y ☐N
	8:00AM		☐Y ☐N
	8:30AM		☐Y ☐N
	9:00AM		☐Y ☐N
	9:30AM		☐Y ☐N
	10:00AM		☐Y ☐N
	10:30AM		☐Y ☐N
	11:00AM		☐Y ☐N
	11:30AM		☐Y ☐N
	12:00PM		☐Y ☐N
	12:30PM		☐Y ☐N
	1:00PM		☐Y ☐N
	1:30PM		☐Y ☐N
	2:00PM		☐Y ☐N
	2:30PM		☐Y ☐N
	3:00PM		☐Y ☐N
	3:30PM		☐Y ☐N
	4:00PM		☐Y ☐N
	4:30PM		☐Y ☐N
	5:00PM		☐Y ☐N
	5:30PM		☐Y ☐N
	6:00PM		☐Y ☐N
	6:30PM		☐Y ☐N
	7:00PM		☐Y ☐N
	7:30PM		☐Y ☐N
	8:00PM		☐Y ☐N
	8:30PM		☐Y ☐N
	9:00PM		☐Y ☐N
	9:30PM		☐Y ☐N

TAKE 5 MINUTES EACH MORNING TO PLAN YOUR DAY.

GET EIGHT HOURS OF SLEEP!

NOTE HIGH PRIORITY TASKS WITH A *

ANALYZE WHY A TASK WAS NOT COMPLETED, THEN MOVE TO NEXT DAY.

ONE POSITIVE

TODAY I GAVE

DAILY
GOAL SLAYERS
PLANNER

SETTING YOURSELF UP FOR SUCCESS DAILY!

DATE

_____ / _____ / _____

SCRIPTURE

MOTIVATIONAL QUOTE

ONE GOAL

ONE FUN THING

*	IMPORTANT TIME	SCHEDULE	SLAYED?
	5:00AM		☐Y ☐N
	5:30AM		☐Y ☐N
	6:00AM		☐Y ☐N
	6:30AM		☐Y ☐N
	7:00AM		☐Y ☐N
	7:30AM		☐Y ☐N
	8:00AM		☐Y ☐N
	8:30AM		☐Y ☐N
	9:00AM		☐Y ☐N
	9:30AM		☐Y ☐N
	10:00AM		☐Y ☐N
	10:30AM		☐Y ☐N
	11:00AM		☐Y ☐N
	11:30AM		☐Y ☐N
	12:00PM		☐Y ☐N
	12:30PM		☐Y ☐N
	1:00PM		☐Y ☐N
	1:30PM		☐Y ☐N
	2:00PM		☐Y ☐N
	2:30PM		☐Y ☐N
	3:00PM		☐Y ☐N
	3:30PM		☐Y ☐N
	4:00PM		☐Y ☐N
	4:30PM		☐Y ☐N
	5:00PM		☐Y ☐N
	5:30PM		☐Y ☐N
	6:00PM		☐Y ☐N
	6:30PM		☐Y ☐N
	7:00PM		☐Y ☐N
	7:30PM		☐Y ☐N
	8:00PM		☐Y ☐N
	8:30PM		☐Y ☐N
	9:00PM		☐Y ☐N
	9:30PM		☐Y ☐N

HEALTH + FITNESS

WATER INTAKE

OZ. OZ. OZ. OZ. OZ.
OZ. OZ. OZ. OZ. OZ.

TAKE 5 MINUTES EACH MORNING TO PLAN YOUR DAY.

GET EIGHT HOURS OF SLEEP!

NOTE HIGH PRIORITY TASKS WITH A *

ANALYZE WHY A TASK WAS NOT COMPLETED. THEN MOVE TO NEXT DAY.

ONE POSITIVE

TODAY I GAVE

DAILY
GOAL SLAYERS
PLANNER

SETTING YOURSELF UP FOR SUCCESS DAILY!

DATE

_____ / _____ / _____

SCRIPTURE

MOTIVATIONAL QUOTE

ONE GOAL

ONE FUN THING

*	IMPORTANT TIME	SCHEDULE	SLAYED?	
	5:00AM		☐Y ☐N	
	5:30AM		☐Y ☐N	
	6:00AM		☐Y ☐N	
	6:30AM		☐Y ☐N	
	7:00AM		☐Y ☐N	
	7:30AM		☐Y ☐N	
	8:00AM		☐Y ☐N	
	8:30AM		☐Y ☐N	
	9:00AM		☐Y ☐N	
	9:30AM		☐Y ☐N	
	10:00AM		☐Y ☐N	
	10:30AM		☐Y ☐N	
	11:00AM		☐Y ☐N	
	11:30AM		☐Y ☐N	
	12:00PM		☐Y ☐N	
	12:30PM		☐Y ☐N	
	1:00PM		☐Y ☐N	
	1:30PM		☐Y ☐N	
	2:00PM		☐Y ☐N	
	2:30PM		☐Y ☐N	
	3:00PM		☐Y ☐N	
	3:30PM		☐Y ☐N	
	4:00PM		☐Y ☐N	
	4:30PM		☐Y ☐N	
	5:00PM		☐Y ☐N	
	5:30PM		☐Y ☐N	
	6:00PM		☐Y ☐N	
	6:30PM		☐Y ☐N	
	7:00PM		☐Y ☐N	
	7:30PM		☐Y ☐N	
	8:00PM		☐Y ☐N	
	8:30PM		☐Y ☐N	
	9:00PM		☐Y ☐N	
	9:30PM		☐Y ☐N	

HEALTH + FITNESS

WATER INTAKE

OZ OZ OZ OZ OZ

OZ OZ OZ OZ OZ

TAKE 5 MINUTES EACH MORNING TO PLAN YOUR DAY.

GET EIGHT HOURS OF SLEEP!

NOTE HIGH PRIORITY TASKS WITH A *

ANALYZE WHY A TASK WAS NOT COMPLETED, THEN MOVE TO NEXT DAY.

ONE POSITIVE

TODAY I GAVE

DAILY
GOAL SLAYERS
PLANNER

SETTING YOURSELF UP FOR SUCCESS DAILY!

DATE

____ / ____ / ____

SCRIPTURE

MOTIVATIONAL QUOTE

ONE GOAL

ONE FUN THING

HEALTH • FITNESS

WATER INTAKE

*	IMPORTANT TIME	SCHEDULE	SLAYED?
	5:00AM		☐Y ☐N
	5:30AM		☐Y ☐N
	6:00AM		☐Y ☐N
	6:30AM		☐Y ☐N
	7:00AM		☐Y ☐N
	7:30AM		☐Y ☐N
	8:00AM		☐Y ☐N
	8:30AM		☐Y ☐N
	9:00AM		☐Y ☐N
	9:30AM		☐Y ☐N
	10:00AM		☐Y ☐N
	10:30AM		☐Y ☐N
	11:00AM		☐Y ☐N
	11:30AM		☐Y ☐N
	12:00PM		☐Y ☐N
	12:30PM		☐Y ☐N
	1:00PM		☐Y ☐N
	1:30PM		☐Y ☐N
	2:00PM		☐Y ☐N
	2:30PM		☐Y ☐N
	3:00PM		☐Y ☐N
	3:30PM		☐Y ☐N
	4:00PM		☐Y ☐N
	4:30PM		☐Y ☐N
	5:00PM		☐Y ☐N
	5:30PM		☐Y ☐N
	6:00PM		☐Y ☐N
	6:30PM		☐Y ☐N
	7:00PM		☐Y ☐N
	7:30PM		☐Y ☐N
	8:00PM		☐Y ☐N
	8:30PM		☐Y ☐N
	9:00PM		☐Y ☐N
	9:30PM		☐Y ☐N

TAKE 5 MINUTES EACH MORNING TO PLAN YOUR DAY.

GET EIGHT HOURS OF SLEEP!

NOTE HIGH PRIORITY TASKS WITH A *

ANALYZE WHY A TASK WAS NOT COMPLETED, THEN MOVE TO NEXT DAY.

ONE POSITIVE

TODAY I GAVE

DAILY
GOAL SLAYERS
PLANNER

SETTING YOURSELF UP FOR SUCCESS DAILY!

DATE
_____ / _____ / _____

SCRIPTURE

MOTIVATIONAL QUOTE

ONE GOAL

ONE FUN THING

*	IMPORTANT TIME	SCHEDULE	SLAYED?
	5:00AM		☐Y ☐N
	5:30AM		☐Y ☐N
	6:00AM		☐Y ☐N
	6:30AM		☐Y ☐N
	7:00AM		☐Y ☐N
	7:30AM		☐Y ☐N
	8:00AM		☐Y ☐N
	8:30AM		☐Y ☐N
	9:00AM		☐Y ☐N
	9:30AM		☐Y ☐N
	10:00AM		☐Y ☐N
	10:30AM		☐Y ☐N
	11:00AM		☐Y ☐N
	11:30AM		☐Y ☐N
	12:00PM		☐Y ☐N
	12:30PM		☐Y ☐N
	1:00PM		☐Y ☐N
	1:30PM		☐Y ☐N
	2:00PM		☐Y ☐N
	2:30PM		☐Y ☐N
	3:00PM		☐Y ☐N
	3:30PM		☐Y ☐N
	4:00PM		☐Y ☐N
	4:30PM		☐Y ☐N
	5:00PM		☐Y ☐N
	5:30PM		☐Y ☐N
	6:00PM		☐Y ☐N
	6:30PM		☐Y ☐N
	7:00PM		☐Y ☐N
	7:30PM		☐Y ☐N
	8:00PM		☐Y ☐N
	8:30PM		☐Y ☐N
	9:00PM		☐Y ☐N
	9:30PM		☐Y ☐N

HEALTH • FITNESS

WATER INTAKE

OZ. OZ. OZ. OZ. OZ.
OZ. OZ. OZ. OZ. OZ.

TAKE 5 MINUTES EACH MORNING TO PLAN YOUR DAY.

GET EIGHT HOURS OF SLEEP!

NOTE HIGH PRIORITY TASKS WITH A *

ANALYZE WHY A TASK WAS NOT COMPLETED, THEN MOVE TO NEXT DAY.

ONE POSITIVE

TODAY I GAVE

DAILY
GOAL SLAYERS
PLANNER

SETTING YOURSELF UP FOR SUCCESS DAILY!

DATE

_____ / _____ / _____

SCRIPTURE

MOTIVATIONAL QUOTE

ONE GOAL

ONE FUN THING

✱	IMPORTANT TIME	SCHEDULE	SLAYED?
	5:00AM		☐Y ☐N
	5:30AM		☐Y ☐N
	6:00AM		☐Y ☐N
	6:30AM		☐Y ☐N
	7:00AM		☐Y ☐N
	7:30AM		☐Y ☐N
	8:00AM		☐Y ☐N
	8:30AM		☐Y ☐N
	9:00AM		☐Y ☐N
	9:30AM		☐Y ☐N
	10:00AM		☐Y ☐N
	10:30AM		☐Y ☐N
	11:00AM		☐Y ☐N
	11:30AM		☐Y ☐N
	12:00PM		☐Y ☐N
	12:30PM		☐Y ☐N
	1:00PM		☐Y ☐N
	1:30PM		☐Y ☐N
	2:00PM		☐Y ☐N
	2:30PM		☐Y ☐N
	3:00PM		☐Y ☐N
	3:30PM		☐Y ☐N
	4:00PM		☐Y ☐N
	4:30PM		☐Y ☐N
	5:00PM		☐Y ☐N
	5:30PM		☐Y ☐N
	6:00PM		☐Y ☐N
	6:30PM		☐Y ☐N
	7:00PM		☐Y ☐N
	7:30PM		☐Y ☐N
	8:00PM		☐Y ☐N
	8:30PM		☐Y ☐N
	9:00PM		☐Y ☐N
	9:30PM		☐Y ☐N

HEALTH • FITNESS

WATER INTAKE

OZ. OZ. OZ. OZ. OZ.
OZ. OZ. OZ. OZ. OZ.

TAKE 5 MINUTES EACH MORNING TO PLAN YOUR DAY.

GET EIGHT HOURS OF SLEEP!

NOTE HIGH PRIORITY TASKS WITH A ✱

ANALYZE WHY A TASK WAS NOT COMPLETED, THEN MOVE TO NEXT DAY.

ONE POSITIVE

TODAY I GAVE

DAILY
GOAL SLAYERS
PLANNER

SETTING YOURSELF UP FOR SUCCESS DAILY!

DATE
____/____/____

SCRIPTURE

MOTIVATIONAL QUOTE

ONE GOAL

ONE FUN THING

HEALTH • FITNESS

WATER INTAKE

OZ OZ OZ OZ OZ

OZ OZ OZ OZ OZ

✱	IMPORTANT TIME	SCHEDULE	SLAYED?
	5:00AM		☐Y ☐N
	5:30AM		☐Y ☐N
	6:00AM		☐Y ☐N
	6:30AM		☐Y ☐N
	7:00AM		☐Y ☐N
	7:30AM		☐Y ☐N
	8:00AM		☐Y ☐N
	8:30AM		☐Y ☐N
	9:00AM		☐Y ☐N
	9:30AM		☐Y ☐N
	10:00AM		☐Y ☐N
	10:30AM		☐Y ☐N
	11:00AM		☐Y ☐N
	11:30AM		☐Y ☐N
	12:00PM		☐Y ☐N
	12:30PM		☐Y ☐N
	1:00PM		☐Y ☐N
	1:30PM		☐Y ☐N
	2:00PM		☐Y ☐N
	2:30PM		☐Y ☐N
	3:00PM		☐Y ☐N
	3:30PM		☐Y ☐N
	4:00PM		☐Y ☐N
	4:30PM		☐Y ☐N
	5:00PM		☐Y ☐N
	5:30PM		☐Y ☐N
	6:00PM		☐Y ☐N
	6:30PM		☐Y ☐N
	7:00PM		☐Y ☐N
	7:30PM		☐Y ☐N
	8:00PM		☐Y ☐N
	8:30PM		☐Y ☐N
	9:00PM		☐Y ☐N
	9:30PM		☐Y ☐N

TAKE 5 MINUTES EACH MORNING TO PLAN YOUR DAY.

GET EIGHT HOURS OF SLEEP!

NOTE HIGH PRIORITY TASKS WITH A ✱

ANALYZE WHY A TASK WAS NOT COMPLETED, THEN MOVE TO NEXT DAY.

ONE POSITIVE

TODAY I GAVE

DAILY
GOAL SLAYERS
PLANNER

SETTING YOURSELF UP FOR SUCCESS DAILY!

DATE

____ / ____ / ____

SCRIPTURE

MOTIVATIONAL QUOTE

ONE GOAL

ONE FUN THING

HEALTH • FITNESS

WATER INTAKE

*	IMPORTANT TIME	SCHEDULE	SLAYED?
	5:00AM		☐Y ☐N
	5:30AM		☐Y ☐N
	6:00AM		☐Y ☐N
	6:30AM		☐Y ☐N
	7:00AM		☐Y ☐N
	7:30AM		☐Y ☐N
	8:00AM		☐Y ☐N
	8:30AM		☐Y ☐N
	9:00AM		☐Y ☐N
	9:30AM		☐Y ☐N
	10:00AM		☐Y ☐N
	10:30AM		☐Y ☐N
	11:00AM		☐Y ☐N
	11:30AM		☐Y ☐N
	12:00PM		☐Y ☐N
	12:30PM		☐Y ☐N
	1:00PM		☐Y ☐N
	1:30PM		☐Y ☐N
	2:00PM		☐Y ☐N
	2:30PM		☐Y ☐N
	3:00PM		☐Y ☐N
	3:30PM		☐Y ☐N
	4:00PM		☐Y ☐N
	4:30PM		☐Y ☐N
	5:00PM		☐Y ☐N
	5:30PM		☐Y ☐N
	6:00PM		☐Y ☐N
	6:30PM		☐Y ☐N
	7:00PM		☐Y ☐N
	7:30PM		☐Y ☐N
	8:00PM		☐Y ☐N
	8:30PM		☐Y ☐N
	9:00PM		☐Y ☐N
	9:30PM		☐Y ☐N

TAKE 5 MINUTES EACH MORNING TO PLAN YOUR DAY.

GET EIGHT HOURS OF SLEEP!

NOTE HIGH PRIORITY TASKS WITH A *

ANALYZE WHY A TASK WAS NOT COMPLETED, THEN MOVE TO NEXT DAY.

ONE POSITIVE

TODAY I GAVE

DAILY
GOAL SLAYERS
PLANNER

SETTING YOURSELF UP FOR SUCCESS DAILY!

DATE
_____ / _____ / _____

SCRIPTURE

MOTIVATIONAL QUOTE

ONE GOAL

ONE FUN THING

HEALTH + FITNESS

WATER INTAKE

*	IMPORTANT TIME	SCHEDULE	SLAYED?
	5:00AM		☐Y ☐N
	5:30AM		☐Y ☐N
	6:00AM		☐Y ☐N
	6:30AM		☐Y ☐N
	7:00AM		☐Y ☐N
	7:30AM		☐Y ☐N
	8:00AM		☐Y ☐N
	8:30AM		☐Y ☐N
	9:00AM		☐Y ☐N
	9:30AM		☐Y ☐N
	10:00AM		☐Y ☐N
	10:30AM		☐Y ☐N
	11:00AM		☐Y ☐N
	11:30AM		☐Y ☐N
	12:00PM		☐Y ☐N
	12:30PM		☐Y ☐N
	1:00PM		☐Y ☐N
	1:30PM		☐Y ☐N
	2:00PM		☐Y ☐N
	2:30PM		☐Y ☐N
	3:00PM		☐Y ☐N
	3:30PM		☐Y ☐N
	4:00PM		☐Y ☐N
	4:30PM		☐Y ☐N
	5:00PM		☐Y ☐N
	5:30PM		☐Y ☐N
	6:00PM		☐Y ☐N
	6:30PM		☐Y ☐N
	7:00PM		☐Y ☐N
	7:30PM		☐Y ☐N
	8:00PM		☐Y ☐N
	8:30PM		☐Y ☐N
	9:00PM		☐Y ☐N
	9:30PM		☐Y ☐N

TAKE 5 MINUTES EACH MORNING TO PLAN YOUR DAY.

GET EIGHT HOURS OF SLEEP!

NOTE HIGH PRIORITY TASKS WITH A *

ANALYZE WHY A TASK WAS NOT COMPLETED, THEN MOVE TO NEXT DAY.

ONE POSITIVE

TODAY I GAVE

DAILY
GOAL SLAYERS
PLANNER

SETTING YOURSELF UP FOR SUCCESS DAILY!

DATE

____ / ____ / ____

SCRIPTURE

MOTIVATIONAL QUOTE

ONE GOAL

ONE FUN THING

✱	IMPORTANT TIME	SCHEDULE	SLAYED?
	5:00AM		☐Y ☐N
	5:30AM		☐Y ☐N
	6:00AM		☐Y ☐N
	6:30AM		☐Y ☐N
	7:00AM		☐Y ☐N
	7:30AM		☐Y ☐N
	8:00AM		☐Y ☐N
	8:30AM		☐Y ☐N
	9:00AM		☐Y ☐N
	9:30AM		☐Y ☐N
	10:00AM		☐Y ☐N
	10:30AM		☐Y ☐N
	11:00AM		☐Y ☐N
	11:30AM		☐Y ☐N
	12:00PM		☐Y ☐N
	12:30PM		☐Y ☐N
	1:00PM		☐Y ☐N
	1:30PM		☐Y ☐N
	2:00PM		☐Y ☐N
	2:30PM		☐Y ☐N
	3:00PM		☐Y ☐N
	3:30PM		☐Y ☐N
	4:00PM		☐Y ☐N
	4:30PM		☐Y ☐N
	5:00PM		☐Y ☐N
	5:30PM		☐Y ☐N
	6:00PM		☐Y ☐N
	6:30PM		☐Y ☐N
	7:00PM		☐Y ☐N
	7:30PM		☐Y ☐N
	8:00PM		☐Y ☐N
	8:30PM		☐Y ☐N
	9:00PM		☐Y ☐N
	9:30PM		☐Y ☐N

HEALTH • FITNESS

WATER INTAKE

OZ. OZ. OZ. OZ. OZ.
OZ. OZ. OZ. OZ. OZ.

TAKE 5 MINUTES EACH MORNING TO PLAN YOUR DAY.

GET EIGHT HOURS OF SLEEP!

NOTE HIGH PRIORITY TASKS WITH A ✱

ANALYZE WHY A TASK WAS NOT COMPLETED, THEN MOVE TO NEXT DAY.

ONE POSITIVE

TODAY I GAVE

DAILY
GOAL SLAYERS
PLANNER

SETTING YOURSELF UP FOR SUCCESS DAILY!

DATE

____ / ____ / ____

SCRIPTURE

MOTIVATIONAL QUOTE

ONE GOAL

ONE FUN THING

*	IMPORTANT TIME	SCHEDULE	SLAYED?
	5:00AM		☐Y ☐N
	5:30AM		☐Y ☐N
	6:00AM		☐Y ☐N
	6:30AM		☐Y ☐N
	7:00AM		☐Y ☐N
	7:30AM		☐Y ☐N
	8:00AM		☐Y ☐N
	8:30AM		☐Y ☐N
	9:00AM		☐Y ☐N
	9:30AM		☐Y ☐N
	10:00AM		☐Y ☐N
	10:30AM		☐Y ☐N
	11:00AM		☐Y ☐N
	11:30AM		☐Y ☐N
	12:00PM		☐Y ☐N
	12:30PM		☐Y ☐N
	1:00PM		☐Y ☐N
	1:30PM		☐Y ☐N
	2:00PM		☐Y ☐N
	2:30PM		☐Y ☐N
	3:00PM		☐Y ☐N
	3:30PM		☐Y ☐N
	4:00PM		☐Y ☐N
	4:30PM		☐Y ☐N
	5:00PM		☐Y ☐N
	5:30PM		☐Y ☐N
	6:00PM		☐Y ☐N
	6:30PM		☐Y ☐N
	7:00PM		☐Y ☐N
	7:30PM		☐Y ☐N
	8:00PM		☐Y ☐N
	8:30PM		☐Y ☐N
	9:00PM		☐Y ☐N
	9:30PM		☐Y ☐N

HEALTH • FITNESS

WATER INTAKE

OZ OZ OZ OZ OZ

OZ OZ OZ OZ OZ

TAKE 5 MINUTES EACH MORNING TO PLAN YOUR DAY.

GET EIGHT HOURS OF SLEEP!

NOTE HIGH PRIORITY TASKS WITH A *

ANALYZE WHY A TASK WAS NOT COMPLETED, THEN MOVE TO NEXT DAY.

ONE POSITIVE

TODAY I GAVE

DAILY
GOAL SLAYERS
PLANNER

SETTING YOURSELF UP FOR SUCCESS DAILY!

DATE

_____ / _____ / _____

SCRIPTURE

MOTIVATIONAL QUOTE

ONE GOAL

ONE FUN THING

✱	IMPORTANT TIME	SCHEDULE	SLAYED?
	5:00AM		☐Y ☐N
	5:30AM		☐Y ☐N
	6:00AM		☐Y ☐N
	6:30AM		☐Y ☐N
	7:00AM		☐Y ☐N
	7:30AM		☐Y ☐N
	8:00AM		☐Y ☐N
	8:30AM		☐Y ☐N
	9:00AM		☐Y ☐N
	9:30AM		☐Y ☐N
	10:00AM		☐Y ☐N
	10:30AM		☐Y ☐N
	11:00AM		☐Y ☐N
	11:30AM		☐Y ☐N
	12:00PM		☐Y ☐N
	12:30PM		☐Y ☐N
	1:00PM		☐Y ☐N
	1:30PM		☐Y ☐N
	2:00PM		☐Y ☐N
	2:30PM		☐Y ☐N
	3:00PM		☐Y ☐N
	3:30PM		☐Y ☐N
	4:00PM		☐Y ☐N
	4:30PM		☐Y ☐N
	5:00PM		☐Y ☐N
	5:30PM		☐Y ☐N
	6:00PM		☐Y ☐N
	6:30PM		☐Y ☐N
	7:00PM		☐Y ☐N
	7:30PM		☐Y ☐N
	8:00PM		☐Y ☐N
	8:30PM		☐Y ☐N
	9:00PM		☐Y ☐N
	9:30PM		☐Y ☐N

HEALTH • FITNESS

WATER INTAKE

OZ OZ OZ OZ OZ
OZ OZ OZ OZ OZ

TAKE 5 MINUTES EACH MORNING TO PLAN YOUR DAY.

GET EIGHT HOURS OF SLEEP!

NOTE HIGH PRIORITY TASKS WITH A ✱

ANALYZE WHY A TASK WAS NOT COMPLETED, THEN MOVE TO NEXT DAY.

ONE POSITIVE

TODAY I GAVE

DAILY
GOAL SLAYERS
PLANNER

SETTING YOURSELF UP FOR SUCCESS DAILY!

DATE

_____ / _____ / _____

SCRIPTURE

MOTIVATIONAL QUOTE

ONE GOAL

ONE FUN THING

HEALTH + FITNESS

WATER INTAKE

OZ. OZ. OZ. OZ. OZ.

OZ. OZ. OZ. OZ. OZ.

*	IMPORTANT TIME	SCHEDULE	SLAYED?
	5:00AM		☐Y ☐N
	5:30AM		☐Y ☐N
	6:00AM		☐Y ☐N
	6:30AM		☐Y ☐N
	7:00AM		☐Y ☐N
	7:30AM		☐Y ☐N
	8:00AM		☐Y ☐N
	8:30AM		☐Y ☐N
	9:00AM		☐Y ☐N
	9:30AM		☐Y ☐N
	10:00AM		☐Y ☐N
	10:30AM		☐Y ☐N
	11:00AM		☐Y ☐N
	11:30AM		☐Y ☐N
	12:00PM		☐Y ☐N
	12:30PM		☐Y ☐N
	1:00PM		☐Y ☐N
	1:30PM		☐Y ☐N
	2:00PM		☐Y ☐N
	2:30PM		☐Y ☐N
	3:00PM		☐Y ☐N
	3:30PM		☐Y ☐N
	4:00PM		☐Y ☐N
	4:30PM		☐Y ☐N
	5:00PM		☐Y ☐N
	5:30PM		☐Y ☐N
	6:00PM		☐Y ☐N
	6:30PM		☐Y ☐N
	7:00PM		☐Y ☐N
	7:30PM		☐Y ☐N
	8:00PM		☐Y ☐N
	8:30PM		☐Y ☐N
	9:00PM		☐Y ☐N
	9:30PM		☐Y ☐N

TAKE 5 MINUTES EACH MORNING TO PLAN YOUR DAY.

GET EIGHT HOURS OF SLEEP!

NOTE HIGH PRIORITY TASKS WITH A *

ANALYZE WHY A TASK WAS NOT COMPLETED, THEN MOVE TO NEXT DAY.

ONE POSITIVE

TODAY I GAVE

DAILY
GOAL SLAYERS
PLANNER

SETTING YOURSELF UP FOR SUCCESS DAILY!

DATE

_____ / _____ / _____

SCRIPTURE

MOTIVATIONAL QUOTE

ONE GOAL

ONE FUN THING

*	IMPORTANT TIME	SCHEDULE	SLAYED?
	5:00AM		☐Y ☐N
	5:30AM		☐Y ☐N
	6:00AM		☐Y ☐N
	6:30AM		☐Y ☐N
	7:00AM		☐Y ☐N
	7:30AM		☐Y ☐N
	8:00AM		☐Y ☐N
	8:30AM		☐Y ☐N
	9:00AM		☐Y ☐N
	9:30AM		☐Y ☐N
	10:00AM		☐Y ☐N
	10:30AM		☐Y ☐N
	11:00AM		☐Y ☐N
	11:30AM		☐Y ☐N
	12:00PM		☐Y ☐N
	12:30PM		☐Y ☐N
	1:00PM		☐Y ☐N
	1:30PM		☐Y ☐N
	2:00PM		☐Y ☐N
	2:30PM		☐Y ☐N
	3:00PM		☐Y ☐N
	3:30PM		☐Y ☐N
	4:00PM		☐Y ☐N
	4:30PM		☐Y ☐N
	5:00PM		☐Y ☐N
	5:30PM		☐Y ☐N
	6:00PM		☐Y ☐N
	6:30PM		☐Y ☐N
	7:00PM		☐Y ☐N
	7:30PM		☐Y ☐N
	8:00PM		☐Y ☐N
	8:30PM		☐Y ☐N
	9:00PM		☐Y ☐N
	9:30PM		☐Y ☐N

HEALTH • FITNESS

WATER INTAKE

OZ. OZ. OZ. OZ. OZ.
OZ. OZ. OZ. OZ. OZ.

TAKE 5 MINUTES EACH MORNING TO PLAN YOUR DAY.

GET EIGHT HOURS OF SLEEP!

NOTE HIGH PRIORITY TASKS WITH A *

ANALYZE WHY A TASK WAS NOT COMPLETED, THEN MOVE TO NEXT DAY.

ONE POSITIVE

TODAY I GAVE

DAILY
GOAL SLAYERS
PLANNER

SETTING YOURSELF UP FOR SUCCESS DAILY!

DATE

_____ / _____ / _____

SCRIPTURE

MOTIVATIONAL QUOTE

ONE GOAL

ONE FUN THING

✱	IMPORTANT TIME	SCHEDULE	SLAYED?
	5:00AM		☐Y ☐N
	5:30AM		☐Y ☐N
	6:00AM		☐Y ☐N
	6:30AM		☐Y ☐N
	7:00AM		☐Y ☐N
	7:30AM		☐Y ☐N
	8:00AM		☐Y ☐N
	8:30AM		☐Y ☐N
	9:00AM		☐Y ☐N
	9:30AM		☐Y ☐N
	10:00AM		☐Y ☐N
	10:30AM		☐Y ☐N
	11:00AM		☐Y ☐N
	11:30AM		☐Y ☐N
	12:00PM		☐Y ☐N
	12:30PM		☐Y ☐N
	1:00PM		☐Y ☐N
	1:30PM		☐Y ☐N
	2:00PM		☐Y ☐N
	2:30PM		☐Y ☐N
	3:00PM		☐Y ☐N
	3:30PM		☐Y ☐N
	4:00PM		☐Y ☐N
	4:30PM		☐Y ☐N
	5:00PM		☐Y ☐N
	5:30PM		☐Y ☐N
	6:00PM		☐Y ☐N
	6:30PM		☐Y ☐N
	7:00PM		☐Y ☐N
	7:30PM		☐Y ☐N
	8:00PM		☐Y ☐N
	8:30PM		☐Y ☐N
	9:00PM		☐Y ☐N
	9:30PM		☐Y ☐N

HEALTH + FITNESS

WATER INTAKE

OZ OZ OZ OZ OZ
OZ OZ OZ OZ OZ

TAKE 5 MINUTES EACH MORNING TO PLAN YOUR DAY.

GET EIGHT HOURS OF SLEEP!

NOTE HIGH PRIORITY TASKS WITH A ✱

ANALYZE WHY A TASK WAS NOT COMPLETED, THEN MOVE TO NEXT DAY.

ONE POSITIVE

TODAY I GAVE

DAILY
GOAL SLAYERS
PLANNER

SETTING YOURSELF UP FOR SUCCESS DAILY!

DATE

____ / ____ / _____

SCRIPTURE

MOTIVATIONAL QUOTE

ONE GOAL

ONE FUN THING

HEALTH • FITNESS

WATER INTAKE

OZ OZ OZ OZ OZ

OZ OZ OZ OZ OZ

*	IMPORTANT TIME	SCHEDULE	SLAYED?
	5:00AM		☐Y ☐N
	5:30AM		☐Y ☐N
	6:00AM		☐Y ☐N
	6:30AM		☐Y ☐N
	7:00AM		☐Y ☐N
	7:30AM		☐Y ☐N
	8:00AM		☐Y ☐N
	8:30AM		☐Y ☐N
	9:00AM		☐Y ☐N
	9:30AM		☐Y ☐N
	10:00AM		☐Y ☐N
	10:30AM		☐Y ☐N
	11:00AM		☐Y ☐N
	11:30AM		☐Y ☐N
	12:00PM		☐Y ☐N
	12:30PM		☐Y ☐N
	1:00PM		☐Y ☐N
	1:30PM		☐Y ☐N
	2:00PM		☐Y ☐N
	2:30PM		☐Y ☐N
	3:00PM		☐Y ☐N
	3:30PM		☐Y ☐N
	4:00PM		☐Y ☐N
	4:30PM		☐Y ☐N
	5:00PM		☐Y ☐N
	5:30PM		☐Y ☐N
	6:00PM		☐Y ☐N
	6:30PM		☐Y ☐N
	7:00PM		☐Y ☐N
	7:30PM		☐Y ☐N
	8:00PM		☐Y ☐N
	8:30PM		☐Y ☐N
	9:00PM		☐Y ☐N
	9:30PM		☐Y ☐N

TAKE 5 MINUTES EACH MORNING TO PLAN YOUR DAY.

GET EIGHT HOURS OF SLEEP!

NOTE HIGH PRIORITY TASKS WITH A ✱

ANALYZE WHY A TASK WAS NOT COMPLETED, THEN MOVE TO NEXT DAY.

ONE POSITIVE

TODAY I GAVE

DAILY
GOAL SLAYERS
PLANNER

SETTING YOURSELF UP FOR SUCCESS DAILY!

DATE

_____ / _____ / _____

SCRIPTURE

MOTIVATIONAL QUOTE

ONE GOAL

ONE FUN THING

HEALTH + FITNESS

WATER INTAKE

OZ. OZ. OZ. OZ. OZ.

OZ. OZ. OZ. OZ. OZ.

*	IMPORTANT TIME	SCHEDULE	SLAYED?
	5:00AM		☐Y ☐N
	5:30AM		☐Y ☐N
	6:00AM		☐Y ☐N
	6:30AM		☐Y ☐N
	7:00AM		☐Y ☐N
	7:30AM		☐Y ☐N
	8.00AM		☐Y ☐N
	8:30AM		☐Y ☐N
	9:00AM		☐Y ☐N
	9:30AM		☐Y ☐N
	10:00AM		☐Y ☐N
	10:30AM		☐Y ☐N
	11:00AM		☐Y ☐N
	11:30AM		☐Y ☐N
	12:00PM		☐Y ☐N
	12:30PM		☐Y ☐N
	1:00PM		☐Y ☐N
	1:30PM		☐Y ☐N
	2:00PM		☐Y ☐N
	2:30PM		☐Y ☐N
	3:00PM		☐Y ☐N
	3:30PM		☐Y ☐N
	4:00PM		☐Y ☐N
	4:30PM		☐Y ☐N
	5:00PM		☐Y ☐N
	5:30PM		☐Y ☐N
	6:00PM		☐Y ☐N
	6:30PM		☐Y ☐N
	7:00PM		☐Y ☐N
	7:30PM		☐Y ☐N
	8:00PM		☐Y ☐N
	8:30PM		☐Y ☐N
	9:00PM		☐Y ☐N
	9:30PM		☐Y ☐N

TAKE 5 MINUTES EACH MORNING TO PLAN YOUR DAY.

GET EIGHT HOURS OF SLEEP!

NOTE HIGH PRIORITY TASKS WITH A *

ANALYZE WHY A TASK WAS NOT COMPLETED, THEN MOVE TO NEXT DAY.

ONE POSITIVE

TODAY I GAVE

DAILY
GOAL SLAYERS
PLANNER

SETTING YOURSELF UP FOR SUCCESS DAILY!

DATE

_____ / _____ / _____

SCRIPTURE

MOTIVATIONAL QUOTE

ONE GOAL

ONE FUN THING

HEALTH • FITNESS

WATER INTAKE

OZ. OZ. OZ. OZ. OZ.

OZ. OZ. OZ. OZ. OZ.

✱	IMPORTANT TIME	SCHEDULE	SLAYED?
	5:00AM		☐Y ☐N
	5:30AM		☐Y ☐N
	6:00AM		☐Y ☐N
	6:30AM		☐Y ☐N
	7:00AM		☐Y ☐N
	7:30AM		☐Y ☐N
	8:00AM		☐Y ☐N
	8:30AM		☐Y ☐N
	9:00AM		☐Y ☐N
	9:30AM		☐Y ☐N
	10:00AM		☐Y ☐N
	10:30AM		☐Y ☐N
	11:00AM		☐Y ☐N
	11:30AM		☐Y ☐N
	12:00PM		☐Y ☐N
	12:30PM		☐Y ☐N
	1:00PM		☐Y ☐N
	1:30PM		☐Y ☐N
	2:00PM		☐Y ☐N
	2:30PM		☐Y ☐N
	3:00PM		☐Y ☐N
	3:30PM		☐Y ☐N
	4:00PM		☐Y ☐N
	4:30PM		☐Y ☐N
	5:00PM		☐Y ☐N
	5:30PM		☐Y ☐N
	6:00PM		☐Y ☐N
	6:30PM		☐Y ☐N
	7:00PM		☐Y ☐N
	7:30PM		☐Y ☐N
	8:00PM		☐Y ☐N
	8:30PM		☐Y ☐N
	9:00PM		☐Y ☐N
	9:30PM		☐Y ☐N

TAKE 5 MINUTES EACH MORNING TO PLAN YOUR DAY.

GET EIGHT HOURS OF SLEEP!

NOTE HIGH PRIORITY TASKS WITH A ✱

ANALYZE WHY A TASK WAS NOT COMPLETED, THEN MOVE TO NEXT DAY.

ONE POSITIVE

TODAY I GAVE

DAILY
GOAL SLAYERS
PLANNER

SETTING YOURSELF UP FOR SUCCESS DAILY!

DATE

_____ / _____ / _____

SCRIPTURE

MOTIVATIONAL QUOTE

ONE GOAL

ONE FUN THING

HEALTH • FITNESS

WATER INTAKE

OZ. OZ. OZ. OZ. OZ.

OZ. OZ. OZ. OZ. OZ.

*	IMPORTANT TIME	SCHEDULE	SLAYED?
	5:00AM		☐Y ☐N
	5:30AM		☐Y ☐N
	6:00AM		☐Y ☐N
	6:30AM		☐Y ☐N
	7:00AM		☐Y ☐N
	7:30AM		☐Y ☐N
	8:00AM		☐Y ☐N
	8:30AM		☐Y ☐N
	9:00AM		☐Y ☐N
	9:30AM		☐Y ☐N
	10:00AM		☐Y ☐N
	10:30AM		☐Y ☐N
	11:00AM		☐Y ☐N
	11:30AM		☐Y ☐N
	12:00PM		☐Y ☐N
	12:30PM		☐Y ☐N
	1:00PM		☐Y ☐N
	1:30PM		☐Y ☐N
	2:00PM		☐Y ☐N
	2:30PM		☐Y ☐N
	3:00PM		☐Y ☐N
	3:30PM		☐Y ☐N
	4:00PM		☐Y ☐N
	4:30PM		☐Y ☐N
	5:00PM		☐Y ☐N
	5:30PM		☐Y ☐N
	6:00PM		☐Y ☐N
	6:30PM		☐Y ☐N
	7:00PM		☐Y ☐N
	7:30PM		☐Y ☐N
	8:00PM		☐Y ☐N
	8:30PM		☐Y ☐N
	9:00PM		☐Y ☐N
	9:30PM		☐Y ☐N

TAKE 5 MINUTES EACH MORNING TO PLAN YOUR DAY.

GET EIGHT HOURS OF SLEEP!

NOTE HIGH PRIORITY TASKS WITH A *

ANALYZE WHY A TASK WAS NOT COMPLETED, THEN MOVE TO NEXT DAY.

ONE POSITIVE

TODAY I GAVE

DAILY
GOAL SLAYERS
PLANNER

SETTING YOURSELF UP FOR SUCCESS DAILY!

DATE

_____ / _____ / _____

SCRIPTURE

MOTIVATIONAL QUOTE

ONE GOAL

ONE FUN THING

*	IMPORTANT TIME	SCHEDULE	SLAYED?
	5:00AM		☐Y ☐N
	5:30AM		☐Y ☐N
	6:00AM		☐Y ☐N
	6:30AM		☐Y ☐N
	7:00AM		☐Y ☐N
	7:30AM		☐Y ☐N
	8:00AM		☐Y ☐N
	8:30AM		☐Y ☐N
	9:00AM		☐Y ☐N
	9:30AM		☐Y ☐N
	10:00AM		☐Y ☐N
	10:30AM		☐Y ☐N
	11:00AM		☐Y ☐N
	11:30AM		☐Y ☐N
	12:00PM		☐Y ☐N
	12:30PM		☐Y ☐N
	1:00PM		☐Y ☐N
	1:30PM		☐Y ☐N
	2:00PM		☐Y ☐N
	2:30PM		☐Y ☐N
	3:00PM		☐Y ☐N
	3:30PM		☐Y ☐N
	4:00PM		☐Y ☐N
	4:30PM		☐Y ☐N
	5:00PM		☐Y ☐N
	5:30PM		☐Y ☐N
	6:00PM		☐Y ☐N
	6:30PM		☐Y ☐N
	7:00PM		☐Y ☐N
	7:30PM		☐Y ☐N
	8:00PM		☐Y ☐N
	8:30PM		☐Y ☐N
	9:00PM		☐Y ☐N
	9:30PM		☐Y ☐N

HEALTH + FITNESS

WATER INTAKE

OZ. OZ. OZ. OZ. OZ.
OZ. OZ. OZ. OZ. OZ.

TAKE 5 MINUTES EACH MORNING TO PLAN YOUR DAY.

GET EIGHT HOURS OF SLEEP!

NOTE HIGH PRIORITY TASKS WITH A *

ANALYZE WHY A TASK WAS NOT COMPLETED, THEN MOVE TO NEXT DAY.

ONE POSITIVE

TODAY I GAVE

DAILY
GOAL SLAYERS
PLANNER

SETTING YOURSELF UP FOR SUCCESS DAILY!

DATE

_____ / _____ / _____

SCRIPTURE

MOTIVATIONAL QUOTE

ONE GOAL

ONE FUN THING

✱	IMPORTANT TIME	SCHEDULE	SLAYED?
	5:00AM		☐Y ☐N
	5:30AM		☐Y ☐N
	6:00AM		☐Y ☐N
	6:30AM		☐Y ☐N
	7:00AM		☐Y ☐N
	7:30AM		☐Y ☐N
	8.00AM		☐Y ☐N
	8:30AM		☐Y ☐N
	9:00AM		☐Y ☐N
	9:30AM		☐Y ☐N
	10:00AM		☐Y ☐N
	10:30AM		☐Y ☐N
	11:00AM		☐Y ☐N
	11:30AM		☐Y ☐N
	12:00PM		☐Y ☐N
	12:30PM		☐Y ☐N
	1:00PM		☐Y ☐N
	1:30PM		☐Y ☐N
	2:00PM		☐Y ☐N
	2:30PM		☐Y ☐N
	3:00PM		☐Y ☐N
	3:30PM		☐Y ☐N
	4:00PM		☐Y ☐N
	4:30PM		☐Y ☐N
	5:00PM		☐Y ☐N
	5:30PM		☐Y ☐N
	6:00PM		☐Y ☐N
	6:30PM		☐Y ☐N
	7:00PM		☐Y ☐N
	7:30PM		☐Y ☐N
	8:00PM		☐Y ☐N
	8:30PM		☐Y ☐N
	9:00PM		☐Y ☐N
	9:30PM		☐Y ☐N

HEALTH + FITNESS

WATER INTAKE

OZ. OZ. OZ. OZ. OZ.

OZ. OZ. OZ. OZ. OZ.

TAKE 5 MINUTES EACH MORNING TO PLAN YOUR DAY.

GET EIGHT HOURS OF SLEEP!

NOTE HIGH PRIORITY TASKS WITH A ✱

ANALYZE WHY A TASK WAS NOT COMPLETED, THEN MOVE TO NEXT DAY.

ONE POSITIVE

TODAY I GAVE

DAILY
GOAL SLAYERS
PLANNER

SETTING YOURSELF UP FOR SUCCESS DAILY!

DATE

____ / ____ / ____

SCRIPTURE

MOTIVATIONAL QUOTE

ONE GOAL

ONE FUN THING

HEALTH • FITNESS

WATER INTAKE

*	IMPORTANT TIME	SCHEDULE	SLAYED?
	5:00AM		☐Y ☐N
	5:30AM		☐Y ☐N
	6:00AM		☐Y ☐N
	6:30AM		☐Y ☐N
	7:00AM		☐Y ☐N
	7:30AM		☐Y ☐N
	8:00AM		☐Y ☐N
	8:30AM		☐Y ☐N
	9:00AM		☐Y ☐N
	9:30AM		☐Y ☐N
	10:00AM		☐Y ☐N
	10:30AM		☐Y ☐N
	11:00AM		☐Y ☐N
	11:30AM		☐Y ☐N
	12:00PM		☐Y ☐N
	12:30PM		☐Y ☐N
	1:00PM		☐Y ☐N
	1:30PM		☐Y ☐N
	2:00PM		☐Y ☐N
	2:30PM		☐Y ☐N
	3:00PM		☐Y ☐N
	3:30PM		☐Y ☐N
	4:00PM		☐Y ☐N
	4:30PM		☐Y ☐N
	5:00PM		☐Y ☐N
	5:30PM		☐Y ☐N
	6:00PM		☐Y ☐N
	6:30PM		☐Y ☐N
	7:00PM		☐Y ☐N
	7:30PM		☐Y ☐N
	8:00PM		☐Y ☐N
	8:30PM		☐Y ☐N
	9:00PM		☐Y ☐N
	9:30PM		☐Y ☐N

TAKE 5 MINUTES EACH MORNING TO PLAN YOUR DAY.

GET EIGHT HOURS OF SLEEP!

NOTE HIGH PRIORITY TASKS WITH A *

ANALYZE WHY A TASK WAS NOT COMPLETED, THEN MOVE TO NEXT DAY.

ONE POSITIVE

TODAY I GAVE

DAILY
GOAL SLAYERS
PLANNER

SETTING YOURSELF UP FOR SUCCESS DAILY!

DATE

_____ / _____ / _____

SCRIPTURE

MOTIVATIONAL QUOTE

ONE GOAL

ONE FUN THING

HEALTH • FITNESS

WATER INTAKE

OZ. OZ. OZ. OZ. OZ.

OZ. OZ. OZ. OZ. OZ.

✱	IMPORTANT TIME	SCHEDULE	SLAYED?
	5:00AM		☐Y ☐N
	5:30AM		☐Y ☐N
	6:00AM		☐Y ☐N
	6:30AM		☐Y ☐N
	7:00AM		☐Y ☐N
	7:30AM		☐Y ☐N
	8:00AM		☐Y ☐N
	8:30AM		☐Y ☐N
	9:00AM		☐Y ☐N
	9:30AM		☐Y ☐N
	10:00AM		☐Y ☐N
	10:30AM		☐Y ☐N
	11:00AM		☐Y ☐N
	11:30AM		☐Y ☐N
	12:00PM		☐Y ☐N
	12:30PM		☐Y ☐N
	1:00PM		☐Y ☐N
	1:30PM		☐Y ☐N
	2:00PM		☐Y ☐N
	2:30PM		☐Y ☐N
	3:00PM		☐Y ☐N
	3:30PM		☐Y ☐N
	4:00PM		☐Y ☐N
	4:30PM		☐Y ☐N
	5:00PM		☐Y ☐N
	5:30PM		☐Y ☐N
	6:00PM		☐Y ☐N
	6:30PM		☐Y ☐N
	7:00PM		☐Y ☐N
	7:30PM		☐Y ☐N
	8:00PM		☐Y ☐N
	8:30PM		☐Y ☐N
	9:00PM		☐Y ☐N
	9:30PM		☐Y ☐N

TAKE 5 MINUTES EACH MORNING TO PLAN YOUR DAY.

GET EIGHT HOURS OF SLEEP!

NOTE HIGH PRIORITY TASKS WITH A ✱

ANALYZE WHY A TASK WAS NOT COMPLETED, THEN MOVE TO NEXT DAY.

ONE POSITIVE

TODAY I GAVE

DAILY
GOAL SLAYERS
PLANNER

SETTING YOURSELF UP FOR SUCCESS DAILY!

DATE

_____ / _____ / _____

SCRIPTURE

MOTIVATIONAL QUOTE

ONE GOAL

ONE FUN THING

✱	IMPORTANT TIME	SCHEDULE	SLAYED?
	5:00AM		☐Y ☐N
	5:30AM		☐Y ☐N
	6:00AM		☐Y ☐N
	6:30AM		☐Y ☐N
	7:00AM		☐Y ☐N
	7:30AM		☐Y ☐N
	8:00AM		☐Y ☐N
	8:30AM		☐Y ☐N
	9:00AM		☐Y ☐N
	9:30AM		☐Y ☐N
	10:00AM		☐Y ☐N
	10:30AM		☐Y ☐N
	11:00AM		☐Y ☐N
	11:30AM		☐Y ☐N
	12:00PM		☐Y ☐N
	12:30PM		☐Y ☐N
	1:00PM		☐Y ☐N
	1:30PM		☐Y ☐N
	2:00PM		☐Y ☐N
	2:30PM		☐Y ☐N
	3:00PM		☐Y ☐N
	3:30PM		☐Y ☐N
	4:00PM		☐Y ☐N
	4:30PM		☐Y ☐N
	5:00PM		☐Y ☐N
	5:30PM		☐Y ☐N
	6:00PM		☐Y ☐N
	6:30PM		☐Y ☐N
	7:00PM		☐Y ☐N
	7:30PM		☐Y ☐N
	8:00PM		☐Y ☐N
	8:30PM		☐Y ☐N
	9:00PM		☐Y ☐N
	9:30PM		☐Y ☐N

HEALTH + FITNESS

WATER INTAKE

OZ. OZ. OZ. OZ. OZ.

OZ. OZ. OZ. OZ. OZ.

TAKE 5 MINUTES EACH MORNING TO PLAN YOUR DAY.

GET EIGHT HOURS OF SLEEP!

NOTE HIGH PRIORITY TASKS WITH A ✱

ANALYZE WHY A TASK WAS NOT COMPLETED, THEN MOVE TO NEXT DAY.

ONE POSITIVE

TODAY I GAVE

DAILY
GOAL SLAYERS
PLANNER

SETTING YOURSELF UP FOR SUCCESS DAILY!

DATE

____ / ____ / ____

SCRIPTURE

MOTIVATIONAL QUOTE

ONE GOAL

ONE FUN THING

✱	IMPORTANT TIME	SCHEDULE	SLAYED?
	5:00AM		☐Y ☐N
	5:30AM		☐Y ☐N
	6:00AM		☐Y ☐N
	6:30AM		☐Y ☐N
	7:00AM		☐Y ☐N
	7:30AM		☐Y ☐N
	8:00AM		☐Y ☐N
	8:30AM		☐Y ☐N
	9:00AM		☐Y ☐N
	9:30AM		☐Y ☐N
	10:00AM		☐Y ☐N
	10:30AM		☐Y ☐N
	11:00AM		☐Y ☐N
	11:30AM		☐Y ☐N
	12:00PM		☐Y ☐N
	12:30PM		☐Y ☐N
	1:00PM		☐Y ☐N
	1:30PM		☐Y ☐N
	2:00PM		☐Y ☐N
	2:30PM		☐Y ☐N
	3:00PM		☐Y ☐N
	3:30PM		☐Y ☐N
	4:00PM		☐Y ☐N
	4:30PM		☐Y ☐N
	5:00PM		☐Y ☐N
	5:30PM		☐Y ☐N
	6:00PM		☐Y ☐N
	6:30PM		☐Y ☐N
	7:00PM		☐Y ☐N
	7:30PM		☐Y ☐N
	8:00PM		☐Y ☐N
	8:30PM		☐Y ☐N
	9:00PM		☐Y ☐N
	9:30PM		☐Y ☐N

HEALTH ✱ FITNESS

WATER INTAKE

OZ. OZ. OZ. OZ. OZ.
OZ. OZ. OZ. OZ. OZ.

TAKE 5 MINUTES EACH MORNING TO PLAN YOUR DAY.

GET EIGHT HOURS OF SLEEP!

NOTE HIGH PRIORITY TASKS WITH A ✱

ANALYZE WHY A TASK WAS NOT COMPLETED, THEN MOVE TO NEXT DAY.

ONE POSITIVE

TODAY I GAVE

DAILY
GOAL SLAYERS
PLANNER

SETTING YOURSELF UP FOR SUCCESS DAILY!

DATE

____ / ____ / ____

SCRIPTURE

MOTIVATIONAL QUOTE

ONE GOAL

ONE FUN THING

HEALTH • FITNESS

WATER INTAKE

✱	IMPORTANT TIME	SCHEDULE	SLAYED?
	5:00AM		☐Y ☐N
	5:30AM		☐Y ☐N
	6:00AM		☐Y ☐N
	6:30AM		☐Y ☐N
	7:00AM		☐Y ☐N
	7:30AM		☐Y ☐N
	8:00AM		☐Y ☐N
	8:30AM		☐Y ☐N
	9:00AM		☐Y ☐N
	9:30AM		☐Y ☐N
	10:00AM		☐Y ☐N
	10:30AM		☐Y ☐N
	11:00AM		☐Y ☐N
	11:30AM		☐Y ☐N
	12:00PM		☐Y ☐N
	12:30PM		☐Y ☐N
	1:00PM		☐Y ☐N
	1:30PM		☐Y ☐N
	2:00PM		☐Y ☐N
	2:30PM		☐Y ☐N
	3:00PM		☐Y ☐N
	3:30PM		☐Y ☐N
	4:00PM		☐Y ☐N
	4:30PM		☐Y ☐N
	5:00PM		☐Y ☐N
	5:30PM		☐Y ☐N
	6:00PM		☐Y ☐N
	6:30PM		☐Y ☐N
	7:00PM		☐Y ☐N
	7:30PM		☐Y ☐N
	8:00PM		☐Y ☐N
	8:30PM		☐Y ☐N
	9:00PM		☐Y ☐N
	9:30PM		☐Y ☐N

TAKE 5 MINUTES EACH MORNING TO PLAN YOUR DAY.

GET EIGHT HOURS OF SLEEP!

NOTE HIGH PRIORITY TASKS WITH A ✱

ANALYZE WHY A TASK WAS NOT COMPLETED, THEN MOVE TO NEXT DAY.

ONE POSITIVE

TODAY I GAVE

DAILY
GOAL SLAYERS
PLANNER

SETTING YOURSELF UP FOR SUCCESS DAILY!

DATE

____ /____ /____

SCRIPTURE

MOTIVATIONAL QUOTE

ONE GOAL

ONE FUN THING

*	IMPORTANT TIME	SCHEDULE	SLAYED?
	5:00AM		☐Y ☐N
	5:30AM		☐Y ☐N
	6:00AM		☐Y ☐N
	6:30AM		☐Y ☐N
	7:00AM		☐Y ☐N
	7:30AM		☐Y ☐N
	8:00AM		☐Y ☐N
	8:30AM		☐Y ☐N
	9:00AM		☐Y ☐N
	9:30AM		☐Y ☐N
	10:00AM		☐Y ☐N
	10:30AM		☐Y ☐N
	11:00AM		☐Y ☐N
	11:30AM		☐Y ☐N
	12:00PM		☐Y ☐N
	12:30PM		☐Y ☐N
	1:00PM		☐Y ☐N
	1:30PM		☐Y ☐N
	2:00PM		☐Y ☐N
	2:30PM		☐Y ☐N
	3:00PM		☐Y ☐N
	3:30PM		☐Y ☐N
	4:00PM		☐Y ☐N
	4:30PM		☐Y ☐N
	5:00PM		☐Y ☐N
	5:30PM		☐Y ☐N
	6:00PM		☐Y ☐N
	6:30PM		☐Y ☐N
	7:00PM		☐Y ☐N
	7:30PM		☐Y ☐N
	8:00PM		☐Y ☐N
	8:30PM		☐Y ☐N
	9:00PM		☐Y ☐N
	9:30PM		☐Y ☐N

HEALTH • FITNESS

WATER INTAKE

OZ OZ OZ OZ OZ
OZ OZ OZ OZ OZ

TAKE 5 MINUTES EACH MORNING TO PLAN YOUR DAY.

GET EIGHT HOURS OF SLEEP!

NOTE HIGH PRIORITY TASKS WITH A *

ANALYZE WHY A TASK WAS NOT COMPLETED, THEN MOVE TO NEXT DAY.

ONE POSITIVE

TODAY I GAVE

DAILY
GOAL SLAYERS
PLANNER

SETTING YOURSELF UP FOR SUCCESS DAILY!

DATE

_____ / _____ / _____

SCRIPTURE

MOTIVATIONAL QUOTE

ONE GOAL

ONE FUN THING

*	IMPORTANT TIME	SCHEDULE	SLAYED?
	5:00AM		☐Y ☐N
	5:30AM		☐Y ☐N
	6:00AM		☐Y ☐N
	6:30AM		☐Y ☐N
	7:00AM		☐Y ☐N
	7:30AM		☐Y ☐N
	8:00AM		☐Y ☐N
	8:30AM		☐Y ☐N
	9:00AM		☐Y ☐N
	9:30AM		☐Y ☐N
	10:00AM		☐Y ☐N
	10:30AM		☐Y ☐N
	11:00AM		☐Y ☐N
	11:30AM		☐Y ☐N
	12:00PM		☐Y ☐N
	12:30PM		☐Y ☐N
	1:00PM		☐Y ☐N
	1:30PM		☐Y ☐N
	2:00PM		☐Y ☐N
	2:30PM		☐Y ☐N
	3:00PM		☐Y ☐N
	3:30PM		☐Y ☐N
	4:00PM		☐Y ☐N
	4:30PM		☐Y ☐N
	5:00PM		☐Y ☐N
	5:30PM		☐Y ☐N
	6:00PM		☐Y ☐N
	6:30PM		☐Y ☐N
	7:00PM		☐Y ☐N
	7:30PM		☐Y ☐N
	8:00PM		☐Y ☐N
	8:30PM		☐Y ☐N
	9:00PM		☐Y ☐N
	9:30PM		☐Y ☐N

HEALTH • FITNESS

WATER INTAKE

OZ OZ OZ OZ OZ
OZ OZ OZ OZ OZ

TAKE 5 MINUTES EACH MORNING TO PLAN YOUR DAY.

GET EIGHT HOURS OF SLEEP!

NOTE HIGH PRIORITY TASKS WITH A *

ANALYZE WHY A TASK WAS NOT COMPLETED, THEN MOVE TO NEXT DAY.

ONE POSITIVE

TODAY I GAVE

DAILY
GOAL SLAYERS
PLANNER

SETTING YOURSELF UP FOR SUCCESS DAILY!

DATE

_____ / _____ / _____

SCRIPTURE

MOTIVATIONAL QUOTE

ONE GOAL

ONE FUN THING

HEALTH + FITNESS

WATER INTAKE

OZ. OZ. OZ. OZ. OZ.

OZ. OZ. OZ. OZ. OZ.

*	IMPORTANT TIME	SCHEDULE	SLAYED?
	5:00AM		☐Y ☐N
	5:30AM		☐Y ☐N
	6:00AM		☐Y ☐N
	6:30AM		☐Y ☐N
	7:00AM		☐Y ☐N
	7:30AM		☐Y ☐N
	8:00AM		☐Y ☐N
	8:30AM		☐Y ☐N
	9:00AM		☐Y ☐N
	9:30AM		☐Y ☐N
	10:00AM		☐Y ☐N
	10:30AM		☐Y ☐N
	11:00AM		☐Y ☐N
	11:30AM		☐Y ☐N
	12:00PM		☐Y ☐N
	12:30PM		☐Y ☐N
	1:00PM		☐Y ☐N
	1:30PM		☐Y ☐N
	2:00PM		☐Y ☐N
	2:30PM		☐Y ☐N
	3:00PM		☐Y ☐N
	3:30PM		☐Y ☐N
	4:00PM		☐Y ☐N
	4:30PM		☐Y ☐N
	5:00PM		☐Y ☐N
	5:30PM		☐Y ☐N
	6:00PM		☐Y ☐N
	6:30PM		☐Y ☐N
	7:00PM		☐Y ☐N
	7:30PM		☐Y ☐N
	8:00PM		☐Y ☐N
	8:30PM		☐Y ☐N
	9:00PM		☐Y ☐N
	9:30PM		☐Y ☐N

TAKE 5 MINUTES EACH MORNING TO PLAN YOUR DAY.

GET EIGHT HOURS OF SLEEP!

NOTE HIGH PRIORITY TASKS WITH A *

ANALYZE WHY A TASK WAS NOT COMPLETED, THEN MOVE TO NEXT DAY.

ONE POSITIVE

TODAY I GAVE

DAILY
GOAL SLAYERS
PLANNER

SETTING YOURSELF UP FOR SUCCESS DAILY!

DATE

_____ / _____ / _____

SCRIPTURE

MOTIVATIONAL QUOTE

ONE GOAL

ONE FUN THING

✱	IMPORTANT TIME	SCHEDULE	SLAYED?
	5:00AM		☐Y ☐N
	5:30AM		☐Y ☐N
	6:00AM		☐Y ☐N
	6:30AM		☐Y ☐N
	7:00AM		☐Y ☐N
	7:30AM		☐Y ☐N
	8:00AM		☐Y ☐N
	8:30AM		☐Y ☐N
	9:00AM		☐Y ☐N
	9:30AM		☐Y ☐N
	10:00AM		☐Y ☐N
	10:30AM		☐Y ☐N
	11:00AM		☐Y ☐N
	11:30AM		☐Y ☐N
	12:00PM		☐Y ☐N
	12:30PM		☐Y ☐N
	1:00PM		☐Y ☐N
	1:30PM		☐Y ☐N
	2:00PM		☐Y ☐N
	2:30PM		☐Y ☐N
	3:00PM		☐Y ☐N
	3:30PM		☐Y ☐N
	4:00PM		☐Y ☐N
	4:30PM		☐Y ☐N
	5:00PM		☐Y ☐N
	5:30PM		☐Y ☐N
	6:00PM		☐Y ☐N
	6:30PM		☐Y ☐N
	7:00PM		☐Y ☐N
	7:30PM		☐Y ☐N
	8:00PM		☐Y ☐N
	8:30PM		☐Y ☐N
	9:00PM		☐Y ☐N
	9:30PM		☐Y ☐N

HEALTH + FITNESS

WATER INTAKE

OZ. OZ. OZ. OZ. OZ.
OZ. OZ. OZ. OZ. OZ.

TAKE 5 MINUTES EACH MORNING TO PLAN YOUR DAY.

GET EIGHT HOURS OF SLEEP!

NOTE HIGH PRIORITY TASKS WITH A ✱

ANALYZE WHY A TASK WAS NOT COMPLETED, THEN MOVE TO NEXT DAY.

ONE POSITIVE

TODAY I GAVE

DAILY
GOAL SLAYERS
PLANNER

SETTING YOURSELF UP FOR SUCCESS DAILY!

DATE

____ / ____ / ____

SCRIPTURE

MOTIVATIONAL QUOTE

ONE GOAL

ONE FUN THING

✱	IMPORTANT TIME	SCHEDULE	SLAYED?
	5:00AM		☐Y ☐N
	5:30AM		☐Y ☐N
	6:00AM		☐Y ☐N
	6:30AM		☐Y ☐N
	7:00AM		☐Y ☐N
	7:30AM		☐Y ☐N
	8:00AM		☐Y ☐N
	8:30AM		☐Y ☐N
	9:00AM		☐Y ☐N
	9:30AM		☐Y ☐N
	10:00AM		☐Y ☐N
	10:30AM		☐Y ☐N
	11:00AM		☐Y ☐N
	11:30AM		☐Y ☐N
	12:00PM		☐Y ☐N
	12:30PM		☐Y ☐N
	1:00PM		☐Y ☐N
	1:30PM		☐Y ☐N
	2:00PM		☐Y ☐N
	2:30PM		☐Y ☐N
	3:00PM		☐Y ☐N
	3:30PM		☐Y ☐N
	4:00PM		☐Y ☐N
	4:30PM		☐Y ☐N
	5:00PM		☐Y ☐N
	5:30PM		☐Y ☐N
	6:00PM		☐Y ☐N
	6:30PM		☐Y ☐N
	7:00PM		☐Y ☐N
	7:30PM		☐Y ☐N
	8:00PM		☐Y ☐N
	8:30PM		☐Y ☐N
	9:00PM		☐Y ☐N
	9:30PM		☐Y ☐N

HEALTH + FITNESS

WATER INTAKE

OZ OZ OZ OZ OZ
OZ OZ OZ OZ OZ

TAKE 5 MINUTES EACH MORNING TO PLAN YOUR DAY.

GET EIGHT HOURS OF SLEEP!

NOTE HIGH PRIORITY TASKS WITH A ✱

ANALYZE WHY A TASK WAS NOT COMPLETED, THEN MOVE TO NEXT DAY.

ONE POSITIVE

TODAY I GAVE

DAILY
GOAL SLAYERS
PLANNER

SETTING YOURSELF UP FOR SUCCESS DAILY!

DATE

____ / ____ / ____

SCRIPTURE

MOTIVATIONAL QUOTE

ONE GOAL

ONE FUN THING

*	IMPORTANT TIME	SCHEDULE	SLAYED?
	5:00AM		☐Y ☐N
	5:30AM		☐Y ☐N
	6:00AM		☐Y ☐N
	6:30AM		☐Y ☐N
	7:00AM		☐Y ☐N
	7:30AM		☐Y ☐N
	8:00AM		☐Y ☐N
	8:30AM		☐Y ☐N
	9:00AM		☐Y ☐N
	9:30AM		☐Y ☐N
	10:00AM		☐Y ☐N
	10:30AM		☐Y ☐N
	11:00AM		☐Y ☐N
	11:30AM		☐Y ☐N
	12:00PM		☐Y ☐N
	12:30PM		☐Y ☐N
	1:00PM		☐Y ☐N
	1:30PM		☐Y ☐N
	2:00PM		☐Y ☐N
	2:30PM		☐Y ☐N
	3:00PM		☐Y ☐N
	3:30PM		☐Y ☐N
	4:00PM		☐Y ☐N
	4:30PM		☐Y ☐N
	5:00PM		☐Y ☐N
	5:30PM		☐Y ☐N
	6:00PM		☐Y ☐N
	6:30PM		☐Y ☐N
	7:00PM		☐Y ☐N
	7:30PM		☐Y ☐N
	8:00PM		☐Y ☐N
	8:30PM		☐Y ☐N
	9:00PM		☐Y ☐N
	9:30PM		☐Y ☐N

HEALTH + FITNESS

WATER INTAKE

OZ. OZ. OZ. OZ. OZ.
OZ. OZ. OZ. OZ. OZ.

TAKE 5 MINUTES EACH MORNING TO PLAN YOUR DAY.

GET EIGHT HOURS OF SLEEP!

NOTE HIGH PRIORITY TASKS WITH A *

ANALYZE WHY A TASK WAS NOT COMPLETED, THEN MOVE TO NEXT DAY.

ONE POSITIVE

TODAY I GAVE

DAILY
GOAL SLAYERS
PLANNER

SETTING YOURSELF UP FOR SUCCESS DAILY!

DATE
____ / ____ / ____

SCRIPTURE

MOTIVATIONAL QUOTE

ONE GOAL

ONE FUN THING

*	IMPORTANT TIME	SCHEDULE	SLAYED?
	5:00AM		□Y □N
	5:30AM		□Y □N
	6:00AM		□Y □N
	6:30AM		□Y □N
	7:00AM		□Y □N
	7:30AM		□Y □N
	8:00AM		□Y □N
	8:30AM		□Y □N
	9:00AM		□Y □N
	9:30AM		□Y □N
	10:00AM		□Y □N
	10:30AM		□Y □N
	11:00AM		□Y □N
	11:30AM		□Y □N
	12:00PM		□Y □N
	12:30PM		□Y □N
	1:00PM		□Y □N
	1:30PM		□Y □N
	2:00PM		□Y □N
	2:30PM		□Y □N
	3:00PM		□Y □N
	3:30PM		□Y □N
	4:00PM		□Y □N
	4:30PM		□Y □N
	5:00PM		□Y □N
	5:30PM		□Y □N
	6:00PM		□Y □N
	6:30PM		□Y □N
	7:00PM		□Y □N
	7:30PM		□Y □N
	8:00PM		□Y □N
	8:30PM		□Y □N
	9:00PM		□Y □N
	9:30PM		□Y □N

HEALTH • FITNESS

WATER INTAKE

OZ. OZ. OZ. OZ. OZ.
OZ. OZ. OZ. OZ. OZ.

TAKE 5 MINUTES EACH MORNING TO PLAN YOUR DAY.

GET EIGHT HOURS OF SLEEP!

NOTE HIGH PRIORITY TASKS WITH A *

ANALYZE WHY A TASK WAS NOT COMPLETED, THEN MOVE TO NEXT DAY.

ONE POSITIVE

TODAY I GAVE

DAILY
GOAL SLAYERS
PLANNER

SETTING YOURSELF UP FOR SUCCESS DAILY!

DATE

_____/_____/_____

SCRIPTURE

MOTIVATIONAL QUOTE

ONE GOAL

ONE FUN THING

HEALTH • FITNESS

WATER INTAKE

*	IMPORTANT TIME	SCHEDULE	SLAYED?
	5:00AM		□Y □N
	5:30AM		□Y □N
	6:00AM		□Y □N
	6:30AM		□Y □N
	7:00AM		□Y □N
	7:30AM		□Y □N
	8:00AM		□Y □N
	8:30AM		□Y □N
	9:00AM		□Y □N
	9:30AM		□Y □N
	10:00AM		□Y □N
	10:30AM		□Y □N
	11:00AM		□Y □N
	11:30AM		□Y □N
	12:00PM		□Y □N
	12:30PM		□Y □N
	1:00PM		□Y □N
	1:30PM		□Y □N
	2:00PM		□Y □N
	2:30PM		□Y □N
	3:00PM		□Y □N
	3:30PM		□Y □N
	4:00PM		□Y □N
	4:30PM		□Y □N
	5:00PM		□Y □N
	5:30PM		□Y □N
	6:00PM		□Y □N
	6:30PM		□Y □N
	7:00PM		□Y □N
	7:30PM		□Y □N
	8:00PM		□Y □N
	8:30PM		□Y □N
	9:00PM		□Y □N
	9:30PM		□Y □N

TAKE 5 MINUTES EACH MORNING TO PLAN YOUR DAY.

GET EIGHT HOURS OF SLEEP!

NOTE HIGH PRIORITY TASKS WITH A *

ANALYZE WHY A TASK WAS NOT COMPLETED, THEN MOVE TO NEXT DAY.

ONE POSITIVE

TODAY I GAVE

DAILY
GOAL SLAYERS
PLANNER

SETTING YOURSELF UP FOR SUCCESS DAILY!

DATE

_____ / _____ / _____

SCRIPTURE

MOTIVATIONAL QUOTE

ONE GOAL

ONE FUN THING

HEALTH • FITNESS

WATER INTAKE

OZ OZ OZ OZ OZ

OZ OZ OZ OZ OZ

*	IMPORTANT TIME	SCHEDULE	SLAYED?
	5:00AM		☐Y ☐N
	5:30AM		☐Y ☐N
	6:00AM		☐Y ☐N
	6:30AM		☐Y ☐N
	7:00AM		☐Y ☐N
	7:30AM		☐Y ☐N
	8:00AM		☐Y ☐N
	8:30AM		☐Y ☐N
	9:00AM		☐Y ☐N
	9:30AM		☐Y ☐N
	10:00AM		☐Y ☐N
	10:30AM		☐Y ☐N
	11:00AM		☐Y ☐N
	11:30AM		☐Y ☐N
	12:00PM		☐Y ☐N
	12:30PM		☐Y ☐N
	1:00PM		☐Y ☐N
	1:30PM		☐Y ☐N
	2:00PM		☐Y ☐N
	2:30PM		☐Y ☐N
	3:00PM		☐Y ☐N
	3:30PM		☐Y ☐N
	4:00PM		☐Y ☐N
	4:30PM		☐Y ☐N
	5:00PM		☐Y ☐N
	5:30PM		☐Y ☐N
	6:00PM		☐Y ☐N
	6:30PM		☐Y ☐N
	7:00PM		☐Y ☐N
	7:30PM		☐Y ☐N
	8:00PM		☐Y ☐N
	8:30PM		☐Y ☐N
	9:00PM		☐Y ☐N
	9:30PM		☐Y ☐N

TAKE 5 MINUTES EACH MORNING TO PLAN YOUR DAY.

GET EIGHT HOURS OF SLEEP!

NOTE HIGH PRIORITY TASKS WITH A *

ANALYZE WHY A TASK WAS NOT COMPLETED, THEN MOVE TO NEXT DAY.

ONE POSITIVE

TODAY I GAVE

DAILY
GOAL SLAYERS
PLANNER

SETTING YOURSELF UP FOR SUCCESS DAILY!

DATE

_____ / _____ / _____

SCRIPTURE

MOTIVATIONAL QUOTE

ONE GOAL

ONE FUN THING

HEALTH • FITNESS

WATER INTAKE

OZ OZ OZ OZ OZ

OZ OZ OZ OZ OZ

✱	IMPORTANT TIME	SCHEDULE	SLAYED?
	5:00AM		☐Y ☐N
	5:30AM		☐Y ☐N
	6:00AM		☐Y ☐N
	6:30AM		☐Y ☐N
	7:00AM		☐Y ☐N
	7:30AM		☐Y ☐N
	8:00AM		☐Y ☐N
	8:30AM		☐Y ☐N
	9:00AM		☐Y ☐N
	9:30AM		☐Y ☐N
	10:00AM		☐Y ☐N
	10:30AM		☐Y ☐N
	11:00AM		☐Y ☐N
	11:30AM		☐Y ☐N
	12:00PM		☐Y ☐N
	12:30PM		☐Y ☐N
	1:00PM		☐Y ☐N
	1:30PM		☐Y ☐N
	2:00PM		☐Y ☐N
	2:30PM		☐Y ☐N
	3:00PM		☐Y ☐N
	3:30PM		☐Y ☐N
	4:00PM		☐Y ☐N
	4:30PM		☐Y ☐N
	5:00PM		☐Y ☐N
	5:30PM		☐Y ☐N
	6:00PM		☐Y ☐N
	6:30PM		☐Y ☐N
	7:00PM		☐Y ☐N
	7:30PM		☐Y ☐N
	8:00PM		☐Y ☐N
	8:30PM		☐Y ☐N
	9:00PM		☐Y ☐N
	9:30PM		☐Y ☐N

TAKE 5 MINUTES EACH MORNING TO PLAN YOUR DAY.

GET EIGHT HOURS OF SLEEP!

NOTE HIGH PRIORITY TASKS WITH A ✱

ANALYZE WHY A TASK WAS NOT COMPLETED, THEN MOVE TO NEXT DAY.

ONE POSITIVE

TODAY I GAVE

DAILY
GOAL SLAYERS
PLANNER

SETTING YOURSELF UP FOR SUCCESS DAILY!

DATE
____ / ____ / ____

SCRIPTURE

MOTIVATIONAL QUOTE

ONE GOAL

ONE FUN THING

HEALTH + FITNESS

WATER INTAKE

*	IMPORTANT TIME	SCHEDULE	SLAYED?
	5:00AM		☐Y ☐N
	5:30AM		☐Y ☐N
	6:00AM		☐Y ☐N
	6:30AM		☐Y ☐N
	7:00AM		☐Y ☐N
	7:30AM		☐Y ☐N
	8:00AM		☐Y ☐N
	8:30AM		☐Y ☐N
	9:00AM		☐Y ☐N
	9:30AM		☐Y ☐N
	10:00AM		☐Y ☐N
	10:30AM		☐Y ☐N
	11:00AM		☐Y ☐N
	11:30AM		☐Y ☐N
	12:00PM		☐Y ☐N
	12:30PM		☐Y ☐N
	1:00PM		☐Y ☐N
	1:30PM		☐Y ☐N
	2:00PM		☐Y ☐N
	2:30PM		☐Y ☐N
	3:00PM		☐Y ☐N
	3:30PM		☐Y ☐N
	4:00PM		☐Y ☐N
	4:30PM		☐Y ☐N
	5:00PM		☐Y ☐N
	5:30PM		☐Y ☐N
	6:00PM		☐Y ☐N
	6:30PM		☐Y ☐N
	7:00PM		☐Y ☐N
	7:30PM		☐Y ☐N
	8:00PM		☐Y ☐N
	8:30PM		☐Y ☐N
	9:00PM		☐Y ☐N
	9:30PM		☐Y ☐N

TAKE 5 MINUTES EACH MORNING TO PLAN YOUR DAY.

GET EIGHT HOURS OF SLEEP!

NOTE HIGH PRIORITY TASKS WITH A *

ANALYZE WHY A TASK WAS NOT COMPLETED, THEN MOVE TO NEXT DAY.

ONE POSITIVE

TODAY I GAVE

DAILY
GOAL SLAYERS
PLANNER

SETTING YOURSELF UP FOR SUCCESS DAILY!

DATE

_____ / _____ / _____

SCRIPTURE

MOTIVATIONAL QUOTE

ONE GOAL

ONE FUN THING

*	IMPORTANT TIME	SCHEDULE	SLAYED?
	5:00AM		☐Y ☐N
	5:30AM		☐Y ☐N
	6:00AM		☐Y ☐N
	6:30AM		☐Y ☐N
	7:00AM		☐Y ☐N
	7:30AM		☐Y ☐N
	8:00AM		☐Y ☐N
	8:30AM		☐Y ☐N
	9:00AM		☐Y ☐N
	9:30AM		☐Y ☐N
	10:00AM		☐Y ☐N
	10:30AM		☐Y ☐N
	11:00AM		☐Y ☐N
	11:30AM		☐Y ☐N
	12:00PM		☐Y ☐N
	12:30PM		☐Y ☐N
	1:00PM		☐Y ☐N
	1:30PM		☐Y ☐N
	2:00PM		☐Y ☐N
	2:30PM		☐Y ☐N
	3:00PM		☐Y ☐N
	3:30PM		☐Y ☐N
	4:00PM		☐Y ☐N
	4:30PM		☐Y ☐N
	5:00PM		☐Y ☐N
	5:30PM		☐Y ☐N
	6:00PM		☐Y ☐N
	6:30PM		☐Y ☐N
	7:00PM		☐Y ☐N
	7:30PM		☐Y ☐N
	8:00PM		☐Y ☐N
	8:30PM		☐Y ☐N
	9:00PM		☐Y ☐N
	9:30PM		☐Y ☐N

HEALTH · FITNESS

WATER INTAKE

OZ OZ OZ OZ OZ

OZ OZ OZ OZ OZ

TAKE 5 MINUTES EACH MORNING TO PLAN YOUR DAY.

GET EIGHT HOURS OF SLEEP!

NOTE HIGH PRIORITY TASKS WITH A *

ANALYZE WHY A TASK WAS NOT COMPLETED, THEN MOVE TO NEXT DAY.

ONE POSITIVE

TODAY I GAVE

DAILY
GOAL SLAYERS
PLANNER

SETTING YOURSELF UP FOR SUCCESS DAILY!

DATE

_____ / _____ / _____

SCRIPTURE

MOTIVATIONAL QUOTE

ONE GOAL

ONE FUN THING

*	IMPORTANT TIME	SCHEDULE	SLAYED?
	5:00AM		☐Y ☐N
	5:30AM		☐Y ☐N
	6:00AM		☐Y ☐N
	6:30AM		☐Y ☐N
	7:00AM		☐Y ☐N
	7:30AM		☐Y ☐N
	8:00AM		☐Y ☐N
	8:30AM		☐Y ☐N
	9:00AM		☐Y ☐N
	9:30AM		☐Y ☐N
	10:00AM		☐Y ☐N
	10:30AM		☐Y ☐N
	11:00AM		☐Y ☐N
	11:30AM		☐Y ☐N
	12:00PM		☐Y ☐N
	12:30PM		☐Y ☐N
	1:00PM		☐Y ☐N
	1:30PM		☐Y ☐N
	2:00PM		☐Y ☐N
	2:30PM		☐Y ☐N
	3:00PM		☐Y ☐N
	3:30PM		☐Y ☐N
	4:00PM		☐Y ☐N
	4:30PM		☐Y ☐N
	5:00PM		☐Y ☐N
	5:30PM		☐Y ☐N
	6:00PM		☐Y ☐N
	6:30PM		☐Y ☐N
	7:00PM		☐Y ☐N
	7:30PM		☐Y ☐N
	8:00PM		☐Y ☐N
	8:30PM		☐Y ☐N
	9:00PM		☐Y ☐N
	9:30PM		☐Y ☐N

HEALTH + FITNESS

WATER INTAKE

OZ OZ OZ OZ OZ

OZ OZ OZ OZ OZ

TAKE 5 MINUTES EACH MORNING TO PLAN YOUR DAY.

GET EIGHT HOURS OF SLEEP!

NOTE HIGH PRIORITY TASKS WITH A *

ANALYZE WHY A TASK WAS NOT COMPLETED, THEN MOVE TO NEXT DAY.

ONE POSITIVE

TODAY I GAVE

DAILY
GOAL SLAYERS
PLANNER

SETTING YOURSELF UP FOR SUCCESS DAILY!

DATE

_____ / _____ / _____

SCRIPTURE

MOTIVATIONAL QUOTE

ONE GOAL

ONE FUN THING

HEALTH + FITNESS

WATER INTAKE

OZ. OZ. OZ. OZ. OZ.
OZ. OZ. OZ. OZ. OZ.

*	IMPORTANT TIME	SCHEDULE	SLAYED?
	5:00AM		☐Y ☐N
	5:30AM		☐Y ☐N
	6:00AM		☐Y ☐N
	6:30AM		☐Y ☐N
	7:00AM		☐Y ☐N
	7:30AM		☐Y ☐N
	8:00AM		☐Y ☐N
	8:30AM		☐Y ☐N
	9:00AM		☐Y ☐N
	9:30AM		☐Y ☐N
	10:00AM		☐Y ☐N
	10:30AM		☐Y ☐N
	11:00AM		☐Y ☐N
	11:30AM		☐Y ☐N
	12:00PM		☐Y ☐N
	12:30PM		☐Y ☐N
	1:00PM		☐Y ☐N
	1:30PM		☐Y ☐N
	2:00PM		☐Y ☐N
	2:30PM		☐Y ☐N
	3:00PM		☐Y ☐N
	3:30PM		☐Y ☐N
	4:00PM		☐Y ☐N
	4:30PM		☐Y ☐N
	5:00PM		☐Y ☐N
	5:30PM		☐Y ☐N
	6:00PM		☐Y ☐N
	6:30PM		☐Y ☐N
	7:00PM		☐Y ☐N
	7:30PM		☐Y ☐N
	8:00PM		☐Y ☐N
	8:30PM		☐Y ☐N
	9:00PM		☐Y ☐N
	9:30PM		☐Y ☐N

TAKE 5 MINUTES EACH MORNING TO PLAN YOUR DAY.

GET EIGHT HOURS OF SLEEP!

NOTE HIGH PRIORITY TASKS WITH A *

ANALYZE WHY A TASK WAS NOT COMPLETED, THEN MOVE TO NEXT DAY.

ONE POSITIVE

TODAY I GAVE

DAILY
GOAL SLAYERS
PLANNER

SETTING YOURSELF UP FOR SUCCESS DAILY!

DATE

_____ / _____ / _____

SCRIPTURE

MOTIVATIONAL QUOTE

ONE GOAL

ONE FUN THING

HEALTH • FITNESS

WATER INTAKE

OZ. OZ. OZ. OZ. OZ.

OZ. OZ. OZ. OZ. OZ.

*	IMPORTANT TIME	SCHEDULE	SLAYED?
	5:00AM		☐Y ☐N
	5:30AM		☐Y ☐N
	6:00AM		☐Y ☐N
	6:30AM		☐Y ☐N
	7:00AM		☐Y ☐N
	7:30AM		☐Y ☐N
	8:00AM		☐Y ☐N
	8:30AM		☐Y ☐N
	9:00AM		☐Y ☐N
	9:30AM		☐Y ☐N
	10:00AM		☐Y ☐N
	10:30AM		☐Y ☐N
	11:00AM		☐Y ☐N
	11:30AM		☐Y ☐N
	12:00PM		☐Y ☐N
	12:30PM		☐Y ☐N
	1:00PM		☐Y ☐N
	1:30PM		☐Y ☐N
	2:00PM		☐Y ☐N
	2:30PM		☐Y ☐N
	3:00PM		☐Y ☐N
	3:30PM		☐Y ☐N
	4:00PM		☐Y ☐N
	4:30PM		☐Y ☐N
	5:00PM		☐Y ☐N
	5:30PM		☐Y ☐N
	6:00PM		☐Y ☐N
	6:30PM		☐Y ☐N
	7:00PM		☐Y ☐N
	7:30PM		☐Y ☐N
	8:00PM		☐Y ☐N
	8:30PM		☐Y ☐N
	9:00PM		☐Y ☐N
	9:30PM		☐Y ☐N

TAKE 5 MINUTES EACH MORNING TO PLAN YOUR DAY.

GET EIGHT HOURS OF SLEEP!

NOTE HIGH PRIORITY TASKS WITH A *

ANALYZE WHY A TASK WAS NOT COMPLETED, THEN MOVE TO NEXT DAY.

ONE POSITIVE

TODAY I GAVE

DAILY
GOAL SLAYERS
PLANNER

SETTING YOURSELF UP FOR SUCCESS DAILY!

DATE

____ / ____ / ____

SCRIPTURE

MOTIVATIONAL QUOTE

ONE GOAL

ONE FUN THING

✱	IMPORTANT TIME	SCHEDULE	SLAYED?
	5:00AM		☐Y ☐N
	5:30AM		☐Y ☐N
	6:00AM		☐Y ☐N
	6:30AM		☐Y ☐N
	7:00AM		☐Y ☐N
	7:30AM		☐Y ☐N
	8:00AM		☐Y ☐N
	8:30AM		☐Y ☐N
	9:00AM		☐Y ☐N
	9:30AM		☐Y ☐N
	10:00AM		☐Y ☐N
	10:30AM		☐Y ☐N
	11:00AM		☐Y ☐N
	11:30AM		☐Y ☐N
	12:00PM		☐Y ☐N
	12:30PM		☐Y ☐N
	1:00PM		☐Y ☐N
	1:30PM		☐Y ☐N
	2:00PM		☐Y ☐N
	2:30PM		☐Y ☐N
	3:00PM		☐Y ☐N
	3:30PM		☐Y ☐N
	4:00PM		☐Y ☐N
	4:30PM		☐Y ☐N
	5:00PM		☐Y ☐N
	5:30PM		☐Y ☐N
	6:00PM		☐Y ☐N
	6:30PM		☐Y ☐N
	7:00PM		☐Y ☐N
	7:30PM		☐Y ☐N
	8:00PM		☐Y ☐N
	8:30PM		☐Y ☐N
	9:00PM		☐Y ☐N
	9:30PM		☐Y ☐N

HEALTH • FITNESS

WATER INTAKE

OZ. OZ. OZ. OZ. OZ.
OZ. OZ. OZ. OZ. OZ.

TAKE 5 MINUTES EACH MORNING TO PLAN YOUR DAY.

GET EIGHT HOURS OF SLEEP!

NOTE HIGH PRIORITY TASKS WITH A ✱

ANALYZE WHY A TASK WAS NOT COMPLETED, THEN MOVE TO NEXT DAY.

ONE POSITIVE

TODAY I GAVE

DAILY
GOAL SLAYERS
PLANNER

SETTING YOURSELF UP FOR SUCCESS DAILY!

DATE

_____ / _____ / _____

SCRIPTURE

MOTIVATIONAL QUOTE

ONE GOAL

ONE FUN THING

✱	IMPORTANT TIME	SCHEDULE	SLAYED?
	5:00AM		☐Y ☐N
	5:30AM		☐Y ☐N
	6:00AM		☐Y ☐N
	6:30AM		☐Y ☐N
	7:00AM		☐Y ☐N
	7:30AM		☐Y ☐N
	8:00AM		☐Y ☐N
	8:30AM		☐Y ☐N
	9:00AM		☐Y ☐N
	9:30AM		☐Y ☐N
	10:00AM		☐Y ☐N
	10:30AM		☐Y ☐N
	11:00AM		☐Y ☐N
	11:30AM		☐Y ☐N
	12:00PM		☐Y ☐N
	12:30PM		☐Y ☐N
	1:00PM		☐Y ☐N
	1:30PM		☐Y ☐N
	2:00PM		☐Y ☐N
	2:30PM		☐Y ☐N
	3:00PM		☐Y ☐N
	3:30PM		☐Y ☐N
	4:00PM		☐Y ☐N
	4:30PM		☐Y ☐N
	5:00PM		☐Y ☐N
	5:30PM		☐Y ☐N
	6:00PM		☐Y ☐N
	6:30PM		☐Y ☐N
	7:00PM		☐Y ☐N
	7:30PM		☐Y ☐N
	8:00PM		☐Y ☐N
	8:30PM		☐Y ☐N
	9:00PM		☐Y ☐N
	9:30PM		☐Y ☐N

HEALTH + FITNESS

WATER INTAKE

OZ OZ OZ OZ OZ

OZ OZ OZ OZ OZ

TAKE 5 MINUTES EACH MORNING TO PLAN YOUR DAY.

GET EIGHT HOURS OF SLEEP!

NOTE HIGH PRIORITY TASKS WITH A ✱

ANALYZE WHY A TASK WAS NOT COMPLETED, THEN MOVE TO NEXT DAY.

ONE POSITIVE

TODAY I GAVE

DAILY
GOAL SLAYERS
PLANNER

SETTING YOURSELF UP FOR SUCCESS DAILY!

DATE

_____ / _____ / _____

SCRIPTURE

MOTIVATIONAL QUOTE

ONE GOAL

ONE FUN THING

✱	IMPORTANT TIME	SCHEDULE	SLAYED?
	5:00AM		☐Y ☐N
	5:30AM		☐Y ☐N
	6:00AM		☐Y ☐N
	6:30AM		☐Y ☐N
	7:00AM		☐Y ☐N
	7:30AM		☐Y ☐N
	8:00AM		☐Y ☐N
	8:30AM		☐Y ☐N
	9:00AM		☐Y ☐N
	9:30AM		☐Y ☐N
	10:00AM		☐Y ☐N
	10:30AM		☐Y ☐N
	11:00AM		☐Y ☐N
	11:30AM		☐Y ☐N
	12:00PM		☐Y ☐N
	12:30PM		☐Y ☐N
	1:00PM		☐Y ☐N
	1:30PM		☐Y ☐N
	2:00PM		☐Y ☐N
	2:30PM		☐Y ☐N
	3:00PM		☐Y ☐N
	3:30PM		☐Y ☐N
	4:00PM		☐Y ☐N
	4:30PM		☐Y ☐N
	5:00PM		☐Y ☐N
	5:30PM		☐Y ☐N
	6:00PM		☐Y ☐N
	6:30PM		☐Y ☐N
	7:00PM		☐Y ☐N
	7:30PM		☐Y ☐N
	8:00PM		☐Y ☐N
	8:30PM		☐Y ☐N
	9:00PM		☐Y ☐N
	9:30PM		☐Y ☐N

HEALTH • FITNESS

WATER INTAKE

OZ. OZ. OZ. OZ. OZ.
OZ. OZ. OZ. OZ. OZ.

TAKE 5 MINUTES EACH MORNING TO PLAN YOUR DAY.

GET EIGHT HOURS OF SLEEP!

NOTE HIGH PRIORITY TASKS WITH A ✱

ANALYZE WHY A TASK WAS NOT COMPLETED, THEN MOVE TO NEXT DAY.

ONE POSITIVE

TODAY I GAVE

DAILY
GOAL SLAYERS
PLANNER

SETTING YOURSELF UP FOR SUCCESS DAILY!

DATE

____ / ____ / ____

SCRIPTURE

MOTIVATIONAL QUOTE

ONE GOAL

ONE FUN THING

*	IMPORTANT TIME	SCHEDULE	SLAYED?
	5:00AM		☐Y ☐N
	5:30AM		☐Y ☐N
	6:00AM		☐Y ☐N
	6:30AM		☐Y ☐N
	7:00AM		☐Y ☐N
	7:30AM		☐Y ☐N
	8:00AM		☐Y ☐N
	8:30AM		☐Y ☐N
	9:00AM		☐Y ☐N
	9:30AM		☐Y ☐N
	10:00AM		☐Y ☐N
	10:30AM		☐Y ☐N
	11:00AM		☐Y ☐N
	11:30AM		☐Y ☐N
	12:00PM		☐Y ☐N
	12:30PM		☐Y ☐N
	1:00PM		☐Y ☐N
	1:30PM		☐Y ☐N
	2:00PM		☐Y ☐N
	2:30PM		☐Y ☐N
	3:00PM		☐Y ☐N
	3:30PM		☐Y ☐N
	4:00PM		☐Y ☐N
	4:30PM		☐Y ☐N
	5:00PM		☐Y ☐N
	5:30PM		☐Y ☐N
	6:00PM		☐Y ☐N
	6:30PM		☐Y ☐N
	7:00PM		☐Y ☐N
	7:30PM		☐Y ☐N
	8:00PM		☐Y ☐N
	8:30PM		☐Y ☐N
	9:00PM		☐Y ☐N
	9:30PM		☐Y ☐N

HEALTH + FITNESS

WATER INTAKE

OZ. OZ. OZ. OZ. OZ.
OZ. OZ. OZ. OZ. OZ.

TAKE 5 MINUTES EACH MORNING TO PLAN YOUR DAY.

GET EIGHT HOURS OF SLEEP!

NOTE HIGH PRIORITY TASKS WITH A *

ANALYZE WHY A TASK WAS NOT COMPLETED, THEN MOVE TO NEXT DAY.

ONE POSITIVE

TODAY I GAVE

DAILY
GOAL SLAYERS
PLANNER

SETTING YOURSELF UP FOR SUCCESS DAILY!

DATE

_____ / _____ / _____

SCRIPTURE

MOTIVATIONAL QUOTE

ONE GOAL

ONE FUN THING

HEALTH • FITNESS

WATER INTAKE

*	IMPORTANT TIME	SCHEDULE	SLAYED?
	5:00AM		☐Y ☐N
	5:30AM		☐Y ☐N
	6:00AM		☐Y ☐N
	6:30AM		☐Y ☐N
	7:00AM		☐Y ☐N
	7:30AM		☐Y ☐N
	8:00AM		☐Y ☐N
	8:30AM		☐Y ☐N
	9:00AM		☐Y ☐N
	9:30AM		☐Y ☐N
	10:00AM		☐Y ☐N
	10:30AM		☐Y ☐N
	11:00AM		☐Y ☐N
	11:30AM		☐Y ☐N
	12:00PM		☐Y ☐N
	12:30PM		☐Y ☐N
	1:00PM		☐Y ☐N
	1:30PM		☐Y ☐N
	2:00PM		☐Y ☐N
	2:30PM		☐Y ☐N
	3:00PM		☐Y ☐N
	3:30PM		☐Y ☐N
	4:00PM		☐Y ☐N
	4:30PM		☐Y ☐N
	5:00PM		☐Y ☐N
	5:30PM		☐Y ☐N
	6:00PM		☐Y ☐N
	6:30PM		☐Y ☐N
	7:00PM		☐Y ☐N
	7:30PM		☐Y ☐N
	8:00PM		☐Y ☐N
	8:30PM		☐Y ☐N
	9:00PM		☐Y ☐N
	9:30PM		☐Y ☐N

TAKE 5 MINUTES EACH MORNING TO PLAN YOUR DAY.

GET EIGHT HOURS OF SLEEP!

NOTE HIGH PRIORITY TASKS WITH A ✱

ANALYZE WHY A TASK WAS NOT COMPLETED, THEN MOVE TO NEXT DAY.

ONE POSITIVE

TODAY I GAVE

DAILY
GOAL SLAYERS
PLANNER

SETTING YOURSELF UP FOR SUCCESS DAILY!

DATE

_____ / _____ / _____

SCRIPTURE

MOTIVATIONAL QUOTE

ONE GOAL

ONE FUN THING

*	IMPORTANT TIME	SCHEDULE	SLAYED?	
	5:00AM		☐Y ☐N	
	5:30AM		☐Y ☐N	
	6:00AM		☐Y ☐N	
	6:30AM		☐Y ☐N	
	7:00AM		☐Y ☐N	
	7:30AM		☐Y ☐N	
	8:00AM		☐Y ☐N	
	8:30AM		☐Y ☐N	
	9:00AM		☐Y ☐N	
	9:30AM		☐Y ☐N	
	10:00AM		☐Y ☐N	
	10:30AM		☐Y ☐N	
	11:00AM		☐Y ☐N	
	11:30AM		☐Y ☐N	
	12:00PM		☐Y ☐N	
	12:30PM		☐Y ☐N	
	1:00PM		☐Y ☐N	
	1:30PM		☐Y ☐N	
	2:00PM		☐Y ☐N	
	2:30PM		☐Y ☐N	
	3:00PM		☐Y ☐N	
	3:30PM		☐Y ☐N	
	4:00PM		☐Y ☐N	
	4:30PM		☐Y ☐N	
	5:00PM		☐Y ☐N	
	5:30PM		☐Y ☐N	
	6:00PM		☐Y ☐N	
	6:30PM		☐Y ☐N	
	7:00PM		☐Y ☐N	
	7:30PM		☐Y ☐N	
	8:00PM		☐Y ☐N	
	8:30PM		☐Y ☐N	
	9:00PM		☐Y ☐N	
	9:30PM		☐Y ☐N	

HEALTH • FITNESS

WATER INTAKE

OZ. OZ. OZ. OZ. OZ.
OZ. OZ. OZ. OZ. OZ.

TAKE 5 MINUTES EACH MORNING TO PLAN YOUR DAY.

GET EIGHT HOURS OF SLEEP!

NOTE HIGH PRIORITY TASKS WITH A *

ANALYZE WHY A TASK WAS NOT COMPLETED, THEN MOVE TO NEXT DAY.

ONE POSITIVE

TODAY I GAVE

DAILY
GOAL SLAYERS
PLANNER

SETTING YOURSELF UP FOR SUCCESS DAILY!

DATE

____ / ____ / ____

SCRIPTURE

MOTIVATIONAL QUOTE

ONE GOAL

ONE FUN THING

✱	IMPORTANT TIME	SCHEDULE	SLAYED?
	5:00AM		☐Y ☐N
	5:30AM		☐Y ☐N
	6:00AM		☐Y ☐N
	6:30AM		☐Y ☐N
	7:00AM		☐Y ☐N
	7:30AM		☐Y ☐N
	8:00AM		☐Y ☐N
	8:30AM		☐Y ☐N
	9:00AM		☐Y ☐N
	9:30AM		☐Y ☐N
	10:00AM		☐Y ☐N
	10:30AM		☐Y ☐N
	11:00AM		☐Y ☐N
	11:30AM		☐Y ☐N
	12:00PM		☐Y ☐N
	12:30PM		☐Y ☐N
	1:00PM		☐Y ☐N
	1:30PM		☐Y ☐N
	2:00PM		☐Y ☐N
	2:30PM		☐Y ☐N
	3:00PM		☐Y ☐N
	3:30PM		☐Y ☐N
	4:00PM		☐Y ☐N
	4:30PM		☐Y ☐N
	5:00PM		☐Y ☐N
	5:30PM		☐Y ☐N
	6:00PM		☐Y ☐N
	6:30PM		☐Y ☐N
	7:00PM		☐Y ☐N
	7:30PM		☐Y ☐N
	8:00PM		☐Y ☐N
	8:30PM		☐Y ☐N
	9:00PM		☐Y ☐N
	9:30PM		☐Y ☐N

HEALTH • FITNESS

WATER INTAKE

OZ. OZ. OZ. OZ. OZ.
OZ. OZ. OZ. OZ. OZ.

TAKE 5 MINUTES EACH MORNING TO PLAN YOUR DAY.

GET EIGHT HOURS OF SLEEP!

NOTE HIGH PRIORITY TASKS WITH A ✱

ANALYZE WHY A TASK WAS NOT COMPLETED, THEN MOVE TO NEXT DAY.

ONE POSITIVE

TODAY I GAVE

DAILY
GOAL SLAYERS
PLANNER

SETTING YOURSELF UP FOR SUCCESS DAILY!

DATE

____ / ____ / ____

SCRIPTURE

MOTIVATIONAL QUOTE

ONE GOAL

ONE FUN THING

HEALTH • FITNESS

*	IMPORTANT TIME	SCHEDULE	SLAYED?
	5:00AM		☐Y ☐N
	5:30AM		☐Y ☐N
	6:00AM		☐Y ☐N
	6:30AM		☐Y ☐N
	7:00AM		☐Y ☐N
	7:30AM		☐Y ☐N
	8:00AM		☐Y ☐N
	8:30AM		☐Y ☐N
	9:00AM		☐Y ☐N
	9:30AM		☐Y ☐N
	10:00AM		☐Y ☐N
	10:30AM		☐Y ☐N
	11:00AM		☐Y ☐N
	11:30AM		☐Y ☐N
	12:00PM		☐Y ☐N
	12:30PM		☐Y ☐N
	1:00PM		☐Y ☐N
	1:30PM		☐Y ☐N
	2:00PM		☐Y ☐N
	2:30PM		☐Y ☐N
	3:00PM		☐Y ☐N
	3:30PM		☐Y ☐N
	4:00PM		☐Y ☐N
	4:30PM		☐Y ☐N
	5:00PM		☐Y ☐N
	5:30PM		☐Y ☐N
	6:00PM		☐Y ☐N
	6:30PM		☐Y ☐N
	7:00PM		☐Y ☐N
	7:30PM		☐Y ☐N
	8:00PM		☐Y ☐N
	8:30PM		☐Y ☐N
	9:00PM		☐Y ☐N
	9:30PM		☐Y ☐N

WATER INTAKE

OZ. OZ. OZ. OZ. OZ.
OZ. OZ. OZ. OZ. OZ.

TAKE 5 MINUTES EACH MORNING TO PLAN YOUR DAY.

GET EIGHT HOURS OF SLEEP!

NOTE HIGH PRIORITY TASKS WITH A *

ANALYZE WHY A TASK WAS NOT COMPLETED, THEN MOVE TO NEXT DAY.

ONE POSITIVE

TODAY I GAVE

DAILY
GOAL SLAYERS
PLANNER

SETTING YOURSELF UP FOR SUCCESS DAILY!

DATE

_____ / _____ / _____

SCRIPTURE

MOTIVATIONAL QUOTE

ONE GOAL

ONE FUN THING

HEALTH • FITNESS

WATER INTAKE

*	IMPORTANT TIME	SCHEDULE	SLAYED?
	5:00AM		☐Y ☐N
	5:30AM		☐Y ☐N
	6:00AM		☐Y ☐N
	6:30AM		☐Y ☐N
	7:00AM		☐Y ☐N
	7:30AM		☐Y ☐N
	8:00AM		☐Y ☐N
	8:30AM		☐Y ☐N
	9:00AM		☐Y ☐N
	9:30AM		☐Y ☐N
	10:00AM		☐Y ☐N
	10:30AM		☐Y ☐N
	11:00AM		☐Y ☐N
	11:30AM		☐Y ☐N
	12:00PM		☐Y ☐N
	12:30PM		☐Y ☐N
	1:00PM		☐Y ☐N
	1:30PM		☐Y ☐N
	2:00PM		☐Y ☐N
	2:30PM		☐Y ☐N
	3:00PM		☐Y ☐N
	3:30PM		☐Y ☐N
	4:00PM		☐Y ☐N
	4:30PM		☐Y ☐N
	5:00PM		☐Y ☐N
	5:30PM		☐Y ☐N
	6:00PM		☐Y ☐N
	6:30PM		☐Y ☐N
	7:00PM		☐Y ☐N
	7:30PM		☐Y ☐N
	8:00PM		☐Y ☐N
	8:30PM		☐Y ☐N
	9:00PM		☐Y ☐N
	9:30PM		☐Y ☐N

TAKE 5 MINUTES EACH MORNING TO PLAN YOUR DAY.

GET EIGHT HOURS OF SLEEP!

NOTE HIGH PRIORITY TASKS WITH A *

ANALYZE WHY A TASK WAS NOT COMPLETED, THEN MOVE TO NEXT DAY.

ONE POSITIVE

TODAY I GAVE

DAILY
GOAL SLAYERS
PLANNER

SETTING YOURSELF UP FOR SUCCESS DAILY!

DATE

_____ / _____ / _____

SCRIPTURE

MOTIVATIONAL QUOTE

ONE GOAL

ONE FUN THING

HEALTH • FITNESS

WATER INTAKE

OZ OZ OZ OZ OZ

OZ OZ OZ OZ OZ

✱	IMPORTANT TIME	SCHEDULE	SLAYED?
	5:00AM		☐Y ☐N
	5:30AM		☐Y ☐N
	6:00AM		☐Y ☐N
	6:30AM		☐Y ☐N
	7:00AM		☐Y ☐N
	7:30AM		☐Y ☐N
	8:00AM		☐Y ☐N
	8:30AM		☐Y ☐N
	9:00AM		☐Y ☐N
	9:30AM		☐Y ☐N
	10:00AM		☐Y ☐N
	10:30AM		☐Y ☐N
	11:00AM		☐Y ☐N
	11:30AM		☐Y ☐N
	12:00PM		☐Y ☐N
	12:30PM		☐Y ☐N
	1:00PM		☐Y ☐N
	1:30PM		☐Y ☐N
	2:00PM		☐Y ☐N
	2:30PM		☐Y ☐N
	3:00PM		☐Y ☐N
	3:30PM		☐Y ☐N
	4:00PM		☐Y ☐N
	4:30PM		☐Y ☐N
	5:00PM		☐Y ☐N
	5:30PM		☐Y ☐N
	6:00PM		☐Y ☐N
	6:30PM		☐Y ☐N
	7:00PM		☐Y ☐N
	7:30PM		☐Y ☐N
	8:00PM		☐Y ☐N
	8:30PM		☐Y ☐N
	9:00PM		☐Y ☐N
	9:30PM		☐Y ☐N

TAKE 5 MINUTES EACH MORNING TO PLAN YOUR DAY.

GET EIGHT HOURS OF SLEEP!

NOTE HIGH PRIORITY TASKS WITH A ✱

ANALYZE WHY A TASK WAS NOT COMPLETED, THEN MOVE TO NEXT DAY.

ONE POSITIVE

TODAY I GAVE

DAILY
GOAL SLAYERS
PLANNER

SETTING YOURSELF UP FOR SUCCESS DAILY!

DATE

_____ / _____ / _____

SCRIPTURE

MOTIVATIONAL QUOTE

ONE GOAL

ONE FUN THING

*	IMPORTANT TIME	SCHEDULE	SLAYED?
	5:00AM		☐Y ☐N
	5:30AM		☐Y ☐N
	6:00AM		☐Y ☐N
	6:30AM		☐Y ☐N
	7:00AM		☐Y ☐N
	7:30AM		☐Y ☐N
	8:00AM		☐Y ☐N
	8:30AM		☐Y ☐N
	9:00AM		☐Y ☐N
	9:30AM		☐Y ☐N
	10:00AM		☐Y ☐N
	10:30AM		☐Y ☐N
	11:00AM		☐Y ☐N
	11:30AM		☐Y ☐N
	12:00PM		☐Y ☐N
	12:30PM		☐Y ☐N
	1:00PM		☐Y ☐N
	1:30PM		☐Y ☐N
	2:00PM		☐Y ☐N
	2:30PM		☐Y ☐N
	3:00PM		☐Y ☐N
	3:30PM		☐Y ☐N
	4:00PM		☐Y ☐N
	4:30PM		☐Y ☐N
	5:00PM		☐Y ☐N
	5:30PM		☐Y ☐N
	6:00PM		☐Y ☐N
	6:30PM		☐Y ☐N
	7:00PM		☐Y ☐N
	7:30PM		☐Y ☐N
	8:00PM		☐Y ☐N
	8:30PM		☐Y ☐N
	9:00PM		☐Y ☐N
	9:30PM		☐Y ☐N

HEALTH • FITNESS

WATER INTAKE

OZ. OZ. OZ. OZ. OZ.
OZ. OZ. OZ. OZ. OZ.

TAKE 5 MINUTES EACH MORNING TO PLAN YOUR DAY.

GET EIGHT HOURS OF SLEEP!

NOTE HIGH PRIORITY TASKS WITH A *

ANALYZE WHY A TASK WAS NOT COMPLETED, THEN MOVE TO NEXT DAY.

ONE POSITIVE

TODAY I GAVE

DAILY
GOAL SLAYERS
PLANNER

SETTING YOURSELF UP FOR SUCCESS DAILY!

DATE

_____ / _____ / _____

SCRIPTURE

MOTIVATIONAL QUOTE

ONE GOAL

ONE FUN THING

*	IMPORTANT TIME	SCHEDULE	SLAYED?
	5:00AM		☐Y ☐N
	5:30AM		☐Y ☐N
	6:00AM		☐Y ☐N
	6:30AM		☐Y ☐N
	7:00AM		☐Y ☐N
	7:30AM		☐Y ☐N
	8:00AM		☐Y ☐N
	8:30AM		☐Y ☐N
	9:00AM		☐Y ☐N
	9:30AM		☐Y ☐N
	10:00AM		☐Y ☐N
	10:30AM		☐Y ☐N
	11:00AM		☐Y ☐N
	11:30AM		☐Y ☐N
	12:00PM		☐Y ☐N
	12:30PM		☐Y ☐N
	1:00PM		☐Y ☐N
	1:30PM		☐Y ☐N
	2:00PM		☐Y ☐N
	2:30PM		☐Y ☐N
	3:00PM		☐Y ☐N
	3:30PM		☐Y ☐N
	4:00PM		☐Y ☐N
	4:30PM		☐Y ☐N
	5:00PM		☐Y ☐N
	5:30PM		☐Y ☐N
	6:00PM		☐Y ☐N
	6:30PM		☐Y ☐N
	7:00PM		☐Y ☐N
	7:30PM		☐Y ☐N
	8:00PM		☐Y ☐N
	8:30PM		☐Y ☐N
	9:00PM		☐Y ☐N
	9:30PM		☐Y ☐N

HEALTH + FITNESS

WATER INTAKE

OZ. OZ. OZ. OZ. OZ.
OZ. OZ. OZ. OZ. OZ.

TAKE 5 MINUTES EACH MORNING TO PLAN YOUR DAY.

GET EIGHT HOURS OF SLEEP!

NOTE HIGH PRIORITY TASKS WITH A *

ANALYZE WHY A TASK WAS NOT COMPLETED, THEN MOVE TO NEXT DAY.

ONE POSITIVE

TODAY I GAVE

DAILY
GOAL SLAYERS
PLANNER

SETTING YOURSELF UP FOR SUCCESS DAILY!

DATE

_____ / _____ / _____

SCRIPTURE

MOTIVATIONAL QUOTE

ONE GOAL

ONE FUN THING

✱	IMPORTANT TIME	SCHEDULE	SLAYED?
	5:00AM		☐Y ☐N
	5:30AM		☐Y ☐N
	6:00AM		☐Y ☐N
	6:30AM		☐Y ☐N
	7:00AM		☐Y ☐N
	7:30AM		☐Y ☐N
	8:00AM		☐Y ☐N
	8:30AM		☐Y ☐N
	9:00AM		☐Y ☐N
	9:30AM		☐Y ☐N
	10:00AM		☐Y ☐N
	10:30AM		☐Y ☐N
	11:00AM		☐Y ☐N
	11:30AM		☐Y ☐N
	12:00PM		☐Y ☐N
	12:30PM		☐Y ☐N
	1:00PM		☐Y ☐N
	1:30PM		☐Y ☐N
	2:00PM		☐Y ☐N
	2:30PM		☐Y ☐N
	3:00PM		☐Y ☐N
	3:30PM		☐Y ☐N
	4:00PM		☐Y ☐N
	4:30PM		☐Y ☐N
	5:00PM		☐Y ☐N
	5:30PM		☐Y ☐N
	6:00PM		☐Y ☐N
	6:30PM		☐Y ☐N
	7:00PM		☐Y ☐N
	7:30PM		☐Y ☐N
	8:00PM		☐Y ☐N
	8:30PM		☐Y ☐N
	9:00PM		☐Y ☐N
	9:30PM		☐Y ☐N

HEALTH • FITNESS

WATER INTAKE

OZ. OZ. OZ. OZ. OZ.
OZ. OZ. OZ. OZ. OZ.

TAKE 5 MINUTES EACH MORNING TO PLAN YOUR DAY.

GET EIGHT HOURS OF SLEEP!

NOTE HIGH PRIORITY TASKS WITH A ✱

ANALYZE WHY A TASK WAS NOT COMPLETED, THEN MOVE TO NEXT DAY.

ONE POSITIVE

TODAY I GAVE

DAILY
GOAL SLAYERS
PLANNER

SETTING YOURSELF UP FOR SUCCESS DAILY!

DATE

____ / ____ / ____

SCRIPTURE

MOTIVATIONAL QUOTE

ONE GOAL

ONE FUN THING

HEALTH + FITNESS

WATER INTAKE

OZ OZ OZ OZ OZ
OZ OZ OZ OZ OZ

*	IMPORTANT TIME	SCHEDULE	SLAYED?
	5:00AM		☐Y ☐N
	5:30AM		☐Y ☐N
	6:00AM		☐Y ☐N
	6:30AM		☐Y ☐N
	7:00AM		☐Y ☐N
	7:30AM		☐Y ☐N
	8:00AM		☐Y ☐N
	8:30AM		☐Y ☐N
	9:00AM		☐Y ☐N
	9:30AM		☐Y ☐N
	10:00AM		☐Y ☐N
	10:30AM		☐Y ☐N
	11:00AM		☐Y ☐N
	11:30AM		☐Y ☐N
	12:00PM		☐Y ☐N
	12:30PM		☐Y ☐N
	1:00PM		☐Y ☐N
	1:30PM		☐Y ☐N
	2:00PM		☐Y ☐N
	2:30PM		☐Y ☐N
	3:00PM		☐Y ☐N
	3:30PM		☐Y ☐N
	4:00PM		☐Y ☐N
	4:30PM		☐Y ☐N
	5:00PM		☐Y ☐N
	5:30PM		☐Y ☐N
	6:00PM		☐Y ☐N
	6:30PM		☐Y ☐N
	7:00PM		☐Y ☐N
	7:30PM		☐Y ☐N
	8:00PM		☐Y ☐N
	8:30PM		☐Y ☐N
	9:00PM		☐Y ☐N
	9:30PM		☐Y ☐N

TAKE 5 MINUTES EACH MORNING TO PLAN YOUR DAY.

GET EIGHT HOURS OF SLEEP!

NOTE HIGH PRIORITY TASKS WITH A *

ANALYZE WHY A TASK WAS NOT COMPLETED, THEN MOVE TO NEXT DAY.

ONE POSITIVE

TODAY I GAVE

DAILY
GOAL SLAYERS
PLANNER

SETTING YOURSELF UP FOR SUCCESS DAILY!

DATE

____ / ____ / ____

SCRIPTURE

MOTIVATIONAL QUOTE

ONE GOAL

ONE FUN THING

✱	IMPORTANT TIME	SCHEDULE	SLAYED?
	5:00AM		☐Y ☐N
	5:30AM		☐Y ☐N
	6:00AM		☐Y ☐N
	6:30AM		☐Y ☐N
	7:00AM		☐Y ☐N
	7:30AM		☐Y ☐N
	8:00AM		☐Y ☐N
	8:30AM		☐Y ☐N
	9:00AM		☐Y ☐N
	9:30AM		☐Y ☐N
	10:00AM		☐Y ☐N
	10:30AM		☐Y ☐N
	11:00AM		☐Y ☐N
	11:30AM		☐Y ☐N
	12:00PM		☐Y ☐N
	12:30PM		☐Y ☐N
	1:00PM		☐Y ☐N
	1:30PM		☐Y ☐N
	2:00PM		☐Y ☐N
	2:30PM		☐Y ☐N
	3:00PM		☐Y ☐N
	3:30PM		☐Y ☐N
	4:00PM		☐Y ☐N
	4:30PM		☐Y ☐N
	5:00PM		☐Y ☐N
	5:30PM		☐Y ☐N
	6:00PM		☐Y ☐N
	6:30PM		☐Y ☐N
	7:00PM		☐Y ☐N
	7:30PM		☐Y ☐N
	8:00PM		☐Y ☐N
	8:30PM		☐Y ☐N
	9:00PM		☐Y ☐N
	9:30PM		☐Y ☐N

HEALTH + FITNESS

WATER INTAKE

OZ. OZ. OZ. OZ. OZ.
OZ. OZ. OZ. OZ. OZ.

TAKE 5 MINUTES EACH MORNING TO PLAN YOUR DAY.

GET EIGHT HOURS OF SLEEP!

NOTE HIGH PRIORITY TASKS WITH A ✱

ANALYZE WHY A TASK WAS NOT COMPLETED, THEN MOVE TO NEXT DAY.

ONE POSITIVE

TODAY I GAVE

DAILY
GOAL SLAYERS
PLANNER

SETTING YOURSELF UP FOR SUCCESS DAILY!

DATE

____ / ____ / ____

SCRIPTURE

MOTIVATIONAL QUOTE

ONE GOAL

ONE FUN THING

*	IMPORTANT TIME	SCHEDULE	SLAYED?
	5:00AM		☐Y ☐N
	5:30AM		☐Y ☐N
	6:00AM		☐Y ☐N
	6:30AM		☐Y ☐N
	7:00AM		☐Y ☐N
	7:30AM		☐Y ☐N
	8:00AM		☐Y ☐N
	8:30AM		☐Y ☐N
	9:00AM		☐Y ☐N
	9:30AM		☐Y ☐N
	10:00AM		☐Y ☐N
	10:30AM		☐Y ☐N
	11:00AM		☐Y ☐N
	11:30AM		☐Y ☐N
	12:00PM		☐Y ☐N
	12:30PM		☐Y ☐N
	1:00PM		☐Y ☐N
	1:30PM		☐Y ☐N
	2:00PM		☐Y ☐N
	2:30PM		☐Y ☐N
	3:00PM		☐Y ☐N
	3:30PM		☐Y ☐N
	4:00PM		☐Y ☐N
	4:30PM		☐Y ☐N
	5:00PM		☐Y ☐N
	5:30PM		☐Y ☐N
	6:00PM		☐Y ☐N
	6:30PM		☐Y ☐N
	7:00PM		☐Y ☐N
	7:30PM		☐Y ☐N
	8:00PM		☐Y ☐N
	8:30PM		☐Y ☐N
	9:00PM		☐Y ☐N
	9:30PM		☐Y ☐N

HEALTH + FITNESS

WATER INTAKE

OZ. OZ. OZ. OZ. OZ.

OZ. OZ. OZ. OZ. OZ.

TAKE 5 MINUTES EACH MORNING TO PLAN YOUR DAY.

GET EIGHT HOURS OF SLEEP!

NOTE HIGH PRIORITY TASKS WITH A *

ANALYZE WHY A TASK WAS NOT COMPLETED, THEN MOVE TO NEXT DAY.

ONE POSITIVE

TODAY I GAVE

DAILY
GOAL SLAYERS
PLANNER

SETTING YOURSELF UP FOR SUCCESS DAILY!

DATE

_____ / _____ / _____

SCRIPTURE

MOTIVATIONAL QUOTE

ONE GOAL

ONE FUN THING

*	IMPORTANT TIME	SCHEDULE	SLAYED?
	5:00AM		☐Y ☐N
	5:30AM		☐Y ☐N
	6:00AM		☐Y ☐N
	6:30AM		☐Y ☐N
	7:00AM		☐Y ☐N
	7:30AM		☐Y ☐N
	8:00AM		☐Y ☐N
	8:30AM		☐Y ☐N
	9:00AM		☐Y ☐N
	9:30AM		☐Y ☐N
	10:00AM		☐Y ☐N
	10:30AM		☐Y ☐N
	11:00AM		☐Y ☐N
	11:30AM		☐Y ☐N
	12:00PM		☐Y ☐N
	12:30PM		☐Y ☐N
	1:00PM		☐Y ☐N
	1:30PM		☐Y ☐N
	2:00PM		☐Y ☐N
	2:30PM		☐Y ☐N
	3:00PM		☐Y ☐N
	3:30PM		☐Y ☐N
	4:00PM		☐Y ☐N
	4:30PM		☐Y ☐N
	5:00PM		☐Y ☐N
	5:30PM		☐Y ☐N
	6:00PM		☐Y ☐N
	6:30PM		☐Y ☐N
	7:00PM		☐Y ☐N
	7:30PM		☐Y ☐N
	8:00PM		☐Y ☐N
	8:30PM		☐Y ☐N
	9:00PM		☐Y ☐N
	9:30PM		☐Y ☐N

HEALTH • FITNESS

WATER INTAKE

OZ. OZ. OZ. OZ. OZ.
OZ. OZ. OZ. OZ. OZ.

TAKE 5 MINUTES EACH MORNING TO PLAN YOUR DAY.

GET EIGHT HOURS OF SLEEP!

NOTE HIGH PRIORITY TASKS WITH A *

ANALYZE WHY A TASK WAS NOT COMPLETED, THEN MOVE TO NEXT DAY.

ONE POSITIVE

TODAY I GAVE

DAILY
GOAL SLAYERS
PLANNER

SETTING YOURSELF UP FOR SUCCESS DAILY!

DATE

____ / ____ / ____

SCRIPTURE

MOTIVATIONAL QUOTE

ONE GOAL

ONE FUN THING

✱	IMPORTANT TIME	SCHEDULE	SLAYED?
	5:00AM		☐Y ☐N
	5:30AM		☐Y ☐N
	6:00AM		☐Y ☐N
	6:30AM		☐Y ☐N
	7:00AM		☐Y ☐N
	7:30AM		☐Y ☐N
	8:00AM		☐Y ☐N
	8:30AM		☐Y ☐N
	9:00AM		☐Y ☐N
	9:30AM		☐Y ☐N
	10:00AM		☐Y ☐N
	10:30AM		☐Y ☐N
	11:00AM		☐Y ☐N
	11:30AM		☐Y ☐N
	12:00PM		☐Y ☐N
	12:30PM		☐Y ☐N
	1:00PM		☐Y ☐N
	1:30PM		☐Y ☐N
	2:00PM		☐Y ☐N
	2:30PM		☐Y ☐N
	3:00PM		☐Y ☐N
	3:30PM		☐Y ☐N
	4:00PM		☐Y ☐N
	4:30PM		☐Y ☐N
	5:00PM		☐Y ☐N
	5:30PM		☐Y ☐N
	6:00PM		☐Y ☐N
	6:30PM		☐Y ☐N
	7:00PM		☐Y ☐N
	7:30PM		☐Y ☐N
	8:00PM		☐Y ☐N
	8:30PM		☐Y ☐N
	9:00PM		☐Y ☐N
	9:30PM		☐Y ☐N

HEALTH • FITNESS

WATER INTAKE

OZ OZ OZ OZ OZ
OZ OZ OZ OZ OZ

TAKE 5 MINUTES EACH MORNING TO PLAN YOUR DAY.

GET EIGHT HOURS OF SLEEP!

NOTE HIGH PRIORITY TASKS WITH A ✱

ANALYZE WHY A TASK WAS NOT COMPLETED, THEN MOVE TO NEXT DAY.

ONE POSITIVE

TODAY I GAVE

DAILY
GOAL SLAYERS
PLANNER

SETTING YOURSELF UP FOR SUCCESS DAILY!

DATE

____ / ____ / ____

SCRIPTURE

MOTIVATIONAL QUOTE

ONE GOAL

ONE FUN THING

HEALTH · FITNESS

WATER INTAKE

OZ. OZ. OZ. OZ. OZ.
OZ. OZ. OZ. OZ. OZ.

*	IMPORTANT TIME	SCHEDULE	SLAYED?
	5:00AM		☐Y ☐N
	5:30AM		☐Y ☐N
	6:00AM		☐Y ☐N
	6:30AM		☐Y ☐N
	7:00AM		☐Y ☐N
	7:30AM		☐Y ☐N
	8:00AM		☐Y ☐N
	8:30AM		☐Y ☐N
	9:00AM		☐Y ☐N
	9:30AM		☐Y ☐N
	10:00AM		☐Y ☐N
	10:30AM		☐Y ☐N
	11:00AM		☐Y ☐N
	11:30AM		☐Y ☐N
	12:00PM		☐Y ☐N
	12:30PM		☐Y ☐N
	1:00PM		☐Y ☐N
	1:30PM		☐Y ☐N
	2:00PM		☐Y ☐N
	2:30PM		☐Y ☐N
	3:00PM		☐Y ☐N
	3:30PM		☐Y ☐N
	4:00PM		☐Y ☐N
	4:30PM		☐Y ☐N
	5:00PM		☐Y ☐N
	5:30PM		☐Y ☐N
	6:00PM		☐Y ☐N
	6:30PM		☐Y ☐N
	7:00PM		☐Y ☐N
	7:30PM		☐Y ☐N
	8:00PM		☐Y ☐N
	8:30PM		☐Y ☐N
	9:00PM		☐Y ☐N
	9:30PM		☐Y ☐N

TAKE 5 MINUTES EACH MORNING TO PLAN YOUR DAY.

GET EIGHT HOURS OF SLEEP!

NOTE HIGH PRIORITY TASKS WITH A *

ANALYZE WHY A TASK WAS NOT COMPLETED, THEN MOVE TO NEXT DAY.

ONE POSITIVE

TODAY I GAVE

DAILY
GOAL SLAYERS
PLANNER

SETTING YOURSELF UP FOR SUCCESS DAILY!

DATE

_____ / _____ / _____

SCRIPTURE

MOTIVATIONAL QUOTE

ONE GOAL

ONE FUN THING

*	IMPORTANT TIME	SCHEDULE	SLAYED?
	5:00AM		☐Y ☐N
	5:30AM		☐Y ☐N
	6:00AM		☐Y ☐N
	6:30AM		☐Y ☐N
	7:00AM		☐Y ☐N
	7:30AM		☐Y ☐N
	8:00AM		☐Y ☐N
	8:30AM		☐Y ☐N
	9:00AM		☐Y ☐N
	9:30AM		☐Y ☐N
	10:00AM		☐Y ☐N
	10:30AM		☐Y ☐N
	11:00AM		☐Y ☐N
	11:30AM		☐Y ☐N
	12:00PM		☐Y ☐N
	12:30PM		☐Y ☐N
	1:00PM		☐Y ☐N
	1:30PM		☐Y ☐N
	2:00PM		☐Y ☐N
	2:30PM		☐Y ☐N
	3:00PM		☐Y ☐N
	3:30PM		☐Y ☐N
	4:00PM		☐Y ☐N
	4:30PM		☐Y ☐N
	5:00PM		☐Y ☐N
	5:30PM		☐Y ☐N
	6:00PM		☐Y ☐N
	6:30PM		☐Y ☐N
	7:00PM		☐Y ☐N
	7:30PM		☐Y ☐N
	8:00PM		☐Y ☐N
	8:30PM		☐Y ☐N
	9:00PM		☐Y ☐N
	9:30PM		☐Y ☐N

HEALTH + FITNESS

WATER INTAKE

OZ. OZ. OZ. OZ. OZ.
OZ. OZ. OZ. OZ. OZ.

TAKE 5 MINUTES EACH MORNING TO PLAN YOUR DAY.

GET EIGHT HOURS OF SLEEP!

NOTE HIGH PRIORITY TASKS WITH A *

ANALYZE WHY A TASK WAS NOT COMPLETED, THEN MOVE TO NEXT DAY.

ONE POSITIVE

TODAY I GAVE

DAILY
GOAL SLAYERS
PLANNER

SETTING YOURSELF UP FOR SUCCESS DAILY!

DATE

_____ / _____ / _____

SCRIPTURE

MOTIVATIONAL QUOTE

ONE GOAL

ONE FUN THING

HEALTH • FITNESS

WATER INTAKE

OZ. OZ. OZ. OZ. OZ.

OZ. OZ. OZ. OZ. OZ.

TAKE 5 MINUTES EACH MORNING TO PLAN YOUR DAY.

GET EIGHT HOURS OF SLEEP!

NOTE HIGH PRIORITY TASKS WITH A *

ANALYZE WHY A TASK WAS NOT COMPLETED, THEN MOVE TO NEXT DAY.

ONE POSITIVE

TODAY I GAVE

*	IMPORTANT TIME	SCHEDULE	SLAYED?
	5:00AM		□Y □N
	5:30AM		□Y □N
	6:00AM		□Y □N
	6:30AM		□Y □N
	7:00AM		□Y □N
	7:30AM		□Y □N
	8:00AM		□Y □N
	8:30AM		□Y □N
	9:00AM		□Y □N
	9:30AM		□Y □N
	10:00AM		□Y □N
	10:30AM		□Y □N
	11:00AM		□Y □N
	11:30AM		□Y □N
	12:00PM		□Y □N
	12:30PM		□Y □N
	1:00PM		□Y □N
	1:30PM		□Y □N
	2:00PM		□Y □N
	2:30PM		□Y □N
	3:00PM		□Y □N
	3:30PM		□Y □N
	4:00PM		□Y □N
	4:30PM		□Y □N
	5:00PM		□Y □N
	5:30PM		□Y □N
	6:00PM		□Y □N
	6:30PM		□Y □N
	7:00PM		□Y □N
	7:30PM		□Y □N
	8:00PM		□Y □N
	8:30PM		□Y □N
	9:00PM		□Y □N
	9:30PM		□Y □N

DAILY
GOAL SLAYERS
PLANNER

SETTING YOURSELF UP FOR SUCCESS DAILY!

DATE

_____ / _____ / _____

SCRIPTURE

MOTIVATIONAL QUOTE

ONE GOAL

ONE FUN THING

HEALTH • FITNESS

WATER INTAKE

OZ. OZ. OZ. OZ. OZ.

OZ. OZ. OZ. OZ. OZ.

✱	IMPORTANT TIME	SCHEDULE	SLAYED?
	5:00AM		☐Y ☐N
	5:30AM		☐Y ☐N
	6:00AM		☐Y ☐N
	6:30AM		☐Y ☐N
	7:00AM		☐Y ☐N
	7:30AM		☐Y ☐N
	8:00AM		☐Y ☐N
	8:30AM		☐Y ☐N
	9:00AM		☐Y ☐N
	9:30AM		☐Y ☐N
	10:00AM		☐Y ☐N
	10:30AM		☐Y ☐N
	11:00AM		☐Y ☐N
	11:30AM		☐Y ☐N
	12:00PM		☐Y ☐N
	12:30PM		☐Y ☐N
	1:00PM		☐Y ☐N
	1:30PM		☐Y ☐N
	2:00PM		☐Y ☐N
	2:30PM		☐Y ☐N
	3:00PM		☐Y ☐N
	3:30PM		☐Y ☐N
	4:00PM		☐Y ☐N
	4:30PM		☐Y ☐N
	5:00PM		☐Y ☐N
	5:30PM		☐Y ☐N
	6:00PM		☐Y ☐N
	6:30PM		☐Y ☐N
	7:00PM		☐Y ☐N
	7:30PM		☐Y ☐N
	8:00PM		☐Y ☐N
	8:30PM		☐Y ☐N
	9:00PM		☐Y ☐N
	9:30PM		☐Y ☐N

TAKE 5 MINUTES EACH MORNING TO PLAN YOUR DAY.

GET EIGHT HOURS OF SLEEP!

NOTE HIGH PRIORITY TASKS WITH A ✱

ANALYZE WHY A TASK WAS NOT COMPLETED, THEN MOVE TO NEXT DAY.

ONE POSITIVE

TODAY I GAVE

DAILY
GOAL SLAYERS
PLANNER

SETTING YOURSELF UP FOR SUCCESS DAILY!

DATE

____ / ____ / ____

SCRIPTURE

MOTIVATIONAL QUOTE

ONE GOAL

ONE FUN THING

HEALTH • FITNESS

WATER INTAKE

*	IMPORTANT TIME	SCHEDULE	SLAYED?
	5:00AM		☐Y ☐N
	5:30AM		☐Y ☐N
	6:00AM		☐Y ☐N
	6:30AM		☐Y ☐N
	7:00AM		☐Y ☐N
	7:30AM		☐Y ☐N
	8:00AM		☐Y ☐N
	8:30AM		☐Y ☐N
	9:00AM		☐Y ☐N
	9:30AM		☐Y ☐N
	10:00AM		☐Y ☐N
	10:30AM		☐Y ☐N
	11:00AM		☐Y ☐N
	11:30AM		☐Y ☐N
	12:00PM		☐Y ☐N
	12:30PM		☐Y ☐N
	1:00PM		☐Y ☐N
	1:30PM		☐Y ☐N
	2:00PM		☐Y ☐N
	2:30PM		☐Y ☐N
	3:00PM		☐Y ☐N
	3:30PM		☐Y ☐N
	4:00PM		☐Y ☐N
	4:30PM		☐Y ☐N
	5:00PM		☐Y ☐N
	5:30PM		☐Y ☐N
	6:00PM		☐Y ☐N
	6:30PM		☐Y ☐N
	7:00PM		☐Y ☐N
	7:30PM		☐Y ☐N
	8:00PM		☐Y ☐N
	8:30PM		☐Y ☐N
	9:00PM		☐Y ☐N
	9:30PM		☐Y ☐N

TAKE 5 MINUTES EACH MORNING TO PLAN YOUR DAY.

GET EIGHT HOURS OF SLEEP!

NOTE HIGH PRIORITY TASKS WITH A *

ANALYZE WHY A TASK WAS NOT COMPLETED, THEN MOVE TO NEXT DAY.

ONE POSITIVE

TODAY I GAVE

DAILY
GOAL SLAYERS
PLANNER

SETTING YOURSELF UP FOR SUCCESS DAILY!

DATE

_____ / _____ / _____

SCRIPTURE

MOTIVATIONAL QUOTE

ONE GOAL

ONE FUN THING

HEALTH • FITNESS

WATER INTAKE

OZ. OZ. OZ. OZ. OZ.

OZ. OZ. OZ. OZ. OZ.

*	IMPORTANT TIME	SCHEDULE	SLAYED?
	5:00AM		☐Y ☐N
	5:30AM		☐Y ☐N
	6:00AM		☐Y ☐N
	6:30AM		☐Y ☐N
	7:00AM		☐Y ☐N
	7:30AM		☐Y ☐N
	8:00AM		☐Y ☐N
	8:30AM		☐Y ☐N
	9:00AM		☐Y ☐N
	9:30AM		☐Y ☐N
	10:00AM		☐Y ☐N
	10:30AM		☐Y ☐N
	11:00AM		☐Y ☐N
	11:30AM		☐Y ☐N
	12:00PM		☐Y ☐N
	12:30PM		☐Y ☐N
	1:00PM		☐Y ☐N
	1:30PM		☐Y ☐N
	2:00PM		☐Y ☐N
	2:30PM		☐Y ☐N
	3:00PM		☐Y ☐N
	3:30PM		☐Y ☐N
	4:00PM		☐Y ☐N
	4:30PM		☐Y ☐N
	5:00PM		☐Y ☐N
	5:30PM		☐Y ☐N
	6:00PM		☐Y ☐N
	6:30PM		☐Y ☐N
	7:00PM		☐Y ☐N
	7:30PM		☐Y ☐N
	8:00PM		☐Y ☐N
	8:30PM		☐Y ☐N
	9:00PM		☐Y ☐N
	9:30PM		☐Y ☐N

TAKE 5 MINUTES EACH MORNING TO PLAN YOUR DAY.

GET EIGHT HOURS OF SLEEP!

NOTE HIGH PRIORITY TASKS WITH A *

ANALYZE WHY A TASK WAS NOT COMPLETED, THEN MOVE TO NEXT DAY.

ONE POSITIVE

TODAY I GAVE

DAILY
GOAL SLAYERS
PLANNER

SETTING YOURSELF UP FOR SUCCESS DAILY!

DATE

_____ / _____ / _____

SCRIPTURE

MOTIVATIONAL QUOTE

ONE GOAL

ONE FUN THING

✱	IMPORTANT TIME	SCHEDULE	SLAYED?
	5:00AM		☐Y ☐N
	5:30AM		☐Y ☐N
	6:00AM		☐Y ☐N
	6:30AM		☐Y ☐N
	7:00AM		☐Y ☐N
	7:30AM		☐Y ☐N
	8:00AM		☐Y ☐N
	8:30AM		☐Y ☐N
	9:00AM		☐Y ☐N
	9:30AM		☐Y ☐N
	10:00AM		☐Y ☐N
	10:30AM		☐Y ☐N
	11:00AM		☐Y ☐N
	11:30AM		☐Y ☐N
	12:00PM		☐Y ☐N
	12:30PM		☐Y ☐N
	1:00PM		☐Y ☐N
	1:30PM		☐Y ☐N
	2:00PM		☐Y ☐N
	2:30PM		☐Y ☐N
	3:00PM		☐Y ☐N
	3:30PM		☐Y ☐N
	4:00PM		☐Y ☐N
	4:30PM		☐Y ☐N
	5:00PM		☐Y ☐N
	5:30PM		☐Y ☐N
	6:00PM		☐Y ☐N
	6:30PM		☐Y ☐N
	7:00PM		☐Y ☐N
	7:30PM		☐Y ☐N
	8:00PM		☐Y ☐N
	8:30PM		☐Y ☐N
	9:00PM		☐Y ☐N
	9:30PM		☐Y ☐N

HEALTH + FITNESS

WATER INTAKE

OZ. OZ. OZ. OZ. OZ.
OZ. OZ. OZ. OZ. OZ.

TAKE 5 MINUTES EACH MORNING TO PLAN YOUR DAY.

GET EIGHT HOURS OF SLEEP!

NOTE HIGH PRIORITY TASKS WITH A ✱

ANALYZE WHY A TASK WAS NOT COMPLETED, THEN MOVE TO NEXT DAY.

ONE POSITIVE

TODAY I GAVE

DAILY GOAL SLAYERS PLANNER

SETTING YOURSELF UP FOR SUCCESS DAILY!

DATE

_____ / _____ / _____

SCRIPTURE

MOTIVATIONAL QUOTE

ONE GOAL

ONE FUN THING

✱	IMPORTANT TIME	SCHEDULE	SLAYED?
	5:00AM		☐Y ☐N
	5:30AM		☐Y ☐N
	6:00AM		☐Y ☐N
	6:30AM		☐Y ☐N
	7:00AM		☐Y ☐N
	7:30AM		☐Y ☐N
	8:00AM		☐Y ☐N
	8:30AM		☐Y ☐N
	9:00AM		☐Y ☐N
	9:30AM		☐Y ☐N
	10:00AM		☐Y ☐N
	10:30AM		☐Y ☐N
	11:00AM		☐Y ☐N
	11:30AM		☐Y ☐N
	12:00PM		☐Y ☐N
	12:30PM		☐Y ☐N
	1:00PM		☐Y ☐N
	1:30PM		☐Y ☐N
	2:00PM		☐Y ☐N
	2:30PM		☐Y ☐N
	3:00PM		☐Y ☐N
	3:30PM		☐Y ☐N
	4:00PM		☐Y ☐N
	4:30PM		☐Y ☐N
	5:00PM		☐Y ☐N
	5:30PM		☐Y ☐N
	6:00PM		☐Y ☐N
	6:30PM		☐Y ☐N
	7:00PM		☐Y ☐N
	7:30PM		☐Y ☐N
	8:00PM		☐Y ☐N
	8:30PM		☐Y ☐N
	9:00PM		☐Y ☐N
	9:30PM		☐Y ☐N

HEALTH • FITNESS

WATER INTAKE

OZ OZ OZ OZ OZ

OZ OZ OZ OZ OZ

TAKE 5 MINUTES EACH MORNING TO PLAN YOUR DAY.

GET EIGHT HOURS OF SLEEP!

NOTE HIGH PRIORITY TASKS WITH A ✱

ANALYZE WHY A TASK WAS NOT COMPLETED, THEN MOVE TO NEXT DAY.

ONE POSITIVE

TODAY I GAVE

DAILY
GOAL SLAYERS
PLANNER

SETTING YOURSELF UP FOR SUCCESS DAILY!

DATE

_____ / _____ / _____

SCRIPTURE

MOTIVATIONAL QUOTE

ONE GOAL

ONE FUN THING

HEALTH • FITNESS

WATER INTAKE

OZ. OZ. OZ. OZ. OZ.

OZ. OZ. OZ. OZ. OZ.

*	IMPORTANT TIME	SCHEDULE	SLAYED?
	5:00AM		☐Y ☐N
	5:30AM		☐Y ☐N
	6:00AM		☐Y ☐N
	6:30AM		☐Y ☐N
	7:00AM		☐Y ☐N
	7:30AM		☐Y ☐N
	8:00AM		☐Y ☐N
	8:30AM		☐Y ☐N
	9:00AM		☐Y ☐N
	9:30AM		☐Y ☐N
	10:00AM		☐Y ☐N
	10:30AM		☐Y ☐N
	11:00AM		☐Y ☐N
	11:30AM		☐Y ☐N
	12:00PM		☐Y ☐N
	12:30PM		☐Y ☐N
	1:00PM		☐Y ☐N
	1:30PM		☐Y ☐N
	2:00PM		☐Y ☐N
	2:30PM		☐Y ☐N
	3:00PM		☐Y ☐N
	3:30PM		☐Y ☐N
	4:00PM		☐Y ☐N
	4:30PM		☐Y ☐N
	5:00PM		☐Y ☐N
	5:30PM		☐Y ☐N
	6:00PM		☐Y ☐N
	6:30PM		☐Y ☐N
	7:00PM		☐Y ☐N
	7:30PM		☐Y ☐N
	8:00PM		☐Y ☐N
	8:30PM		☐Y ☐N
	9:00PM		☐Y ☐N
	9:30PM		☐Y ☐N

TAKE 5 MINUTES EACH MORNING TO PLAN YOUR DAY.

GET EIGHT HOURS OF SLEEP!

NOTE HIGH PRIORITY TASKS WITH A *

ANALYZE WHY A TASK WAS NOT COMPLETED, THEN MOVE TO NEXT DAY.

ONE POSITIVE

TODAY I GAVE

DAILY
GOAL SLAYERS
PLANNER

SETTING YOURSELF UP FOR SUCCESS DAILY!

DATE

____ / ____ / ____

SCRIPTURE

MOTIVATIONAL QUOTE

ONE GOAL

ONE FUN THING

*	IMPORTANT TIME	SCHEDULE	SLAYED?
	5:00AM		☐Y ☐N
	5:30AM		☐Y ☐N
	6:00AM		☐Y ☐N
	6:30AM		☐Y ☐N
	7:00AM		☐Y ☐N
	7:30AM		☐Y ☐N
	8:00AM		☐Y ☐N
	8:30AM		☐Y ☐N
	9:00AM		☐Y ☐N
	9:30AM		☐Y ☐N
	10:00AM		☐Y ☐N
	10:30AM		☐Y ☐N
	11:00AM		☐Y ☐N
	11:30AM		☐Y ☐N
	12:00PM		☐Y ☐N
	12:30PM		☐Y ☐N
	1:00PM		☐Y ☐N
	1:30PM		☐Y ☐N
	2:00PM		☐Y ☐N
	2:30PM		☐Y ☐N
	3:00PM		☐Y ☐N
	3:30PM		☐Y ☐N
	4:00PM		☐Y ☐N
	4:30PM		☐Y ☐N
	5:00PM		☐Y ☐N
	5:30PM		☐Y ☐N
	6:00PM		☐Y ☐N
	6:30PM		☐Y ☐N
	7:00PM		☐Y ☐N
	7:30PM		☐Y ☐N
	8:00PM		☐Y ☐N
	8:30PM		☐Y ☐N
	9:00PM		☐Y ☐N
	9:30PM		☐Y ☐N

HEALTH + FITNESS

WATER INTAKE

OZ. OZ. OZ. OZ. OZ.
OZ. OZ. OZ. OZ. OZ.

TAKE 5 MINUTES EACH MORNING TO PLAN YOUR DAY.

GET EIGHT HOURS OF SLEEP!

NOTE HIGH PRIORITY TASKS WITH A *

ANALYZE WHY A TASK WAS NOT COMPLETED, THEN MOVE TO NEXT DAY.

ONE POSITIVE

TODAY I GAVE

DAILY
GOAL SLAYERS
PLANNER

SETTING YOURSELF UP FOR SUCCESS DAILY!

DATE

_____ / _____ / _____

SCRIPTURE

MOTIVATIONAL QUOTE

ONE GOAL

ONE FUN THING

✱	IMPORTANT TIME	SCHEDULE	SLAYED?
	5:00AM		☐Y ☐N
	5:30AM		☐Y ☐N
	6:00AM		☐Y ☐N
	6:30AM		☐Y ☐N
	7:00AM		☐Y ☐N
	7:30AM		☐Y ☐N
	8:00AM		☐Y ☐N
	8:30AM		☐Y ☐N
	9:00AM		☐Y ☐N
	9:30AM		☐Y ☐N
	10:00AM		☐Y ☐N
	10:30AM		☐Y ☐N
	11:00AM		☐Y ☐N
	11:30AM		☐Y ☐N
	12:00PM		☐Y ☐N
	12:30PM		☐Y ☐N
	1:00PM		☐Y ☐N
	1:30PM		☐Y ☐N
	2:00PM		☐Y ☐N
	2:30PM		☐Y ☐N
	3:00PM		☐Y ☐N
	3:30PM		☐Y ☐N
	4:00PM		☐Y ☐N
	4:30PM		☐Y ☐N
	5:00PM		☐Y ☐N
	5:30PM		☐Y ☐N
	6:00PM		☐Y ☐N
	6:30PM		☐Y ☐N
	7:00PM		☐Y ☐N
	7:30PM		☐Y ☐N
	8:00PM		☐Y ☐N
	8:30PM		☐Y ☐N
	9:00PM		☐Y ☐N
	9:30PM		☐Y ☐N

HEALTH • FITNESS

WATER INTAKE

OZ OZ OZ OZ OZ
OZ OZ OZ OZ OZ

TAKE 5 MINUTES EACH MORNING TO PLAN YOUR DAY.

GET EIGHT HOURS OF SLEEP!

NOTE HIGH PRIORITY TASKS WITH A ✱

ANALYZE WHY A TASK WAS NOT COMPLETED, THEN MOVE TO NEXT DAY.

ONE POSITIVE

TODAY I GAVE

DATE

_____ / _____ / _____

SCRIPTURE

MOTIVATIONAL QUOTE

ONE GOAL

ONE FUN THING

HEALTH + FITNESS

WATER INTAKE

*	IMPORTANT TIME	SCHEDULE	SLAYED?
	5:00AM		☐Y ☐N
	5:30AM		☐Y ☐N
	6:00AM		☐Y ☐N
	6:30AM		☐Y ☐N
	7:00AM		☐Y ☐N
	7:30AM		☐Y ☐N
	8:00AM		☐Y ☐N
	8:30AM		☐Y ☐N
	9:00AM		☐Y ☐N
	9:30AM		☐Y ☐N
	10:00AM		☐Y ☐N
	10:30AM		☐Y ☐N
	11:00AM		☐Y ☐N
	11:30AM		☐Y ☐N
	12:00PM		☐Y ☐N
	12:30PM		☐Y ☐N
	1:00PM		☐Y ☐N
	1:30PM		☐Y ☐N
	2:00PM		☐Y ☐N
	2:30PM		☐Y ☐N
	3:00PM		☐Y ☐N
	3:30PM		☐Y ☐N
	4:00PM		☐Y ☐N
	4:30PM		☐Y ☐N
	5:00PM		☐Y ☐N
	5:30PM		☐Y ☐N
	6:00PM		☐Y ☐N
	6:30PM		☐Y ☐N
	7:00PM		☐Y ☐N
	7:30PM		☐Y ☐N
	8:00PM		☐Y ☐N
	8:30PM		☐Y ☐N
	9:00PM		☐Y ☐N
	9:30PM		☐Y ☐N

TAKE 5 MINUTES EACH MORNING TO PLAN YOUR DAY.

GET EIGHT HOURS OF SLEEP!

NOTE HIGH PRIORITY TASKS WITH A *

ANALYZE WHY A TASK WAS NOT COMPLETED, THEN MOVE TO NEXT DAY.

ONE POSITIVE

TODAY I GAVE

DAILY
GOAL SLAYERS
PLANNER

SETTING YOURSELF UP FOR SUCCESS DAILY!

DATE

____ / ____ / ____

SCRIPTURE

MOTIVATIONAL QUOTE

ONE GOAL

ONE FUN THING

HEALTH + FITNESS

WATER INTAKE

OZ. OZ. OZ. OZ. OZ.
OZ. OZ. OZ. OZ. OZ.

*	IMPORTANT TIME	SCHEDULE	SLAYED?
	5:00AM		☐Y ☐N
	5:30AM		☐Y ☐N
	6:00AM		☐Y ☐N
	6:30AM		☐Y ☐N
	7:00AM		☐Y ☐N
	7:30AM		☐Y ☐N
	8:00AM		☐Y ☐N
	8:30AM		☐Y ☐N
	9:00AM		☐Y ☐N
	9:30AM		☐Y ☐N
	10:00AM		☐Y ☐N
	10:30AM		☐Y ☐N
	11:00AM		☐Y ☐N
	11:30AM		☐Y ☐N
	12:00PM		☐Y ☐N
	12:30PM		☐Y ☐N
	1:00PM		☐Y ☐N
	1:30PM		☐Y ☐N
	2:00PM		☐Y ☐N
	2:30PM		☐Y ☐N
	3:00PM		☐Y ☐N
	3:30PM		☐Y ☐N
	4:00PM		☐Y ☐N
	4:30PM		☐Y ☐N
	5:00PM		☐Y ☐N
	5:30PM		☐Y ☐N
	6:00PM		☐Y ☐N
	6:30PM		☐Y ☐N
	7:00PM		☐Y ☐N
	7:30PM		☐Y ☐N
	8:00PM		☐Y ☐N
	8:30PM		☐Y ☐N
	9:00PM		☐Y ☐N
	9:30PM		☐Y ☐N

TAKE 5 MINUTES EACH MORNING TO PLAN YOUR DAY.

GET EIGHT HOURS OF SLEEP!

NOTE HIGH PRIORITY TASKS WITH A *

ANALYZE WHY A TASK WAS NOT COMPLETED, THEN MOVE TO NEXT DAY.

ONE POSITIVE

TODAY I GAVE

DAILY
GOAL SLAYERS
PLANNER

SETTING YOURSELF UP FOR SUCCESS DAILY!

DATE

_____ / _____ / _____

SCRIPTURE

MOTIVATIONAL QUOTE

ONE GOAL

ONE FUN THING

*	IMPORTANT TIME	SCHEDULE	SLAYED?
	5:00AM		☐Y ☐N
	5:30AM		☐Y ☐N
	6:00AM		☐Y ☐N
	6:30AM		☐Y ☐N
	7:00AM		☐Y ☐N
	7:30AM		☐Y ☐N
	8:00AM		☐Y ☐N
	8:30AM		☐Y ☐N
	9:00AM		☐Y ☐N
	9:30AM		☐Y ☐N
	10:00AM		☐Y ☐N
	10:30AM		☐Y ☐N
	11:00AM		☐Y ☐N
	11:30AM		☐Y ☐N
	12:00PM		☐Y ☐N
	12:30PM		☐Y ☐N
	1:00PM		☐Y ☐N
	1:30PM		☐Y ☐N
	2:00PM		☐Y ☐N
	2:30PM		☐Y ☐N
	3:00PM		☐Y ☐N
	3:30PM		☐Y ☐N
	4:00PM		☐Y ☐N
	4:30PM		☐Y ☐N
	5:00PM		☐Y ☐N
	5:30PM		☐Y ☐N
	6:00PM		☐Y ☐N
	6:30PM		☐Y ☐N
	7:00PM		☐Y ☐N
	7:30PM		☐Y ☐N
	8:00PM		☐Y ☐N
	8:30PM		☐Y ☐N
	9:00PM		☐Y ☐N
	9:30PM		☐Y ☐N

HEALTH + FITNESS

WATER INTAKE

OZ. OZ. OZ. OZ. OZ.
OZ. OZ. OZ. OZ. OZ.

TAKE 5 MINUTES EACH MORNING TO PLAN YOUR DAY.

GET EIGHT HOURS OF SLEEP!

NOTE HIGH PRIORITY TASKS WITH A *

ANALYZE WHY A TASK WAS NOT COMPLETED, THEN MOVE TO NEXT DAY.

ONE POSITIVE

TODAY I GAVE

DAILY
GOAL SLAYERS
PLANNER

SETTING YOURSELF UP FOR SUCCESS DAILY!

DATE

_____ / _____ / _____

SCRIPTURE

MOTIVATIONAL QUOTE

ONE GOAL

ONE FUN THING

*	IMPORTANT TIME	SCHEDULE	SLAYED?
	5:00AM		☐Y ☐N
	5:30AM		☐Y ☐N
	6:00AM		☐Y ☐N
	6:30AM		☐Y ☐N
	7:00AM		☐Y ☐N
	7:30AM		☐Y ☐N
	8:00AM		☐Y ☐N
	8:30AM		☐Y ☐N
	9:00AM		☐Y ☐N
	9:30AM		☐Y ☐N
	10:00AM		☐Y ☐N
	10:30AM		☐Y ☐N
	11:00AM		☐Y ☐N
	11:30AM		☐Y ☐N
	12:00PM		☐Y ☐N
	12:30PM		☐Y ☐N
	1:00PM		☐Y ☐N
	1:30PM		☐Y ☐N
	2:00PM		☐Y ☐N
	2:30PM		☐Y ☐N
	3:00PM		☐Y ☐N
	3:30PM		☐Y ☐N
	4:00PM		☐Y ☐N
	4:30PM		☐Y ☐N
	5:00PM		☐Y ☐N
	5:30PM		☐Y ☐N
	6:00PM		☐Y ☐N
	6:30PM		☐Y ☐N
	7:00PM		☐Y ☐N
	7:30PM		☐Y ☐N
	8:00PM		☐Y ☐N
	8:30PM		☐Y ☐N
	9:00PM		☐Y ☐N
	9:30PM		☐Y ☐N

HEALTH + FITNESS

WATER INTAKE

OZ. OZ. OZ. OZ. OZ.
OZ. OZ. OZ. OZ. OZ.

TAKE 5 MINUTES EACH MORNING TO PLAN YOUR DAY.

GET EIGHT HOURS OF SLEEP!

NOTE HIGH PRIORITY TASKS WITH A *

ANALYZE WHY A TASK WAS NOT COMPLETED, THEN MOVE TO NEXT DAY.

ONE POSITIVE

TODAY I GAVE

DAILY
GOAL SLAYERS
PLANNER

SETTING YOURSELF UP FOR SUCCESS DAILY!

DATE

_____ / _____ / _____

SCRIPTURE

MOTIVATIONAL QUOTE

ONE GOAL

ONE FUN THING

*	IMPORTANT TIME	SCHEDULE	SLAYED?
	5:00AM		☐Y ☐N
	5:30AM		☐Y ☐N
	6:00AM		☐Y ☐N
	6:30AM		☐Y ☐N
	7:00AM		☐Y ☐N
	7:30AM		☐Y ☐N
	8:00AM		☐Y ☐N
	8:30AM		☐Y ☐N
	9:00AM		☐Y ☐N
	9:30AM		☐Y ☐N
	10:00AM		☐Y ☐N
	10:30AM		☐Y ☐N
	11:00AM		☐Y ☐N
	11:30AM		☐Y ☐N
	12:00PM		☐Y ☐N
	12:30PM		☐Y ☐N
	1:00PM		☐Y ☐N
	1:30PM		☐Y ☐N
	2:00PM		☐Y ☐N
	2:30PM		☐Y ☐N
	3:00PM		☐Y ☐N
	3:30PM		☐Y ☐N
	4:00PM		☐Y ☐N
	4:30PM		☐Y ☐N
	5:00PM		☐Y ☐N
	5:30PM		☐Y ☐N
	6:00PM		☐Y ☐N
	6:30PM		☐Y ☐N
	7:00PM		☐Y ☐N
	7:30PM		☐Y ☐N
	8:00PM		☐Y ☐N
	8:30PM		☐Y ☐N
	9:00PM		☐Y ☐N
	9:30PM		☐Y ☐N

HEALTH • FITNESS

WATER INTAKE

OZ OZ OZ OZ OZ

OZ OZ OZ OZ OZ

TAKE 5 MINUTES EACH MORNING TO PLAN YOUR DAY.

GET EIGHT HOURS OF SLEEP!

NOTE HIGH PRIORITY TASKS WITH A *

ANALYZE WHY A TASK WAS NOT COMPLETED, THEN MOVE TO NEXT DAY.

ONE POSITIVE

TODAY I GAVE

DAILY
GOAL SLAYERS
PLANNER

SETTING YOURSELF UP FOR SUCCESS DAILY!

DATE

_____ / _____ / _____

SCRIPTURE

MOTIVATIONAL QUOTE

ONE GOAL

ONE FUN THING

HEALTH + FITNESS

WATER INTAKE

*	IMPORTANT TIME	SCHEDULE	SLAYED?
	5:00AM		☐Y ☐N
	5:30AM		☐Y ☐N
	6:00AM		☐Y ☐N
	6:30AM		☐Y ☐N
	7:00AM		☐Y ☐N
	7:30AM		☐Y ☐N
	8:00AM		☐Y ☐N
	8:30AM		☐Y ☐N
	9:00AM		☐Y ☐N
	9:30AM		☐Y ☐N
	10:00AM		☐Y ☐N
	10:30AM		☐Y ☐N
	11:00AM		☐Y ☐N
	11:30AM		☐Y ☐N
	12:00PM		☐Y ☐N
	12:30PM		☐Y ☐N
	1:00PM		☐Y ☐N
	1:30PM		☐Y ☐N
	2:00PM		☐Y ☐N
	2:30PM		☐Y ☐N
	3:00PM		☐Y ☐N
	3:30PM		☐Y ☐N
	4:00PM		☐Y ☐N
	4:30PM		☐Y ☐N
	5:00PM		☐Y ☐N
	5:30PM		☐Y ☐N
	6:00PM		☐Y ☐N
	6:30PM		☐Y ☐N
	7:00PM		☐Y ☐N
	7:30PM		☐Y ☐N
	8:00PM		☐Y ☐N
	8:30PM		☐Y ☐N
	9:00PM		☐Y ☐N
	9:30PM		☐Y ☐N

TAKE 5 MINUTES EACH MORNING TO PLAN YOUR DAY.

GET EIGHT HOURS OF SLEEP!

NOTE HIGH PRIORITY TASKS WITH A *

ANALYZE WHY A TASK WAS NOT COMPLETED, THEN MOVE TO NEXT DAY.

ONE POSITIVE

TODAY I GAVE

DAILY
GOAL SLAYERS
PLANNER

SETTING YOURSELF UP FOR SUCCESS DAILY!

DATE

_____ / _____ / _____

SCRIPTURE

MOTIVATIONAL QUOTE

ONE GOAL

ONE FUN THING

*	IMPORTANT TIME	SCHEDULE	SLAYED?
	5:00AM		☐Y ☐N
	5:30AM		☐Y ☐N
	6:00AM		☐Y ☐N
	6:30AM		☐Y ☐N
	7:00AM		☐Y ☐N
	7:30AM		☐Y ☐N
	8:00AM		☐Y ☐N
	8:30AM		☐Y ☐N
	9:00AM		☐Y ☐N
	9:30AM		☐Y ☐N
	10:00AM		☐Y ☐N
	10:30AM		☐Y ☐N
	11:00AM		☐Y ☐N
	11:30AM		☐Y ☐N
	12:00PM		☐Y ☐N
	12:30PM		☐Y ☐N
	1:00PM		☐Y ☐N
	1:30PM		☐Y ☐N
	2:00PM		☐Y ☐N
	2:30PM		☐Y ☐N
	3:00PM		☐Y ☐N
	3:30PM		☐Y ☐N
	4:00PM		☐Y ☐N
	4:30PM		☐Y ☐N
	5:00PM		☐Y ☐N
	5:30PM		☐Y ☐N
	6:00PM		☐Y ☐N
	6:30PM		☐Y ☐N
	7:00PM		☐Y ☐N
	7:30PM		☐Y ☐N
	8:00PM		☐Y ☐N
	8:30PM		☐Y ☐N
	9:00PM		☐Y ☐N
	9:30PM		☐Y ☐N

HEALTH • FITNESS

WATER INTAKE

OZ. OZ. OZ. OZ. OZ.

OZ. OZ. OZ. OZ. OZ.

TAKE 5 MINUTES EACH MORNING TO PLAN YOUR DAY.

GET EIGHT HOURS OF SLEEP!

NOTE HIGH PRIORITY TASKS WITH A *

ANALYZE WHY A TASK WAS NOT COMPLETED, THEN MOVE TO NEXT DAY.

ONE POSITIVE

TODAY I GAVE

DAILY
GOAL SLAYERS
PLANNER

SETTING YOURSELF UP FOR SUCCESS DAILY!

DATE
_____ / _____ / _____

SCRIPTURE

MOTIVATIONAL QUOTE

ONE GOAL

ONE FUN THING

HEALTH + FITNESS

WATER INTAKE

OZ OZ OZ OZ OZ
OZ OZ OZ OZ OZ

✱	IMPORTANT TIME	SCHEDULE	SLAYED?
	5:00AM		☐Y ☐N
	5:30AM		☐Y ☐N
	6:00AM		☐Y ☐N
	6:30AM		☐Y ☐N
	7:00AM		☐Y ☐N
	7:30AM		☐Y ☐N
	8:00AM		☐Y ☐N
	8:30AM		☐Y ☐N
	9:00AM		☐Y ☐N
	9:30AM		☐Y ☐N
	10:00AM		☐Y ☐N
	10:30AM		☐Y ☐N
	11:00AM		☐Y ☐N
	11:30AM		☐Y ☐N
	12:00PM		☐Y ☐N
	12:30PM		☐Y ☐N
	1:00PM		☐Y ☐N
	1:30PM		☐Y ☐N
	2:00PM		☐Y ☐N
	2:30PM		☐Y ☐N
	3:00PM		☐Y ☐N
	3:30PM		☐Y ☐N
	4:00PM		☐Y ☐N
	4:30PM		☐Y ☐N
	5:00PM		☐Y ☐N
	5:30PM		☐Y ☐N
	6:00PM		☐Y ☐N
	6:30PM		☐Y ☐N
	7:00PM		☐Y ☐N
	7:30PM		☐Y ☐N
	8:00PM		☐Y ☐N
	8:30PM		☐Y ☐N
	9:00PM		☐Y ☐N
	9:30PM		☐Y ☐N

TAKE 5 MINUTES EACH MORNING TO PLAN YOUR DAY.

GET EIGHT HOURS OF SLEEP!

NOTE HIGH PRIORITY TASKS WITH A ✱

ANALYZE WHY A TASK WAS NOT COMPLETED, THEN MOVE TO NEXT DAY.

ONE POSITIVE

TODAY I GAVE

DAILY
GOAL SLAYERS
PLANNER

SETTING YOURSELF UP FOR SUCCESS DAILY!

DATE

_____ / _____ / _____

SCRIPTURE

MOTIVATIONAL QUOTE

ONE GOAL

ONE FUN THING

*	IMPORTANT TIME	SCHEDULE	SLAYED?
	5:00AM		☐Y ☐N
	5:30AM		☐Y ☐N
	6:00AM		☐Y ☐N
	6:30AM		☐Y ☐N
	7:00AM		☐Y ☐N
	7:30AM		☐Y ☐N
	8:00AM		☐Y ☐N
	8:30AM		☐Y ☐N
	9:00AM		☐Y ☐N
	9:30AM		☐Y ☐N
	10:00AM		☐Y ☐N
	10:30AM		☐Y ☐N
	11:00AM		☐Y ☐N
	11:30AM		☐Y ☐N
	12:00PM		☐Y ☐N
	12:30PM		☐Y ☐N
	1:00PM		☐Y ☐N
	1:30PM		☐Y ☐N
	2:00PM		☐Y ☐N
	2:30PM		☐Y ☐N
	3:00PM		☐Y ☐N
	3:30PM		☐Y ☐N
	4:00PM		☐Y ☐N
	4:30PM		☐Y ☐N
	5:00PM		☐Y ☐N
	5:30PM		☐Y ☐N
	6:00PM		☐Y ☐N
	6:30PM		☐Y ☐N
	7:00PM		☐Y ☐N
	7:30PM		☐Y ☐N
	8:00PM		☐Y ☐N
	8:30PM		☐Y ☐N
	9:00PM		☐Y ☐N
	9:30PM		☐Y ☐N

HEALTH + FITNESS

WATER INTAKE

OZ OZ OZ OZ OZ
OZ OZ OZ OZ OZ

TAKE 5 MINUTES EACH MORNING TO PLAN YOUR DAY.

GET EIGHT HOURS OF SLEEP!

NOTE HIGH PRIORITY TASKS WITH A *

ANALYZE WHY A TASK WAS NOT COMPLETED, THEN MOVE TO NEXT DAY.

ONE POSITIVE

TODAY I GAVE

DAILY
GOAL SLAYERS
PLANNER

SETTING YOURSELF UP FOR SUCCESS DAILY!

DATE

_____ / _____ / _____

SCRIPTURE

MOTIVATIONAL QUOTE

ONE GOAL

ONE FUN THING

*	IMPORTANT TIME	SCHEDULE	SLAYED?
	5:00AM		☐Y ☐N
	5:30AM		☐Y ☐N
	6:00AM		☐Y ☐N
	6:30AM		☐Y ☐N
	7:00AM		☐Y ☐N
	7:30AM		☐Y ☐N
	8:00AM		☐Y ☐N
	8:30AM		☐Y ☐N
	9:00AM		☐Y ☐N
	9:30AM		☐Y ☐N
	10:00AM		☐Y ☐N
	10:30AM		☐Y ☐N
	11:00AM		☐Y ☐N
	11:30AM		☐Y ☐N
	12:00PM		☐Y ☐N
	12:30PM		☐Y ☐N
	1:00PM		☐Y ☐N
	1:30PM		☐Y ☐N
	2:00PM		☐Y ☐N
	2:30PM		☐Y ☐N
	3:00PM		☐Y ☐N
	3:30PM		☐Y ☐N
	4:00PM		☐Y ☐N
	4:30PM		☐Y ☐N
	5:00PM		☐Y ☐N
	5:30PM		☐Y ☐N
	6:00PM		☐Y ☐N
	6:30PM		☐Y ☐N
	7:00PM		☐Y ☐N
	7:30PM		☐Y ☐N
	8:00PM		☐Y ☐N
	8:30PM		☐Y ☐N
	9:00PM		☐Y ☐N
	9:30PM		☐Y ☐N

HEALTH + FITNESS

WATER INTAKE

OZ OZ OZ OZ OZ

OZ OZ OZ OZ OZ

TAKE 5 MINUTES EACH MORNING TO PLAN YOUR DAY.

GET EIGHT HOURS OF SLEEP!

NOTE HIGH PRIORITY TASKS WITH A *

ANALYZE WHY A TASK WAS NOT COMPLETED, THEN MOVE TO NEXT DAY.

ONE POSITIVE

TODAY I GAVE

DAILY
GOAL SLAYERS
PLANNER

SETTING YOURSELF UP FOR SUCCESS DAILY!

DATE

_____ / _____ / _____

SCRIPTURE

MOTIVATIONAL QUOTE

ONE GOAL

ONE FUN THING

✱	IMPORTANT TIME	SCHEDULE	SLAYED?
	5:00AM		☐Y ☐N
	5:30AM		☐Y ☐N
	6:00AM		☐Y ☐N
	6:30AM		☐Y ☐N
	7:00AM		☐Y ☐N
	7:30AM		☐Y ☐N
	8:00AM		☐Y ☐N
	8:30AM		☐Y ☐N
	9:00AM		☐Y ☐N
	9:30AM		☐Y ☐N
	10:00AM		☐Y ☐N
	10:30AM		☐Y ☐N
	11:00AM		☐Y ☐N
	11:30AM		☐Y ☐N
	12:00PM		☐Y ☐N
	12:30PM		☐Y ☐N
	1:00PM		☐Y ☐N
	1:30PM		☐Y ☐N
	2:00PM		☐Y ☐N
	2:30PM		☐Y ☐N
	3:00PM		☐Y ☐N
	3:30PM		☐Y ☐N
	4:00PM		☐Y ☐N
	4:30PM		☐Y ☐N
	5:00PM		☐Y ☐N
	5:30PM		☐Y ☐N
	6:00PM		☐Y ☐N
	6:30PM		☐Y ☐N
	7:00PM		☐Y ☐N
	7:30PM		☐Y ☐N
	8:00PM		☐Y ☐N
	8:30PM		☐Y ☐N
	9:00PM		☐Y ☐N
	9:30PM		☐Y ☐N

HEALTH • FITNESS

WATER INTAKE

OZ. OZ. OZ. OZ. OZ.

OZ. OZ. OZ. OZ. OZ.

TAKE 5 MINUTES EACH MORNING TO PLAN YOUR DAY.

GET EIGHT HOURS OF SLEEP!

NOTE HIGH PRIORITY TASKS WITH A ✱

ANALYZE WHY A TASK WAS NOT COMPLETED, THEN MOVE TO NEXT DAY.

ONE POSITIVE

TODAY I GAVE

DAILY
GOAL SLAYERS
PLANNER

SETTING YOURSELF UP FOR SUCCESS DAILY!

DATE

_____ / _____ / _____

SCRIPTURE

MOTIVATIONAL QUOTE

ONE GOAL

ONE FUN THING

✱	IMPORTANT TIME	SCHEDULE	SLAYED?
	5:00AM		☐Y ☐N
	5:30AM		☐Y ☐N
	6:00AM		☐Y ☐N
	6:30AM		☐Y ☐N
	7:00AM		☐Y ☐N
	7:30AM		☐Y ☐N
	8:00AM		☐Y ☐N
	8:30AM		☐Y ☐N
	9:00AM		☐Y ☐N
	9:30AM		☐Y ☐N
	10:00AM		☐Y ☐N
	10:30AM		☐Y ☐N
	11:00AM		☐Y ☐N
	11:30AM		☐Y ☐N
	12:00PM		☐Y ☐N
	12:30PM		☐Y ☐N
	1:00PM		☐Y ☐N
	1:30PM		☐Y ☐N
	2:00PM		☐Y ☐N
	2:30PM		☐Y ☐N
	3:00PM		☐Y ☐N
	3:30PM		☐Y ☐N
	4:00PM		☐Y ☐N
	4:30PM		☐Y ☐N
	5:00PM		☐Y ☐N
	5:30PM		☐Y ☐N
	6:00PM		☐Y ☐N
	6:30PM		☐Y ☐N
	7:00PM		☐Y ☐N
	7:30PM		☐Y ☐N
	8:00PM		☐Y ☐N
	8:30PM		☐Y ☐N
	9:00PM		☐Y ☐N
	9:30PM		☐Y ☐N

HEALTH • FITNESS

WATER INTAKE

OZ. OZ. OZ. OZ. OZ.
OZ. OZ. OZ. OZ. OZ.

TAKE 5 MINUTES EACH MORNING TO PLAN YOUR DAY.

GET EIGHT HOURS OF SLEEP!

NOTE HIGH PRIORITY TASKS WITH A ✱

ANALYZE WHY A TASK WAS NOT COMPLETED, THEN MOVE TO NEXT DAY.

ONE POSITIVE

TODAY I GAVE

DAILY
GOAL SLAYERS
PLANNER

SETTING YOURSELF UP FOR SUCCESS DAILY!

DATE

_____ / _____ / _____

SCRIPTURE

MOTIVATIONAL QUOTE

ONE GOAL

ONE FUN THING

HEALTH + FITNESS

WATER INTAKE

✱	IMPORTANT TIME	SCHEDULE	SLAYED?
	5:00AM		☐Y ☐N
	5:30AM		☐Y ☐N
	6:00AM		☐Y ☐N
	6:30AM		☐Y ☐N
	7:00AM		☐Y ☐N
	7:30AM		☐Y ☐N
	8:00AM		☐Y ☐N
	8:30AM		☐Y ☐N
	9:00AM		☐Y ☐N
	9:30AM		☐Y ☐N
	10:00AM		☐Y ☐N
	10:30AM		☐Y ☐N
	11:00AM		☐Y ☐N
	11:30AM		☐Y ☐N
	12:00PM		☐Y ☐N
	12:30PM		☐Y ☐N
	1:00PM		☐Y ☐N
	1:30PM		☐Y ☐N
	2:00PM		☐Y ☐N
	2:30PM		☐Y ☐N
	3:00PM		☐Y ☐N
	3:30PM		☐Y ☐N
	4:00PM		☐Y ☐N
	4:30PM		☐Y ☐N
	5:00PM		☐Y ☐N
	5:30PM		☐Y ☐N
	6:00PM		☐Y ☐N
	6:30PM		☐Y ☐N
	7:00PM		☐Y ☐N
	7:30PM		☐Y ☐N
	8:00PM		☐Y ☐N
	8:30PM		☐Y ☐N
	9:00PM		☐Y ☐N
	9:30PM		☐Y ☐N

TAKE 5 MINUTES EACH MORNING TO PLAN YOUR DAY.

GET EIGHT HOURS OF SLEEP!

NOTE HIGH PRIORITY TASKS WITH A ✱

ANALYZE WHY A TASK WAS NOT COMPLETED, THEN MOVE TO NEXT DAY.

ONE POSITIVE

TODAY I GAVE

DAILY
GOAL SLAYERS
PLANNER

SETTING YOURSELF UP FOR SUCCESS DAILY!

DATE
_____/_____/_____

SCRIPTURE

MOTIVATIONAL QUOTE

ONE GOAL

ONE FUN THING

*	IMPORTANT TIME	SCHEDULE	SLAYED?
	5:00AM		☐Y ☐N
	5:30AM		☐Y ☐N
	6:00AM		☐Y ☐N
	6:30AM		☐Y ☐N
	7:00AM		☐Y ☐N
	7:30AM		☐Y ☐N
	8:00AM		☐Y ☐N
	8:30AM		☐Y ☐N
	9:00AM		☐Y ☐N
	9:30AM		☐Y ☐N
	10:00AM		☐Y ☐N
	10:30AM		☐Y ☐N
	11:00AM		☐Y ☐N
	11:30AM		☐Y ☐N
	12:00PM		☐Y ☐N
	12:30PM		☐Y ☐N
	1:00PM		☐Y ☐N
	1:30PM		☐Y ☐N
	2:00PM		☐Y ☐N
	2:30PM		☐Y ☐N
	3:00PM		☐Y ☐N
	3:30PM		☐Y ☐N
	4:00PM		☐Y ☐N
	4:30PM		☐Y ☐N
	5:00PM		☐Y ☐N
	5:30PM		☐Y ☐N
	6:00PM		☐Y ☐N
	6:30PM		☐Y ☐N
	7:00PM		☐Y ☐N
	7:30PM		☐Y ☐N
	8:00PM		☐Y ☐N
	8:30PM		☐Y ☐N
	9:00PM		☐Y ☐N
	9:30PM		☐Y ☐N

HEALTH + FITNESS

WATER INTAKE

OZ. OZ. OZ. OZ. OZ.
OZ. OZ. OZ. OZ. OZ.

TAKE 5 MINUTES EACH MORNING TO PLAN YOUR DAY.

GET EIGHT HOURS OF SLEEP!

NOTE HIGH PRIORITY TASKS WITH A *

ANALYZE WHY A TASK WAS NOT COMPLETED, THEN MOVE TO NEXT DAY.

ONE POSITIVE

TODAY I GAVE

DAILY
GOAL SLAYERS
PLANNER

SETTING YOURSELF UP FOR SUCCESS DAILY!

DATE

_____ / _____ / _____

SCRIPTURE

MOTIVATIONAL QUOTE

ONE GOAL

ONE FUN THING

✱	IMPORTANT TIME	SCHEDULE	SLAYED?
	5:00AM		☐Y ☐N
	5:30AM		☐Y ☐N
	6:00AM		☐Y ☐N
	6:30AM		☐Y ☐N
	7:00AM		☐Y ☐N
	7:30AM		☐Y ☐N
	8:00AM		☐Y ☐N
	8:30AM		☐Y ☐N
	9:00AM		☐Y ☐N
	9:30AM		☐Y ☐N
	10:00AM		☐Y ☐N
	10:30AM		☐Y ☐N
	11:00AM		☐Y ☐N
	11:30AM		☐Y ☐N
	12:00PM		☐Y ☐N
	12:30PM		☐Y ☐N
	1:00PM		☐Y ☐N
	1:30PM		☐Y ☐N
	2:00PM		☐Y ☐N
	2:30PM		☐Y ☐N
	3:00PM		☐Y ☐N
	3:30PM		☐Y ☐N
	4:00PM		☐Y ☐N
	4:30PM		☐Y ☐N
	5:00PM		☐Y ☐N
	5:30PM		☐Y ☐N
	6:00PM		☐Y ☐N
	6:30PM		☐Y ☐N
	7:00PM		☐Y ☐N
	7:30PM		☐Y ☐N
	8:00PM		☐Y ☐N
	8:30PM		☐Y ☐N
	9:00PM		☐Y ☐N
	9:30PM		☐Y ☐N

HEALTH • FITNESS

WATER INTAKE

OZ. OZ. OZ. OZ. OZ.
OZ. OZ. OZ. OZ. OZ.

TAKE 5 MINUTES EACH MORNING TO PLAN YOUR DAY.

GET EIGHT HOURS OF SLEEP!

NOTE HIGH PRIORITY TASKS WITH A ✱

ANALYZE WHY A TASK WAS NOT COMPLETED, THEN MOVE TO NEXT DAY.

ONE POSITIVE

TODAY I GAVE

DAILY
GOAL SLAYERS
PLANNER

SETTING YOURSELF UP FOR SUCCESS DAILY!

DATE
_____ / _____ / _____

SCRIPTURE

MOTIVATIONAL QUOTE

ONE GOAL

ONE FUN THING

HEALTH • FITNESS

WATER INTAKE

OZ. OZ. OZ. OZ. OZ.
OZ. OZ. OZ. OZ. OZ.

✱	IMPORTANT TIME	SCHEDULE	SLAYED?
	5:00AM		☐Y ☐N
	5:30AM		☐Y ☐N
	6:00AM		☐Y ☐N
	6:30AM		☐Y ☐N
	7:00AM		☐Y ☐N
	7:30AM		☐Y ☐N
	8:00AM		☐Y ☐N
	8:30AM		☐Y ☐N
	9:00AM		☐Y ☐N
	9:30AM		☐Y ☐N
	10:00AM		☐Y ☐N
	10:30AM		☐Y ☐N
	11:00AM		☐Y ☐N
	11:30AM		☐Y ☐N
	12:00PM		☐Y ☐N
	12:30PM		☐Y ☐N
	1:00PM		☐Y ☐N
	1:30PM		☐Y ☐N
	2:00PM		☐Y ☐N
	2:30PM		☐Y ☐N
	3:00PM		☐Y ☐N
	3:30PM		☐Y ☐N
	4:00PM		☐Y ☐N
	4:30PM		☐Y ☐N
	5:00PM		☐Y ☐N
	5:30PM		☐Y ☐N
	6:00PM		☐Y ☐N
	6:30PM		☐Y ☐N
	7:00PM		☐Y ☐N
	7:30PM		☐Y ☐N
	8:00PM		☐Y ☐N
	8:30PM		☐Y ☐N
	9:00PM		☐Y ☐N
	9:30PM		☐Y ☐N

TAKE 5 MINUTES EACH MORNING TO PLAN YOUR DAY.

GET EIGHT HOURS OF SLEEP!

NOTE HIGH PRIORITY TASKS WITH A ✱

ANALYZE WHY A TASK WAS NOT COMPLETED, THEN MOVE TO NEXT DAY.

ONE POSITIVE

TODAY I GAVE

DAILY
GOAL SLAYERS
PLANNER

SETTING YOURSELF UP FOR SUCCESS DAILY!

DATE

_____ / _____ / _____

SCRIPTURE

MOTIVATIONAL QUOTE

ONE GOAL

ONE FUN THING

✱	IMPORTANT TIME	SCHEDULE	SLAYED?
	5:00AM		☐Y ☐N
	5:30AM		☐Y ☐N
	6:00AM		☐Y ☐N
	6:30AM		☐Y ☐N
	7:00AM		☐Y ☐N
	7:30AM		☐Y ☐N
	8:00AM		☐Y ☐N
	8:30AM		☐Y ☐N
	9:00AM		☐Y ☐N
	9:30AM		☐Y ☐N
	10:00AM		☐Y ☐N
	10:30AM		☐Y ☐N
	11:00AM		☐Y ☐N
	11:30AM		☐Y ☐N
	12:00PM		☐Y ☐N
	12:30PM		☐Y ☐N
	1:00PM		☐Y ☐N
	1:30PM		☐Y ☐N
	2:00PM		☐Y ☐N
	2:30PM		☐Y ☐N
	3:00PM		☐Y ☐N
	3:30PM		☐Y ☐N
	4:00PM		☐Y ☐N
	4:30PM		☐Y ☐N
	5:00PM		☐Y ☐N
	5:30PM		☐Y ☐N
	6:00PM		☐Y ☐N
	6:30PM		☐Y ☐N
	7:00PM		☐Y ☐N
	7:30PM		☐Y ☐N
	8:00PM		☐Y ☐N
	8:30PM		☐Y ☐N
	9:00PM		☐Y ☐N
	9:30PM		☐Y ☐N

HEALTH + FITNESS

WATER INTAKE

OZ OZ OZ OZ OZ

OZ OZ OZ OZ OZ

TAKE 5 MINUTES EACH MORNING TO PLAN YOUR DAY.

GET EIGHT HOURS OF SLEEP!

NOTE HIGH PRIORITY TASKS WITH A ✱

ANALYZE WHY A TASK WAS NOT COMPLETED, THEN MOVE TO NEXT DAY.

ONE POSITIVE

TODAY I GAVE

DAILY
GOAL SLAYERS
PLANNER

SETTING YOURSELF UP FOR SUCCESS DAILY!

DATE

____ / ____ / ____

SCRIPTURE

MOTIVATIONAL QUOTE

ONE GOAL

ONE FUN THING

HEALTH · FITNESS

WATER INTAKE

OZ OZ OZ OZ OZ
OZ OZ OZ OZ OZ

✻	IMPORTANT TIME	SCHEDULE	SLAYED?
	5:00AM		☐Y ☐N
	5:30AM		☐Y ☐N
	6:00AM		☐Y ☐N
	6:30AM		☐Y ☐N
	7:00AM		☐Y ☐N
	7:30AM		☐Y ☐N
	8:00AM		☐Y ☐N
	8:30AM		☐Y ☐N
	9:00AM		☐Y ☐N
	9:30AM		☐Y ☐N
	10:00AM		☐Y ☐N
	10:30AM		☐Y ☐N
	11:00AM		☐Y ☐N
	11:30AM		☐Y ☐N
	12:00PM		☐Y ☐N
	12:30PM		☐Y ☐N
	1:00PM		☐Y ☐N
	1:30PM		☐Y ☐N
	2:00PM		☐Y ☐N
	2:30PM		☐Y ☐N
	3:00PM		☐Y ☐N
	3:30PM		☐Y ☐N
	4:00PM		☐Y ☐N
	4:30PM		☐Y ☐N
	5:00PM		☐Y ☐N
	5:30PM		☐Y ☐N
	6:00PM		☐Y ☐N
	6:30PM		☐Y ☐N
	7:00PM		☐Y ☐N
	7:30PM		☐Y ☐N
	8:00PM		☐Y ☐N
	8:30PM		☐Y ☐N
	9:00PM		☐Y ☐N
	9:30PM		☐Y ☐N

TAKE 5 MINUTES EACH MORNING TO PLAN YOUR DAY.

GET EIGHT HOURS OF SLEEP!

NOTE HIGH PRIORITY TASKS WITH A ✻

ANALYZE WHY A TASK WAS NOT COMPLETED, THEN MOVE TO NEXT DAY.

ONE POSITIVE

TODAY I GAVE

DAILY
GOAL SLAYERS
PLANNER

SETTING YOURSELF UP FOR SUCCESS DAILY!

DATE

_____ / _____ / _____

SCRIPTURE

MOTIVATIONAL QUOTE

ONE GOAL

ONE FUN THING

*	IMPORTANT TIME	SCHEDULE	SLAYED?
	5:00AM		☐Y ☐N
	5:30AM		☐Y ☐N
	6:00AM		☐Y ☐N
	6:30AM		☐Y ☐N
	7:00AM		☐Y ☐N
	7:30AM		☐Y ☐N
	8:00AM		☐Y ☐N
	8:30AM		☐Y ☐N
	9:00AM		☐Y ☐N
	9:30AM		☐Y ☐N
	10:00AM		☐Y ☐N
	10:30AM		☐Y ☐N
	11:00AM		☐Y ☐N
	11:30AM		☐Y ☐N
	12:00PM		☐Y ☐N
	12:30PM		☐Y ☐N
	1:00PM		☐Y ☐N
	1:30PM		☐Y ☐N
	2:00PM		☐Y ☐N
	2:30PM		☐Y ☐N
	3:00PM		☐Y ☐N
	3:30PM		☐Y ☐N
	4:00PM		☐Y ☐N
	4:30PM		☐Y ☐N
	5:00PM		☐Y ☐N
	5:30PM		☐Y ☐N
	6:00PM		☐Y ☐N
	6:30PM		☐Y ☐N
	7:00PM		☐Y ☐N
	7:30PM		☐Y ☐N
	8:00PM		☐Y ☐N
	8:30PM		☐Y ☐N
	9:00PM		☐Y ☐N
	9:30PM		☐Y ☐N

HEALTH • FITNESS

WATER INTAKE

OZ. OZ. OZ. OZ. OZ.
OZ. OZ. OZ. OZ. OZ.

TAKE 5 MINUTES EACH MORNING TO PLAN YOUR DAY.

GET EIGHT HOURS OF SLEEP!

NOTE HIGH PRIORITY TASKS WITH A *

ANALYZE WHY A TASK WAS NOT COMPLETED, THEN MOVE TO NEXT DAY.

ONE POSITIVE

TODAY I GAVE

DAILY
GOAL SLAYERS
PLANNER

SETTING YOURSELF UP FOR SUCCESS DAILY!

DATE

_____ / _____ / _____

SCRIPTURE

MOTIVATIONAL QUOTE

ONE GOAL

ONE FUN THING

*	IMPORTANT TIME	SCHEDULE	SLAYED?
	5:00AM		☐Y ☐N
	5:30AM		☐Y ☐N
	6:00AM		☐Y ☐N
	6:30AM		☐Y ☐N
	7:00AM		☐Y ☐N
	7:30AM		☐Y ☐N
	8:00AM		☐Y ☐N
	8:30AM		☐Y ☐N
	9:00AM		☐Y ☐N
	9:30AM		☐Y ☐N
	10:00AM		☐Y ☐N
	10:30AM		☐Y ☐N
	11:00AM		☐Y ☐N
	11:30AM		☐Y ☐N
	12:00PM		☐Y ☐N
	12:30PM		☐Y ☐N
	1:00PM		☐Y ☐N
	1:30PM		☐Y ☐N
	2:00PM		☐Y ☐N
	2:30PM		☐Y ☐N
	3:00PM		☐Y ☐N
	3:30PM		☐Y ☐N
	4:00PM		☐Y ☐N
	4:30PM		☐Y ☐N
	5:00PM		☐Y ☐N
	5:30PM		☐Y ☐N
	6:00PM		☐Y ☐N
	6:30PM		☐Y ☐N
	7:00PM		☐Y ☐N
	7:30PM		☐Y ☐N
	8:00PM		☐Y ☐N
	8:30PM		☐Y ☐N
	9:00PM		☐Y ☐N
	9:30PM		☐Y ☐N

HEALTH • FITNESS

WATER INTAKE

OZ. OZ. OZ. OZ. OZ.
OZ. OZ. OZ. OZ. OZ.

TAKE 5 MINUTES EACH MORNING TO PLAN YOUR DAY.

GET EIGHT HOURS OF SLEEP!

NOTE HIGH PRIORITY TASKS WITH A *

ANALYZE WHY A TASK WAS NOT COMPLETED, THEN MOVE TO NEXT DAY.

ONE POSITIVE

TODAY I GAVE

DAILY
GOAL SLAYERS
PLANNER

SETTING YOURSELF UP FOR SUCCESS DAILY!

DATE

_____ / _____ / _____

SCRIPTURE

MOTIVATIONAL QUOTE

ONE GOAL

ONE FUN THING

HEALTH + FITNESS

WATER INTAKE

*	IMPORTANT TIME	SCHEDULE	SLAYED?
	5:00AM		☐Y ☐N
	5:30AM		☐Y ☐N
	6:00AM		☐Y ☐N
	6:30AM		☐Y ☐N
	7:00AM		☐Y ☐N
	7:30AM		☐Y ☐N
	8:00AM		☐Y ☐N
	8:30AM		☐Y ☐N
	9:00AM		☐Y ☐N
	9:30AM		☐Y ☐N
	10:00AM		☐Y ☐N
	10:30AM		☐Y ☐N
	11:00AM		☐Y ☐N
	11:30AM		☐Y ☐N
	12:00PM		☐Y ☐N
	12:30PM		☐Y ☐N
	1:00PM		☐Y ☐N
	1:30PM		☐Y ☐N
	2:00PM		☐Y ☐N
	2:30PM		☐Y ☐N
	3:00PM		☐Y ☐N
	3:30PM		☐Y ☐N
	4:00PM		☐Y ☐N
	4:30PM		☐Y ☐N
	5:00PM		☐Y ☐N
	5:30PM		☐Y ☐N
	6:00PM		☐Y ☐N
	6:30PM		☐Y ☐N
	7:00PM		☐Y ☐N
	7:30PM		☐Y ☐N
	8:00PM		☐Y ☐N
	8:30PM		☐Y ☐N
	9:00PM		☐Y ☐N
	9:30PM		☐Y ☐N

TAKE 5 MINUTES EACH MORNING TO PLAN YOUR DAY.

GET EIGHT HOURS OF SLEEP!

NOTE HIGH PRIORITY TASKS WITH A *

ANALYZE WHY A TASK WAS NOT COMPLETED, THEN MOVE TO NEXT DAY.

ONE POSITIVE

TODAY I GAVE

DAILY
GOAL SLAYERS
PLANNER

SETTING YOURSELF UP FOR SUCCESS DAILY!

DATE

_____ / _____ / _____

SCRIPTURE

MOTIVATIONAL QUOTE

ONE GOAL

ONE FUN THING

HEALTH + FITNESS

WATER INTAKE

*	IMPORTANT TIME	SCHEDULE	SLAYED?
	5:00AM		☐Y ☐N
	5:30AM		☐Y ☐N
	6:00AM		☐Y ☐N
	6:30AM		☐Y ☐N
	7:00AM		☐Y ☐N
	7:30AM		☐Y ☐N
	8:00AM		☐Y ☐N
	8:30AM		☐Y ☐N
	9:00AM		☐Y ☐N
	9:30AM		☐Y ☐N
	10:00AM		☐Y ☐N
	10:30AM		☐Y ☐N
	11:00AM		☐Y ☐N
	11:30AM		☐Y ☐N
	12:00PM		☐Y ☐N
	12:30PM		☐Y ☐N
	1:00PM		☐Y ☐N
	1:30PM		☐Y ☐N
	2:00PM		☐Y ☐N
	2:30PM		☐Y ☐N
	3:00PM		☐Y ☐N
	3:30PM		☐Y ☐N
	4:00PM		☐Y ☐N
	4:30PM		☐Y ☐N
	5:00PM		☐Y ☐N
	5:30PM		☐Y ☐N
	6:00PM		☐Y ☐N
	6:30PM		☐Y ☐N
	7:00PM		☐Y ☐N
	7:30PM		☐Y ☐N
	8:00PM		☐Y ☐N
	8:30PM		☐Y ☐N
	9:00PM		☐Y ☐N
	9:30PM		☐Y ☐N

TAKE 5 MINUTES EACH MORNING TO PLAN YOUR DAY.

GET EIGHT HOURS OF SLEEP!

NOTE HIGH PRIORITY TASKS WITH A *

ANALYZE WHY A TASK WAS NOT COMPLETED, THEN MOVE TO NEXT DAY.

ONE POSITIVE

TODAY I GAVE

DAILY
GOAL SLAYERS
PLANNER

SETTING YOURSELF UP FOR SUCCESS DAILY!

DATE

_____ / _____ / _____

SCRIPTURE

MOTIVATIONAL QUOTE

ONE GOAL

ONE FUN THING

*	IMPORTANT TIME	SCHEDULE	SLAYED?
	5:00AM		☐Y ☐N
	5:30AM		☐Y ☐N
	6:00AM		☐Y ☐N
	6:30AM		☐Y ☐N
	7:00AM		☐Y ☐N
	7:30AM		☐Y ☐N
	8:00AM		☐Y ☐N
	8:30AM		☐Y ☐N
	9:00AM		☐Y ☐N
	9:30AM		☐Y ☐N
	10:00AM		☐Y ☐N
	10:30AM		☐Y ☐N
	11:00AM		☐Y ☐N
	11:30AM		☐Y ☐N
	12:00PM		☐Y ☐N
	12:30PM		☐Y ☐N
	1:00PM		☐Y ☐N
	1:30PM		☐Y ☐N
	2:00PM		☐Y ☐N
	2:30PM		☐Y ☐N
	3:00PM		☐Y ☐N
	3:30PM		☐Y ☐N
	4:00PM		☐Y ☐N
	4:30PM		☐Y ☐N
	5:00PM		☐Y ☐N
	5:30PM		☐Y ☐N
	6:00PM		☐Y ☐N
	6:30PM		☐Y ☐N
	7:00PM		☐Y ☐N
	7:30PM		☐Y ☐N
	8:00PM		☐Y ☐N
	8:30PM		☐Y ☐N
	9:00PM		☐Y ☐N
	9:30PM		☐Y ☐N

HEALTH + FITNESS

WATER INTAKE

OZ. OZ. OZ. OZ. OZ.
OZ. OZ. OZ. OZ. OZ.

TAKE 5 MINUTES EACH MORNING TO PLAN YOUR DAY.

GET EIGHT HOURS OF SLEEP!

NOTE HIGH PRIORITY TASKS WITH A *

ANALYZE WHY A TASK WAS NOT COMPLETED, THEN MOVE TO NEXT DAY.

ONE POSITIVE

TODAY I GAVE

DAILY
GOAL SLAYERS
PLANNER

SETTING YOURSELF UP FOR SUCCESS DAILY!

DATE

_____ / _____ / _____

SCRIPTURE

MOTIVATIONAL QUOTE

ONE GOAL

ONE FUN THING

HEALTH • FITNESS

WATER INTAKE

OZ. OZ. OZ. OZ. OZ.

OZ. OZ. OZ. OZ. OZ.

✱	IMPORTANT TIME	SCHEDULE	SLAYED?
	5:00AM		☐Y ☐N
	5:30AM		☐Y ☐N
	6:00AM		☐Y ☐N
	6:30AM		☐Y ☐N
	7:00AM		☐Y ☐N
	7:30AM		☐Y ☐N
	8:00AM		☐Y ☐N
	8:30AM		☐Y ☐N
	9:00AM		☐Y ☐N
	9:30AM		☐Y ☐N
	10:00AM		☐Y ☐N
	10:30AM		☐Y ☐N
	11:00AM		☐Y ☐N
	11:30AM		☐Y ☐N
	12:00PM		☐Y ☐N
	12:30PM		☐Y ☐N
	1:00PM		☐Y ☐N
	1:30PM		☐Y ☐N
	2:00PM		☐Y ☐N
	2:30PM		☐Y ☐N
	3:00PM		☐Y ☐N
	3:30PM		☐Y ☐N
	4:00PM		☐Y ☐N
	4:30PM		☐Y ☐N
	5:00PM		☐Y ☐N
	5:30PM		☐Y ☐N
	6:00PM		☐Y ☐N
	6:30PM		☐Y ☐N
	7:00PM		☐Y ☐N
	7:30PM		☐Y ☐N
	8:00PM		☐Y ☐N
	8:30PM		☐Y ☐N
	9:00PM		☐Y ☐N
	9:30PM		☐Y ☐N

TAKE 5 MINUTES EACH MORNING TO PLAN YOUR DAY.

GET EIGHT HOURS OF SLEEP!

NOTE HIGH PRIORITY TASKS WITH A ✱

ANALYZE WHY A TASK WAS NOT COMPLETED, THEN MOVE TO NEXT DAY.

ONE POSITIVE

TODAY I GAVE

DAILY
GOAL SLAYERS
PLANNER

SETTING YOURSELF UP FOR SUCCESS DAILY!

DATE

_____ / _____ / _____

SCRIPTURE

MOTIVATIONAL QUOTE

ONE GOAL

ONE FUN THING

HEALTH + FITNESS

WATER INTAKE

✳	IMPORTANT TIME	SCHEDULE	SLAYED?
	5:00AM		☐Y ☐N
	5:30AM		☐Y ☐N
	6:00AM		☐Y ☐N
	6:30AM		☐Y ☐N
	7:00AM		☐Y ☐N
	7:30AM		☐Y ☐N
	8:00AM		☐Y ☐N
	8:30AM		☐Y ☐N
	9:00AM		☐Y ☐N
	9:30AM		☐Y ☐N
	10:00AM		☐Y ☐N
	10:30AM		☐Y ☐N
	11:00AM		☐Y ☐N
	11:30AM		☐Y ☐N
	12:00PM		☐Y ☐N
	12:30PM		☐Y ☐N
	1:00PM		☐Y ☐N
	1:30PM		☐Y ☐N
	2:00PM		☐Y ☐N
	2:30PM		☐Y ☐N
	3:00PM		☐Y ☐N
	3:30PM		☐Y ☐N
	4:00PM		☐Y ☐N
	4:30PM		☐Y ☐N
	5:00PM		☐Y ☐N
	5:30PM		☐Y ☐N
	6:00PM		☐Y ☐N
	6:30PM		☐Y ☐N
	7:00PM		☐Y ☐N
	7:30PM		☐Y ☐N
	8:00PM		☐Y ☐N
	8:30PM		☐Y ☐N
	9:00PM		☐Y ☐N
	9:30PM		☐Y ☐N

TAKE 5 MINUTES EACH MORNING TO PLAN YOUR DAY.

GET EIGHT HOURS OF SLEEP!

NOTE HIGH PRIORITY TASKS WITH A ✳

ANALYZE WHY A TASK WAS NOT COMPLETED, THEN MOVE TO NEXT DAY.

ONE POSITIVE

TODAY I GAVE

DAILY
GOAL SLAYERS
PLANNER

SETTING YOURSELF UP FOR SUCCESS DAILY!

DATE

____ / ____ / ____

SCRIPTURE

MOTIVATIONAL QUOTE

ONE GOAL

ONE FUN THING

*	IMPORTANT TIME	SCHEDULE	SLAYED?
	5:00AM		☐Y ☐N
	5:30AM		☐Y ☐N
	6:00AM		☐Y ☐N
	6:30AM		☐Y ☐N
	7:00AM		☐Y ☐N
	7:30AM		☐Y ☐N
	8:00AM		☐Y ☐N
	8:30AM		☐Y ☐N
	9:00AM		☐Y ☐N
	9:30AM		☐Y ☐N
	10:00AM		☐Y ☐N
	10:30AM		☐Y ☐N
	11:00AM		☐Y ☐N
	11:30AM		☐Y ☐N
	12:00PM		☐Y ☐N
	12:30PM		☐Y ☐N
	1:00PM		☐Y ☐N
	1:30PM		☐Y ☐N
	2:00PM		☐Y ☐N
	2:30PM		☐Y ☐N
	3:00PM		☐Y ☐N
	3:30PM		☐Y ☐N
	4:00PM		☐Y ☐N
	4:30PM		☐Y ☐N
	5:00PM		☐Y ☐N
	5:30PM		☐Y ☐N
	6:00PM		☐Y ☐N
	6:30PM		☐Y ☐N
	7:00PM		☐Y ☐N
	7:30PM		☐Y ☐N
	8:00PM		☐Y ☐N
	8:30PM		☐Y ☐N
	9:00PM		☐Y ☐N
	9:30PM		☐Y ☐N

HEALTH • FITNESS

WATER INTAKE

OZ OZ OZ OZ OZ
OZ OZ OZ OZ OZ

TAKE 5 MINUTES EACH MORNING TO PLAN YOUR DAY.

GET EIGHT HOURS OF SLEEP!

NOTE HIGH PRIORITY TASKS WITH A *

ANALYZE WHY A TASK WAS NOT COMPLETED, THEN MOVE TO NEXT DAY.

ONE POSITIVE

TODAY I GAVE

DAILY
GOAL SLAYERS
PLANNER

SETTING YOURSELF UP FOR SUCCESS DAILY!

DATE

_____ / _____ / _____

SCRIPTURE

MOTIVATIONAL QUOTE

ONE GOAL

ONE FUN THING

HEALTH + FITNESS

WATER INTAKE

OZ. OZ. OZ. OZ. OZ.

OZ. OZ. OZ. OZ. OZ.

✱	IMPORTANT TIME	SCHEDULE	SLAYED?
	5:00AM		☐Y ☐N
	5:30AM		☐Y ☐N
	6:00AM		☐Y ☐N
	6:30AM		☐Y ☐N
	7:00AM		☐Y ☐N
	7:30AM		☐Y ☐N
	8:00AM		☐Y ☐N
	8:30AM		☐Y ☐N
	9:00AM		☐Y ☐N
	9:30AM		☐Y ☐N
	10:00AM		☐Y ☐N
	10:30AM		☐Y ☐N
	11:00AM		☐Y ☐N
	11:30AM		☐Y ☐N
	12:00PM		☐Y ☐N
	12:30PM		☐Y ☐N
	1:00PM		☐Y ☐N
	1:30PM		☐Y ☐N
	2:00PM		☐Y ☐N
	2:30PM		☐Y ☐N
	3:00PM		☐Y ☐N
	3:30PM		☐Y ☐N
	4:00PM		☐Y ☐N
	4:30PM		☐Y ☐N
	5:00PM		☐Y ☐N
	5:30PM		☐Y ☐N
	6:00PM		☐Y ☐N
	6:30PM		☐Y ☐N
	7:00PM		☐Y ☐N
	7:30PM		☐Y ☐N
	8:00PM		☐Y ☐N
	8:30PM		☐Y ☐N
	9:00PM		☐Y ☐N
	9:30PM		☐Y ☐N

TAKE 5 MINUTES EACH MORNING TO PLAN YOUR DAY.

GET EIGHT HOURS OF SLEEP!

NOTE HIGH PRIORITY TASKS WITH A ✱

ANALYZE WHY A TASK WAS NOT COMPLETED, THEN MOVE TO NEXT DAY.

ONE POSITIVE

TODAY I GAVE

DAILY
GOAL SLAYERS
PLANNER

SETTING YOURSELF UP FOR SUCCESS DAILY!

DATE
_____/_____/_____

SCRIPTURE

MOTIVATIONAL QUOTE

ONE GOAL

ONE FUN THING

HEALTH • FITNESS

WATER INTAKE

OZ OZ OZ OZ OZ

OZ OZ OZ OZ OZ

*	IMPORTANT TIME	SCHEDULE	SLAYED?
	5:00AM		☐Y ☐N
	5:30AM		☐Y ☐N
	6:00AM		☐Y ☐N
	6:30AM		☐Y ☐N
	7:00AM		☐Y ☐N
	7:30AM		☐Y ☐N
	8:00AM		☐Y ☐N
	8:30AM		☐Y ☐N
	9:00AM		☐Y ☐N
	9:30AM		☐Y ☐N
	10:00AM		☐Y ☐N
	10:30AM		☐Y ☐N
	11:00AM		☐Y ☐N
	11:30AM		☐Y ☐N
	12:00PM		☐Y ☐N
	12:30PM		☐Y ☐N
	1:00PM		☐Y ☐N
	1:30PM		☐Y ☐N
	2:00PM		☐Y ☐N
	2:30PM		☐Y ☐N
	3:00PM		☐Y ☐N
	3:30PM		☐Y ☐N
	4:00PM		☐Y ☐N
	4:30PM		☐Y ☐N
	5:00PM		☐Y ☐N
	5:30PM		☐Y ☐N
	6:00PM		☐Y ☐N
	6:30PM		☐Y ☐N
	7:00PM		☐Y ☐N
	7:30PM		☐Y ☐N
	8:00PM		☐Y ☐N
	8:30PM		☐Y ☐N
	9:00PM		☐Y ☐N
	9:30PM		☐Y ☐N

TAKE 5 MINUTES EACH MORNING TO PLAN YOUR DAY.

GET EIGHT HOURS OF SLEEP!

NOTE HIGH PRIORITY TASKS WITH A *

ANALYZE WHY A TASK WAS NOT COMPLETED, THEN MOVE TO NEXT DAY.

ONE POSITIVE

TODAY I GAVE

DAILY
GOAL SLAYERS
PLANNER

SETTING YOURSELF UP FOR SUCCESS DAILY!

DATE
____/____/____

SCRIPTURE

MOTIVATIONAL QUOTE

ONE GOAL

ONE FUN THING

HEALTH + FITNESS

WATER INTAKE

OZ. OZ. OZ. OZ. OZ.

OZ. OZ. OZ. OZ. OZ.

✱	IMPORTANT TIME	SCHEDULE	SLAYED?
	5:00AM		☐Y ☐N
	5:30AM		☐Y ☐N
	6:00AM		☐Y ☐N
	6:30AM		☐Y ☐N
	7:00AM		☐Y ☐N
	7:30AM		☐Y ☐N
	8:00AM		☐Y ☐N
	8:30AM		☐Y ☐N
	9:00AM		☐Y ☐N
	9:30AM		☐Y ☐N
	10:00AM		☐Y ☐N
	10:30AM		☐Y ☐N
	11:00AM		☐Y ☐N
	11:30AM		☐Y ☐N
	12:00PM		☐Y ☐N
	12:30PM		☐Y ☐N
	1:00PM		☐Y ☐N
	1:30PM		☐Y ☐N
	2:00PM		☐Y ☐N
	2:30PM		☐Y ☐N
	3:00PM		☐Y ☐N
	3:30PM		☐Y ☐N
	4:00PM		☐Y ☐N
	4:30PM		☐Y ☐N
	5:00PM		☐Y ☐N
	5:30PM		☐Y ☐N
	6:00PM		☐Y ☐N
	6:30PM		☐Y ☐N
	7:00PM		☐Y ☐N
	7:30PM		☐Y ☐N
	8:00PM		☐Y ☐N
	8:30PM		☐Y ☐N
	9:00PM		☐Y ☐N
	9:30PM		☐Y ☐N

TAKE 5 MINUTES EACH MORNING TO PLAN YOUR DAY.

GET EIGHT HOURS OF SLEEP!

NOTE HIGH PRIORITY TASKS WITH A ✱

ANALYZE WHY A TASK WAS NOT COMPLETED, THEN MOVE TO NEXT DAY.

ONE POSITIVE

TODAY I GAVE

DAILY GOAL SLAYERS PLANNER

SETTING YOURSELF UP FOR SUCCESS DAILY!

DATE

____ / ____ / ____

SCRIPTURE

MOTIVATIONAL QUOTE

ONE GOAL

ONE FUN THING

*	IMPORTANT TIME	SCHEDULE	SLAYED?
	5:00AM		☐Y ☐N
	5:30AM		☐Y ☐N
	6:00AM		☐Y ☐N
	6:30AM		☐Y ☐N
	7:00AM		☐Y ☐N
	7:30AM		☐Y ☐N
	8:00AM		☐Y ☐N
	8:30AM		☐Y ☐N
	9:00AM		☐Y ☐N
	9:30AM		☐Y ☐N
	10:00AM		☐Y ☐N
	10:30AM		☐Y ☐N
	11:00AM		☐Y ☐N
	11:30AM		☐Y ☐N
	12:00PM		☐Y ☐N
	12:30PM		☐Y ☐N
	1:00PM		☐Y ☐N
	1:30PM		☐Y ☐N
	2:00PM		☐Y ☐N
	2:30PM		☐Y ☐N
	3:00PM		☐Y ☐N
	3:30PM		☐Y ☐N
	4:00PM		☐Y ☐N
	4:30PM		☐Y ☐N
	5:00PM		☐Y ☐N
	5:30PM		☐Y ☐N
	6:00PM		☐Y ☐N
	6:30PM		☐Y ☐N
	7:00PM		☐Y ☐N
	7:30PM		☐Y ☐N
	8:00PM		☐Y ☐N
	8:30PM		☐Y ☐N
	9:00PM		☐Y ☐N
	9:30PM		☐Y ☐N

HEALTH + FITNESS

WATER INTAKE

OZ. OZ. OZ. OZ. OZ.
OZ. OZ. OZ. OZ. OZ.

TAKE 5 MINUTES EACH MORNING TO PLAN YOUR DAY.

GET EIGHT HOURS OF SLEEP!

NOTE HIGH PRIORITY TASKS WITH A *

ANALYZE WHY A TASK WAS NOT COMPLETED, THEN MOVE TO NEXT DAY.

ONE POSITIVE

TODAY I GAVE

DAILY
GOAL SLAYERS
PLANNER

SETTING YOURSELF UP FOR SUCCESS DAILY!

DATE

_____ / _____ / _____

SCRIPTURE

MOTIVATIONAL QUOTE

ONE GOAL

ONE FUN THING

HEALTH + FITNESS

*	IMPORTANT TIME	SCHEDULE	SLAYED?
	5:00AM		☐Y ☐N
	5:30AM		☐Y ☐N
	6:00AM		☐Y ☐N
	6:30AM		☐Y ☐N
	7:00AM		☐Y ☐N
	7:30AM		☐Y ☐N
	8:00AM		☐Y ☐N
	8:30AM		☐Y ☐N
	9:00AM		☐Y ☐N
	9:30AM		☐Y ☐N
	10:00AM		☐Y ☐N
	10:30AM		☐Y ☐N
	11:00AM		☐Y ☐N
	11:30AM		☐Y ☐N
	12:00PM		☐Y ☐N
	12:30PM		☐Y ☐N
	1:00PM		☐Y ☐N
	1:30PM		☐Y ☐N
	2:00PM		☐Y ☐N
	2:30PM		☐Y ☐N
	3:00PM		☐Y ☐N
	3:30PM		☐Y ☐N
	4:00PM		☐Y ☐N
	4:30PM		☐Y ☐N
	5:00PM		☐Y ☐N
	5:30PM		☐Y ☐N
	6:00PM		☐Y ☐N
	6:30PM		☐Y ☐N
	7:00PM		☐Y ☐N
	7:30PM		☐Y ☐N
	8:00PM		☐Y ☐N
	8:30PM		☐Y ☐N
	9:00PM		☐Y ☐N
	9:30PM		☐Y ☐N

WATER INTAKE

OZ. OZ. OZ. OZ. OZ.
OZ. OZ. OZ. OZ. OZ.

TAKE 5 MINUTES EACH MORNING TO PLAN YOUR DAY.

GET EIGHT HOURS OF SLEEP!

NOTE HIGH PRIORITY TASKS WITH A *

ANALYZE WHY A TASK WAS NOT COMPLETED, THEN MOVE TO NEXT DAY.

ONE POSITIVE

TODAY I GAVE

DAILY
GOAL SLAYERS
PLANNER

SETTING YOURSELF UP FOR SUCCESS DAILY!

DATE

_____ / _____ / _____

SCRIPTURE

MOTIVATIONAL QUOTE

ONE GOAL

ONE FUN THING

HEALTH · FITNESS

WATER INTAKE

OZ. OZ. OZ. OZ. OZ.

OZ. OZ. OZ. OZ. OZ.

*	IMPORTANT TIME	SCHEDULE	SLAYED?
	5:00AM		☐Y ☐N
	5:30AM		☐Y ☐N
	6:00AM		☐Y ☐N
	6:30AM		☐Y ☐N
	7:00AM		☐Y ☐N
	7:30AM		☐Y ☐N
	8:00AM		☐Y ☐N
	8:30AM		☐Y ☐N
	9:00AM		☐Y ☐N
	9:30AM		☐Y ☐N
	10:00AM		☐Y ☐N
	10:30AM		☐Y ☐N
	11:00AM		☐Y ☐N
	11:30AM		☐Y ☐N
	12:00PM		☐Y ☐N
	12:30PM		☐Y ☐N
	1:00PM		☐Y ☐N
	1:30PM		☐Y ☐N
	2:00PM		☐Y ☐N
	2:30PM		☐Y ☐N
	3:00PM		☐Y ☐N
	3:30PM		☐Y ☐N
	4:00PM		☐Y ☐N
	4:30PM		☐Y ☐N
	5:00PM		☐Y ☐N
	5:30PM		☐Y ☐N
	6:00PM		☐Y ☐N
	6:30PM		☐Y ☐N
	7:00PM		☐Y ☐N
	7:30PM		☐Y ☐N
	8:00PM		☐Y ☐N
	8:30PM		☐Y ☐N
	9:00PM		☐Y ☐N
	9:30PM		☐Y ☐N

TAKE 5 MINUTES EACH MORNING TO PLAN YOUR DAY.

GET EIGHT HOURS OF SLEEP!

NOTE HIGH PRIORITY TASKS WITH A *

ANALYZE WHY A TASK WAS NOT COMPLETED, THEN MOVE TO NEXT DAY.

ONE POSITIVE

TODAY I GAVE

DAILY
GOAL SLAYERS
PLANNER

SETTING YOURSELF UP FOR SUCCESS DAILY!

DATE

_____ / _____ / _____

SCRIPTURE

MOTIVATIONAL QUOTE

ONE GOAL

ONE FUN THING

HEALTH + FITNESS

WATER INTAKE

OZ OZ OZ OZ OZ

OZ OZ OZ OZ OZ

*	IMPORTANT TIME	SCHEDULE	SLAYED?
	5:00AM		☐Y ☐N
	5:30AM		☐Y ☐N
	6:00AM		☐Y ☐N
	6:30AM		☐Y ☐N
	7:00AM		☐Y ☐N
	7:30AM		☐Y ☐N
	8:00AM		☐Y ☐N
	8:30AM		☐Y ☐N
	9:00AM		☐Y ☐N
	9:30AM		☐Y ☐N
	10:00AM		☐Y ☐N
	10:30AM		☐Y ☐N
	11:00AM		☐Y ☐N
	11:30AM		☐Y ☐N
	12:00PM		☐Y ☐N
	12:30PM		☐Y ☐N
	1:00PM		☐Y ☐N
	1:30PM		☐Y ☐N
	2:00PM		☐Y ☐N
	2:30PM		☐Y ☐N
	3:00PM		☐Y ☐N
	3:30PM		☐Y ☐N
	4:00PM		☐Y ☐N
	4:30PM		☐Y ☐N
	5:00PM		☐Y ☐N
	5:30PM		☐Y ☐N
	6:00PM		☐Y ☐N
	6:30PM		☐Y ☐N
	7:00PM		☐Y ☐N
	7:30PM		☐Y ☐N
	8:00PM		☐Y ☐N
	8:30PM		☐Y ☐N
	9:00PM		☐Y ☐N
	9:30PM		☐Y ☐N

TAKE 5 MINUTES EACH MORNING TO PLAN YOUR DAY.

GET EIGHT HOURS OF SLEEP!

NOTE HIGH PRIORITY TASKS WITH A *

ANALYZE WHY A TASK WAS NOT COMPLETED, THEN MOVE TO NEXT DAY.

ONE POSITIVE

TODAY I GAVE

DAILY
GOAL SLAYERS
PLANNER

SETTING YOURSELF UP FOR SUCCESS DAILY!

DATE

_____ / _____ / _____

SCRIPTURE

MOTIVATIONAL QUOTE

ONE GOAL

ONE FUN THING

✱	IMPORTANT TIME	SCHEDULE	SLAYED?
	5:00AM		☐Y ☐N
	5:30AM		☐Y ☐N
	6:00AM		☐Y ☐N
	6:30AM		☐Y ☐N
	7:00AM		☐Y ☐N
	7:30AM		☐Y ☐N
	8:00AM		☐Y ☐N
	8:30AM		☐Y ☐N
	9:00AM		☐Y ☐N
	9:30AM		☐Y ☐N
	10:00AM		☐Y ☐N
	10:30AM		☐Y ☐N
	11:00AM		☐Y ☐N
	11:30AM		☐Y ☐N
	12:00PM		☐Y ☐N
	12:30PM		☐Y ☐N
	1:00PM		☐Y ☐N
	1:30PM		☐Y ☐N
	2:00PM		☐Y ☐N
	2:30PM		☐Y ☐N
	3:00PM		☐Y ☐N
	3:30PM		☐Y ☐N
	4:00PM		☐Y ☐N
	4:30PM		☐Y ☐N
	5:00PM		☐Y ☐N
	5:30PM		☐Y ☐N
	6:00PM		☐Y ☐N
	6:30PM		☐Y ☐N
	7:00PM		☐Y ☐N
	7:30PM		☐Y ☐N
	8:00PM		☐Y ☐N
	8:30PM		☐Y ☐N
	9:00PM		☐Y ☐N
	9:30PM		☐Y ☐N

HEALTH + FITNESS

WATER INTAKE

OZ. OZ. OZ. OZ. OZ.
OZ. OZ. OZ. OZ. OZ.

TAKE 5 MINUTES EACH MORNING TO PLAN YOUR DAY.

GET EIGHT HOURS OF SLEEP!

NOTE HIGH PRIORITY TASKS WITH A ✱

ANALYZE WHY A TASK WAS NOT COMPLETED, THEN MOVE TO NEXT DAY.

ONE POSITIVE

TODAY I GAVE

DAILY
GOAL SLAYERS
PLANNER

SETTING YOURSELF UP FOR SUCCESS DAILY!

DATE

_____ / _____ / _____

SCRIPTURE

MOTIVATIONAL QUOTE

ONE GOAL

ONE FUN THING

HEALTH + FITNESS

WATER INTAKE

*	IMPORTANT TIME	SCHEDULE	SLAYED?
	5:00AM		☐Y ☐N
	5:30AM		☐Y ☐N
	6:00AM		☐Y ☐N
	6:30AM		☐Y ☐N
	7:00AM		☐Y ☐N
	7:30AM		☐Y ☐N
	8:00AM		☐Y ☐N
	8:30AM		☐Y ☐N
	9:00AM		☐Y ☐N
	9:30AM		☐Y ☐N
	10:00AM		☐Y ☐N
	10:30AM		☐Y ☐N
	11:00AM		☐Y ☐N
	11:30AM		☐Y ☐N
	12:00PM		☐Y ☐N
	12:30PM		☐Y ☐N
	1:00PM		☐Y ☐N
	1:30PM		☐Y ☐N
	2:00PM		☐Y ☐N
	2:30PM		☐Y ☐N
	3:00PM		☐Y ☐N
	3:30PM		☐Y ☐N
	4:00PM		☐Y ☐N
	4:30PM		☐Y ☐N
	5:00PM		☐Y ☐N
	5:30PM		☐Y ☐N
	6:00PM		☐Y ☐N
	6:30PM		☐Y ☐N
	7:00PM		☐Y ☐N
	7:30PM		☐Y ☐N
	8:00PM		☐Y ☐N
	8:30PM		☐Y ☐N
	9:00PM		☐Y ☐N
	9:30PM		☐Y ☐N

OZ. OZ. OZ. OZ. OZ.
OZ. OZ. OZ. OZ. OZ.

TAKE 5 MINUTES EACH MORNING TO PLAN YOUR DAY.

GET EIGHT HOURS OF SLEEP!

NOTE HIGH PRIORITY TASKS WITH A *

ANALYZE WHY A TASK WAS NOT COMPLETED, THEN MOVE TO NEXT DAY.

ONE POSITIVE

TODAY I GAVE

DAILY
GOAL SLAYERS
PLANNER

SETTING YOURSELF UP FOR SUCCESS DAILY!

DATE

_____ / _____ / _____

SCRIPTURE

MOTIVATIONAL QUOTE

ONE GOAL

ONE FUN THING

*	IMPORTANT TIME	SCHEDULE	SLAYED?
	5:00AM		☐Y ☐N
	5:30AM		☐Y ☐N
	6:00AM		☐Y ☐N
	6:30AM		☐Y ☐N
	7:00AM		☐Y ☐N
	7:30AM		☐Y ☐N
	8:00AM		☐Y ☐N
	8:30AM		☐Y ☐N
	9:00AM		☐Y ☐N
	9:30AM		☐Y ☐N
	10:00AM		☐Y ☐N
	10:30AM		☐Y ☐N
	11:00AM		☐Y ☐N
	11:30AM		☐Y ☐N
	12:00PM		☐Y ☐N
	12:30PM		☐Y ☐N
	1:00PM		☐Y ☐N
	1:30PM		☐Y ☐N
	2:00PM		☐Y ☐N
	2:30PM		☐Y ☐N
	3:00PM		☐Y ☐N
	3:30PM		☐Y ☐N
	4:00PM		☐Y ☐N
	4:30PM		☐Y ☐N
	5:00PM		☐Y ☐N
	5:30PM		☐Y ☐N
	6:00PM		☐Y ☐N
	6:30PM		☐Y ☐N
	7:00PM		☐Y ☐N
	7:30PM		☐Y ☐N
	8:00PM		☐Y ☐N
	8:30PM		☐Y ☐N
	9:00PM		☐Y ☐N
	9:30PM		☐Y ☐N

HEALTH • FITNESS

WATER INTAKE

OZ. OZ. OZ. OZ. OZ.
OZ. OZ. OZ. OZ. OZ.

TAKE 5 MINUTES EACH MORNING TO PLAN YOUR DAY.

GET EIGHT HOURS OF SLEEP!

NOTE HIGH PRIORITY TASKS WITH A *

ANALYZE WHY A TASK WAS NOT COMPLETED, THEN MOVE TO NEXT DAY.

ONE POSITIVE

TODAY I GAVE

DAILY
GOAL SLAYERS
PLANNER

SETTING YOURSELF UP FOR SUCCESS DAILY!

DATE

_____ / _____ / _____

SCRIPTURE

MOTIVATIONAL QUOTE

ONE GOAL

ONE FUN THING

✱	IMPORTANT TIME	SCHEDULE	SLAYED?
	5:00AM		☐Y ☐N
	5:30AM		☐Y ☐N
	6:00AM		☐Y ☐N
	6:30AM		☐Y ☐N
	7:00AM		☐Y ☐N
	7:30AM		☐Y ☐N
	8:00AM		☐Y ☐N
	8:30AM		☐Y ☐N
	9:00AM		☐Y ☐N
	9:30AM		☐Y ☐N
	10:00AM		☐Y ☐N
	10:30AM		☐Y ☐N
	11:00AM		☐Y ☐N
	11:30AM		☐Y ☐N
	12:00PM		☐Y ☐N
	12:30PM		☐Y ☐N
	1:00PM		☐Y ☐N
	1:30PM		☐Y ☐N
	2:00PM		☐Y ☐N
	2:30PM		☐Y ☐N
	3:00PM		☐Y ☐N
	3:30PM		☐Y ☐N
	4:00PM		☐Y ☐N
	4:30PM		☐Y ☐N
	5:00PM		☐Y ☐N
	5:30PM		☐Y ☐N
	6:00PM		☐Y ☐N
	6:30PM		☐Y ☐N
	7:00PM		☐Y ☐N
	7:30PM		☐Y ☐N
	8:00PM		☐Y ☐N
	8:30PM		☐Y ☐N
	9:00PM		☐Y ☐N
	9:30PM		☐Y ☐N

HEALTH + FITNESS

WATER INTAKE

OZ OZ OZ OZ OZ
OZ OZ OZ OZ OZ

TAKE 5 MINUTES EACH MORNING TO PLAN YOUR DAY.

GET EIGHT HOURS OF SLEEP!

NOTE HIGH PRIORITY TASKS WITH A ✱

ANALYZE WHY A TASK WAS NOT COMPLETED, THEN MOVE TO NEXT DAY.

ONE POSITIVE

TODAY I GAVE

DAILY
GOAL SLAYERS
PLANNER

SETTING YOURSELF UP FOR SUCCESS DAILY!

DATE

_____ / _____ / _____

SCRIPTURE

MOTIVATIONAL QUOTE

ONE GOAL

ONE FUN THING

*	IMPORTANT TIME	SCHEDULE	SLAYED?
	5:00AM		☐Y ☐N
	5:30AM		☐Y ☐N
	6:00AM		☐Y ☐N
	6:30AM		☐Y ☐N
	7:00AM		☐Y ☐N
	7:30AM		☐Y ☐N
	8:00AM		☐Y ☐N
	8:30AM		☐Y ☐N
	9:00AM		☐Y ☐N
	9:30AM		☐Y ☐N
	10:00AM		☐Y ☐N
	10:30AM		☐Y ☐N
	11:00AM		☐Y ☐N
	11:30AM		☐Y ☐N
	12:00PM		☐Y ☐N
	12:30PM		☐Y ☐N
	1:00PM		☐Y ☐N
	1:30PM		☐Y ☐N
	2:00PM		☐Y ☐N
	2:30PM		☐Y ☐N
	3:00PM		☐Y ☐N
	3:30PM		☐Y ☐N
	4:00PM		☐Y ☐N
	4:30PM		☐Y ☐N
	5:00PM		☐Y ☐N
	5:30PM		☐Y ☐N
	6:00PM		☐Y ☐N
	6:30PM		☐Y ☐N
	7:00PM		☐Y ☐N
	7:30PM		☐Y ☐N
	8:00PM		☐Y ☐N
	8:30PM		☐Y ☐N
	9:00PM		☐Y ☐N
	9:30PM		☐Y ☐N

HEALTH • FITNESS

WATER INTAKE

OZ OZ OZ OZ OZ
OZ OZ OZ OZ OZ

TAKE 5 MINUTES EACH MORNING TO PLAN YOUR DAY.

GET EIGHT HOURS OF SLEEP!

NOTE HIGH PRIORITY TASKS WITH A *

ANALYZE WHY A TASK WAS NOT COMPLETED, THEN MOVE TO NEXT DAY.

ONE POSITIVE

TODAY I GAVE

DAILY
GOAL SLAYERS
PLANNER

SETTING YOURSELF UP FOR SUCCESS DAILY!

DATE

_____ / _____ / _____

SCRIPTURE

MOTIVATIONAL QUOTE

ONE GOAL

ONE FUN THING

*	IMPORTANT TIME	SCHEDULE	SLAYED?
	5:00AM		□Y □N
	5:30AM		□Y □N
	6:00AM		□Y □N
	6:30AM		□Y □N
	7:00AM		□Y □N
	7:30AM		□Y □N
	8:00AM		□Y □N
	8:30AM		□Y □N
	9:00AM		□Y □N
	9:30AM		□Y □N
	10:00AM		□Y □N
	10:30AM		□Y □N
	11:00AM		□Y □N
	11:30AM		□Y □N
	12:00PM		□Y □N
	12:30PM		□Y □N
	1:00PM		□Y □N
	1:30PM		□Y □N
	2:00PM		□Y □N
	2:30PM		□Y □N
	3:00PM		□Y □N
	3:30PM		□Y □N
	4:00PM		□Y □N
	4:30PM		□Y □N
	5:00PM		□Y □N
	5:30PM		□Y □N
	6:00PM		□Y □N
	6:30PM		□Y □N
	7:00PM		□Y □N
	7:30PM		□Y □N
	8:00PM		□Y □N
	8:30PM		□Y □N
	9:00PM		□Y □N
	9:30PM		□Y □N

HEALTH + FITNESS

WATER INTAKE

OZ. OZ. OZ. OZ. OZ.
OZ. OZ. OZ. OZ. OZ.

TAKE 5 MINUTES EACH MORNING TO PLAN YOUR DAY.

GET EIGHT HOURS OF SLEEP!

NOTE HIGH PRIORITY TASKS WITH A *

ANALYZE WHY A TASK WAS NOT COMPLETED, THEN MOVE TO NEXT DAY.

ONE POSITIVE

TODAY I GAVE

DAILY
GOAL SLAYERS
PLANNER

SETTING YOURSELF UP FOR SUCCESS DAILY!

DATE

_____ / _____ / _____

SCRIPTURE

MOTIVATIONAL QUOTE

ONE GOAL

ONE FUN THING

✳	IMPORTANT TIME	SCHEDULE	SLAYED?
	5:00AM		☐Y ☐N
	5:30AM		☐Y ☐N
	6:00AM		☐Y ☐N
	6:30AM		☐Y ☐N
	7:00AM		☐Y ☐N
	7:30AM		☐Y ☐N
	8:00AM		☐Y ☐N
	8:30AM		☐Y ☐N
	9:00AM		☐Y ☐N
	9:30AM		☐Y ☐N
	10:00AM		☐Y ☐N
	10:30AM		☐Y ☐N
	11:00AM		☐Y ☐N
	11:30AM		☐Y ☐N
	12:00PM		☐Y ☐N
	12:30PM		☐Y ☐N
	1:00PM		☐Y ☐N
	1:30PM		☐Y ☐N
	2:00PM		☐Y ☐N
	2:30PM		☐Y ☐N
	3:00PM		☐Y ☐N
	3:30PM		☐Y ☐N
	4:00PM		☐Y ☐N
	4:30PM		☐Y ☐N
	5:00PM		☐Y ☐N
	5:30PM		☐Y ☐N
	6:00PM		☐Y ☐N
	6:30PM		☐Y ☐N
	7:00PM		☐Y ☐N
	7:30PM		☐Y ☐N
	8:00PM		☐Y ☐N
	8:30PM		☐Y ☐N
	9:00PM		☐Y ☐N
	9:30PM		☐Y ☐N

HEALTH • FITNESS

WATER INTAKE

OZ. OZ. OZ. OZ. OZ.

OZ. OZ. OZ. OZ. OZ.

TAKE 5 MINUTES EACH MORNING TO PLAN YOUR DAY.

GET EIGHT HOURS OF SLEEP!

NOTE HIGH PRIORITY TASKS WITH A ✳

ANALYZE WHY A TASK WAS NOT COMPLETED, THEN MOVE TO NEXT DAY.

ONE POSITIVE

TODAY I GAVE

DAILY
GOAL SLAYERS
PLANNER

SETTING YOURSELF UP FOR SUCCESS DAILY!

DATE

_____ / _____ / _____

SCRIPTURE

MOTIVATIONAL QUOTE

ONE GOAL

ONE FUN THING

✱	IMPORTANT TIME	SCHEDULE	SLAYED?
	5:00AM		☐Y ☐N
	5:30AM		☐Y ☐N
	6:00AM		☐Y ☐N
	6:30AM		☐Y ☐N
	7:00AM		☐Y ☐N
	7:30AM		☐Y ☐N
	8:00AM		☐Y ☐N
	8:30AM		☐Y ☐N
	9:00AM		☐Y ☐N
	9:30AM		☐Y ☐N
	10:00AM		☐Y ☐N
	10:30AM		☐Y ☐N
	11:00AM		☐Y ☐N
	11:30AM		☐Y ☐N
	12:00PM		☐Y ☐N
	12:30PM		☐Y ☐N
	1:00PM		☐Y ☐N
	1:30PM		☐Y ☐N
	2:00PM		☐Y ☐N
	2:30PM		☐Y ☐N
	3:00PM		☐Y ☐N
	3:30PM		☐Y ☐N
	4:00PM		☐Y ☐N
	4:30PM		☐Y ☐N
	5:00PM		☐Y ☐N
	5:30PM		☐Y ☐N
	6:00PM		☐Y ☐N
	6:30PM		☐Y ☐N
	7:00PM		☐Y ☐N
	7:30PM		☐Y ☐N
	8:00PM		☐Y ☐N
	8:30PM		☐Y ☐N
	9:00PM		☐Y ☐N
	9:30PM		☐Y ☐N

HEALTH • FITNESS

WATER INTAKE

OZ. OZ. OZ. OZ. OZ.
OZ. OZ. OZ. OZ. OZ.

TAKE 5 MINUTES EACH MORNING TO PLAN YOUR DAY.

GET EIGHT HOURS OF SLEEP!

NOTE HIGH PRIORITY TASKS WITH A ✱

ANALYZE WHY A TASK WAS NOT COMPLETED. THEN MOVE TO NEXT DAY.

ONE POSITIVE

TODAY I GAVE

DAILY
GOAL SLAYERS
PLANNER

SETTING YOURSELF UP FOR SUCCESS DAILY!

DATE

____ / ____ / ____

SCRIPTURE

MOTIVATIONAL QUOTE

ONE GOAL

ONE FUN THING

HEALTH + FITNESS

WATER INTAKE

*	IMPORTANT TIME	SCHEDULE	SLAYED?
	5:00AM		☐Y ☐N
	5:30AM		☐Y ☐N
	6:00AM		☐Y ☐N
	6:30AM		☐Y ☐N
	7:00AM		☐Y ☐N
	7:30AM		☐Y ☐N
	8:00AM		☐Y ☐N
	8:30AM		☐Y ☐N
	9:00AM		☐Y ☐N
	9:30AM		☐Y ☐N
	10:00AM		☐Y ☐N
	10:30AM		☐Y ☐N
	11:00AM		☐Y ☐N
	11:30AM		☐Y ☐N
	12:00PM		☐Y ☐N
	12:30PM		☐Y ☐N
	1:00PM		☐Y ☐N
	1:30PM		☐Y ☐N
	2:00PM		☐Y ☐N
	2:30PM		☐Y ☐N
	3:00PM		☐Y ☐N
	3:30PM		☐Y ☐N
	4:00PM		☐Y ☐N
	4:30PM		☐Y ☐N
	5:00PM		☐Y ☐N
	5:30PM		☐Y ☐N
	6:00PM		☐Y ☐N
	6:30PM		☐Y ☐N
	7:00PM		☐Y ☐N
	7:30PM		☐Y ☐N
	8:00PM		☐Y ☐N
	8:30PM		☐Y ☐N
	9:00PM		☐Y ☐N
	9:30PM		☐Y ☐N

TAKE 5 MINUTES EACH MORNING TO PLAN YOUR DAY.

GET EIGHT HOURS OF SLEEP!

NOTE HIGH PRIORITY TASKS WITH A *

ANALYZE WHY A TASK WAS NOT COMPLETED, THEN MOVE TO NEXT DAY.

ONE POSITIVE

TODAY I GAVE

DAILY
GOAL SLAYERS
PLANNER

SETTING YOURSELF UP FOR SUCCESS DAILY!

DATE

_____ / _____ / _____

SCRIPTURE

MOTIVATIONAL QUOTE

ONE GOAL

ONE FUN THING

✱	IMPORTANT TIME	SCHEDULE	SLAYED?
	5:00AM		☐Y ☐N
	5:30AM		☐Y ☐N
	6:00AM		☐Y ☐N
	6:30AM		☐Y ☐N
	7:00AM		☐Y ☐N
	7:30AM		☐Y ☐N
	8:00AM		☐Y ☐N
	8:30AM		☐Y ☐N
	9:00AM		☐Y ☐N
	9:30AM		☐Y ☐N
	10:00AM		☐Y ☐N
	10:30AM		☐Y ☐N
	11:00AM		☐Y ☐N
	11:30AM		☐Y ☐N
	12:00PM		☐Y ☐N
	12:30PM		☐Y ☐N
	1:00PM		☐Y ☐N
	1:30PM		☐Y ☐N
	2:00PM		☐Y ☐N
	2:30PM		☐Y ☐N
	3:00PM		☐Y ☐N
	3:30PM		☐Y ☐N
	4:00PM		☐Y ☐N
	4:30PM		☐Y ☐N
	5:00PM		☐Y ☐N
	5:30PM		☐Y ☐N
	6:00PM		☐Y ☐N
	6:30PM		☐Y ☐N
	7:00PM		☐Y ☐N
	7:30PM		☐Y ☐N
	8:00PM		☐Y ☐N
	8:30PM		☐Y ☐N
	9:00PM		☐Y ☐N
	9:30PM		☐Y ☐N

HEALTH • FITNESS

WATER INTAKE

OZ. OZ. OZ. OZ. OZ.
OZ. OZ. OZ. OZ. OZ.

TAKE 5 MINUTES EACH MORNING TO PLAN YOUR DAY.

GET EIGHT HOURS OF SLEEP!

NOTE HIGH PRIORITY TASKS WITH A ✱

ANALYZE WHY A TASK WAS NOT COMPLETED, THEN MOVE TO NEXT DAY.

ONE POSITIVE

TODAY I GAVE

DAILY
GOAL SLAYERS
PLANNER

SETTING YOURSELF UP FOR SUCCESS DAILY!

DATE

_____ / _____ / _____

SCRIPTURE

MOTIVATIONAL QUOTE

ONE GOAL

ONE FUN THING

HEALTH • FITNESS

WATER INTAKE

OZ. OZ. OZ. OZ. OZ.

OZ. OZ. OZ. OZ. OZ.

✱	IMPORTANT TIME	SCHEDULE	SLAYED?
	5:00AM		☐Y ☐N
	5:30AM		☐Y ☐N
	6:00AM		☐Y ☐N
	6:30AM		☐Y ☐N
	7:00AM		☐Y ☐N
	7:30AM		☐Y ☐N
	8:00AM		☐Y ☐N
	8:30AM		☐Y ☐N
	9:00AM		☐Y ☐N
	9:30AM		☐Y ☐N
	10:00AM		☐Y ☐N
	10:30AM		☐Y ☐N
	11:00AM		☐Y ☐N
	11:30AM		☐Y ☐N
	12:00PM		☐Y ☐N
	12:30PM		☐Y ☐N
	1:00PM		☐Y ☐N
	1:30PM		☐Y ☐N
	2:00PM		☐Y ☐N
	2:30PM		☐Y ☐N
	3:00PM		☐Y ☐N
	3:30PM		☐Y ☐N
	4:00PM		☐Y ☐N
	4:30PM		☐Y ☐N
	5:00PM		☐Y ☐N
	5:30PM		☐Y ☐N
	6:00PM		☐Y ☐N
	6:30PM		☐Y ☐N
	7:00PM		☐Y ☐N
	7:30PM		☐Y ☐N
	8:00PM		☐Y ☐N
	8:30PM		☐Y ☐N
	9:00PM		☐Y ☐N
	9:30PM		☐Y ☐N

TAKE 5 MINUTES EACH MORNING TO PLAN YOUR DAY.

GET EIGHT HOURS OF SLEEP!

NOTE HIGH PRIORITY TASKS WITH A ✱

ANALYZE WHY A TASK WAS NOT COMPLETED, THEN MOVE TO NEXT DAY.

ONE POSITIVE

TODAY I GAVE

DAILY
GOAL SLAYERS
PLANNER

SETTING YOURSELF UP FOR SUCCESS DAILY!

DATE
_____ / _____ / _____

SCRIPTURE

MOTIVATIONAL QUOTE

ONE GOAL

ONE FUN THING

HEALTH • FITNESS

WATER INTAKE

OZ. OZ. OZ. OZ. OZ.
OZ. OZ. OZ. OZ. OZ.

*	IMPORTANT TIME	SCHEDULE	SLAYED?
	5:00AM		☐Y ☐N
	5:30AM		☐Y ☐N
	6:00AM		☐Y ☐N
	6:30AM		☐Y ☐N
	7:00AM		☐Y ☐N
	7:30AM		☐Y ☐N
	8:00AM		☐Y ☐N
	8:30AM		☐Y ☐N
	9:00AM		☐Y ☐N
	9:30AM		☐Y ☐N
	10:00AM		☐Y ☐N
	10:30AM		☐Y ☐N
	11:00AM		☐Y ☐N
	11:30AM		☐Y ☐N
	12:00PM		☐Y ☐N
	12:30PM		☐Y ☐N
	1:00PM		☐Y ☐N
	1:30PM		☐Y ☐N
	2:00PM		☐Y ☐N
	2:30PM		☐Y ☐N
	3:00PM		☐Y ☐N
	3:30PM		☐Y ☐N
	4:00PM		☐Y ☐N
	4:30PM		☐Y ☐N
	5:00PM		☐Y ☐N
	5:30PM		☐Y ☐N
	6:00PM		☐Y ☐N
	6:30PM		☐Y ☐N
	7:00PM		☐Y ☐N
	7:30PM		☐Y ☐N
	8:00PM		☐Y ☐N
	8:30PM		☐Y ☐N
	9:00PM		☐Y ☐N
	9:30PM		☐Y ☐N

TAKE 5 MINUTES EACH MORNING TO PLAN YOUR DAY.

GET EIGHT HOURS OF SLEEP!

NOTE HIGH PRIORITY TASKS WITH A *

ANALYZE WHY A TASK WAS NOT COMPLETED, THEN MOVE TO NEXT DAY.

ONE POSITIVE

TODAY I GAVE

DAILY
GOAL SLAYERS
PLANNER

SETTING YOURSELF UP FOR SUCCESS DAILY!

DATE

_____ / _____ / _____

SCRIPTURE

MOTIVATIONAL QUOTE

ONE GOAL

ONE FUN THING

*	IMPORTANT TIME	SCHEDULE	SLAYED?
	5:00AM		☐Y ☐N
	5:30AM		☐Y ☐N
	6:00AM		☐Y ☐N
	6:30AM		☐Y ☐N
	7:00AM		☐Y ☐N
	7:30AM		☐Y ☐N
	8:00AM		☐Y ☐N
	8:30AM		☐Y ☐N
	9:00AM		☐Y ☐N
	9:30AM		☐Y ☐N
	10:00AM		☐Y ☐N
	10:30AM		☐Y ☐N
	11:00AM		☐Y ☐N
	11:30AM		☐Y ☐N
	12:00PM		☐Y ☐N
	12:30PM		☐Y ☐N
	1:00PM		☐Y ☐N
	1:30PM		☐Y ☐N
	2:00PM		☐Y ☐N
	2:30PM		☐Y ☐N
	3:00PM		☐Y ☐N
	3:30PM		☐Y ☐N
	4:00PM		☐Y ☐N
	4:30PM		☐Y ☐N
	5:00PM		☐Y ☐N
	5:30PM		☐Y ☐N
	6:00PM		☐Y ☐N
	6:30PM		☐Y ☐N
	7:00PM		☐Y ☐N
	7:30PM		☐Y ☐N
	8:00PM		☐Y ☐N
	8:30PM		☐Y ☐N
	9:00PM		☐Y ☐N
	9:30PM		☐Y ☐N

HEALTH + FITNESS

WATER INTAKE

OZ OZ OZ OZ OZ

OZ OZ OZ OZ OZ

TAKE 5 MINUTES EACH MORNING TO PLAN YOUR DAY.

GET EIGHT HOURS OF SLEEP!

NOTE HIGH PRIORITY TASKS WITH A *

ANALYZE WHY A TASK WAS NOT COMPLETED, THEN MOVE TO NEXT DAY.

ONE POSITIVE

TODAY I GAVE

DAILY
GOAL SLAYERS
PLANNER

SETTING YOURSELF UP FOR SUCCESS DAILY!

DATE

_____ / _____ / _____

SCRIPTURE

MOTIVATIONAL QUOTE

ONE GOAL

ONE FUN THING

✱	IMPORTANT TIME	SCHEDULE	SLAYED?
	5:00AM		☐Y ☐N
	5:30AM		☐Y ☐N
	6:00AM		☐Y ☐N
	6:30AM		☐Y ☐N
	7:00AM		☐Y ☐N
	7:30AM		☐Y ☐N
	8:00AM		☐Y ☐N
	8:30AM		☐Y ☐N
	9:00AM		☐Y ☐N
	9:30AM		☐Y ☐N
	10:00AM		☐Y ☐N
	10:30AM		☐Y ☐N
	11:00AM		☐Y ☐N
	11:30AM		☐Y ☐N
	12:00PM		☐Y ☐N
	12:30PM		☐Y ☐N
	1:00PM		☐Y ☐N
	1:30PM		☐Y ☐N
	2:00PM		☐Y ☐N
	2:30PM		☐Y ☐N
	3:00PM		☐Y ☐N
	3:30PM		☐Y ☐N
	4:00PM		☐Y ☐N
	4:30PM		☐Y ☐N
	5:00PM		☐Y ☐N
	5:30PM		☐Y ☐N
	6:00PM		☐Y ☐N
	6:30PM		☐Y ☐N
	7:00PM		☐Y ☐N
	7:30PM		☐Y ☐N
	8:00PM		☐Y ☐N
	8:30PM		☐Y ☐N
	9:00PM		☐Y ☐N
	9:30PM		☐Y ☐N

HEALTH • FITNESS

WATER INTAKE

OZ. OZ. OZ. OZ. OZ.

OZ. OZ. OZ. OZ. OZ.

TAKE 5 MINUTES EACH MORNING TO PLAN YOUR DAY.

GET EIGHT HOURS OF SLEEP!

NOTE HIGH PRIORITY TASKS WITH A ✱

ANALYZE WHY A TASK WAS NOT COMPLETED, THEN MOVE TO NEXT DAY.

ONE POSITIVE

TODAY I GAVE

DAILY
GOAL SLAYERS
PLANNER

SETTING YOURSELF UP FOR SUCCESS DAILY!

DATE

_____ / _____ / _____

SCRIPTURE

MOTIVATIONAL QUOTE

ONE GOAL

ONE FUN THING

HEALTH · FITNESS

WATER INTAKE

OZ. OZ. OZ. OZ. OZ.

OZ. OZ. OZ. OZ. OZ.

*	IMPORTANT TIME	SCHEDULE	SLAYED?
	5:00AM		☐ Y ☐ N
	5:30AM		☐ Y ☐ N
	6:00AM		☐ Y ☐ N
	6:30AM		☐ Y ☐ N
	7:00AM		☐ Y ☐ N
	7:30AM		☐ Y ☐ N
	8:00AM		☐ Y ☐ N
	8:30AM		☐ Y ☐ N
	9:00AM		☐ Y ☐ N
	9:30AM		☐ Y ☐ N
	10:00AM		☐ Y ☐ N
	10:30AM		☐ Y ☐ N
	11:00AM		☐ Y ☐ N
	11:30AM		☐ Y ☐ N
	12:00PM		☐ Y ☐ N
	12:30PM		☐ Y ☐ N
	1:00PM		☐ Y ☐ N
	1:30PM		☐ Y ☐ N
	2:00PM		☐ Y ☐ N
	2:30PM		☐ Y ☐ N
	3:00PM		☐ Y ☐ N
	3:30PM		☐ Y ☐ N
	4:00PM		☐ Y ☐ N
	4:30PM		☐ Y ☐ N
	5:00PM		☐ Y ☐ N
	5:30PM		☐ Y ☐ N
	6:00PM		☐ Y ☐ N
	6:30PM		☐ Y ☐ N
	7:00PM		☐ Y ☐ N
	7:30PM		☐ Y ☐ N
	8:00PM		☐ Y ☐ N
	8:30PM		☐ Y ☐ N
	9:00PM		☐ Y ☐ N
	9:30PM		☐ Y ☐ N

TAKE 5 MINUTES EACH MORNING TO PLAN YOUR DAY.

GET EIGHT HOURS OF SLEEP!

NOTE HIGH PRIORITY TASKS WITH A *

ANALYZE WHY A TASK WAS NOT COMPLETED, THEN MOVE TO NEXT DAY.

ONE POSITIVE

TODAY I GAVE

DAILY
GOAL SLAYERS
PLANNER

SETTING YOURSELF UP FOR SUCCESS DAILY!

DATE

_____ / _____ / _____

SCRIPTURE

MOTIVATIONAL QUOTE

ONE GOAL

ONE FUN THING

✱	IMPORTANT TIME	SCHEDULE	SLAYED?
	5:00AM		☐Y ☐N
	5:30AM		☐Y ☐N
	6:00AM		☐Y ☐N
	6:30AM		☐Y ☐N
	7:00AM		☐Y ☐N
	7:30AM		☐Y ☐N
	8:00AM		☐Y ☐N
	8:30AM		☐Y ☐N
	9:00AM		☐Y ☐N
	9:30AM		☐Y ☐N
	10:00AM		☐Y ☐N
	10:30AM		☐Y ☐N
	11:00AM		☐Y ☐N
	11:30AM		☐Y ☐N
	12:00PM		☐Y ☐N
	12:30PM		☐Y ☐N
	1:00PM		☐Y ☐N
	1:30PM		☐Y ☐N
	2:00PM		☐Y ☐N
	2:30PM		☐Y ☐N
	3:00PM		☐Y ☐N
	3:30PM		☐Y ☐N
	4:00PM		☐Y ☐N
	4:30PM		☐Y ☐N
	5:00PM		☐Y ☐N
	5:30PM		☐Y ☐N
	6:00PM		☐Y ☐N
	6:30PM		☐Y ☐N
	7:00PM		☐Y ☐N
	7:30PM		☐Y ☐N
	8:00PM		☐Y ☐N
	8:30PM		☐Y ☐N
	9:00PM		☐Y ☐N
	9:30PM		☐Y ☐N

HEALTH • FITNESS

WATER INTAKE

OZ OZ OZ OZ OZ
OZ OZ OZ OZ OZ

TAKE 5 MINUTES EACH MORNING TO PLAN YOUR DAY.

GET EIGHT HOURS OF SLEEP!

NOTE HIGH PRIORITY TASKS WITH A ✱

ANALYZE WHY A TASK WAS NOT COMPLETED, THEN MOVE TO NEXT DAY.

ONE POSITIVE

TODAY I GAVE

DAILY
GOAL SLAYERS
PLANNER

SETTING YOURSELF UP FOR SUCCESS DAILY!

DATE

____ / ____ / ____

SCRIPTURE

MOTIVATIONAL QUOTE

ONE GOAL

ONE FUN THING

HEALTH • FITNESS

WATER INTAKE

OZ OZ OZ OZ OZ

OZ OZ OZ OZ OZ

*	IMPORTANT TIME	SCHEDULE	SLAYED?
	5:00AM		☐Y ☐N
	5:30AM		☐Y ☐N
	6:00AM		☐Y ☐N
	6:30AM		☐Y ☐N
	7:00AM		☐Y ☐N
	7:30AM		☐Y ☐N
	8:00AM		☐Y ☐N
	8:30AM		☐Y ☐N
	9:00AM		☐Y ☐N
	9:30AM		☐Y ☐N
	10:00AM		☐Y ☐N
	10:30AM		☐Y ☐N
	11:00AM		☐Y ☐N
	11:30AM		☐Y ☐N
	12:00PM		☐Y ☐N
	12:30PM		☐Y ☐N
	1:00PM		☐Y ☐N
	1:30PM		☐Y ☐N
	2:00PM		☐Y ☐N
	2:30PM		☐Y ☐N
	3:00PM		☐Y ☐N
	3:30PM		☐Y ☐N
	4:00PM		☐Y ☐N
	4:30PM		☐Y ☐N
	5:00PM		☐Y ☐N
	5:30PM		☐Y ☐N
	6:00PM		☐Y ☐N
	6:30PM		☐Y ☐N
	7:00PM		☐Y ☐N
	7:30PM		☐Y ☐N
	8:00PM		☐Y ☐N
	8:30PM		☐Y ☐N
	9:00PM		☐Y ☐N
	9:30PM		☐Y ☐N

TAKE 5 MINUTES EACH MORNING TO PLAN YOUR DAY.

GET EIGHT HOURS OF SLEEP!

NOTE HIGH PRIORITY TASKS WITH A *

ANALYZE WHY A TASK WAS NOT COMPLETED, THEN MOVE TO NEXT DAY.

ONE POSITIVE

TODAY I GAVE

DAILY
GOAL SLAYERS
PLANNER

SETTING YOURSELF UP FOR SUCCESS DAILY!

DATE

_____ / _____ / _____

SCRIPTURE

MOTIVATIONAL QUOTE

ONE GOAL

ONE FUN THING

HEALTH + FITNESS

WATER INTAKE

OZ. OZ. OZ. OZ. OZ.

OZ. OZ. OZ. OZ. OZ.

✳	IMPORTANT TIME	SCHEDULE	SLAYED?
	5:00AM		☐Y ☐N
	5:30AM		☐Y ☐N
	6:00AM		☐Y ☐N
	6:30AM		☐Y ☐N
	7:00AM		☐Y ☐N
	7:30AM		☐Y ☐N
	8:00AM		☐Y ☐N
	8:30AM		☐Y ☐N
	9:00AM		☐Y ☐N
	9:30AM		☐Y ☐N
	10:00AM		☐Y ☐N
	10:30AM		☐Y ☐N
	11:00AM		☐Y ☐N
	11:30AM		☐Y ☐N
	12:00PM		☐Y ☐N
	12:30PM		☐Y ☐N
	1:00PM		☐Y ☐N
	1:30PM		☐Y ☐N
	2:00PM		☐Y ☐N
	2:30PM		☐Y ☐N
	3:00PM		☐Y ☐N
	3:30PM		☐Y ☐N
	4:00PM		☐Y ☐N
	4:30PM		☐Y ☐N
	5:00PM		☐Y ☐N
	5:30PM		☐Y ☐N
	6:00PM		☐Y ☐N
	6:30PM		☐Y ☐N
	7:00PM		☐Y ☐N
	7:30PM		☐Y ☐N
	8:00PM		☐Y ☐N
	8:30PM		☐Y ☐N
	9:00PM		☐Y ☐N
	9:30PM		☐Y ☐N

TAKE 5 MINUTES EACH MORNING TO PLAN YOUR DAY.

GET EIGHT HOURS OF SLEEP!

NOTE HIGH PRIORITY TASKS WITH A ✳

ANALYZE WHY A TASK WAS NOT COMPLETED, THEN MOVE TO NEXT DAY.

ONE POSITIVE

TODAY I GAVE

DAILY
GOAL SLAYERS
PLANNER

SETTING YOURSELF UP FOR SUCCESS DAILY!

DATE

_____ / _____ / _____

SCRIPTURE

MOTIVATIONAL QUOTE

ONE GOAL

ONE FUN THING

HEALTH • FITNESS

WATER INTAKE

*	IMPORTANT TIME	SCHEDULE	SLAYED?
	5:00AM		☐Y ☐N
	5:30AM		☐Y ☐N
	6:00AM		☐Y ☐N
	6:30AM		☐Y ☐N
	7:00AM		☐Y ☐N
	7:30AM		☐Y ☐N
	8:00AM		☐Y ☐N
	8:30AM		☐Y ☐N
	9:00AM		☐Y ☐N
	9:30AM		☐Y ☐N
	10:00AM		☐Y ☐N
	10:30AM		☐Y ☐N
	11:00AM		☐Y ☐N
	11:30AM		☐Y ☐N
	12:00PM		☐Y ☐N
	12:30PM		☐Y ☐N
	1:00PM		☐Y ☐N
	1:30PM		☐Y ☐N
	2:00PM		☐Y ☐N
	2:30PM		☐Y ☐N
	3:00PM		☐Y ☐N
	3:30PM		☐Y ☐N
	4:00PM		☐Y ☐N
	4:30PM		☐Y ☐N
	5:00PM		☐Y ☐N
	5:30PM		☐Y ☐N
	6:00PM		☐Y ☐N
	6:30PM		☐Y ☐N
	7:00PM		☐Y ☐N
	7:30PM		☐Y ☐N
	8:00PM		☐Y ☐N
	8:30PM		☐Y ☐N
	9:00PM		☐Y ☐N
	9:30PM		☐Y ☐N

TAKE 5 MINUTES EACH MORNING TO PLAN YOUR DAY.

GET EIGHT HOURS OF SLEEP!

NOTE HIGH PRIORITY TASKS WITH A *

ANALYZE WHY A TASK WAS NOT COMPLETED, THEN MOVE TO NEXT DAY.

ONE POSITIVE

TODAY I GAVE

DAILY
GOAL SLAYERS
PLANNER

SETTING YOURSELF UP FOR SUCCESS DAILY!

DATE

_____/_____/_____

SCRIPTURE

MOTIVATIONAL QUOTE

ONE GOAL

ONE FUN THING

✱	IMPORTANT TIME	SCHEDULE	SLAYED?
	5:00AM		☐Y ☐N
	5:30AM		☐Y ☐N
	6:00AM		☐Y ☐N
	6:30AM		☐Y ☐N
	7:00AM		☐Y ☐N
	7:30AM		☐Y ☐N
	8:00AM		☐Y ☐N
	8:30AM		☐Y ☐N
	9:00AM		☐Y ☐N
	9:30AM		☐Y ☐N
	10:00AM		☐Y ☐N
	10:30AM		☐Y ☐N
	11:00AM		☐Y ☐N
	11:30AM		☐Y ☐N
	12:00PM		☐Y ☐N
	12:30PM		☐Y ☐N
	1:00PM		☐Y ☐N
	1:30PM		☐Y ☐N
	2:00PM		☐Y ☐N
	2:30PM		☐Y ☐N
	3:00PM		☐Y ☐N
	3:30PM		☐Y ☐N
	4:00PM		☐Y ☐N
	4:30PM		☐Y ☐N
	5:00PM		☐Y ☐N
	5:30PM		☐Y ☐N
	6:00PM		☐Y ☐N
	6:30PM		☐Y ☐N
	7:00PM		☐Y ☐N
	7:30PM		☐Y ☐N
	8:00PM		☐Y ☐N
	8:30PM		☐Y ☐N
	9:00PM		☐Y ☐N
	9:30PM		☐Y ☐N

HEALTH + FITNESS

WATER INTAKE

OZ OZ OZ OZ OZ

OZ OZ OZ OZ OZ

TAKE 5 MINUTES EACH MORNING TO PLAN YOUR DAY.

GET EIGHT HOURS OF SLEEP!

NOTE HIGH PRIORITY TASKS WITH A ✱

ANALYZE WHY A TASK WAS NOT COMPLETED, THEN MOVE TO NEXT DAY.

ONE POSITIVE

TODAY I GAVE

DAILY
GOAL SLAYERS
PLANNER

SETTING YOURSELF UP FOR SUCCESS DAILY!

DATE

_____/_____/_____

SCRIPTURE

MOTIVATIONAL QUOTE

ONE GOAL

ONE FUN THING

HEALTH • FITNESS

✷	IMPORTANT TIME	SCHEDULE	SLAYED?
	5:00AM		☐Y ☐N
	5:30AM		☐Y ☐N
	6:00AM		☐Y ☐N
	6:30AM		☐Y ☐N
	7:00AM		☐Y ☐N
	7:30AM		☐Y ☐N
	8:00AM		☐Y ☐N
	8:30AM		☐Y ☐N
	9:00AM		☐Y ☐N
	9:30AM		☐Y ☐N
	10:00AM		☐Y ☐N
	10:30AM		☐Y ☐N
	11:00AM		☐Y ☐N
	11:30AM		☐Y ☐N
	12:00PM		☐Y ☐N
	12:30PM		☐Y ☐N
	1:00PM		☐Y ☐N
	1:30PM		☐Y ☐N
	2:00PM		☐Y ☐N
	2:30PM		☐Y ☐N
	3:00PM		☐Y ☐N
	3:30PM		☐Y ☐N
	4:00PM		☐Y ☐N
	4:30PM		☐Y ☐N
	5:00PM		☐Y ☐N
	5:30PM		☐Y ☐N
	6:00PM		☐Y ☐N
	6:30PM		☐Y ☐N
	7:00PM		☐Y ☐N
	7:30PM		☐Y ☐N
	8:00PM		☐Y ☐N
	8:30PM		☐Y ☐N
	9:00PM		☐Y ☐N
	9:30PM		☐Y ☐N

WATER INTAKE

OZ. OZ. OZ. OZ. OZ.
OZ. OZ. OZ. OZ. OZ.

TAKE 5 MINUTES EACH MORNING TO PLAN YOUR DAY.

GET EIGHT HOURS OF SLEEP!

NOTE HIGH PRIORITY TASKS WITH A ✷

ANALYZE WHY A TASK WAS NOT COMPLETED, THEN MOVE TO NEXT DAY.

ONE POSITIVE

TODAY I GAVE

DAILY
GOAL SLAYERS
PLANNER

SETTING YOURSELF UP FOR SUCCESS DAILY!

DATE

_____ / _____ / _____

SCRIPTURE

MOTIVATIONAL QUOTE

ONE GOAL

ONE FUN THING

HEALTH + FITNESS

WATER INTAKE

*	IMPORTANT TIME	SCHEDULE	SLAYED?
	5:00AM		☐Y ☐N
	5:30AM		☐Y ☐N
	6:00AM		☐Y ☐N
	6:30AM		☐Y ☐N
	7:00AM		☐Y ☐N
	7:30AM		☐Y ☐N
	8:00AM		☐Y ☐N
	8:30AM		☐Y ☐N
	9:00AM		☐Y ☐N
	9:30AM		☐Y ☐N
	10:00AM		☐Y ☐N
	10:30AM		☐Y ☐N
	11:00AM		☐Y ☐N
	11:30AM		☐Y ☐N
	12:00PM		☐Y ☐N
	12:30PM		☐Y ☐N
	1:00PM		☐Y ☐N
	1:30PM		☐Y ☐N
	2:00PM		☐Y ☐N
	2:30PM		☐Y ☐N
	3:00PM		☐Y ☐N
	3:30PM		☐Y ☐N
	4:00PM		☐Y ☐N
	4:30PM		☐Y ☐N
	5:00PM		☐Y ☐N
	5:30PM		☐Y ☐N
	6:00PM		☐Y ☐N
	6:30PM		☐Y ☐N
	7:00PM		☐Y ☐N
	7:30PM		☐Y ☐N
	8:00PM		☐Y ☐N
	8:30PM		☐Y ☐N
	9:00PM		☐Y ☐N
	9:30PM		☐Y ☐N

TAKE 5 MINUTES EACH MORNING TO PLAN YOUR DAY.

GET EIGHT HOURS OF SLEEP!

NOTE HIGH PRIORITY TASKS WITH A *

ANALYZE WHY A TASK WAS NOT COMPLETED, THEN MOVE TO NEXT DAY.

ONE POSITIVE

TODAY I GAVE

DAILY
GOAL SLAYERS
PLANNER

SETTING YOURSELF UP FOR SUCCESS DAILY!

DATE

____ / ____ / ____

SCRIPTURE

MOTIVATIONAL QUOTE

ONE GOAL

ONE FUN THING

HEALTH • FITNESS

WATER INTAKE

*	IMPORTANT TIME	SCHEDULE	SLAYED?
	5:00AM		☐Y ☐N
	5:30AM		☐Y ☐N
	6:00AM		☐Y ☐N
	6:30AM		☐Y ☐N
	7:00AM		☐Y ☐N
	7:30AM		☐Y ☐N
	8:00AM		☐Y ☐N
	8:30AM		☐Y ☐N
	9:00AM		☐Y ☐N
	9:30AM		☐Y ☐N
	10:00AM		☐Y ☐N
	10:30AM		☐Y ☐N
	11:00AM		☐Y ☐N
	11:30AM		☐Y ☐N
	12:00PM		☐Y ☐N
	12:30PM		☐Y ☐N
	1:00PM		☐Y ☐N
	1:30PM		☐Y ☐N
	2:00PM		☐Y ☐N
	2:30PM		☐Y ☐N
	3:00PM		☐Y ☐N
	3:30PM		☐Y ☐N
	4:00PM		☐Y ☐N
	4:30PM		☐Y ☐N
	5:00PM		☐Y ☐N
	5:30PM		☐Y ☐N
	6:00PM		☐Y ☐N
	6:30PM		☐Y ☐N
	7:00PM		☐Y ☐N
	7:30PM		☐Y ☐N
	8:00PM		☐Y ☐N
	8:30PM		☐Y ☐N
	9:00PM		☐Y ☐N
	9:30PM		☐Y ☐N

TAKE 5 MINUTES EACH MORNING TO PLAN YOUR DAY.

GET EIGHT HOURS OF SLEEP!

NOTE HIGH PRIORITY TASKS WITH A *

ANALYZE WHY A TASK WAS NOT COMPLETED, THEN MOVE TO NEXT DAY.

ONE POSITIVE

TODAY I GAVE

DAILY
GOAL SLAYERS
PLANNER

SETTING YOURSELF UP FOR SUCCESS DAILY!

DATE

_____ / _____ / _____

SCRIPTURE

MOTIVATIONAL QUOTE

ONE GOAL

ONE FUN THING

✱	IMPORTANT TIME	SCHEDULE	SLAYED?
	5:00AM		☐Y ☐N
	5:30AM		☐Y ☐N
	6:00AM		☐Y ☐N
	6:30AM		☐Y ☐N
	7:00AM		☐Y ☐N
	7:30AM		☐Y ☐N
	8:00AM		☐Y ☐N
	8:30AM		☐Y ☐N
	9:00AM		☐Y ☐N
	9:30AM		☐Y ☐N
	10:00AM		☐Y ☐N
	10:30AM		☐Y ☐N
	11:00AM		☐Y ☐N
	11:30AM		☐Y ☐N
	12:00PM		☐Y ☐N
	12:30PM		☐Y ☐N
	1:00PM		☐Y ☐N
	1:30PM		☐Y ☐N
	2:00PM		☐Y ☐N
	2:30PM		☐Y ☐N
	3:00PM		☐Y ☐N
	3:30PM		☐Y ☐N
	4:00PM		☐Y ☐N
	4:30PM		☐Y ☐N
	5:00PM		☐Y ☐N
	5:30PM		☐Y ☐N
	6:00PM		☐Y ☐N
	6:30PM		☐Y ☐N
	7:00PM		☐Y ☐N
	7:30PM		☐Y ☐N
	8:00PM		☐Y ☐N
	8:30PM		☐Y ☐N
	9:00PM		☐Y ☐N
	9:30PM		☐Y ☐N

HEALTH • FITNESS

WATER INTAKE

OZ. OZ. OZ. OZ. OZ.

OZ. OZ. OZ. OZ. OZ.

TAKE 5 MINUTES EACH MORNING TO PLAN YOUR DAY.

GET EIGHT HOURS OF SLEEP!

NOTE HIGH PRIORITY TASKS WITH A ✱

ANALYZE WHY A TASK WAS NOT COMPLETED, THEN MOVE TO NEXT DAY.

ONE POSITIVE

TODAY I GAVE

DAILY
GOAL SLAYERS
PLANNER

SETTING YOURSELF UP FOR SUCCESS DAILY!

DATE

_____ / _____ / _____

SCRIPTURE

MOTIVATIONAL QUOTE

ONE GOAL

ONE FUN THING

✱	IMPORTANT TIME	SCHEDULE	SLAYED?
	5:00AM		☐Y ☐N
	5:30AM		☐Y ☐N
	6:00AM		☐Y ☐N
	6:30AM		☐Y ☐N
	7:00AM		☐Y ☐N
	7:30AM		☐Y ☐N
	8:00AM		☐Y ☐N
	8:30AM		☐Y ☐N
	9:00AM		☐Y ☐N
	9:30AM		☐Y ☐N
	10:00AM		☐Y ☐N
	10:30AM		☐Y ☐N
	11:00AM		☐Y ☐N
	11:30AM		☐Y ☐N
	12:00PM		☐Y ☐N
	12:30PM		☐Y ☐N
	1:00PM		☐Y ☐N
	1:30PM		☐Y ☐N
	2:00PM		☐Y ☐N
	2:30PM		☐Y ☐N
	3:00PM		☐Y ☐N
	3:30PM		☐Y ☐N
	4:00PM		☐Y ☐N
	4:30PM		☐Y ☐N
	5:00PM		☐Y ☐N
	5:30PM		☐Y ☐N
	6:00PM		☐Y ☐N
	6:30PM		☐Y ☐N
	7:00PM		☐Y ☐N
	7:30PM		☐Y ☐N
	8:00PM		☐Y ☐N
	8:30PM		☐Y ☐N
	9:00PM		☐Y ☐N
	9:30PM		☐Y ☐N

HEALTH + FITNESS

WATER INTAKE

OZ. OZ. OZ. OZ. OZ.
OZ. OZ. OZ. OZ. OZ.

TAKE 5 MINUTES EACH MORNING TO PLAN YOUR DAY.

GET EIGHT HOURS OF SLEEP!

NOTE HIGH PRIORITY TASKS WITH A ✱

ANALYZE WHY A TASK WAS NOT COMPLETED, THEN MOVE TO NEXT DAY.

ONE POSITIVE

TODAY I GAVE

DAILY
GOAL SLAYERS
PLANNER

SETTING YOURSELF UP FOR SUCCESS DAILY!

DATE

_____/_____/_____

SCRIPTURE

MOTIVATIONAL QUOTE

ONE GOAL

ONE FUN THING

HEALTH • FITNESS

WATER INTAKE

✳	IMPORTANT TIME	SCHEDULE	SLAYED?
	5:00AM		☐Y ☐N
	5:30AM		☐Y ☐N
	6:00AM		☐Y ☐N
	6:30AM		☐Y ☐N
	7:00AM		☐Y ☐N
	7:30AM		☐Y ☐N
	8:00AM		☐Y ☐N
	8:30AM		☐Y ☐N
	9:00AM		☐Y ☐N
	9:30AM		☐Y ☐N
	10:00AM		☐Y ☐N
	10:30AM		☐Y ☐N
	11:00AM		☐Y ☐N
	11:30AM		☐Y ☐N
	12:00PM		☐Y ☐N
	12:30PM		☐Y ☐N
	1:00PM		☐Y ☐N
	1:30PM		☐Y ☐N
	2:00PM		☐Y ☐N
	2:30PM		☐Y ☐N
	3:00PM		☐Y ☐N
	3:30PM		☐Y ☐N
	4:00PM		☐Y ☐N
	4:30PM		☐Y ☐N
	5:00PM		☐Y ☐N
	5:30PM		☐Y ☐N
	6:00PM		☐Y ☐N
	6:30PM		☐Y ☐N
	7:00PM		☐Y ☐N
	7:30PM		☐Y ☐N
	8:00PM		☐Y ☐N
	8:30PM		☐Y ☐N
	9:00PM		☐Y ☐N
	9:30PM		☐Y ☐N

TAKE 5 MINUTES EACH MORNING TO PLAN YOUR DAY.

GET EIGHT HOURS OF SLEEP!

NOTE HIGH PRIORITY TASKS WITH A ✳

ANALYZE WHY A TASK WAS NOT COMPLETED, THEN MOVE TO NEXT DAY.

ONE POSITIVE

TODAY I GAVE

DAILY
GOAL SLAYERS
PLANNER

SETTING YOURSELF UP FOR SUCCESS DAILY!

DATE

_____ / _____ / _____

SCRIPTURE

MOTIVATIONAL QUOTE

ONE GOAL

ONE FUN THING

HEALTH • FITNESS

WATER INTAKE

OZ. OZ. OZ. OZ. OZ.

OZ. OZ. OZ. OZ. OZ.

*	IMPORTANT TIME	SCHEDULE	SLAYED?
	5:00AM		☐Y ☐N
	5:30AM		☐Y ☐N
	6:00AM		☐Y ☐N
	6:30AM		☐Y ☐N
	7:00AM		☐Y ☐N
	7:30AM		☐Y ☐N
	8:00AM		☐Y ☐N
	8:30AM		☐Y ☐N
	9:00AM		☐Y ☐N
	9:30AM		☐Y ☐N
	10:00AM		☐Y ☐N
	10:30AM		☐Y ☐N
	11:00AM		☐Y ☐N
	11:30AM		☐Y ☐N
	12:00PM		☐Y ☐N
	12:30PM		☐Y ☐N
	1:00PM		☐Y ☐N
	1:30PM		☐Y ☐N
	2:00PM		☐Y ☐N
	2:30PM		☐Y ☐N
	3:00PM		☐Y ☐N
	3:30PM		☐Y ☐N
	4:00PM		☐Y ☐N
	4:30PM		☐Y ☐N
	5:00PM		☐Y ☐N
	5:30PM		☐Y ☐N
	6:00PM		☐Y ☐N
	6:30PM		☐Y ☐N
	7:00PM		☐Y ☐N
	7:30PM		☐Y ☐N
	8:00PM		☐Y ☐N
	8:30PM		☐Y ☐N
	9:00PM		☐Y ☐N
	9:30PM		☐Y ☐N

TAKE 5 MINUTES EACH MORNING TO PLAN YOUR DAY.

GET EIGHT HOURS OF SLEEP!

NOTE HIGH PRIORITY TASKS WITH A *

ANALYZE WHY A TASK WAS NOT COMPLETED, THEN MOVE TO NEXT DAY.

ONE POSITIVE

TODAY I GAVE

DAILY
GOAL SLAYERS
PLANNER

SETTING YOURSELF UP FOR SUCCESS DAILY!

DATE

____ / ____ / ____

SCRIPTURE

MOTIVATIONAL QUOTE

ONE GOAL

ONE FUN THING

HEALTH + FITNESS

WATER INTAKE

OZ. OZ. OZ. OZ. OZ.

OZ. OZ. OZ. OZ. OZ.

✳	IMPORTANT TIME	SCHEDULE	SLAYED?
	5:00AM		☐Y ☐N
	5:30AM		☐Y ☐N
	6:00AM		☐Y ☐N
	6:30AM		☐Y ☐N
	7:00AM		☐Y ☐N
	7:30AM		☐Y ☐N
	8:00AM		☐Y ☐N
	8:30AM		☐Y ☐N
	9:00AM		☐Y ☐N
	9:30AM		☐Y ☐N
	10:00AM		☐Y ☐N
	10:30AM		☐Y ☐N
	11:00AM		☐Y ☐N
	11:30AM		☐Y ☐N
	12:00PM		☐Y ☐N
	12:30PM		☐Y ☐N
	1:00PM		☐Y ☐N
	1:30PM		☐Y ☐N
	2:00PM		☐Y ☐N
	2:30PM		☐Y ☐N
	3:00PM		☐Y ☐N
	3:30PM		☐Y ☐N
	4:00PM		☐Y ☐N
	4:30PM		☐Y ☐N
	5:00PM		☐Y ☐N
	5:30PM		☐Y ☐N
	6:00PM		☐Y ☐N
	6:30PM		☐Y ☐N
	7:00PM		☐Y ☐N
	7:30PM		☐Y ☐N
	8:00PM		☐Y ☐N
	8:30PM		☐Y ☐N
	9:00PM		☐Y ☐N
	9:30PM		☐Y ☐N

TAKE 5 MINUTES EACH MORNING TO PLAN YOUR DAY.

GET EIGHT HOURS OF SLEEP!

NOTE HIGH PRIORITY TASKS WITH A ✳

ANALYZE WHY A TASK WAS NOT COMPLETED, THEN MOVE TO NEXT DAY.

ONE POSITIVE

TODAY I GAVE

DAILY
GOAL SLAYERS
PLANNER

SETTING YOURSELF UP FOR SUCCESS DAILY!

DATE
_____ / _____ / _____

SCRIPTURE

MOTIVATIONAL QUOTE

ONE GOAL

ONE FUN THING

HEALTH + FITNESS

WATER INTAKE

*	IMPORTANT TIME	SCHEDULE	SLAYED?
	5:00AM		☐Y ☐N
	5:30AM		☐Y ☐N
	6:00AM		☐Y ☐N
	6:30AM		☐Y ☐N
	7:00AM		☐Y ☐N
	7:30AM		☐Y ☐N
	8:00AM		☐Y ☐N
	8:30AM		☐Y ☐N
	9:00AM		☐Y ☐N
	9:30AM		☐Y ☐N
	10:00AM		☐Y ☐N
	10:30AM		☐Y ☐N
	11:00AM		☐Y ☐N
	11:30AM		☐Y ☐N
	12:00PM		☐Y ☐N
	12:30PM		☐Y ☐N
	1:00PM		☐Y ☐N
	1:30PM		☐Y ☐N
	2:00PM		☐Y ☐N
	2:30PM		☐Y ☐N
	3:00PM		☐Y ☐N
	3:30PM		☐Y ☐N
	4:00PM		☐Y ☐N
	4:30PM		☐Y ☐N
	5:00PM		☐Y ☐N
	5:30PM		☐Y ☐N
	6:00PM		☐Y ☐N
	6:30PM		☐Y ☐N
	7:00PM		☐Y ☐N
	7:30PM		☐Y ☐N
	8:00PM		☐Y ☐N
	8:30PM		☐Y ☐N
	9:00PM		☐Y ☐N
	9:30PM		☐Y ☐N

TAKE 5 MINUTES EACH MORNING TO PLAN YOUR DAY.

GET EIGHT HOURS OF SLEEP!

NOTE HIGH PRIORITY TASKS WITH A *

ANALYZE WHY A TASK WAS NOT COMPLETED, THEN MOVE TO NEXT DAY.

ONE POSITIVE

TODAY I GAVE

DAILY
GOAL SLAYERS
PLANNER

SETTING YOURSELF UP FOR SUCCESS DAILY!

DATE

_____/_____/_____

SCRIPTURE

MOTIVATIONAL QUOTE

ONE GOAL

ONE FUN THING

*	IMPORTANT TIME	SCHEDULE	SLAYED?
	5:00AM		☐Y ☐N
	5:30AM		☐Y ☐N
	6:00AM		☐Y ☐N
	6:30AM		☐Y ☐N
	7:00AM		☐Y ☐N
	7:30AM		☐Y ☐N
	8:00AM		☐Y ☐N
	8:30AM		☐Y ☐N
	9:00AM		☐Y ☐N
	9:30AM		☐Y ☐N
	10:00AM		☐Y ☐N
	10:30AM		☐Y ☐N
	11:00AM		☐Y ☐N
	11:30AM		☐Y ☐N
	12:00PM		☐Y ☐N
	12:30PM		☐Y ☐N
	1:00PM		☐Y ☐N
	1:30PM		☐Y ☐N
	2:00PM		☐Y ☐N
	2:30PM		☐Y ☐N
	3:00PM		☐Y ☐N
	3:30PM		☐Y ☐N
	4:00PM		☐Y ☐N
	4:30PM		☐Y ☐N
	5:00PM		☐Y ☐N
	5:30PM		☐Y ☐N
	6:00PM		☐Y ☐N
	6:30PM		☐Y ☐N
	7:00PM		☐Y ☐N
	7:30PM		☐Y ☐N
	8:00PM		☐Y ☐N
	8:30PM		☐Y ☐N
	9:00PM		☐Y ☐N
	9:30PM		☐Y ☐N

HEALTH • FITNESS

WATER INTAKE

OZ. OZ. OZ. OZ. OZ.
OZ. OZ. OZ. OZ. OZ.

TAKE 5 MINUTES EACH MORNING TO PLAN YOUR DAY.

GET EIGHT HOURS OF SLEEP!

NOTE HIGH PRIORITY TASKS WITH A *

ANALYZE WHY A TASK WAS NOT COMPLETED, THEN MOVE TO NEXT DAY.

ONE POSITIVE

TODAY I GAVE

DAILY
GOAL SLAYERS
PLANNER

SETTING YOURSELF UP FOR SUCCESS DAILY!

DATE

_____ / _____ / _____

SCRIPTURE

MOTIVATIONAL QUOTE

ONE GOAL

ONE FUN THING

HEALTH • FITNESS

WATER INTAKE

*	IMPORTANT TIME	SCHEDULE	SLAYED?
	5:00AM		☐Y ☐N
	5:30AM		☐Y ☐N
	6:00AM		☐Y ☐N
	6:30AM		☐Y ☐N
	7:00AM		☐Y ☐N
	7:30AM		☐Y ☐N
	8:00AM		☐Y ☐N
	8:30AM		☐Y ☐N
	9:00AM		☐Y ☐N
	9:30AM		☐Y ☐N
	10:00AM		☐Y ☐N
	10:30AM		☐Y ☐N
	11:00AM		☐Y ☐N
	11:30AM		☐Y ☐N
	12:00PM		☐Y ☐N
	12:30PM		☐Y ☐N
	1:00PM		☐Y ☐N
	1:30PM		☐Y ☐N
	2:00PM		☐Y ☐N
	2:30PM		☐Y ☐N
	3:00PM		☐Y ☐N
	3:30PM		☐Y ☐N
	4:00PM		☐Y ☐N
	4:30PM		☐Y ☐N
	5:00PM		☐Y ☐N
	5:30PM		☐Y ☐N
	6:00PM		☐Y ☐N
	6:30PM		☐Y ☐N
	7:00PM		☐Y ☐N
	7:30PM		☐Y ☐N
	8:00PM		☐Y ☐N
	8:30PM		☐Y ☐N
	9:00PM		☐Y ☐N
	9:30PM		☐Y ☐N

TAKE 5 MINUTES EACH MORNING TO PLAN YOUR DAY.

GET EIGHT HOURS OF SLEEP!

NOTE HIGH PRIORITY TASKS WITH A *

ANALYZE WHY A TASK WAS NOT COMPLETED, THEN MOVE TO NEXT DAY.

ONE POSITIVE

TODAY I GAVE

DAILY
GOAL SLAYERS
PLANNER

SETTING YOURSELF UP FOR SUCCESS DAILY!

DATE

_____ / _____ / _____

SCRIPTURE

MOTIVATIONAL QUOTE

ONE GOAL

ONE FUN THING

HEALTH • FITNESS

WATER INTAKE

OZ OZ OZ OZ OZ

OZ OZ OZ OZ OZ

TAKE 5 MINUTES EACH MORNING TO PLAN YOUR DAY.

GET EIGHT HOURS OF SLEEP!

NOTE HIGH PRIORITY TASKS WITH A *

ANALYZE WHY A TASK WAS NOT COMPLETED, THEN MOVE TO NEXT DAY.

*	IMPORTANT TIME	SCHEDULE	SLAYED?
	5:00AM		☐Y ☐N
	5:30AM		☐Y ☐N
	6:00AM		☐Y ☐N
	6:30AM		☐Y ☐N
	7:00AM		☐Y ☐N
	7:30AM		☐Y ☐N
	8:00AM		☐Y ☐N
	8:30AM		☐Y ☐N
	9:00AM		☐Y ☐N
	9:30AM		☐Y ☐N
	10:00AM		☐Y ☐N
	10:30AM		☐Y ☐N
	11:00AM		☐Y ☐N
	11:30AM		☐Y ☐N
	12:00PM		☐Y ☐N
	12:30PM		☐Y ☐N
	1:00PM		☐Y ☐N
	1:30PM		☐Y ☐N
	2:00PM		☐Y ☐N
	2:30PM		☐Y ☐N
	3:00PM		☐Y ☐N
	3:30PM		☐Y ☐N
	4:00PM		☐Y ☐N
	4:30PM		☐Y ☐N
	5:00PM		☐Y ☐N
	5:30PM		☐Y ☐N
	6:00PM		☐Y ☐N
	6:30PM		☐Y ☐N
	7:00PM		☐Y ☐N
	7:30PM		☐Y ☐N
	8:00PM		☐Y ☐N
	8:30PM		☐Y ☐N
	9:00PM		☐Y ☐N
	9:30PM		☐Y ☐N

ONE POSITIVE

TODAY I GAVE

DAILY
GOAL SLAYERS
PLANNER

SETTING YOURSELF UP FOR SUCCESS DAILY!

DATE

_____ / _____ / _____

SCRIPTURE

MOTIVATIONAL QUOTE

ONE GOAL

ONE FUN THING

✱	IMPORTANT TIME	SCHEDULE	SLAYED?
	5:00AM		☐Y ☐N
	5:30AM		☐Y ☐N
	6:00AM		☐Y ☐N
	6:30AM		☐Y ☐N
	7:00AM		☐Y ☐N
	7:30AM		☐Y ☐N
	8:00AM		☐Y ☐N
	8:30AM		☐Y ☐N
	9:00AM		☐Y ☐N
	9:30AM		☐Y ☐N
	10:00AM		☐Y ☐N
	10:30AM		☐Y ☐N
	11:00AM		☐Y ☐N
	11:30AM		☐Y ☐N
	12:00PM		☐Y ☐N
	12:30PM		☐Y ☐N
	1:00PM		☐Y ☐N
	1:30PM		☐Y ☐N
	2:00PM		☐Y ☐N
	2:30PM		☐Y ☐N
	3:00PM		☐Y ☐N
	3:30PM		☐Y ☐N
	4:00PM		☐Y ☐N
	4:30PM		☐Y ☐N
	5:00PM		☐Y ☐N
	5:30PM		☐Y ☐N
	6:00PM		☐Y ☐N
	6:30PM		☐Y ☐N
	7:00PM		☐Y ☐N
	7:30PM		☐Y ☐N
	8:00PM		☐Y ☐N
	8:30PM		☐Y ☐N
	9:00PM		☐Y ☐N
	9:30PM		☐Y ☐N

HEALTH • FITNESS

WATER INTAKE

OZ. OZ. OZ. OZ. OZ.
OZ. OZ. OZ. OZ. OZ.

TAKE 5 MINUTES EACH MORNING TO PLAN YOUR DAY.

GET EIGHT HOURS OF SLEEP!

NOTE HIGH PRIORITY TASKS WITH A ✱

ANALYZE WHY A TASK WAS NOT COMPLETED, THEN MOVE TO NEXT DAY.

ONE POSITIVE

TODAY I GAVE

DAILY
GOAL SLAYERS
PLANNER

SETTING YOURSELF UP FOR SUCCESS DAILY!

DATE

_____ / _____ / _____

SCRIPTURE

MOTIVATIONAL QUOTE

ONE GOAL

ONE FUN THING

HEALTH + FITNESS

WATER INTAKE

OZ. OZ. OZ. OZ. OZ.

OZ. OZ. OZ. OZ. OZ.

*	IMPORTANT TIME	SCHEDULE	SLAYED?
	5:00AM		☐Y ☐N
	5:30AM		☐Y ☐N
	6:00AM		☐Y ☐N
	6:30AM		☐Y ☐N
	7:00AM		☐Y ☐N
	7:30AM		☐Y ☐N
	8:00AM		☐Y ☐N
	8:30AM		☐Y ☐N
	9:00AM		☐Y ☐N
	9:30AM		☐Y ☐N
	10:00AM		☐Y ☐N
	10:30AM		☐Y ☐N
	11:00AM		☐Y ☐N
	11:30AM		☐Y ☐N
	12:00PM		☐Y ☐N
	12:30PM		☐Y ☐N
	1:00PM		☐Y ☐N
	1:30PM		☐Y ☐N
	2:00PM		☐Y ☐N
	2:30PM		☐Y ☐N
	3:00PM		☐Y ☐N
	3:30PM		☐Y ☐N
	4:00PM		☐Y ☐N
	4:30PM		☐Y ☐N
	5:00PM		☐Y ☐N
	5:30PM		☐Y ☐N
	6:00PM		☐Y ☐N
	6:30PM		☐Y ☐N
	7:00PM		☐Y ☐N
	7:30PM		☐Y ☐N
	8:00PM		☐Y ☐N
	8:30PM		☐Y ☐N
	9:00PM		☐Y ☐N
	9:30PM		☐Y ☐N

TAKE 5 MINUTES EACH MORNING TO PLAN YOUR DAY.

GET EIGHT HOURS OF SLEEP!

NOTE HIGH PRIORITY TASKS WITH A *

ANALYZE WHY A TASK WAS NOT COMPLETED, THEN MOVE TO NEXT DAY.

ONE POSITIVE

TODAY I GAVE

DAILY
GOAL SLAYERS
PLANNER

SETTING YOURSELF UP FOR SUCCESS DAILY!

DATE

_____ / _____ / _____

SCRIPTURE

MOTIVATIONAL QUOTE

ONE GOAL

ONE FUN THING

HEALTH · FITNESS

WATER INTAKE

OZ. OZ. OZ. OZ. OZ.

OZ. OZ. OZ. OZ. OZ.

*	IMPORTANT TIME	SCHEDULE	SLAYED?
	5:00AM		☐Y ☐N
	5:30AM		☐Y ☐N
	6:00AM		☐Y ☐N
	6:30AM		☐Y ☐N
	7:00AM		☐Y ☐N
	7:30AM		☐Y ☐N
	8:00AM		☐Y ☐N
	8:30AM		☐Y ☐N
	9:00AM		☐Y ☐N
	9:30AM		☐Y ☐N
	10:00AM		☐Y ☐N
	10:30AM		☐Y ☐N
	11:00AM		☐Y ☐N
	11:30AM		☐Y ☐N
	12:00PM		☐Y ☐N
	12:30PM		☐Y ☐N
	1:00PM		☐Y ☐N
	1:30PM		☐Y ☐N
	2:00PM		☐Y ☐N
	2:30PM		☐Y ☐N
	3:00PM		☐Y ☐N
	3:30PM		☐Y ☐N
	4:00PM		☐Y ☐N
	4:30PM		☐Y ☐N
	5:00PM		☐Y ☐N
	5:30PM		☐Y ☐N
	6:00PM		☐Y ☐N
	6:30PM		☐Y ☐N
	7:00PM		☐Y ☐N
	7:30PM		☐Y ☐N
	8:00PM		☐Y ☐N
	8:30PM		☐Y ☐N
	9:00PM		☐Y ☐N
	9:30PM		☐Y ☐N

TAKE 5 MINUTES EACH MORNING TO PLAN YOUR DAY.

GET EIGHT HOURS OF SLEEP!

NOTE HIGH PRIORITY TASKS WITH A *

ANALYZE WHY A TASK WAS NOT COMPLETED, THEN MOVE TO NEXT DAY.

ONE POSITIVE

TODAY I GAVE

DAILY
GOAL SLAYERS
PLANNER

SETTING YOURSELF UP FOR SUCCESS DAILY!

DATE

_____ / _____ / _____

SCRIPTURE

MOTIVATIONAL QUOTE

ONE GOAL

ONE FUN THING

HEALTH • FITNESS

WATER INTAKE

OZ OZ OZ OZ OZ

OZ OZ OZ OZ OZ

✱	IMPORTANT TIME	SCHEDULE	SLAYED?
	5:00AM		☐Y ☐N
	5:30AM		☐Y ☐N
	6:00AM		☐Y ☐N
	6:30AM		☐Y ☐N
	7:00AM		☐Y ☐N
	7:30AM		☐Y ☐N
	8:00AM		☐Y ☐N
	8:30AM		☐Y ☐N
	9:00AM		☐Y ☐N
	9:30AM		☐Y ☐N
	10:00AM		☐Y ☐N
	10:30AM		☐Y ☐N
	11:00AM		☐Y ☐N
	11:30AM		☐Y ☐N
	12:00PM		☐Y ☐N
	12:30PM		☐Y ☐N
	1:00PM		☐Y ☐N
	1:30PM		☐Y ☐N
	2:00PM		☐Y ☐N
	2:30PM		☐Y ☐N
	3:00PM		☐Y ☐N
	3:30PM		☐Y ☐N
	4:00PM		☐Y ☐N
	4:30PM		☐Y ☐N
	5:00PM		☐Y ☐N
	5:30PM		☐Y ☐N
	6:00PM		☐Y ☐N
	6:30PM		☐Y ☐N
	7:00PM		☐Y ☐N
	7:30PM		☐Y ☐N
	8:00PM		☐Y ☐N
	8:30PM		☐Y ☐N
	9:00PM		☐Y ☐N
	9:30PM		☐Y ☐N

TAKE 5 MINUTES EACH MORNING TO PLAN YOUR DAY.

GET EIGHT HOURS OF SLEEP!

NOTE HIGH PRIORITY TASKS WITH A ✱

ANALYZE WHY A TASK WAS NOT COMPLETED, THEN MOVE TO NEXT DAY.

ONE POSITIVE

TODAY I GAVE

DAILY
GOAL SLAYERS
PLANNER

SETTING YOURSELF UP FOR SUCCESS DAILY!

DATE

_____ / _____ / _____

SCRIPTURE

MOTIVATIONAL QUOTE

ONE GOAL

ONE FUN THING

✱	IMPORTANT TIME	SCHEDULE	SLAYED?
	5:00AM		☐Y ☐N
	5:30AM		☐Y ☐N
	6:00AM		☐Y ☐N
	6:30AM		☐Y ☐N
	7:00AM		☐Y ☐N
	7:30AM		☐Y ☐N
	8:00AM		☐Y ☐N
	8:30AM		☐Y ☐N
	9:00AM		☐Y ☐N
	9:30AM		☐Y ☐N
	10:00AM		☐Y ☐N
	10:30AM		☐Y ☐N
	11:00AM		☐Y ☐N
	11:30AM		☐Y ☐N
	12:00PM		☐Y ☐N
	12:30PM		☐Y ☐N
	1:00PM		☐Y ☐N
	1:30PM		☐Y ☐N
	2:00PM		☐Y ☐N
	2:30PM		☐Y ☐N
	3:00PM		☐Y ☐N
	3:30PM		☐Y ☐N
	4:00PM		☐Y ☐N
	4:30PM		☐Y ☐N
	5:00PM		☐Y ☐N
	5:30PM		☐Y ☐N
	6:00PM		☐Y ☐N
	6:30PM		☐Y ☐N
	7:00PM		☐Y ☐N
	7:30PM		☐Y ☐N
	8:00PM		☐Y ☐N
	8:30PM		☐Y ☐N
	9:00PM		☐Y ☐N
	9:30PM		☐Y ☐N

HEALTH • FITNESS

WATER INTAKE

OZ. OZ. OZ. OZ. OZ.
OZ. OZ. OZ. OZ. OZ.

TAKE 5 MINUTES EACH MORNING TO PLAN YOUR DAY.

GET EIGHT HOURS OF SLEEP!

NOTE HIGH PRIORITY TASKS WITH A ✱

ANALYZE WHY A TASK WAS NOT COMPLETED, THEN MOVE TO NEXT DAY.

ONE POSITIVE

TODAY I GAVE

DAILY
GOAL SLAYERS
PLANNER

SETTING YOURSELF UP FOR SUCCESS DAILY!

DATE

_____ / _____ / _____

SCRIPTURE

MOTIVATIONAL QUOTE

ONE GOAL

ONE FUN THING

*	IMPORTANT TIME	SCHEDULE	SLAYED?
	5:00AM		☐Y ☐N
	5:30AM		☐Y ☐N
	6:00AM		☐Y ☐N
	6:30AM		☐Y ☐N
	7:00AM		☐Y ☐N
	7:30AM		☐Y ☐N
	8:00AM		☐Y ☐N
	8:30AM		☐Y ☐N
	9:00AM		☐Y ☐N
	9:30AM		☐Y ☐N
	10:00AM		☐Y ☐N
	10:30AM		☐Y ☐N
	11:00AM		☐Y ☐N
	11:30AM		☐Y ☐N
	12:00PM		☐Y ☐N
	12:30PM		☐Y ☐N
	1:00PM		☐Y ☐N
	1:30PM		☐Y ☐N
	2:00PM		☐Y ☐N
	2:30PM		☐Y ☐N
	3:00PM		☐Y ☐N
	3:30PM		☐Y ☐N
	4:00PM		☐Y ☐N
	4:30PM		☐Y ☐N
	5:00PM		☐Y ☐N
	5:30PM		☐Y ☐N
	6:00PM		☐Y ☐N
	6:30PM		☐Y ☐N
	7:00PM		☐Y ☐N
	7:30PM		☐Y ☐N
	8:00PM		☐Y ☐N
	8:30PM		☐Y ☐N
	9:00PM		☐Y ☐N
	9:30PM		☐Y ☐N

HEALTH • FITNESS

WATER INTAKE

OZ. OZ. OZ. OZ. OZ.

OZ. OZ. OZ. OZ. OZ.

TAKE 5 MINUTES EACH MORNING TO PLAN YOUR DAY.

GET EIGHT HOURS OF SLEEP!

NOTE HIGH PRIORITY TASKS WITH A *

ANALYZE WHY A TASK WAS NOT COMPLETED, THEN MOVE TO NEXT DAY.

ONE POSITIVE

TODAY I GAVE

DAILY
GOAL SLAYERS
PLANNER

SETTING YOURSELF UP FOR SUCCESS DAILY!

DATE

_____/_____/_____

SCRIPTURE

MOTIVATIONAL QUOTE

ONE GOAL

ONE FUN THING

*	IMPORTANT TIME	SCHEDULE	SLAYED?
	5:00AM		☐Y ☐N
	5:30AM		☐Y ☐N
	6:00AM		☐Y ☐N
	6:30AM		☐Y ☐N
	7:00AM		☐Y ☐N
	7:30AM		☐Y ☐N
	8:00AM		☐Y ☐N
	8:30AM		☐Y ☐N
	9:00AM		☐Y ☐N
	9:30AM		☐Y ☐N
	10:00AM		☐Y ☐N
	10:30AM		☐Y ☐N
	11:00AM		☐Y ☐N
	11:30AM		☐Y ☐N
	12:00PM		☐Y ☐N
	12:30PM		☐Y ☐N
	1:00PM		☐Y ☐N
	1:30PM		☐Y ☐N
	2:00PM		☐Y ☐N
	2:30PM		☐Y ☐N
	3:00PM		☐Y ☐N
	3:30PM		☐Y ☐N
	4:00PM		☐Y ☐N
	4:30PM		☐Y ☐N
	5:00PM		☐Y ☐N
	5:30PM		☐Y ☐N
	6:00PM		☐Y ☐N
	6:30PM		☐Y ☐N
	7:00PM		☐Y ☐N
	7:30PM		☐Y ☐N
	8:00PM		☐Y ☐N
	8:30PM		☐Y ☐N
	9:00PM		☐Y ☐N
	9:30PM		☐Y ☐N

HEALTH • FITNESS

WATER INTAKE

OZ. OZ. OZ. OZ. OZ.
OZ. OZ. OZ. OZ. OZ.

TAKE 5 MINUTES EACH MORNING TO PLAN YOUR DAY.

GET EIGHT HOURS OF SLEEP!

NOTE HIGH PRIORITY TASKS WITH A *

ANALYZE WHY A TASK WAS NOT COMPLETED, THEN MOVE TO NEXT DAY.

ONE POSITIVE

TODAY I GAVE

DAILY
GOAL SLAYERS
PLANNER

SETTING YOURSELF UP FOR SUCCESS DAILY!

DATE

____ / ____ / ____

SCRIPTURE

MOTIVATIONAL QUOTE

ONE GOAL

ONE FUN THING

HEALTH • FITNESS

WATER INTAKE

OZ. OZ. OZ. OZ. OZ.

OZ. OZ. OZ. OZ. OZ.

✱	IMPORTANT TIME	SCHEDULE	SLAYED?
	5:00AM		☐Y ☐N
	5:30AM		☐Y ☐N
	6:00AM		☐Y ☐N
	6:30AM		☐Y ☐N
	7:00AM		☐Y ☐N
	7:30AM		☐Y ☐N
	8:00AM		☐Y ☐N
	8:30AM		☐Y ☐N
	9:00AM		☐Y ☐N
	9:30AM		☐Y ☐N
	10:00AM		☐Y ☐N
	10:30AM		☐Y ☐N
	11:00AM		☐Y ☐N
	11:30AM		☐Y ☐N
	12:00PM		☐Y ☐N
	12:30PM		☐Y ☐N
	1:00PM		☐Y ☐N
	1:30PM		☐Y ☐N
	2:00PM		☐Y ☐N
	2:30PM		☐Y ☐N
	3:00PM		☐Y ☐N
	3:30PM		☐Y ☐N
	4:00PM		☐Y ☐N
	4:30PM		☐Y ☐N
	5:00PM		☐Y ☐N
	5:30PM		☐Y ☐N
	6:00PM		☐Y ☐N
	6:30PM		☐Y ☐N
	7:00PM		☐Y ☐N
	7:30PM		☐Y ☐N
	8:00PM		☐Y ☐N
	8:30PM		☐Y ☐N
	9:00PM		☐Y ☐N
	9:30PM		☐Y ☐N

TAKE 5 MINUTES EACH MORNING TO PLAN YOUR DAY.

GET EIGHT HOURS OF SLEEP!

NOTE HIGH PRIORITY TASKS WITH A ✱

ANALYZE WHY A TASK WAS NOT COMPLETED, THEN MOVE TO NEXT DAY.

ONE POSITIVE

TODAY I GAVE

DAILY
GOAL SLAYERS
PLANNER

SETTING YOURSELF UP FOR SUCCESS DAILY!

DATE

____ / ____ / ____

SCRIPTURE

MOTIVATIONAL QUOTE

ONE GOAL

ONE FUN THING

*	IMPORTANT TIME	SCHEDULE	SLAYED?
	5:00AM		☐Y ☐N
	5:30AM		☐Y ☐N
	6:00AM		☐Y ☐N
	6:30AM		☐Y ☐N
	7:00AM		☐Y ☐N
	7:30AM		☐Y ☐N
	8:00AM		☐Y ☐N
	8:30AM		☐Y ☐N
	9:00AM		☐Y ☐N
	9:30AM		☐Y ☐N
	10:00AM		☐Y ☐N
	10:30AM		☐Y ☐N
	11:00AM		☐Y ☐N
	11:30AM		☐Y ☐N
	12:00PM		☐Y ☐N
	12:30PM		☐Y ☐N
	1:00PM		☐Y ☐N
	1:30PM		☐Y ☐N
	2:00PM		☐Y ☐N
	2:30PM		☐Y ☐N
	3:00PM		☐Y ☐N
	3:30PM		☐Y ☐N
	4:00PM		☐Y ☐N
	4:30PM		☐Y ☐N
	5:00PM		☐Y ☐N
	5:30PM		☐Y ☐N
	6:00PM		☐Y ☐N
	6:30PM		☐Y ☐N
	7:00PM		☐Y ☐N
	7:30PM		☐Y ☐N
	8:00PM		☐Y ☐N
	8:30PM		☐Y ☐N
	9:00PM		☐Y ☐N
	9:30PM		☐Y ☐N

HEALTH • FITNESS

WATER INTAKE

OZ. OZ. OZ. OZ. OZ.
OZ. OZ. OZ. OZ. OZ.

TAKE 5 MINUTES EACH MORNING TO PLAN YOUR DAY.

GET EIGHT HOURS OF SLEEP!

NOTE HIGH PRIORITY TASKS WITH A *

ANALYZE WHY A TASK WAS NOT COMPLETED, THEN MOVE TO NEXT DAY.

ONE POSITIVE

TODAY I GAVE

DAILY
GOAL SLAYERS
PLANNER

SETTING YOURSELF UP FOR SUCCESS DAILY!

DATE

_____ / _____ / _____

SCRIPTURE

MOTIVATIONAL QUOTE

ONE GOAL

ONE FUN THING

HEALTH + FITNESS

WATER INTAKE

OZ. OZ. OZ. OZ. OZ.

OZ. OZ. OZ. OZ. OZ.

✱	IMPORTANT TIME	SCHEDULE	SLAYED?
	5:00AM		☐Y ☐N
	5:30AM		☐Y ☐N
	6:00AM		☐Y ☐N
	6:30AM		☐Y ☐N
	7:00AM		☐Y ☐N
	7:30AM		☐Y ☐N
	8:00AM		☐Y ☐N
	8:30AM		☐Y ☐N
	9:00AM		☐Y ☐N
	9:30AM		☐Y ☐N
	10:00AM		☐Y ☐N
	10:30AM		☐Y ☐N
	11:00AM		☐Y ☐N
	11:30AM		☐Y ☐N
	12:00PM		☐Y ☐N
	12:30PM		☐Y ☐N
	1:00PM		☐Y ☐N
	1:30PM		☐Y ☐N
	2:00PM		☐Y ☐N
	2:30PM		☐Y ☐N
	3:00PM		☐Y ☐N
	3:30PM		☐Y ☐N
	4:00PM		☐Y ☐N
	4:30PM		☐Y ☐N
	5:00PM		☐Y ☐N
	5:30PM		☐Y ☐N
	6:00PM		☐Y ☐N
	6:30PM		☐Y ☐N
	7:00PM		☐Y ☐N
	7:30PM		☐Y ☐N
	8:00PM		☐Y ☐N
	8:30PM		☐Y ☐N
	9:00PM		☐Y ☐N
	9:30PM		☐Y ☐N

TAKE 5 MINUTES EACH MORNING TO PLAN YOUR DAY.

GET EIGHT HOURS OF SLEEP!

NOTE HIGH PRIORITY TASKS WITH A ✱

ANALYZE WHY A TASK WAS NOT COMPLETED, THEN MOVE TO NEXT DAY.

ONE POSITIVE

TODAY I GAVE

DAILY GOAL SLAYERS PLANNER

SETTING YOURSELF UP FOR SUCCESS DAILY!

DATE

_____/_____/_____

SCRIPTURE

MOTIVATIONAL QUOTE

ONE GOAL

ONE FUN THING

HEALTH • FITNESS

WATER INTAKE

✱	IMPORTANT TIME	SCHEDULE	SLAYED?
	5:00AM		☐Y ☐N
	5:30AM		☐Y ☐N
	6:00AM		☐Y ☐N
	6:30AM		☐Y ☐N
	7:00AM		☐Y ☐N
	7:30AM		☐Y ☐N
	8:00AM		☐Y ☐N
	8:30AM		☐Y ☐N
	9:00AM		☐Y ☐N
	9:30AM		☐Y ☐N
	10:00AM		☐Y ☐N
	10:30AM		☐Y ☐N
	11:00AM		☐Y ☐N
	11:30AM		☐Y ☐N
	12:00PM		☐Y ☐N
	12:30PM		☐Y ☐N
	1:00PM		☐Y ☐N
	1:30PM		☐Y ☐N
	2:00PM		☐Y ☐N
	2:30PM		☐Y ☐N
	3:00PM		☐Y ☐N
	3:30PM		☐Y ☐N
	4:00PM		☐Y ☐N
	4:30PM		☐Y ☐N
	5:00PM		☐Y ☐N
	5:30PM		☐Y ☐N
	6:00PM		☐Y ☐N
	6:30PM		☐Y ☐N
	7:00PM		☐Y ☐N
	7:30PM		☐Y ☐N
	8:00PM		☐Y ☐N
	8:30PM		☐Y ☐N
	9:00PM		☐Y ☐N
	9:30PM		☐Y ☐N

TAKE 5 MINUTES EACH MORNING TO PLAN YOUR DAY.

GET EIGHT HOURS OF SLEEP!

NOTE HIGH PRIORITY TASKS WITH A ✱

ANALYZE WHY A TASK WAS NOT COMPLETED, THEN MOVE TO NEXT DAY.

ONE POSITIVE

TODAY I GAVE

DAILY
GOAL SLAYERS
PLANNER

SETTING YOURSELF UP FOR SUCCESS DAILY!

DATE

_____ / _____ / _____

SCRIPTURE

MOTIVATIONAL QUOTE

ONE GOAL

ONE FUN THING

*	IMPORTANT TIME	SCHEDULE	SLAYED?
	5:00AM		☐Y ☐N
	5:30AM		☐Y ☐N
	6:00AM		☐Y ☐N
	6:30AM		☐Y ☐N
	7:00AM		☐Y ☐N
	7:30AM		☐Y ☐N
	8:00AM		☐Y ☐N
	8:30AM		☐Y ☐N
	9:00AM		☐Y ☐N
	9:30AM		☐Y ☐N
	10:00AM		☐Y ☐N
	10:30AM		☐Y ☐N
	11:00AM		☐Y ☐N
	11:30AM		☐Y ☐N
	12:00PM		☐Y ☐N
	12:30PM		☐Y ☐N
	1:00PM		☐Y ☐N
	1:30PM		☐Y ☐N
	2:00PM		☐Y ☐N
	2:30PM		☐Y ☐N
	3:00PM		☐Y ☐N
	3:30PM		☐Y ☐N
	4:00PM		☐Y ☐N
	4:30PM		☐Y ☐N
	5:00PM		☐Y ☐N
	5:30PM		☐Y ☐N
	6:00PM		☐Y ☐N
	6:30PM		☐Y ☐N
	7:00PM		☐Y ☐N
	7:30PM		☐Y ☐N
	8:00PM		☐Y ☐N
	8:30PM		☐Y ☐N
	9:00PM		☐Y ☐N
	9:30PM		☐Y ☐N

HEALTH • FITNESS

WATER INTAKE

OZ OZ OZ OZ OZ
OZ OZ OZ OZ OZ

TAKE 5 MINUTES EACH MORNING TO PLAN YOUR DAY.

GET EIGHT HOURS OF SLEEP!

NOTE HIGH PRIORITY TASKS WITH A *

ANALYZE WHY A TASK WAS NOT COMPLETED, THEN MOVE TO NEXT DAY.

ONE POSITIVE

TODAY I GAVE

DAILY
GOAL SLAYERS
PLANNER

SETTING YOURSELF UP FOR SUCCESS DAILY!

DATE

____ / ____ / ____

SCRIPTURE

MOTIVATIONAL QUOTE

ONE GOAL

ONE FUN THING

HEALTH + FITNESS

WATER INTAKE

*	IMPORTANT TIME	SCHEDULE	SLAYED?
	5:00AM		☐Y ☐N
	5:30AM		☐Y ☐N
	6:00AM		☐Y ☐N
	6:30AM		☐Y ☐N
	7:00AM		☐Y ☐N
	7:30AM		☐Y ☐N
	8:00AM		☐Y ☐N
	8:30AM		☐Y ☐N
	9:00AM		☐Y ☐N
	9:30AM		☐Y ☐N
	10:00AM		☐Y ☐N
	10:30AM		☐Y ☐N
	11:00AM		☐Y ☐N
	11:30AM		☐Y ☐N
	12:00PM		☐Y ☐N
	12:30PM		☐Y ☐N
	1:00PM		☐Y ☐N
	1:30PM		☐Y ☐N
	2:00PM		☐Y ☐N
	2:30PM		☐Y ☐N
	3:00PM		☐Y ☐N
	3:30PM		☐Y ☐N
	4:00PM		☐Y ☐N
	4:30PM		☐Y ☐N
	5:00PM		☐Y ☐N
	5:30PM		☐Y ☐N
	6:00PM		☐Y ☐N
	6:30PM		☐Y ☐N
	7:00PM		☐Y ☐N
	7:30PM		☐Y ☐N
	8:00PM		☐Y ☐N
	8:30PM		☐Y ☐N
	9:00PM		☐Y ☐N
	9:30PM		☐Y ☐N

TAKE 5 MINUTES EACH MORNING TO PLAN YOUR DAY.

GET EIGHT HOURS OF SLEEP!

NOTE HIGH PRIORITY TASKS WITH A *

ANALYZE WHY A TASK WAS NOT COMPLETED, THEN MOVE TO NEXT DAY.

ONE POSITIVE

TODAY I GAVE

DAILY
GOAL SLAYERS
PLANNER

SETTING YOURSELF UP FOR SUCCESS DAILY!

DATE

_____/_____/_____

SCRIPTURE

MOTIVATIONAL QUOTE

ONE GOAL

ONE FUN THING

✱	IMPORTANT TIME	SCHEDULE	SLAYED?
	5:00AM		☐Y ☐N
	5:30AM		☐Y ☐N
	6:00AM		☐Y ☐N
	6:30AM		☐Y ☐N
	7:00AM		☐Y ☐N
	7:30AM		☐Y ☐N
	8:00AM		☐Y ☐N
	8:30AM		☐Y ☐N
	9:00AM		☐Y ☐N
	9:30AM		☐Y ☐N
	10:00AM		☐Y ☐N
	10:30AM		☐Y ☐N
	11:00AM		☐Y ☐N
	11:30AM		☐Y ☐N
	12:00PM		☐Y ☐N
	12:30PM		☐Y ☐N
	1:00PM		☐Y ☐N
	1:30PM		☐Y ☐N
	2:00PM		☐Y ☐N
	2:30PM		☐Y ☐N
	3:00PM		☐Y ☐N
	3:30PM		☐Y ☐N
	4:00PM		☐Y ☐N
	4:30PM		☐Y ☐N
	5:00PM		☐Y ☐N
	5:30PM		☐Y ☐N
	6:00PM		☐Y ☐N
	6:30PM		☐Y ☐N
	7:00PM		☐Y ☐N
	7:30PM		☐Y ☐N
	8:00PM		☐Y ☐N
	8:30PM		☐Y ☐N
	9:00PM		☐Y ☐N
	9:30PM		☐Y ☐N

HEALTH + FITNESS

WATER INTAKE

OZ. OZ. OZ. OZ. OZ.

OZ. OZ. OZ. OZ. OZ.

TAKE 5 MINUTES EACH MORNING TO PLAN YOUR DAY.

GET EIGHT HOURS OF SLEEP!

NOTE HIGH PRIORITY TASKS WITH A ✱

ANALYZE WHY A TASK WAS NOT COMPLETED, THEN MOVE TO NEXT DAY.

ONE POSITIVE

TODAY I GAVE

DAILY
GOAL SLAYERS
PLANNER

SETTING YOURSELF UP FOR SUCCESS DAILY!

DATE

_____ / _____ / _____

SCRIPTURE

MOTIVATIONAL QUOTE

ONE GOAL

ONE FUN THING

HEALTH • FITNESS

WATER INTAKE

OZ. OZ. OZ. OZ. OZ.
OZ. OZ. OZ. OZ. OZ.

*	IMPORTANT TIME	SCHEDULE	SLAYED?
	5:00AM		☐Y ☐N
	5:30AM		☐Y ☐N
	6:00AM		☐Y ☐N
	6:30AM		☐Y ☐N
	7:00AM		☐Y ☐N
	7:30AM		☐Y ☐N
	8:00AM		☐Y ☐N
	8:30AM		☐Y ☐N
	9:00AM		☐Y ☐N
	9:30AM		☐Y ☐N
	10:00AM		☐Y ☐N
	10:30AM		☐Y ☐N
	11:00AM		☐Y ☐N
	11:30AM		☐Y ☐N
	12:00PM		☐Y ☐N
	12:30PM		☐Y ☐N
	1:00PM		☐Y ☐N
	1:30PM		☐Y ☐N
	2:00PM		☐Y ☐N
	2:30PM		☐Y ☐N
	3:00PM		☐Y ☐N
	3:30PM		☐Y ☐N
	4:00PM		☐Y ☐N
	4:30PM		☐Y ☐N
	5:00PM		☐Y ☐N
	5:30PM		☐Y ☐N
	6:00PM		☐Y ☐N
	6:30PM		☐Y ☐N
	7:00PM		☐Y ☐N
	7:30PM		☐Y ☐N
	8:00PM		☐Y ☐N
	8:30PM		☐Y ☐N
	9:00PM		☐Y ☐N
	9:30PM		☐Y ☐N

TAKE 5 MINUTES EACH MORNING TO PLAN YOUR DAY.

GET EIGHT HOURS OF SLEEP!

NOTE HIGH PRIORITY TASKS WITH A *

ANALYZE WHY A TASK WAS NOT COMPLETED, THEN MOVE TO NEXT DAY.

ONE POSITIVE

TODAY I GAVE

DAILY
GOAL SLAYERS
PLANNER

SETTING YOURSELF UP FOR SUCCESS DAILY!

DATE

_____ / _____ / _____

SCRIPTURE

MOTIVATIONAL QUOTE

ONE GOAL

ONE FUN THING

*	IMPORTANT TIME	SCHEDULE	SLAYED?
	5:00AM		☐Y ☐N
	5:30AM		☐Y ☐N
	6:00AM		☐Y ☐N
	6:30AM		☐Y ☐N
	7:00AM		☐Y ☐N
	7:30AM		☐Y ☐N
	8:00AM		☐Y ☐N
	8:30AM		☐Y ☐N
	9:00AM		☐Y ☐N
	9:30AM		☐Y ☐N
	10:00AM		☐Y ☐N
	10:30AM		☐Y ☐N
	11:00AM		☐Y ☐N
	11:30AM		☐Y ☐N
	12:00PM		☐Y ☐N
	12:30PM		☐Y ☐N
	1:00PM		☐Y ☐N
	1:30PM		☐Y ☐N
	2:00PM		☐Y ☐N
	2:30PM		☐Y ☐N
	3:00PM		☐Y ☐N
	3:30PM		☐Y ☐N
	4:00PM		☐Y ☐N
	4:30PM		☐Y ☐N
	5:00PM		☐Y ☐N
	5:30PM		☐Y ☐N
	6:00PM		☐Y ☐N
	6:30PM		☐Y ☐N
	7:00PM		☐Y ☐N
	7:30PM		☐Y ☐N
	8:00PM		☐Y ☐N
	8:30PM		☐Y ☐N
	9:00PM		☐Y ☐N
	9:30PM		☐Y ☐N

HEALTH • FITNESS

WATER INTAKE

OZ. OZ. OZ. OZ. OZ.

OZ. OZ. OZ. OZ. OZ.

TAKE 5 MINUTES EACH MORNING TO PLAN YOUR DAY.

GET EIGHT HOURS OF SLEEP!

NOTE HIGH PRIORITY TASKS WITH A *

ANALYZE WHY A TASK WAS NOT COMPLETED, THEN MOVE TO NEXT DAY.

ONE POSITIVE

TODAY I GAVE

DAILY
GOAL SLAYERS
PLANNER

SETTING YOURSELF UP FOR SUCCESS DAILY!

DATE

_____ / _____ / _____

SCRIPTURE

MOTIVATIONAL QUOTE

ONE GOAL

ONE FUN THING

HEALTH + FITNESS

*	IMPORTANT TIME	SCHEDULE	SLAYED?
	5:00AM		☐Y ☐N
	5:30AM		☐Y ☐N
	6:00AM		☐Y ☐N
	6:30AM		☐Y ☐N
	7:00AM		☐Y ☐N
	7:30AM		☐Y ☐N
	8:00AM		☐Y ☐N
	8:30AM		☐Y ☐N
	9:00AM		☐Y ☐N
	9:30AM		☐Y ☐N
	10:00AM		☐Y ☐N
	10:30AM		☐Y ☐N
	11:00AM		☐Y ☐N
	11:30AM		☐Y ☐N
	12:00PM		☐Y ☐N
	12:30PM		☐Y ☐N
	1:00PM		☐Y ☐N
	1:30PM		☐Y ☐N
	2:00PM		☐Y ☐N
	2:30PM		☐Y ☐N
	3:00PM		☐Y ☐N
	3:30PM		☐Y ☐N
	4:00PM		☐Y ☐N
	4:30PM		☐Y ☐N
	5:00PM		☐Y ☐N
	5:30PM		☐Y ☐N
	6:00PM		☐Y ☐N
	6:30PM		☐Y ☐N
	7:00PM		☐Y ☐N
	7:30PM		☐Y ☐N
	8:00PM		☐Y ☐N
	8:30PM		☐Y ☐N
	9:00PM		☐Y ☐N
	9:30PM		☐Y ☐N

WATER INTAKE

OZ OZ OZ OZ OZ
OZ OZ OZ OZ OZ

TAKE 5 MINUTES EACH MORNING TO PLAN YOUR DAY.

GET EIGHT HOURS OF SLEEP!

NOTE HIGH PRIORITY TASKS WITH A *

ANALYZE WHY A TASK WAS NOT COMPLETED, THEN MOVE TO NEXT DAY.

ONE POSITIVE

TODAY I GAVE

DAILY
GOAL SLAYERS
PLANNER

SETTING YOURSELF UP FOR SUCCESS DAILY!

DATE

_____ / _____ / _____

SCRIPTURE

MOTIVATIONAL QUOTE

ONE GOAL

ONE FUN THING

HEALTH • FITNESS

WATER INTAKE

OZ. OZ. OZ. OZ. OZ.

OZ. OZ. OZ. OZ. OZ.

✱	IMPORTANT TIME	SCHEDULE	SLAYED?
	5:00AM		☐Y ☐N
	5:30AM		☐Y ☐N
	6:00AM		☐Y ☐N
	6:30AM		☐Y ☐N
	7:00AM		☐Y ☐N
	7:30AM		☐Y ☐N
	8:00AM		☐Y ☐N
	8:30AM		☐Y ☐N
	9:00AM		☐Y ☐N
	9:30AM		☐Y ☐N
	10:00AM		☐Y ☐N
	10:30AM		☐Y ☐N
	11:00AM		☐Y ☐N
	11:30AM		☐Y ☐N
	12:00PM		☐Y ☐N
	12:30PM		☐Y ☐N
	1:00PM		☐Y ☐N
	1:30PM		☐Y ☐N
	2:00PM		☐Y ☐N
	2:30PM		☐Y ☐N
	3:00PM		☐Y ☐N
	3:30PM		☐Y ☐N
	4:00PM		☐Y ☐N
	4:30PM		☐Y ☐N
	5:00PM		☐Y ☐N
	5:30PM		☐Y ☐N
	6:00PM		☐Y ☐N
	6:30PM		☐Y ☐N
	7:00PM		☐Y ☐N
	7:30PM		☐Y ☐N
	8:00PM		☐Y ☐N
	8:30PM		☐Y ☐N
	9:00PM		☐Y ☐N
	9:30PM		☐Y ☐N

TAKE 5 MINUTES EACH MORNING TO PLAN YOUR DAY.

GET EIGHT HOURS OF SLEEP!

NOTE HIGH PRIORITY TASKS WITH A ✱

ANALYZE WHY A TASK WAS NOT COMPLETED, THEN MOVE TO NEXT DAY.

ONE POSITIVE

TODAY I GAVE

DAILY
GOAL SLAYERS
PLANNER

SETTING YOURSELF UP FOR SUCCESS DAILY!

DATE

____ / ____ / ____

SCRIPTURE

MOTIVATIONAL QUOTE

ONE GOAL

ONE FUN THING

HEALTH • FITNESS

WATER INTAKE

OZ. OZ. OZ. OZ. OZ.

OZ. OZ. OZ. OZ. OZ.

*	IMPORTANT TIME	SCHEDULE	SLAYED?
	5:00AM		☐Y ☐N
	5:30AM		☐Y ☐N
	6:00AM		☐Y ☐N
	6:30AM		☐Y ☐N
	7:00AM		☐Y ☐N
	7:30AM		☐Y ☐N
	8:00AM		☐Y ☐N
	8:30AM		☐Y ☐N
	9:00AM		☐Y ☐N
	9:30AM		☐Y ☐N
	10:00AM		☐Y ☐N
	10:30AM		☐Y ☐N
	11:00AM		☐Y ☐N
	11:30AM		☐Y ☐N
	12:00PM		☐Y ☐N
	12:30PM		☐Y ☐N
	1:00PM		☐Y ☐N
	1:30PM		☐Y ☐N
	2:00PM		☐Y ☐N
	2:30PM		☐Y ☐N
	3:00PM		☐Y ☐N
	3:30PM		☐Y ☐N
	4:00PM		☐Y ☐N
	4:30PM		☐Y ☐N
	5:00PM		☐Y ☐N
	5:30PM		☐Y ☐N
	6:00PM		☐Y ☐N
	6:30PM		☐Y ☐N
	7:00PM		☐Y ☐N
	7:30PM		☐Y ☐N
	8:00PM		☐Y ☐N
	8:30PM		☐Y ☐N
	9:00PM		☐Y ☐N
	9:30PM		☐Y ☐N

TAKE 5 MINUTES EACH MORNING TO PLAN YOUR DAY.

GET EIGHT HOURS OF SLEEP!

NOTE HIGH PRIORITY TASKS WITH A *

ANALYZE WHY A TASK WAS NOT COMPLETED, THEN MOVE TO NEXT DAY.

ONE POSITIVE

TODAY I GAVE

DAILY
GOAL SLAYERS
PLANNER

SETTING YOURSELF UP FOR SUCCESS DAILY!

DATE

_____ / _____ / _____

SCRIPTURE

MOTIVATIONAL QUOTE

ONE GOAL

ONE FUN THING

HEALTH • FITNESS

WATER INTAKE

OZ. OZ. OZ. OZ. OZ.

OZ. OZ. OZ. OZ. OZ.

✱	IMPORTANT TIME	SCHEDULE	SLAYED?
	5:00AM		☐Y ☐N
	5:30AM		☐Y ☐N
	6:00AM		☐Y ☐N
	6:30AM		☐Y ☐N
	7:00AM		☐Y ☐N
	7:30AM		☐Y ☐N
	8:00AM		☐Y ☐N
	8:30AM		☐Y ☐N
	9:00AM		☐Y ☐N
	9:30AM		☐Y ☐N
	10:00AM		☐Y ☐N
	10:30AM		☐Y ☐N
	11:00AM		☐Y ☐N
	11:30AM		☐Y ☐N
	12:00PM		☐Y ☐N
	12:30PM		☐Y ☐N
	1:00PM		☐Y ☐N
	1:30PM		☐Y ☐N
	2:00PM		☐Y ☐N
	2:30PM		☐Y ☐N
	3:00PM		☐Y ☐N
	3:30PM		☐Y ☐N
	4:00PM		☐Y ☐N
	4:30PM		☐Y ☐N
	5:00PM		☐Y ☐N
	5:30PM		☐Y ☐N
	6:00PM		☐Y ☐N
	6:30PM		☐Y ☐N
	7:00PM		☐Y ☐N
	7:30PM		☐Y ☐N
	8:00PM		☐Y ☐N
	8:30PM		☐Y ☐N
	9:00PM		☐Y ☐N
	9:30PM		☐Y ☐N

TAKE 5 MINUTES EACH MORNING TO PLAN YOUR DAY.

GET EIGHT HOURS OF SLEEP!

NOTE HIGH PRIORITY TASKS WITH A ✱

ANALYZE WHY A TASK WAS NOT COMPLETED, THEN MOVE TO NEXT DAY.

ONE POSITIVE

TODAY I GAVE

DAILY
GOAL SLAYERS
PLANNER

SETTING YOURSELF UP FOR SUCCESS DAILY!

DATE

_____/_____/_____

SCRIPTURE

MOTIVATIONAL QUOTE

ONE GOAL

ONE FUN THING

*	IMPORTANT TIME	SCHEDULE	SLAYED?
	5:00AM		☐Y ☐N
	5:30AM		☐Y ☐N
	6:00AM		☐Y ☐N
	6:30AM		☐Y ☐N
	7:00AM		☐Y ☐N
	7:30AM		☐Y ☐N
	8:00AM		☐Y ☐N
	8:30AM		☐Y ☐N
	9:00AM		☐Y ☐N
	9:30AM		☐Y ☐N
	10:00AM		☐Y ☐N
	10:30AM		☐Y ☐N
	11:00AM		☐Y ☐N
	11:30AM		☐Y ☐N
	12:00PM		☐Y ☐N
	12:30PM		☐Y ☐N
	1:00PM		☐Y ☐N
	1:30PM		☐Y ☐N
	2:00PM		☐Y ☐N
	2:30PM		☐Y ☐N
	3:00PM		☐Y ☐N
	3:30PM		☐Y ☐N
	4:00PM		☐Y ☐N
	4:30PM		☐Y ☐N
	5:00PM		☐Y ☐N
	5:30PM		☐Y ☐N
	6:00PM		☐Y ☐N
	6:30PM		☐Y ☐N
	7:00PM		☐Y ☐N
	7:30PM		☐Y ☐N
	8:00PM		☐Y ☐N
	8:30PM		☐Y ☐N
	9:00PM		☐Y ☐N
	9:30PM		☐Y ☐N

HEALTH • FITNESS

WATER INTAKE

OZ. OZ. OZ. OZ. OZ.
OZ. OZ. OZ. OZ. OZ.

TAKE 5 MINUTES EACH MORNING TO PLAN YOUR DAY.

GET EIGHT HOURS OF SLEEP!

NOTE HIGH PRIORITY TASKS WITH A *

ANALYZE WHY A TASK WAS NOT COMPLETED, THEN MOVE TO NEXT DAY.

ONE POSITIVE

TODAY I GAVE

DAILY GOAL SLAYERS PLANNER

SETTING YOURSELF UP FOR SUCCESS DAILY!

DATE

_____ / _____ / _____

SCRIPTURE

MOTIVATIONAL QUOTE

ONE GOAL

ONE FUN THING

*	IMPORTANT TIME	SCHEDULE	SLAYED?
	5:00AM		☐Y ☐N
	5:30AM		☐Y ☐N
	6:00AM		☐Y ☐N
	6:30AM		☐Y ☐N
	7:00AM		☐Y ☐N
	7:30AM		☐Y ☐N
	8:00AM		☐Y ☐N
	8:30AM		☐Y ☐N
	9:00AM		☐Y ☐N
	9:30AM		☐Y ☐N
	10:00AM		☐Y ☐N
	10:30AM		☐Y ☐N
	11:00AM		☐Y ☐N
	11:30AM		☐Y ☐N
	12:00PM		☐Y ☐N
	12:30PM		☐Y ☐N
	1:00PM		☐Y ☐N
	1:30PM		☐Y ☐N
	2:00PM		☐Y ☐N
	2:30PM		☐Y ☐N
	3:00PM		☐Y ☐N
	3:30PM		☐Y ☐N
	4:00PM		☐Y ☐N
	4:30PM		☐Y ☐N
	5:00PM		☐Y ☐N
	5:30PM		☐Y ☐N
	6:00PM		☐Y ☐N
	6:30PM		☐Y ☐N
	7:00PM		☐Y ☐N
	7:30PM		☐Y ☐N
	8:00PM		☐Y ☐N
	8:30PM		☐Y ☐N
	9:00PM		☐Y ☐N
	9:30PM		☐Y ☐N

HEALTH + FITNESS

WATER INTAKE

OZ. OZ. OZ. OZ. OZ.
OZ. OZ. OZ. OZ. OZ.

TAKE 5 MINUTES EACH MORNING TO PLAN YOUR DAY.

GET EIGHT HOURS OF SLEEP!

NOTE HIGH PRIORITY TASKS WITH A *

ANALYZE WHY A TASK WAS NOT COMPLETED, THEN MOVE TO NEXT DAY.

ONE POSITIVE

TODAY I GAVE

DAILY
GOAL SLAYERS
PLANNER

SETTING YOURSELF UP FOR SUCCESS DAILY!

DATE

_____ / _____ / _____

SCRIPTURE

MOTIVATIONAL QUOTE

ONE GOAL

ONE FUN THING

HEALTH + FITNESS

WATER INTAKE

*	IMPORTANT TIME	SCHEDULE	SLAYED?
	5:00AM		☐Y ☐N
	5:30AM		☐Y ☐N
	6:00AM		☐Y ☐N
	6:30AM		☐Y ☐N
	7:00AM		☐Y ☐N
	7:30AM		☐Y ☐N
	8:00AM		☐Y ☐N
	8:30AM		☐Y ☐N
	9:00AM		☐Y ☐N
	9:30AM		☐Y ☐N
	10:00AM		☐Y ☐N
	10:30AM		☐Y ☐N
	11:00AM		☐Y ☐N
	11:30AM		☐Y ☐N
	12:00PM		☐Y ☐N
	12:30PM		☐Y ☐N
	1:00PM		☐Y ☐N
	1:30PM		☐Y ☐N
	2:00PM		☐Y ☐N
	2:30PM		☐Y ☐N
	3:00PM		☐Y ☐N
	3:30PM		☐Y ☐N
	4:00PM		☐Y ☐N
	4:30PM		☐Y ☐N
	5:00PM		☐Y ☐N
	5:30PM		☐Y ☐N
	6:00PM		☐Y ☐N
	6:30PM		☐Y ☐N
	7:00PM		☐Y ☐N
	7:30PM		☐Y ☐N
	8:00PM		☐Y ☐N
	8:30PM		☐Y ☐N
	9:00PM		☐Y ☐N
	9:30PM		☐Y ☐N

TAKE 5 MINUTES EACH MORNING TO PLAN YOUR DAY.

GET EIGHT HOURS OF SLEEP!

NOTE HIGH PRIORITY TASKS WITH A *

ANALYZE WHY A TASK WAS NOT COMPLETED, THEN MOVE TO NEXT DAY.

ONE POSITIVE

TODAY I GAVE

DAILY
GOAL SLAYERS
PLANNER

SETTING YOURSELF UP FOR SUCCESS DAILY!

DATE

_____ / _____ / _____

SCRIPTURE

MOTIVATIONAL QUOTE

ONE GOAL

ONE FUN THING

HEALTH + FITNESS

*	IMPORTANT TIME	SCHEDULE	SLAYED?
	5:00AM		☐Y ☐N
	5:30AM		☐Y ☐N
	6:00AM		☐Y ☐N
	6:30AM		☐Y ☐N
	7:00AM		☐Y ☐N
	7:30AM		☐Y ☐N
	8:00AM		☐Y ☐N
	8:30AM		☐Y ☐N
	9:00AM		☐Y ☐N
	9:30AM		☐Y ☐N
	10:00AM		☐Y ☐N
	10:30AM		☐Y ☐N
	11:00AM		☐Y ☐N
	11:30AM		☐Y ☐N
	12:00PM		☐Y ☐N
	12:30PM		☐Y ☐N
	1:00PM		☐Y ☐N
	1:30PM		☐Y ☐N
	2:00PM		☐Y ☐N
	2:30PM		☐Y ☐N
	3:00PM		☐Y ☐N
	3:30PM		☐Y ☐N
	4:00PM		☐Y ☐N
	4:30PM		☐Y ☐N
	5:00PM		☐Y ☐N
	5:30PM		☐Y ☐N
	6:00PM		☐Y ☐N
	6:30PM		☐Y ☐N
	7:00PM		☐Y ☐N
	7:30PM		☐Y ☐N
	8:00PM		☐Y ☐N
	8:30PM		☐Y ☐N
	9:00PM		☐Y ☐N
	9:30PM		☐Y ☐N

WATER INTAKE

OZ OZ OZ OZ OZ
OZ OZ OZ OZ OZ

TAKE 5 MINUTES EACH MORNING TO PLAN YOUR DAY.

GET EIGHT HOURS OF SLEEP!

NOTE HIGH PRIORITY TASKS WITH A *

ANALYZE WHY A TASK WAS NOT COMPLETED, THEN MOVE TO NEXT DAY.

ONE POSITIVE

TODAY I GAVE

DAILY
GOAL SLAYERS
PLANNER

SETTING YOURSELF UP FOR SUCCESS DAILY!

DATE

____/____/____

SCRIPTURE

MOTIVATIONAL QUOTE

ONE GOAL

ONE FUN THING

HEALTH • FITNESS

WATER INTAKE

✳	IMPORTANT TIME	SCHEDULE	SLAYED?
	5:00AM		☐Y ☐N
	5:30AM		☐Y ☐N
	6:00AM		☐Y ☐N
	6:30AM		☐Y ☐N
	7:00AM		☐Y ☐N
	7:30AM		☐Y ☐N
	8:00AM		☐Y ☐N
	8:30AM		☐Y ☐N
	9:00AM		☐Y ☐N
	9:30AM		☐Y ☐N
	10:00AM		☐Y ☐N
	10:30AM		☐Y ☐N
	11:00AM		☐Y ☐N
	11:30AM		☐Y ☐N
	12:00PM		☐Y ☐N
	12:30PM		☐Y ☐N
	1:00PM		☐Y ☐N
	1:30PM		☐Y ☐N
	2:00PM		☐Y ☐N
	2:30PM		☐Y ☐N
	3:00PM		☐Y ☐N
	3:30PM		☐Y ☐N
	4:00PM		☐Y ☐N
	4:30PM		☐Y ☐N
	5:00PM		☐Y ☐N
	5:30PM		☐Y ☐N
	6:00PM		☐Y ☐N
	6:30PM		☐Y ☐N
	7:00PM		☐Y ☐N
	7:30PM		☐Y ☐N
	8:00PM		☐Y ☐N
	8:30PM		☐Y ☐N
	9:00PM		☐Y ☐N
	9:30PM		☐Y ☐N

TAKE 5 MINUTES EACH MORNING TO PLAN YOUR DAY.

GET EIGHT HOURS OF SLEEP!

NOTE HIGH PRIORITY TASKS WITH A ✳

ANALYZE WHY A TASK WAS NOT COMPLETED, THEN MOVE TO NEXT DAY.

ONE POSITIVE

TODAY I GAVE

DAILY
GOAL SLAYERS
PLANNER

SETTING YOURSELF UP FOR SUCCESS DAILY!

DATE

_____ / _____ / _____

SCRIPTURE

MOTIVATIONAL QUOTE

ONE GOAL

ONE FUN THING

✱	IMPORTANT TIME	SCHEDULE	SLAYED?
	5:00AM		☐Y ☐N
	5:30AM		☐Y ☐N
	6:00AM		☐Y ☐N
	6:30AM		☐Y ☐N
	7:00AM		☐Y ☐N
	7:30AM		☐Y ☐N
	8:00AM		☐Y ☐N
	8:30AM		☐Y ☐N
	9:00AM		☐Y ☐N
	9:30AM		☐Y ☐N
	10:00AM		☐Y ☐N
	10:30AM		☐Y ☐N
	11:00AM		☐Y ☐N
	11:30AM		☐Y ☐N
	12:00PM		☐Y ☐N
	12:30PM		☐Y ☐N
	1:00PM		☐Y ☐N
	1:30PM		☐Y ☐N
	2:00PM		☐Y ☐N
	2:30PM		☐Y ☐N
	3:00PM		☐Y ☐N
	3:30PM		☐Y ☐N
	4:00PM		☐Y ☐N
	4:30PM		☐Y ☐N
	5:00PM		☐Y ☐N
	5:30PM		☐Y ☐N
	6:00PM		☐Y ☐N
	6:30PM		☐Y ☐N
	7:00PM		☐Y ☐N
	7:30PM		☐Y ☐N
	8:00PM		☐Y ☐N
	8:30PM		☐Y ☐N
	9:00PM		☐Y ☐N
	9:30PM		☐Y ☐N

HEALTH + FITNESS

WATER INTAKE

OZ. OZ. OZ. OZ. OZ.

OZ. OZ. OZ. OZ. OZ.

TAKE 5 MINUTES EACH MORNING TO PLAN YOUR DAY.

GET EIGHT HOURS OF SLEEP!

NOTE HIGH PRIORITY TASKS WITH A ✱

ANALYZE WHY A TASK WAS NOT COMPLETED, THEN MOVE TO NEXT DAY.

ONE POSITIVE

TODAY I GAVE

DAILY
GOAL SLAYERS
PLANNER

SETTING YOURSELF UP FOR SUCCESS DAILY!

DATE

____ / ____ / ____

SCRIPTURE

MOTIVATIONAL QUOTE

ONE GOAL

ONE FUN THING

HEALTH • FITNESS

WATER INTAKE

OZ. OZ. OZ. OZ. OZ.

OZ. OZ. OZ. OZ. OZ.

*	IMPORTANT TIME	SCHEDULE	SLAYED?
	5:00AM		☐Y ☐N
	5:30AM		☐Y ☐N
	6:00AM		☐Y ☐N
	6:30AM		☐Y ☐N
	7:00AM		☐Y ☐N
	7:30AM		☐Y ☐N
	8:00AM		☐Y ☐N
	8:30AM		☐Y ☐N
	9:00AM		☐Y ☐N
	9:30AM		☐Y ☐N
	10:00AM		☐Y ☐N
	10:30AM		☐Y ☐N
	11:00AM		☐Y ☐N
	11:30AM		☐Y ☐N
	12:00PM		☐Y ☐N
	12:30PM		☐Y ☐N
	1:00PM		☐Y ☐N
	1:30PM		☐Y ☐N
	2:00PM		☐Y ☐N
	2:30PM		☐Y ☐N
	3:00PM		☐Y ☐N
	3:30PM		☐Y ☐N
	4:00PM		☐Y ☐N
	4:30PM		☐Y ☐N
	5:00PM		☐Y ☐N
	5:30PM		☐Y ☐N
	6:00PM		☐Y ☐N
	6:30PM		☐Y ☐N
	7:00PM		☐Y ☐N
	7:30PM		☐Y ☐N
	8:00PM		☐Y ☐N
	8:30PM		☐Y ☐N
	9:00PM		☐Y ☐N
	9:30PM		☐Y ☐N

TAKE 5 MINUTES EACH MORNING TO PLAN YOUR DAY.

GET EIGHT HOURS OF SLEEP!

NOTE HIGH PRIORITY TASKS WITH A *

ANALYZE WHY A TASK WAS NOT COMPLETED, THEN MOVE TO NEXT DAY.

ONE POSITIVE

TODAY I GAVE

DAILY
GOAL SLAYERS
PLANNER

SETTING YOURSELF UP FOR SUCCESS DAILY!

DATE

_____ / _____ / _____

SCRIPTURE

MOTIVATIONAL QUOTE

ONE GOAL

ONE FUN THING

HEALTH + FITNESS

WATER INTAKE

✱	IMPORTANT TIME	SCHEDULE	SLAYED?
	5:00AM		☐Y ☐N
	5:30AM		☐Y ☐N
	6:00AM		☐Y ☐N
	6:30AM		☐Y ☐N
	7:00AM		☐Y ☐N
	7:30AM		☐Y ☐N
	8:00AM		☐Y ☐N
	8:30AM		☐Y ☐N
	9:00AM		☐Y ☐N
	9:30AM		☐Y ☐N
	10:00AM		☐Y ☐N
	10:30AM		☐Y ☐N
	11:00AM		☐Y ☐N
	11:30AM		☐Y ☐N
	12:00PM		☐Y ☐N
	12:30PM		☐Y ☐N
	1:00PM		☐Y ☐N
	1:30PM		☐Y ☐N
	2:00PM		☐Y ☐N
	2:30PM		☐Y ☐N
	3:00PM		☐Y ☐N
	3:30PM		☐Y ☐N
	4:00PM		☐Y ☐N
	4:30PM		☐Y ☐N
	5:00PM		☐Y ☐N
	5:30PM		☐Y ☐N
	6:00PM		☐Y ☐N
	6:30PM		☐Y ☐N
	7:00PM		☐Y ☐N
	7:30PM		☐Y ☐N
	8:00PM		☐Y ☐N
	8:30PM		☐Y ☐N
	9:00PM		☐Y ☐N
	9:30PM		☐Y ☐N

TAKE 5 MINUTES EACH MORNING TO PLAN YOUR DAY.

GET EIGHT HOURS OF SLEEP!

NOTE HIGH PRIORITY TASKS WITH A ✱

ANALYZE WHY A TASK WAS NOT COMPLETED, THEN MOVE TO NEXT DAY.

ONE POSITIVE

TODAY I GAVE

DAILY
GOAL SLAYERS
PLANNER

SETTING YOURSELF UP FOR SUCCESS DAILY!

DATE

____ / ____ / ____

SCRIPTURE

MOTIVATIONAL QUOTE

ONE GOAL

ONE FUN THING

HEALTH + FITNESS

WATER INTAKE

OZ OZ OZ OZ OZ
OZ OZ OZ OZ OZ

*	IMPORTANT TIME	SCHEDULE	SLAYED?
	5:00AM		☐Y ☐N
	5:30AM		☐Y ☐N
	6:00AM		☐Y ☐N
	6:30AM		☐Y ☐N
	7:00AM		☐Y ☐N
	7:30AM		☐Y ☐N
	8:00AM		☐Y ☐N
	8:30AM		☐Y ☐N
	9:00AM		☐Y ☐N
	9:30AM		☐Y ☐N
	10:00AM		☐Y ☐N
	10:30AM		☐Y ☐N
	11:00AM		☐Y ☐N
	11:30AM		☐Y ☐N
	12:00PM		☐Y ☐N
	12:30PM		☐Y ☐N
	1:00PM		☐Y ☐N
	1:30PM		☐Y ☐N
	2:00PM		☐Y ☐N
	2:30PM		☐Y ☐N
	3:00PM		☐Y ☐N
	3:30PM		☐Y ☐N
	4:00PM		☐Y ☐N
	4:30PM		☐Y ☐N
	5:00PM		☐Y ☐N
	5:30PM		☐Y ☐N
	6:00PM		☐Y ☐N
	6:30PM		☐Y ☐N
	7:00PM		☐Y ☐N
	7:30PM		☐Y ☐N
	8:00PM		☐Y ☐N
	8:30PM		☐Y ☐N
	9:00PM		☐Y ☐N
	9:30PM		☐Y ☐N

TAKE 5 MINUTES EACH MORNING TO PLAN YOUR DAY.

GET EIGHT HOURS OF SLEEP!

NOTE HIGH PRIORITY TASKS WITH A ✴

ANALYZE WHY A TASK WAS NOT COMPLETED, THEN MOVE TO NEXT DAY.

ONE POSITIVE

TODAY I GAVE

DAILY
GOAL SLAYERS
PLANNER

SETTING YOURSELF UP FOR SUCCESS DAILY!

DATE

_____ / _____ / _____

SCRIPTURE

MOTIVATIONAL QUOTE

ONE GOAL

ONE FUN THING

HEALTH + FITNESS

WATER INTAKE

OZ. OZ. OZ. OZ. OZ.

OZ. OZ. OZ. OZ. OZ.

*	IMPORTANT TIME	SCHEDULE	SLAYED?
	5:00AM		☐Y ☐N
	5:30AM		☐Y ☐N
	6:00AM		☐Y ☐N
	6:30AM		☐Y ☐N
	7:00AM		☐Y ☐N
	7:30AM		☐Y ☐N
	8:00AM		☐Y ☐N
	8:30AM		☐Y ☐N
	9:00AM		☐Y ☐N
	9:30AM		☐Y ☐N
	10:00AM		☐Y ☐N
	10:30AM		☐Y ☐N
	11:00AM		☐Y ☐N
	11:30AM		☐Y ☐N
	12:00PM		☐Y ☐N
	12:30PM		☐Y ☐N
	1:00PM		☐Y ☐N
	1:30PM		☐Y ☐N
	2:00PM		☐Y ☐N
	2:30PM		☐Y ☐N
	3:00PM		☐Y ☐N
	3:30PM		☐Y ☐N
	4:00PM		☐Y ☐N
	4:30PM		☐Y ☐N
	5:00PM		☐Y ☐N
	5:30PM		☐Y ☐N
	6:00PM		☐Y ☐N
	6:30PM		☐Y ☐N
	7:00PM		☐Y ☐N
	7:30PM		☐Y ☐N
	8:00PM		☐Y ☐N
	8:30PM		☐Y ☐N
	9:00PM		☐Y ☐N
	9:30PM		☐Y ☐N

TAKE 5 MINUTES EACH MORNING TO PLAN YOUR DAY.

GET EIGHT HOURS OF SLEEP!

NOTE HIGH PRIORITY TASKS WITH A *

ANALYZE WHY A TASK WAS NOT COMPLETED, THEN MOVE TO NEXT DAY.

ONE POSITIVE

TODAY I GAVE

DAILY
GOAL SLAYERS
PLANNER

SETTING YOURSELF UP FOR SUCCESS DAILY!

DATE

_____ / _____ / _____

SCRIPTURE

MOTIVATIONAL QUOTE

ONE GOAL

ONE FUN THING

*	IMPORTANT TIME	SCHEDULE	SLAYED?
	5:00AM		☐Y ☐N
	5:30AM		☐Y ☐N
	6:00AM		☐Y ☐N
	6:30AM		☐Y ☐N
	7:00AM		☐Y ☐N
	7:30AM		☐Y ☐N
	8:00AM		☐Y ☐N
	8:30AM		☐Y ☐N
	9:00AM		☐Y ☐N
	9:30AM		☐Y ☐N
	10:00AM		☐Y ☐N
	10:30AM		☐Y ☐N
	11:00AM		☐Y ☐N
	11:30AM		☐Y ☐N
	12:00PM		☐Y ☐N
	12:30PM		☐Y ☐N
	1:00PM		☐Y ☐N
	1:30PM		☐Y ☐N
	2:00PM		☐Y ☐N
	2:30PM		☐Y ☐N
	3:00PM		☐Y ☐N
	3:30PM		☐Y ☐N
	4:00PM		☐Y ☐N
	4:30PM		☐Y ☐N
	5:00PM		☐Y ☐N
	5:30PM		☐Y ☐N
	6:00PM		☐Y ☐N
	6:30PM		☐Y ☐N
	7:00PM		☐Y ☐N
	7:30PM		☐Y ☐N
	8:00PM		☐Y ☐N
	8:30PM		☐Y ☐N
	9:00PM		☐Y ☐N
	9:30PM		☐Y ☐N

HEALTH • FITNESS

WATER INTAKE

OZ. OZ. OZ. OZ. OZ.
OZ. OZ. OZ. OZ. OZ.

TAKE 5 MINUTES EACH MORNING TO PLAN YOUR DAY.

GET EIGHT HOURS OF SLEEP!

NOTE HIGH PRIORITY TASKS WITH A *

ANALYZE WHY A TASK WAS NOT COMPLETED, THEN MOVE TO NEXT DAY.

ONE POSITIVE

TODAY I GAVE

DAILY
GOAL SLAYERS
PLANNER

SETTING YOURSELF UP FOR SUCCESS DAILY!

DATE

_____ / _____ / _____

SCRIPTURE

MOTIVATIONAL QUOTE

ONE GOAL

ONE FUN THING

HEALTH • FITNESS

WATER INTAKE

OZ OZ OZ OZ OZ
OZ OZ OZ OZ OZ

*	IMPORTANT TIME	SCHEDULE	SLAYED?
	5:00AM		☐Y ☐N
	5:30AM		☐Y ☐N
	6:00AM		☐Y ☐N
	6:30AM		☐Y ☐N
	7:00AM		☐Y ☐N
	7:30AM		☐Y ☐N
	8:00AM		☐Y ☐N
	8:30AM		☐Y ☐N
	9:00AM		☐Y ☐N
	9:30AM		☐Y ☐N
	10:00AM		☐Y ☐N
	10:30AM		☐Y ☐N
	11:00AM		☐Y ☐N
	11:30AM		☐Y ☐N
	12:00PM		☐Y ☐N
	12:30PM		☐Y ☐N
	1:00PM		☐Y ☐N
	1:30PM		☐Y ☐N
	2:00PM		☐Y ☐N
	2:30PM		☐Y ☐N
	3:00PM		☐Y ☐N
	3:30PM		☐Y ☐N
	4:00PM		☐Y ☐N
	4:30PM		☐Y ☐N
	5:00PM		☐Y ☐N
	5:30PM		☐Y ☐N
	6:00PM		☐Y ☐N
	6:30PM		☐Y ☐N
	7:00PM		☐Y ☐N
	7:30PM		☐Y ☐N
	8:00PM		☐Y ☐N
	8:30PM		☐Y ☐N
	9:00PM		☐Y ☐N
	9:30PM		☐Y ☐N

TAKE 5 MINUTES EACH MORNING TO PLAN YOUR DAY.

GET EIGHT HOURS OF SLEEP!

NOTE HIGH PRIORITY TASKS WITH A *

ANALYZE WHY A TASK WAS NOT COMPLETED, THEN MOVE TO NEXT DAY.

ONE POSITIVE

TODAY I GAVE

DAILY
GOAL SLAYERS
PLANNER

SETTING YOURSELF UP FOR SUCCESS DAILY!

DATE

_____ / _____ / _____

SCRIPTURE

MOTIVATIONAL QUOTE

ONE GOAL

ONE FUN THING

*	IMPORTANT TIME	SCHEDULE	SLAYED?
	5:00AM		☐Y ☐N
	5:30AM		☐Y ☐N
	6:00AM		☐Y ☐N
	6:30AM		☐Y ☐N
	7:00AM		☐Y ☐N
	7:30AM		☐Y ☐N
	8:00AM		☐Y ☐N
	8:30AM		☐Y ☐N
	9:00AM		☐Y ☐N
	9:30AM		☐Y ☐N
	10:00AM		☐Y ☐N
	10:30AM		☐Y ☐N
	11:00AM		☐Y ☐N
	11:30AM		☐Y ☐N
	12:00PM		☐Y ☐N
	12:30PM		☐Y ☐N
	1:00PM		☐Y ☐N
	1:30PM		☐Y ☐N
	2:00PM		☐Y ☐N
	2:30PM		☐Y ☐N
	3:00PM		☐Y ☐N
	3:30PM		☐Y ☐N
	4:00PM		☐Y ☐N
	4:30PM		☐Y ☐N
	5:00PM		☐Y ☐N
	5:30PM		☐Y ☐N
	6:00PM		☐Y ☐N
	6:30PM		☐Y ☐N
	7:00PM		☐Y ☐N
	7:30PM		☐Y ☐N
	8:00PM		☐Y ☐N
	8:30PM		☐Y ☐N
	9:00PM		☐Y ☐N
	9:30PM		☐Y ☐N

HEALTH + FITNESS

WATER INTAKE

OZ. OZ. OZ. OZ. OZ.
OZ. OZ. OZ. OZ. OZ.

TAKE 5 MINUTES EACH MORNING TO PLAN YOUR DAY.

GET EIGHT HOURS OF SLEEP!

NOTE HIGH PRIORITY TASKS WITH A *

ANALYZE WHY A TASK WAS NOT COMPLETED, THEN MOVE TO NEXT DAY.

ONE POSITIVE

TODAY I GAVE

DAILY
GOAL SLAYERS
PLANNER

SETTING YOURSELF UP FOR SUCCESS DAILY!

DATE
____/____/____

SCRIPTURE

MOTIVATIONAL QUOTE

ONE GOAL

ONE FUN THING

HEALTH + FITNESS

WATER INTAKE

OZ. OZ. OZ. OZ. OZ.
OZ. OZ. OZ. OZ. OZ.

TAKE 5 MINUTES EACH MORNING TO PLAN YOUR DAY.

GET EIGHT HOURS OF SLEEP!

NOTE HIGH PRIORITY TASKS WITH A ✳

ANALYZE WHY A TASK WAS NOT COMPLETED, THEN MOVE TO NEXT DAY.

ONE POSITIVE

TODAY I GAVE

✳	IMPORTANT TIME	SCHEDULE	SLAYED?
	5:00AM		☐Y ☐N
	5:30AM		☐Y ☐N
	6:00AM		☐Y ☐N
	6:30AM		☐Y ☐N
	7:00AM		☐Y ☐N
	7:30AM		☐Y ☐N
	8:00AM		☐Y ☐N
	8:30AM		☐Y ☐N
	9:00AM		☐Y ☐N
	9:30AM		☐Y ☐N
	10:00AM		☐Y ☐N
	10:30AM		☐Y ☐N
	11:00AM		☐Y ☐N
	11:30AM		☐Y ☐N
	12:00PM		☐Y ☐N
	12:30PM		☐Y ☐N
	1:00PM		☐Y ☐N
	1:30PM		☐Y ☐N
	2:00PM		☐Y ☐N
	2:30PM		☐Y ☐N
	3:00PM		☐Y ☐N
	3:30PM		☐Y ☐N
	4:00PM		☐Y ☐N
	4:30PM		☐Y ☐N
	5:00PM		☐Y ☐N
	5:30PM		☐Y ☐N
	6:00PM		☐Y ☐N
	6:30PM		☐Y ☐N
	7:00PM		☐Y ☐N
	7:30PM		☐Y ☐N
	8:00PM		☐Y ☐N
	8:30PM		☐Y ☐N
	9:00PM		☐Y ☐N
	9:30PM		☐Y ☐N

DAILY
GOAL SLAYERS
PLANNER

SETTING YOURSELF UP FOR SUCCESS DAILY!

DATE

_____ / _____ / _____

SCRIPTURE

MOTIVATIONAL QUOTE

ONE GOAL

ONE FUN THING

HEALTH • FITNESS

WATER INTAKE

OZ. OZ. OZ. OZ. OZ.

OZ. OZ. OZ. OZ. OZ.

✱	IMPORTANT TIME	SCHEDULE	SLAYED?
	5:00AM		☐Y ☐N
	5:30AM		☐Y ☐N
	6:00AM		☐Y ☐N
	6:30AM		☐Y ☐N
	7:00AM		☐Y ☐N
	7:30AM		☐Y ☐N
	8:00AM		☐Y ☐N
	8:30AM		☐Y ☐N
	9:00AM		☐Y ☐N
	9:30AM		☐Y ☐N
	10:00AM		☐Y ☐N
	10:30AM		☐Y ☐N
	11:00AM		☐Y ☐N
	11:30AM		☐Y ☐N
	12:00PM		☐Y ☐N
	12:30PM		☐Y ☐N
	1:00PM		☐Y ☐N
	1:30PM		☐Y ☐N
	2:00PM		☐Y ☐N
	2:30PM		☐Y ☐N
	3:00PM		☐Y ☐N
	3:30PM		☐Y ☐N
	4:00PM		☐Y ☐N
	4:30PM		☐Y ☐N
	5:00PM		☐Y ☐N
	5:30PM		☐Y ☐N
	6:00PM		☐Y ☐N
	6:30PM		☐Y ☐N
	7:00PM		☐Y ☐N
	7:30PM		☐Y ☐N
	8:00PM		☐Y ☐N
	8:30PM		☐Y ☐N
	9:00PM		☐Y ☐N
	9:30PM		☐Y ☐N

TAKE 5 MINUTES EACH MORNING TO PLAN YOUR DAY.

GET EIGHT HOURS OF SLEEP!

NOTE HIGH PRIORITY TASKS WITH A ✱

ANALYZE WHY A TASK WAS NOT COMPLETED, THEN MOVE TO NEXT DAY.

ONE POSITIVE

TODAY I GAVE

DAILY
GOAL SLAYERS
PLANNER

SETTING YOURSELF UP FOR SUCCESS DAILY!

DATE

_____ / _____ / _____

SCRIPTURE

MOTIVATIONAL QUOTE

ONE GOAL

ONE FUN THING

✱	IMPORTANT TIME	SCHEDULE	SLAYED?
	5:00AM		☐Y ☐N
	5:30AM		☐Y ☐N
	6:00AM		☐Y ☐N
	6:30AM		☐Y ☐N
	7:00AM		☐Y ☐N
	7:30AM		☐Y ☐N
	8.00AM		☐Y ☐N
	8:30AM		☐Y ☐N
	9:00AM		☐Y ☐N
	9:30AM		☐Y ☐N
	10:00AM		☐Y ☐N
	10:30AM		☐Y ☐N
	11:00AM		☐Y ☐N
	11:30AM		☐Y ☐N
	12:00PM		☐Y ☐N
	12:30PM		☐Y ☐N
	1:00PM		☐Y ☐N
	1:30PM		☐Y ☐N
	2:00PM		☐Y ☐N
	2:30PM		☐Y ☐N
	3:00PM		☐Y ☐N
	3:30PM		☐Y ☐N
	4:00PM		☐Y ☐N
	4:30PM		☐Y ☐N
	5:00PM		☐Y ☐N
	5:30PM		☐Y ☐N
	6:00PM		☐Y ☐N
	6:30PM		☐Y ☐N
	7:00PM		☐Y ☐N
	7:30PM		☐Y ☐N
	8:00PM		☐Y ☐N
	8:30PM		☐Y ☐N
	9:00PM		☐Y ☐N
	9:30PM		☐Y ☐N

HEALTH + FITNESS

WATER INTAKE

OZ OZ OZ OZ OZ
OZ OZ OZ OZ OZ

TAKE 5 MINUTES EACH MORNING TO PLAN YOUR DAY.

GET EIGHT HOURS OF SLEEP!

NOTE HIGH PRIORITY TASKS WITH A ✱

ANALYZE WHY A TASK WAS NOT COMPLETED, THEN MOVE TO NEXT DAY.

ONE POSITIVE

TODAY I GAVE

DAILY
GOAL SLAYERS
PLANNER

SETTING YOURSELF UP FOR SUCCESS DAILY!

DATE

____ / ____ / ____

SCRIPTURE

MOTIVATIONAL QUOTE

ONE GOAL

ONE FUN THING

HEALTH • FITNESS

WATER INTAKE

✱	IMPORTANT TIME	SCHEDULE	SLAYED?
	5:00AM		☐Y ☐N
	5:30AM		☐Y ☐N
	6:00AM		☐Y ☐N
	6:30AM		☐Y ☐N
	7:00AM		☐Y ☐N
	7:30AM		☐Y ☐N
	8:00AM		☐Y ☐N
	8:30AM		☐Y ☐N
	9:00AM		☐Y ☐N
	9:30AM		☐Y ☐N
	10:00AM		☐Y ☐N
	10:30AM		☐Y ☐N
	11:00AM		☐Y ☐N
	11:30AM		☐Y ☐N
	12:00PM		☐Y ☐N
	12:30PM		☐Y ☐N
	1:00PM		☐Y ☐N
	1:30PM		☐Y ☐N
	2:00PM		☐Y ☐N
	2:30PM		☐Y ☐N
	3:00PM		☐Y ☐N
	3:30PM		☐Y ☐N
	4:00PM		☐Y ☐N
	4:30PM		☐Y ☐N
	5:00PM		☐Y ☐N
	5:30PM		☐Y ☐N
	6:00PM		☐Y ☐N
	6:30PM		☐Y ☐N
	7:00PM		☐Y ☐N
	7:30PM		☐Y ☐N
	8:00PM		☐Y ☐N
	8:30PM		☐Y ☐N
	9:00PM		☐Y ☐N
	9:30PM		☐Y ☐N

TAKE 5 MINUTES EACH MORNING TO PLAN YOUR DAY.

GET EIGHT HOURS OF SLEEP!

NOTE HIGH PRIORITY TASKS WITH A ✱

ANALYZE WHY A TASK WAS NOT COMPLETED, THEN MOVE TO NEXT DAY.

ONE POSITIVE

TODAY I GAVE

DAILY
GOAL SLAYERS
PLANNER

SETTING YOURSELF UP FOR SUCCESS DAILY!

DATE

_____ / _____ / _____

SCRIPTURE

MOTIVATIONAL QUOTE

ONE GOAL

ONE FUN THING

HEALTH + FITNESS

*	IMPORTANT TIME	SCHEDULE	SLAYED?
	5:00AM		☐Y ☐N
	5:30AM		☐Y ☐N
	6:00AM		☐Y ☐N
	6:30AM		☐Y ☐N
	7:00AM		☐Y ☐N
	7:30AM		☐Y ☐N
	8:00AM		☐Y ☐N
	8:30AM		☐Y ☐N
	9:00AM		☐Y ☐N
	9:30AM		☐Y ☐N
	10:00AM		☐Y ☐N
	10:30AM		☐Y ☐N
	11:00AM		☐Y ☐N
	11:30AM		☐Y ☐N
	12:00PM		☐Y ☐N
	12:30PM		☐Y ☐N
	1:00PM		☐Y ☐N
	1:30PM		☐Y ☐N
	2:00PM		☐Y ☐N
	2:30PM		☐Y ☐N
	3:00PM		☐Y ☐N
	3:30PM		☐Y ☐N
	4:00PM		☐Y ☐N
	4:30PM		☐Y ☐N
	5:00PM		☐Y ☐N
	5:30PM		☐Y ☐N
	6:00PM		☐Y ☐N
	6:30PM		☐Y ☐N
	7:00PM		☐Y ☐N
	7:30PM		☐Y ☐N
	8:00PM		☐Y ☐N
	8:30PM		☐Y ☐N
	9:00PM		☐Y ☐N
	9:30PM		☐Y ☐N

WATER INTAKE

OZ. OZ. OZ. OZ. OZ.
OZ. OZ. OZ. OZ. OZ.

TAKE 5 MINUTES EACH MORNING TO PLAN YOUR DAY.

GET EIGHT HOURS OF SLEEP!

NOTE HIGH PRIORITY TASKS WITH A *

ANALYZE WHY A TASK WAS NOT COMPLETED, THEN MOVE TO NEXT DAY.

ONE POSITIVE

TODAY I GAVE

DAILY
GOAL SLAYERS
PLANNER

SETTING YOURSELF UP FOR SUCCESS DAILY!

DATE

____ / ____ / ____

SCRIPTURE

MOTIVATIONAL QUOTE

ONE GOAL

ONE FUN THING

HEALTH • FITNESS

WATER INTAKE

OZ. OZ. OZ. OZ. OZ.

OZ. OZ. OZ. OZ. OZ.

*	IMPORTANT TIME	SCHEDULE	SLAYED?
	5:00AM		☐Y ☐N
	5:30AM		☐Y ☐N
	6:00AM		☐Y ☐N
	6:30AM		☐Y ☐N
	7:00AM		☐Y ☐N
	7:30AM		☐Y ☐N
	8:00AM		☐Y ☐N
	8:30AM		☐Y ☐N
	9:00AM		☐Y ☐N
	9:30AM		☐Y ☐N
	10:00AM		☐Y ☐N
	10:30AM		☐Y ☐N
	11:00AM		☐Y ☐N
	11:30AM		☐Y ☐N
	12:00PM		☐Y ☐N
	12:30PM		☐Y ☐N
	1:00PM		☐Y ☐N
	1:30PM		☐Y ☐N
	2:00PM		☐Y ☐N
	2:30PM		☐Y ☐N
	3:00PM		☐Y ☐N
	3:30PM		☐Y ☐N
	4:00PM		☐Y ☐N
	4:30PM		☐Y ☐N
	5:00PM		☐Y ☐N
	5:30PM		☐Y ☐N
	6:00PM		☐Y ☐N
	6:30PM		☐Y ☐N
	7:00PM		☐Y ☐N
	7:30PM		☐Y ☐N
	8:00PM		☐Y ☐N
	8:30PM		☐Y ☐N
	9:00PM		☐Y ☐N
	9:30PM		☐Y ☐N

TAKE 5 MINUTES EACH MORNING TO PLAN YOUR DAY.

GET EIGHT HOURS OF SLEEP!

NOTE HIGH PRIORITY TASKS WITH A ✱

ANALYZE WHY A TASK WAS NOT COMPLETED, THEN MOVE TO NEXT DAY.

ONE POSITIVE

TODAY I GAVE

DAILY
GOAL SLAYERS
PLANNER

SETTING YOURSELF UP FOR SUCCESS DAILY!

DATE

_____ / _____ / _____

SCRIPTURE

MOTIVATIONAL QUOTE

ONE GOAL

ONE FUN THING

HEALTH • FITNESS

✱	IMPORTANT TIME	SCHEDULE	SLAYED?
	5:00AM		☐Y ☐N
	5:30AM		☐Y ☐N
	6:00AM		☐Y ☐N
	6:30AM		☐Y ☐N
	7:00AM		☐Y ☐N
	7:30AM		☐Y ☐N
	8:00AM		☐Y ☐N
	8:30AM		☐Y ☐N
	9:00AM		☐Y ☐N
	9:30AM		☐Y ☐N
	10:00AM		☐Y ☐N
	10:30AM		☐Y ☐N
	11:00AM		☐Y ☐N
	11:30AM		☐Y ☐N
	12:00PM		☐Y ☐N
	12:30PM		☐Y ☐N
	1:00PM		☐Y ☐N
	1:30PM		☐Y ☐N
	2:00PM		☐Y ☐N
	2:30PM		☐Y ☐N
	3:00PM		☐Y ☐N
	3:30PM		☐Y ☐N
	4:00PM		☐Y ☐N
	4:30PM		☐Y ☐N
	5:00PM		☐Y ☐N
	5:30PM		☐Y ☐N
	6:00PM		☐Y ☐N
	6:30PM		☐Y ☐N
	7:00PM		☐Y ☐N
	7:30PM		☐Y ☐N
	8:00PM		☐Y ☐N
	8:30PM		☐Y ☐N
	9:00PM		☐Y ☐N
	9:30PM		☐Y ☐N

WATER INTAKE

OZ. OZ. OZ. OZ. OZ.
OZ. OZ. OZ. OZ. OZ.

TAKE 5 MINUTES EACH MORNING TO PLAN YOUR DAY.

GET EIGHT HOURS OF SLEEP!

NOTE HIGH PRIORITY TASKS WITH A ✱

ANALYZE WHY A TASK WAS NOT COMPLETED, THEN MOVE TO NEXT DAY.

ONE POSITIVE

TODAY I GAVE

DAILY
GOAL SLAYERS
PLANNER

SETTING YOURSELF UP FOR SUCCESS DAILY!

DATE

_____ / _____ / _____

SCRIPTURE

MOTIVATIONAL QUOTE

ONE GOAL

ONE FUN THING

✱	IMPORTANT TIME	SCHEDULE	SLAYED?
	5:00AM		☐Y ☐N
	5:30AM		☐Y ☐N
	6:00AM		☐Y ☐N
	6:30AM		☐Y ☐N
	7:00AM		☐Y ☐N
	7:30AM		☐Y ☐N
	8:00AM		☐Y ☐N
	8:30AM		☐Y ☐N
	9:00AM		☐Y ☐N
	9:30AM		☐Y ☐N
	10:00AM		☐Y ☐N
	10:30AM		☐Y ☐N
	11:00AM		☐Y ☐N
	11:30AM		☐Y ☐N
	12:00PM		☐Y ☐N
	12:30PM		☐Y ☐N
	1:00PM		☐Y ☐N
	1:30PM		☐Y ☐N
	2:00PM		☐Y ☐N
	2:30PM		☐Y ☐N
	3:00PM		☐Y ☐N
	3:30PM		☐Y ☐N
	4:00PM		☐Y ☐N
	4:30PM		☐Y ☐N
	5:00PM		☐Y ☐N
	5:30PM		☐Y ☐N
	6:00PM		☐Y ☐N
	6:30PM		☐Y ☐N
	7:00PM		☐Y ☐N
	7:30PM		☐Y ☐N
	8:00PM		☐Y ☐N
	8:30PM		☐Y ☐N
	9:00PM		☐Y ☐N
	9:30PM		☐Y ☐N

HEALTH • FITNESS

WATER INTAKE

OZ OZ OZ OZ OZ
OZ OZ OZ OZ OZ

TAKE 5 MINUTES EACH MORNING TO PLAN YOUR DAY.

GET EIGHT HOURS OF SLEEP!

NOTE HIGH PRIORITY TASKS WITH A ✱

ANALYZE WHY A TASK WAS NOT COMPLETED, THEN MOVE TO NEXT DAY.

ONE POSITIVE

TODAY I GAVE

DAILY
GOAL SLAYERS
PLANNER

SETTING YOURSELF UP FOR SUCCESS DAILY!

DATE

_____ / _____ / _____

SCRIPTURE

MOTIVATIONAL QUOTE

ONE GOAL

ONE FUN THING

*	IMPORTANT TIME	SCHEDULE	SLAYED?
	5:00AM		☐Y ☐N
	5:30AM		☐Y ☐N
	6:00AM		☐Y ☐N
	6:30AM		☐Y ☐N
	7:00AM		☐Y ☐N
	7:30AM		☐Y ☐N
	8:00AM		☐Y ☐N
	8:30AM		☐Y ☐N
	9:00AM		☐Y ☐N
	9:30AM		☐Y ☐N
	10:00AM		☐Y ☐N
	10:30AM		☐Y ☐N
	11:00AM		☐Y ☐N
	11:30AM		☐Y ☐N
	12:00PM		☐Y ☐N
	12:30PM		☐Y ☐N
	1:00PM		☐Y ☐N
	1:30PM		☐Y ☐N
	2:00PM		☐Y ☐N
	2:30PM		☐Y ☐N
	3:00PM		☐Y ☐N
	3:30PM		☐Y ☐N
	4:00PM		☐Y ☐N
	4:30PM		☐Y ☐N
	5:00PM		☐Y ☐N
	5:30PM		☐Y ☐N
	6:00PM		☐Y ☐N
	6:30PM		☐Y ☐N
	7:00PM		☐Y ☐N
	7:30PM		☐Y ☐N
	8:00PM		☐Y ☐N
	8:30PM		☐Y ☐N
	9:00PM		☐Y ☐N
	9:30PM		☐Y ☐N

HEALTH + FITNESS

WATER INTAKE

OZ. OZ. OZ. OZ. OZ.
OZ. OZ. OZ. OZ. OZ.

TAKE 5 MINUTES EACH MORNING TO PLAN YOUR DAY.

GET EIGHT HOURS OF SLEEP!

NOTE HIGH PRIORITY TASKS WITH A *

ANALYZE WHY A TASK WAS NOT COMPLETED, THEN MOVE TO NEXT DAY.

ONE POSITIVE

TODAY I GAVE

DAILY
GOAL SLAYERS
PLANNER

SETTING YOURSELF UP FOR SUCCESS DAILY!

DATE

_____ / _____ / _____

SCRIPTURE

MOTIVATIONAL QUOTE

ONE GOAL

ONE FUN THING

*	IMPORTANT TIME	SCHEDULE	SLAYED?
	5:00AM		☐Y ☐N
	5:30AM		☐Y ☐N
	6:00AM		☐Y ☐N
	6:30AM		☐Y ☐N
	7:00AM		☐Y ☐N
	7:30AM		☐Y ☐N
	8:00AM		☐Y ☐N
	8:30AM		☐Y ☐N
	9:00AM		☐Y ☐N
	9:30AM		☐Y ☐N
	10:00AM		☐Y ☐N
	10:30AM		☐Y ☐N
	11:00AM		☐Y ☐N
	11:30AM		☐Y ☐N
	12:00PM		☐Y ☐N
	12:30PM		☐Y ☐N
	1:00PM		☐Y ☐N
	1:30PM		☐Y ☐N
	2:00PM		☐Y ☐N
	2:30PM		☐Y ☐N
	3:00PM		☐Y ☐N
	3:30PM		☐Y ☐N
	4:00PM		☐Y ☐N
	4:30PM		☐Y ☐N
	5:00PM		☐Y ☐N
	5:30PM		☐Y ☐N
	6:00PM		☐Y ☐N
	6:30PM		☐Y ☐N
	7:00PM		☐Y ☐N
	7:30PM		☐Y ☐N
	8:00PM		☐Y ☐N
	8:30PM		☐Y ☐N
	9:00PM		☐Y ☐N
	9:30PM		☐Y ☐N

HEALTH • FITNESS

WATER INTAKE

OZ. OZ. OZ. OZ. OZ.
OZ. OZ. OZ. OZ. OZ.

TAKE 5 MINUTES EACH MORNING TO PLAN YOUR DAY.

GET EIGHT HOURS OF SLEEP!

NOTE HIGH PRIORITY TASKS WITH A *

ANALYZE WHY A TASK WAS NOT COMPLETED, THEN MOVE TO NEXT DAY.

ONE POSITIVE

TODAY I GAVE

DAILY
GOAL SLAYERS
PLANNER

SETTING YOURSELF UP FOR SUCCESS DAILY!

DATE
_____ / _____ / _____

SCRIPTURE

MOTIVATIONAL QUOTE

ONE GOAL

ONE FUN THING

*	IMPORTANT TIME	SCHEDULE	SLAYED?
	5:00AM		☐Y ☐N
	5:30AM		☐Y ☐N
	6:00AM		☐Y ☐N
	6:30AM		☐Y ☐N
	7:00AM		☐Y ☐N
	7:30AM		☐Y ☐N
	8:00AM		☐Y ☐N
	8:30AM		☐Y ☐N
	9:00AM		☐Y ☐N
	9:30AM		☐Y ☐N
	10:00AM		☐Y ☐N
	10:30AM		☐Y ☐N
	11:00AM		☐Y ☐N
	11:30AM		☐Y ☐N
	12:00PM		☐Y ☐N
	12:30PM		☐Y ☐N
	1:00PM		☐Y ☐N
	1:30PM		☐Y ☐N
	2:00PM		☐Y ☐N
	2:30PM		☐Y ☐N
	3:00PM		☐Y ☐N
	3:30PM		☐Y ☐N
	4:00PM		☐Y ☐N
	4:30PM		☐Y ☐N
	5:00PM		☐Y ☐N
	5:30PM		☐Y ☐N
	6:00PM		☐Y ☐N
	6:30PM		☐Y ☐N
	7:00PM		☐Y ☐N
	7:30PM		☐Y ☐N
	8:00PM		☐Y ☐N
	8:30PM		☐Y ☐N
	9:00PM		☐Y ☐N
	9:30PM		☐Y ☐N

HEALTH • FITNESS

WATER INTAKE

OZ. OZ. OZ. OZ. OZ.

OZ. OZ. OZ. OZ. OZ.

TAKE 5 MINUTES EACH MORNING TO PLAN YOUR DAY.

GET EIGHT HOURS OF SLEEP!

NOTE HIGH PRIORITY TASKS WITH A *

ANALYZE WHY A TASK WAS NOT COMPLETED, THEN MOVE TO NEXT DAY.

ONE POSITIVE

TODAY I GAVE

DAILY
GOAL SLAYERS
PLANNER

SETTING YOURSELF UP FOR SUCCESS DAILY!

DATE

_____ / _____ / _____

SCRIPTURE

MOTIVATIONAL QUOTE

ONE GOAL

ONE FUN THING

HEALTH • FITNESS

WATER INTAKE

OZ. OZ. OZ. OZ. OZ.
OZ. OZ. OZ. OZ. OZ.

*	IMPORTANT TIME	SCHEDULE	SLAYED?
	5:00AM		☐Y ☐N
	5:30AM		☐Y ☐N
	6:00AM		☐Y ☐N
	6:30AM		☐Y ☐N
	7:00AM		☐Y ☐N
	7:30AM		☐Y ☐N
	8:00AM		☐Y ☐N
	8:30AM		☐Y ☐N
	9:00AM		☐Y ☐N
	9:30AM		☐Y ☐N
	10:00AM		☐Y ☐N
	10:30AM		☐Y ☐N
	11:00AM		☐Y ☐N
	11:30AM		☐Y ☐N
	12:00PM		☐Y ☐N
	12:30PM		☐Y ☐N
	1:00PM		☐Y ☐N
	1:30PM		☐Y ☐N
	2:00PM		☐Y ☐N
	2:30PM		☐Y ☐N
	3:00PM		☐Y ☐N
	3:30PM		☐Y ☐N
	4:00PM		☐Y ☐N
	4:30PM		☐Y ☐N
	5:00PM		☐Y ☐N
	5:30PM		☐Y ☐N
	6:00PM		☐Y ☐N
	6:30PM		☐Y ☐N
	7:00PM		☐Y ☐N
	7:30PM		☐Y ☐N
	8:00PM		☐Y ☐N
	8:30PM		☐Y ☐N
	9:00PM		☐Y ☐N
	9:30PM		☐Y ☐N

TAKE 5 MINUTES EACH MORNING TO PLAN YOUR DAY.

GET EIGHT HOURS OF SLEEP!

NOTE HIGH PRIORITY TASKS WITH A *

ANALYZE WHY A TASK WAS NOT COMPLETED, THEN MOVE TO NEXT DAY.

ONE POSITIVE

TODAY I GAVE

DAILY
GOAL SLAYERS
PLANNER

SETTING YOURSELF UP FOR SUCCESS DAILY!

DATE

____/____/_____

SCRIPTURE

MOTIVATIONAL QUOTE

ONE GOAL

ONE FUN THING

HEALTH + FITNESS

WATER INTAKE

OZ. OZ. OZ. OZ. OZ.

OZ. OZ. OZ. OZ. OZ.

✳	IMPORTANT TIME	SCHEDULE	SLAYED?
	5:00AM		☐Y ☐N
	5:30AM		☐Y ☐N
	6:00AM		☐Y ☐N
	6:30AM		☐Y ☐N
	7:00AM		☐Y ☐N
	7:30AM		☐Y ☐N
	8:00AM		☐Y ☐N
	8:30AM		☐Y ☐N
	9:00AM		☐Y ☐N
	9:30AM		☐Y ☐N
	10:00AM		☐Y ☐N
	10:30AM		☐Y ☐N
	11:00AM		☐Y ☐N
	11:30AM		☐Y ☐N
	12:00PM		☐Y ☐N
	12:30PM		☐Y ☐N
	1:00PM		☐Y ☐N
	1:30PM		☐Y ☐N
	2:00PM		☐Y ☐N
	2:30PM		☐Y ☐N
	3:00PM		☐Y ☐N
	3:30PM		☐Y ☐N
	4:00PM		☐Y ☐N
	4:30PM		☐Y ☐N
	5:00PM		☐Y ☐N
	5:30PM		☐Y ☐N
	6:00PM		☐Y ☐N
	6:30PM		☐Y ☐N
	7:00PM		☐Y ☐N
	7:30PM		☐Y ☐N
	8:00PM		☐Y ☐N
	8:30PM		☐Y ☐N
	9:00PM		☐Y ☐N
	9:30PM		☐Y ☐N

TAKE 5 MINUTES EACH MORNING TO PLAN YOUR DAY.

GET EIGHT HOURS OF SLEEP!

NOTE HIGH PRIORITY TASKS WITH A ✳

ANALYZE WHY A TASK WAS NOT COMPLETED, THEN MOVE TO NEXT DAY.

ONE POSITIVE

TODAY I GAVE

DAILY
GOAL SLAYERS
PLANNER

SETTING YOURSELF UP FOR SUCCESS DAILY!

DATE

_____/_____/_____

SCRIPTURE

MOTIVATIONAL QUOTE

ONE GOAL

ONE FUN THING

HEALTH • FITNESS

WATER INTAKE

*	IMPORTANT TIME	SCHEDULE	SLAYED?
	5:00AM		☐Y ☐N
	5:30AM		☐Y ☐N
	6:00AM		☐Y ☐N
	6:30AM		☐Y ☐N
	7:00AM		☐Y ☐N
	7:30AM		☐Y ☐N
	8:00AM		☐Y ☐N
	8:30AM		☐Y ☐N
	9:00AM		☐Y ☐N
	9:30AM		☐Y ☐N
	10:00AM		☐Y ☐N
	10:30AM		☐Y ☐N
	11:00AM		☐Y ☐N
	11:30AM		☐Y ☐N
	12:00PM		☐Y ☐N
	12:30PM		☐Y ☐N
	1:00PM		☐Y ☐N
	1:30PM		☐Y ☐N
	2:00PM		☐Y ☐N
	2:30PM		☐Y ☐N
	3:00PM		☐Y ☐N
	3:30PM		☐Y ☐N
	4:00PM		☐Y ☐N
	4:30PM		☐Y ☐N
	5:00PM		☐Y ☐N
	5:30PM		☐Y ☐N
	6:00PM		☐Y ☐N
	6:30PM		☐Y ☐N
	7:00PM		☐Y ☐N
	7:30PM		☐Y ☐N
	8:00PM		☐Y ☐N
	8:30PM		☐Y ☐N
	9:00PM		☐Y ☐N
	9:30PM		☐Y ☐N

TAKE 5 MINUTES EACH MORNING TO PLAN YOUR DAY.

GET EIGHT HOURS OF SLEEP!

NOTE HIGH PRIORITY TASKS WITH A *

ANALYZE WHY A TASK WAS NOT COMPLETED, THEN MOVE TO NEXT DAY.

ONE POSITIVE

TODAY I GAVE

DAILY
GOAL SLAYERS
PLANNER

SETTING YOURSELF UP FOR SUCCESS DAILY!

DATE

_____ / _____ / _____

SCRIPTURE

MOTIVATIONAL QUOTE

ONE GOAL

ONE FUN THING

*	IMPORTANT TIME	SCHEDULE	SLAYED?
	5:00AM		☐Y ☐N
	5:30AM		☐Y ☐N
	6:00AM		☐Y ☐N
	6:30AM		☐Y ☐N
	7:00AM		☐Y ☐N
	7:30AM		☐Y ☐N
	8:00AM		☐Y ☐N
	8:30AM		☐Y ☐N
	9:00AM		☐Y ☐N
	9:30AM		☐Y ☐N
	10:00AM		☐Y ☐N
	10:30AM		☐Y ☐N
	11:00AM		☐Y ☐N
	11:30AM		☐Y ☐N
	12:00PM		☐Y ☐N
	12:30PM		☐Y ☐N
	1:00PM		☐Y ☐N
	1:30PM		☐Y ☐N
	2:00PM		☐Y ☐N
	2:30PM		☐Y ☐N
	3:00PM		☐Y ☐N
	3:30PM		☐Y ☐N
	4:00PM		☐Y ☐N
	4:30PM		☐Y ☐N
	5:00PM		☐Y ☐N
	5:30PM		☐Y ☐N
	6:00PM		☐Y ☐N
	6:30PM		☐Y ☐N
	7:00PM		☐Y ☐N
	7:30PM		☐Y ☐N
	8:00PM		☐Y ☐N
	8:30PM		☐Y ☐N
	9:00PM		☐Y ☐N
	9:30PM		☐Y ☐N

HEALTH + FITNESS

WATER INTAKE

OZ OZ OZ OZ OZ

OZ OZ OZ OZ OZ

TAKE 5 MINUTES EACH MORNING TO PLAN YOUR DAY.

GET EIGHT HOURS OF SLEEP!

NOTE HIGH PRIORITY TASKS WITH A *

ANALYZE WHY A TASK WAS NOT COMPLETED, THEN MOVE TO NEXT DAY.

ONE POSITIVE

TODAY I GAVE

DAILY
GOAL SLAYERS
PLANNER

SETTING YOURSELF UP FOR SUCCESS DAILY!

DATE

____ / ____ / ____

SCRIPTURE

MOTIVATIONAL QUOTE

ONE GOAL

ONE FUN THING

HEALTH + FITNESS

WATER INTAKE

OZ. OZ. OZ. OZ. OZ.
OZ. OZ. OZ. OZ. OZ.

*	IMPORTANT TIME	SCHEDULE	SLAYED?
	5:00AM		☐Y ☐N
	5:30AM		☐Y ☐N
	6:00AM		☐Y ☐N
	6:30AM		☐Y ☐N
	7:00AM		☐Y ☐N
	7:30AM		☐Y ☐N
	8:00AM		☐Y ☐N
	8:30AM		☐Y ☐N
	9:00AM		☐Y ☐N
	9:30AM		☐Y ☐N
	10:00AM		☐Y ☐N
	10:30AM		☐Y ☐N
	11:00AM		☐Y ☐N
	11:30AM		☐Y ☐N
	12:00PM		☐Y ☐N
	12:30PM		☐Y ☐N
	1:00PM		☐Y ☐N
	1:30PM		☐Y ☐N
	2:00PM		☐Y ☐N
	2:30PM		☐Y ☐N
	3:00PM		☐Y ☐N
	3:30PM		☐Y ☐N
	4:00PM		☐Y ☐N
	4:30PM		☐Y ☐N
	5:00PM		☐Y ☐N
	5:30PM		☐Y ☐N
	6:00PM		☐Y ☐N
	6:30PM		☐Y ☐N
	7:00PM		☐Y ☐N
	7:30PM		☐Y ☐N
	8:00PM		☐Y ☐N
	8:30PM		☐Y ☐N
	9:00PM		☐Y ☐N
	9:30PM		☐Y ☐N

TAKE 5 MINUTES EACH MORNING TO PLAN YOUR DAY.

GET EIGHT HOURS OF SLEEP!

NOTE HIGH PRIORITY TASKS WITH A *

ANALYZE WHY A TASK WAS NOT COMPLETED, THEN MOVE TO NEXT DAY.

ONE POSITIVE

TODAY I GAVE

DAILY
GOAL SLAYERS
PLANNER

SETTING YOURSELF UP FOR SUCCESS DAILY!

DATE

____ / ____ / ____

SCRIPTURE

MOTIVATIONAL QUOTE

ONE GOAL

ONE FUN THING

HEALTH + FITNESS

WATER INTAKE

OZ. OZ. OZ. OZ. OZ.

OZ. OZ. OZ. OZ. OZ.

TAKE 5 MINUTES EACH MORNING TO PLAN YOUR DAY.

GET EIGHT HOURS OF SLEEP!

NOTE HIGH PRIORITY TASKS WITH A ✱

ANALYZE WHY A TASK WAS NOT COMPLETED, THEN MOVE TO NEXT DAY.

ONE POSITIVE

TODAY I GAVE

✱	IMPORTANT TIME	SCHEDULE	SLAYED?
	5:00AM		☐Y ☐N
	5:30AM		☐Y ☐N
	6:00AM		☐Y ☐N
	6:30AM		☐Y ☐N
	7:00AM		☐Y ☐N
	7:30AM		☐Y ☐N
	8:00AM		☐Y ☐N
	8:30AM		☐Y ☐N
	9:00AM		☐Y ☐N
	9:30AM		☐Y ☐N
	10:00AM		☐Y ☐N
	10:30AM		☐Y ☐N
	11:00AM		☐Y ☐N
	11:30AM		☐Y ☐N
	12:00PM		☐Y ☐N
	12:30PM		☐Y ☐N
	1:00PM		☐Y ☐N
	1:30PM		☐Y ☐N
	2:00PM		☐Y ☐N
	2:30PM		☐Y ☐N
	3:00PM		☐Y ☐N
	3:30PM		☐Y ☐N
	4:00PM		☐Y ☐N
	4:30PM		☐Y ☐N
	5:00PM		☐Y ☐N
	5:30PM		☐Y ☐N
	6:00PM		☐Y ☐N
	6:30PM		☐Y ☐N
	7:00PM		☐Y ☐N
	7:30PM		☐Y ☐N
	8:00PM		☐Y ☐N
	8:30PM		☐Y ☐N
	9:00PM		☐Y ☐N
	9:30PM		☐Y ☐N

DAILY
GOAL SLAYERS
PLANNER

SETTING YOURSELF UP FOR SUCCESS DAILY!

DATE

_____ / _____ / _____

SCRIPTURE

MOTIVATIONAL QUOTE

ONE GOAL

ONE FUN THING

*	IMPORTANT TIME	SCHEDULE	SLAYED?
	5:00AM		☐Y ☐N
	5:30AM		☐Y ☐N
	6:00AM		☐Y ☐N
	6:30AM		☐Y ☐N
	7:00AM		☐Y ☐N
	7:30AM		☐Y ☐N
	8:00AM		☐Y ☐N
	8:30AM		☐Y ☐N
	9:00AM		☐Y ☐N
	9:30AM		☐Y ☐N
	10:00AM		☐Y ☐N
	10:30AM		☐Y ☐N
	11:00AM		☐Y ☐N
	11:30AM		☐Y ☐N
	12:00PM		☐Y ☐N
	12:30PM		☐Y ☐N
	1:00PM		☐Y ☐N
	1:30PM		☐Y ☐N
	2:00PM		☐Y ☐N
	2:30PM		☐Y ☐N
	3:00PM		☐Y ☐N
	3:30PM		☐Y ☐N
	4:00PM		☐Y ☐N
	4:30PM		☐Y ☐N
	5:00PM		☐Y ☐N
	5:30PM		☐Y ☐N
	6:00PM		☐Y ☐N
	6:30PM		☐Y ☐N
	7:00PM		☐Y ☐N
	7:30PM		☐Y ☐N
	8:00PM		☐Y ☐N
	8:30PM		☐Y ☐N
	9:00PM		☐Y ☐N
	9:30PM		☐Y ☐N

HEALTH • FITNESS

WATER INTAKE

OZ. OZ. OZ. OZ. OZ.
OZ. OZ. OZ. OZ. OZ.

TAKE 5 MINUTES EACH MORNING TO PLAN YOUR DAY.

GET EIGHT HOURS OF SLEEP!

NOTE HIGH PRIORITY TASKS WITH A *

ANALYZE WHY A TASK WAS NOT COMPLETED, THEN MOVE TO NEXT DAY.

ONE POSITIVE

TODAY I GAVE

DAILY
GOAL SLAYERS
PLANNER

SETTING YOURSELF UP FOR SUCCESS DAILY!

DATE

____ / ____ / ____

SCRIPTURE

MOTIVATIONAL QUOTE

ONE GOAL

ONE FUN THING

✱	IMPORTANT TIME	SCHEDULE	SLAYED?
	5:00AM		☐Y ☐N
	5:30AM		☐Y ☐N
	6:00AM		☐Y ☐N
	6:30AM		☐Y ☐N
	7:00AM		☐Y ☐N
	7:30AM		☐Y ☐N
	8:00AM		☐Y ☐N
	8:30AM		☐Y ☐N
	9:00AM		☐Y ☐N
	9:30AM		☐Y ☐N
	10:00AM		☐Y ☐N
	10:30AM		☐Y ☐N
	11:00AM		☐Y ☐N
	11:30AM		☐Y ☐N
	12:00PM		☐Y ☐N
	12:30PM		☐Y ☐N
	1:00PM		☐Y ☐N
	1:30PM		☐Y ☐N
	2:00PM		☐Y ☐N
	2:30PM		☐Y ☐N
	3:00PM		☐Y ☐N
	3:30PM		☐Y ☐N
	4:00PM		☐Y ☐N
	4:30PM		☐Y ☐N
	5:00PM		☐Y ☐N
	5:30PM		☐Y ☐N
	6:00PM		☐Y ☐N
	6:30PM		☐Y ☐N
	7:00PM		☐Y ☐N
	7:30PM		☐Y ☐N
	8:00PM		☐Y ☐N
	8:30PM		☐Y ☐N
	9:00PM		☐Y ☐N
	9:30PM		☐Y ☐N

HEALTH • FITNESS

WATER INTAKE

OZ. OZ. OZ. OZ. OZ.
OZ. OZ. OZ. OZ. OZ.

TAKE 5 MINUTES EACH MORNING TO PLAN YOUR DAY.

GET EIGHT HOURS OF SLEEP!

NOTE HIGH PRIORITY TASKS WITH A ✱

ANALYZE WHY A TASK WAS NOT COMPLETED, THEN MOVE TO NEXT DAY.

ONE POSITIVE

TODAY I GAVE

DAILY
GOAL SLAYERS
PLANNER

SETTING YOURSELF UP FOR SUCCESS DAILY!

DATE
_____ / _____ / _____

SCRIPTURE

MOTIVATIONAL QUOTE

ONE GOAL

ONE FUN THING

HEALTH • FITNESS

WATER INTAKE

OZ OZ OZ OZ OZ
OZ OZ OZ OZ OZ

*	IMPORTANT TIME	SCHEDULE	SLAYED?
	5:00AM		☐Y ☐N
	5:30AM		☐Y ☐N
	6:00AM		☐Y ☐N
	6:30AM		☐Y ☐N
	7:00AM		☐Y ☐N
	7:30AM		☐Y ☐N
	8:00AM		☐Y ☐N
	8:30AM		☐Y ☐N
	9:00AM		☐Y ☐N
	9:30AM		☐Y ☐N
	10:00AM		☐Y ☐N
	10:30AM		☐Y ☐N
	11:00AM		☐Y ☐N
	11:30AM		☐Y ☐N
	12:00PM		☐Y ☐N
	12:30PM		☐Y ☐N
	1:00PM		☐Y ☐N
	1:30PM		☐Y ☐N
	2:00PM		☐Y ☐N
	2:30PM		☐Y ☐N
	3:00PM		☐Y ☐N
	3:30PM		☐Y ☐N
	4:00PM		☐Y ☐N
	4:30PM		☐Y ☐N
	5:00PM		☐Y ☐N
	5:30PM		☐Y ☐N
	6:00PM		☐Y ☐N
	6:30PM		☐Y ☐N
	7:00PM		☐Y ☐N
	7:30PM		☐Y ☐N
	8:00PM		☐Y ☐N
	8:30PM		☐Y ☐N
	9:00PM		☐Y ☐N
	9:30PM		☐Y ☐N

TAKE 5 MINUTES EACH MORNING TO PLAN YOUR DAY.

GET EIGHT HOURS OF SLEEP!

NOTE HIGH PRIORITY TASKS WITH A *

ANALYZE WHY A TASK WAS NOT COMPLETED, THEN MOVE TO NEXT DAY.

ONE POSITIVE

TODAY I GAVE

DAILY
GOAL SLAYERS
PLANNER

SETTING YOURSELF UP FOR SUCCESS DAILY!

DATE

_____ / _____ / _____

SCRIPTURE

MOTIVATIONAL QUOTE

ONE GOAL

ONE FUN THING

HEALTH • FITNESS

WATER INTAKE

✱	IMPORTANT TIME	SCHEDULE	SLAYED?
	5:00AM		☐Y ☐N
	5:30AM		☐Y ☐N
	6:00AM		☐Y ☐N
	6:30AM		☐Y ☐N
	7:00AM		☐Y ☐N
	7:30AM		☐Y ☐N
	8:00AM		☐Y ☐N
	8:30AM		☐Y ☐N
	9:00AM		☐Y ☐N
	9:30AM		☐Y ☐N
	10:00AM		☐Y ☐N
	10:30AM		☐Y ☐N
	11:00AM		☐Y ☐N
	11:30AM		☐Y ☐N
	12:00PM		☐Y ☐N
	12:30PM		☐Y ☐N
	1:00PM		☐Y ☐N
	1:30PM		☐Y ☐N
	2:00PM		☐Y ☐N
	2:30PM		☐Y ☐N
	3:00PM		☐Y ☐N
	3:30PM		☐Y ☐N
	4:00PM		☐Y ☐N
	4:30PM		☐Y ☐N
	5:00PM		☐Y ☐N
	5:30PM		☐Y ☐N
	6:00PM		☐Y ☐N
	6:30PM		☐Y ☐N
	7:00PM		☐Y ☐N
	7:30PM		☐Y ☐N
	8:00PM		☐Y ☐N
	8:30PM		☐Y ☐N
	9:00PM		☐Y ☐N
	9:30PM		☐Y ☐N

TAKE 5 MINUTES EACH MORNING TO PLAN YOUR DAY.

GET EIGHT HOURS OF SLEEP!

NOTE HIGH PRIORITY TASKS WITH A ✱

ANALYZE WHY A TASK WAS NOT COMPLETED, THEN MOVE TO NEXT DAY.

ONE POSITIVE

TODAY I GAVE

DAILY
GOAL SLAYERS
PLANNER

SETTING YOURSELF UP FOR SUCCESS DAILY!

DATE

_____ / _____ / _____

SCRIPTURE

MOTIVATIONAL QUOTE

ONE GOAL

ONE FUN THING

HEALTH · FITNESS

WATER INTAKE

OZ. OZ. OZ. OZ. OZ.

OZ. OZ. OZ. OZ. OZ.

*	IMPORTANT TIME	SCHEDULE	SLAYED?
	5:00AM		☐Y ☐N
	5:30AM		☐Y ☐N
	6:00AM		☐Y ☐N
	6:30AM		☐Y ☐N
	7:00AM		☐Y ☐N
	7:30AM		☐Y ☐N
	8:00AM		☐Y ☐N
	8:30AM		☐Y ☐N
	9:00AM		☐Y ☐N
	9:30AM		☐Y ☐N
	10:00AM		☐Y ☐N
	10:30AM		☐Y ☐N
	11:00AM		☐Y ☐N
	11:30AM		☐Y ☐N
	12:00PM		☐Y ☐N
	12:30PM		☐Y ☐N
	1:00PM		☐Y ☐N
	1:30PM		☐Y ☐N
	2:00PM		☐Y ☐N
	2:30PM		☐Y ☐N
	3:00PM		☐Y ☐N
	3:30PM		☐Y ☐N
	4:00PM		☐Y ☐N
	4:30PM		☐Y ☐N
	5:00PM		☐Y ☐N
	5:30PM		☐Y ☐N
	6:00PM		☐Y ☐N
	6:30PM		☐Y ☐N
	7:00PM		☐Y ☐N
	7:30PM		☐Y ☐N
	8:00PM		☐Y ☐N
	8:30PM		☐Y ☐N
	9:00PM		☐Y ☐N
	9:30PM		☐Y ☐N

TAKE 5 MINUTES EACH MORNING TO PLAN YOUR DAY.

GET EIGHT HOURS OF SLEEP!

NOTE HIGH PRIORITY TASKS WITH A *

ANALYZE WHY A TASK WAS NOT COMPLETED, THEN MOVE TO NEXT DAY.

ONE POSITIVE

TODAY I GAVE

DAILY
GOAL SLAYERS
PLANNER

SETTING YOURSELF UP FOR SUCCESS DAILY!

DATE
_____ / _____ / _____

SCRIPTURE

MOTIVATIONAL QUOTE

ONE GOAL

ONE FUN THING

HEALTH + FITNESS

WATER INTAKE

*	IMPORTANT TIME	SCHEDULE	SLAYED?
	5:00AM		☐Y ☐N
	5:30AM		☐Y ☐N
	6:00AM		☐Y ☐N
	6:30AM		☐Y ☐N
	7:00AM		☐Y ☐N
	7:30AM		☐Y ☐N
	8:00AM		☐Y ☐N
	8:30AM		☐Y ☐N
	9:00AM		☐Y ☐N
	9:30AM		☐Y ☐N
	10:00AM		☐Y ☐N
	10:30AM		☐Y ☐N
	11:00AM		☐Y ☐N
	11:30AM		☐Y ☐N
	12:00PM		☐Y ☐N
	12:30PM		☐Y ☐N
	1:00PM		☐Y ☐N
	1:30PM		☐Y ☐N
	2:00PM		☐Y ☐N
	2:30PM		☐Y ☐N
	3:00PM		☐Y ☐N
	3:30PM		☐Y ☐N
	4:00PM		☐Y ☐N
	4:30PM		☐Y ☐N
	5:00PM		☐Y ☐N
	5:30PM		☐Y ☐N
	6:00PM		☐Y ☐N
	6:30PM		☐Y ☐N
	7:00PM		☐Y ☐N
	7:30PM		☐Y ☐N
	8:00PM		☐Y ☐N
	8:30PM		☐Y ☐N
	9:00PM		☐Y ☐N
	9:30PM		☐Y ☐N

TAKE 5 MINUTES EACH MORNING TO PLAN YOUR DAY.

GET EIGHT HOURS OF SLEEP!

NOTE HIGH PRIORITY TASKS WITH A *

ANALYZE WHY A TASK WAS NOT COMPLETED, THEN MOVE TO NEXT DAY.

ONE POSITIVE

TODAY I GAVE

DAILY
GOAL SLAYERS
PLANNER

SETTING YOURSELF UP FOR SUCCESS DAILY!

DATE

_____ / _____ / _____

SCRIPTURE

MOTIVATIONAL QUOTE

ONE GOAL

ONE FUN THING

HEALTH • FITNESS

WATER INTAKE

*	IMPORTANT TIME	SCHEDULE	SLAYED?
	5:00AM		☐Y ☐N
	5:30AM		☐Y ☐N
	6:00AM		☐Y ☐N
	6:30AM		☐Y ☐N
	7:00AM		☐Y ☐N
	7:30AM		☐Y ☐N
	8:00AM		☐Y ☐N
	8:30AM		☐Y ☐N
	9:00AM		☐Y ☐N
	9:30AM		☐Y ☐N
	10:00AM		☐Y ☐N
	10:30AM		☐Y ☐N
	11:00AM		☐Y ☐N
	11:30AM		☐Y ☐N
	12:00PM		☐Y ☐N
	12:30PM		☐Y ☐N
	1:00PM		☐Y ☐N
	1:30PM		☐Y ☐N
	2:00PM		☐Y ☐N
	2:30PM		☐Y ☐N
	3:00PM		☐Y ☐N
	3:30PM		☐Y ☐N
	4:00PM		☐Y ☐N
	4:30PM		☐Y ☐N
	5:00PM		☐Y ☐N
	5:30PM		☐Y ☐N
	6:00PM		☐Y ☐N
	6:30PM		☐Y ☐N
	7:00PM		☐Y ☐N
	7:30PM		☐Y ☐N
	8:00PM		☐Y ☐N
	8:30PM		☐Y ☐N
	9:00PM		☐Y ☐N
	9:30PM		☐Y ☐N

TAKE 5 MINUTES EACH MORNING TO PLAN YOUR DAY.

GET EIGHT HOURS OF SLEEP!

NOTE HIGH PRIORITY TASKS WITH A *

ANALYZE WHY A TASK WAS NOT COMPLETED, THEN MOVE TO NEXT DAY.

ONE POSITIVE

TODAY I GAVE

DAILY
GOAL SLAYERS
PLANNER

SETTING YOURSELF UP FOR SUCCESS DAILY!

DATE

_____ / _____ / _____

SCRIPTURE

MOTIVATIONAL QUOTE

ONE GOAL

ONE FUN THING

HEALTH • FITNESS

WATER INTAKE

OZ. OZ. OZ. OZ. OZ.

OZ. OZ. OZ. OZ. OZ.

*	IMPORTANT TIME	SCHEDULE	SLAYED?
	5:00AM		☐Y ☐N
	5:30AM		☐Y ☐N
	6:00AM		☐Y ☐N
	6:30AM		☐Y ☐N
	7:00AM		☐Y ☐N
	7:30AM		☐Y ☐N
	8:00AM		☐Y ☐N
	8:30AM		☐Y ☐N
	9:00AM		☐Y ☐N
	9:30AM		☐Y ☐N
	10:00AM		☐Y ☐N
	10:30AM		☐Y ☐N
	11:00AM		☐Y ☐N
	11:30AM		☐Y ☐N
	12:00PM		☐Y ☐N
	12:30PM		☐Y ☐N
	1:00PM		☐Y ☐N
	1:30PM		☐Y ☐N
	2:00PM		☐Y ☐N
	2:30PM		☐Y ☐N
	3:00PM		☐Y ☐N
	3:30PM		☐Y ☐N
	4:00PM		☐Y ☐N
	4:30PM		☐Y ☐N
	5:00PM		☐Y ☐N
	5:30PM		☐Y ☐N
	6:00PM		☐Y ☐N
	6:30PM		☐Y ☐N
	7:00PM		☐Y ☐N
	7:30PM		☐Y ☐N
	8:00PM		☐Y ☐N
	8:30PM		☐Y ☐N
	9:00PM		☐Y ☐N
	9:30PM		☐Y ☐N

TAKE 5 MINUTES EACH MORNING TO PLAN YOUR DAY.

GET EIGHT HOURS OF SLEEP!

NOTE HIGH PRIORITY TASKS WITH A *

ANALYZE WHY A TASK WAS NOT COMPLETED, THEN MOVE TO NEXT DAY.

ONE POSITIVE

TODAY I GAVE

DAILY
GOAL SLAYERS
PLANNER

SETTING YOURSELF UP FOR SUCCESS DAILY!

DATE

_____ / _____ / _____

SCRIPTURE

MOTIVATIONAL QUOTE

ONE GOAL

ONE FUN THING

HEALTH • FITNESS

WATER INTAKE

OZ OZ OZ OZ OZ

OZ OZ OZ OZ OZ

*	IMPORTANT TIME	SCHEDULE	SLAYED?
	5:00AM		☐Y ☐N
	5:30AM		☐Y ☐N
	6:00AM		☐Y ☐N
	6:30AM		☐Y ☐N
	7:00AM		☐Y ☐N
	7:30AM		☐Y ☐N
	8:00AM		☐Y ☐N
	8:30AM		☐Y ☐N
	9:00AM		☐Y ☐N
	9:30AM		☐Y ☐N
	10:00AM		☐Y ☐N
	10:30AM		☐Y ☐N
	11:00AM		☐Y ☐N
	11:30AM		☐Y ☐N
	12:00PM		☐Y ☐N
	12:30PM		☐Y ☐N
	1:00PM		☐Y ☐N
	1:30PM		☐Y ☐N
	2:00PM		☐Y ☐N
	2:30PM		☐Y ☐N
	3:00PM		☐Y ☐N
	3:30PM		☐Y ☐N
	4:00PM		☐Y ☐N
	4:30PM		☐Y ☐N
	5:00PM		☐Y ☐N
	5:30PM		☐Y ☐N
	6:00PM		☐Y ☐N
	6:30PM		☐Y ☐N
	7:00PM		☐Y ☐N
	7:30PM		☐Y ☐N
	8:00PM		☐Y ☐N
	8:30PM		☐Y ☐N
	9:00PM		☐Y ☐N
	9:30PM		☐Y ☐N

TAKE 5 MINUTES EACH MORNING TO PLAN YOUR DAY.

GET EIGHT HOURS OF SLEEP!

NOTE HIGH PRIORITY TASKS WITH A *

ANALYZE WHY A TASK WAS NOT COMPLETED, THEN MOVE TO NEXT DAY.

ONE POSITIVE

TODAY I GAVE

DAILY
GOAL SLAYERS
PLANNER

SETTING YOURSELF UP FOR SUCCESS DAILY!

DATE

_____ / _____ / _____

SCRIPTURE

MOTIVATIONAL QUOTE

ONE GOAL

ONE FUN THING

*	IMPORTANT TIME	SCHEDULE	SLAYED?
	5:00AM		☐Y ☐N
	5:30AM		☐Y ☐N
	6:00AM		☐Y ☐N
	6:30AM		☐Y ☐N
	7:00AM		☐Y ☐N
	7:30AM		☐Y ☐N
	8:00AM		☐Y ☐N
	8:30AM		☐Y ☐N
	9:00AM		☐Y ☐N
	9:30AM		☐Y ☐N
	10:00AM		☐Y ☐N
	10:30AM		☐Y ☐N
	11:00AM		☐Y ☐N
	11:30AM		☐Y ☐N
	12:00PM		☐Y ☐N
	12:30PM		☐Y ☐N
	1:00PM		☐Y ☐N
	1:30PM		☐Y ☐N
	2:00PM		☐Y ☐N
	2:30PM		☐Y ☐N
	3:00PM		☐Y ☐N
	3:30PM		☐Y ☐N
	4:00PM		☐Y ☐N
	4:30PM		☐Y ☐N
	5:00PM		☐Y ☐N
	5:30PM		☐Y ☐N
	6:00PM		☐Y ☐N
	6:30PM		☐Y ☐N
	7:00PM		☐Y ☐N
	7:30PM		☐Y ☐N
	8:00PM		☐Y ☐N
	8:30PM		☐Y ☐N
	9:00PM		☐Y ☐N
	9:30PM		☐Y ☐N

HEALTH • FITNESS

WATER INTAKE

OZ. OZ. OZ. OZ. OZ.

OZ. OZ. OZ. OZ. OZ.

TAKE 5 MINUTES EACH MORNING TO PLAN YOUR DAY.

GET EIGHT HOURS OF SLEEP!

NOTE HIGH PRIORITY TASKS WITH A *

ANALYZE WHY A TASK WAS NOT COMPLETED, THEN MOVE TO NEXT DAY.

ONE POSITIVE

TODAY I GAVE

DAILY
GOAL SLAYERS
PLANNER

SETTING YOURSELF UP FOR SUCCESS DAILY!

DATE

_____/_____/_____

SCRIPTURE

MOTIVATIONAL QUOTE

ONE GOAL

ONE FUN THING

HEALTH • FITNESS

WATER INTAKE

OZ OZ OZ OZ OZ

OZ OZ OZ OZ OZ

*	IMPORTANT TIME	SCHEDULE	SLAYED?
	5:00AM		☐Y ☐N
	5:30AM		☐Y ☐N
	6:00AM		☐Y ☐N
	6:30AM		☐Y ☐N
	7:00AM		☐Y ☐N
	7:30AM		☐Y ☐N
	8:00AM		☐Y ☐N
	8:30AM		☐Y ☐N
	9:00AM		☐Y ☐N
	9:30AM		☐Y ☐N
	10:00AM		☐Y ☐N
	10:30AM		☐Y ☐N
	11:00AM		☐Y ☐N
	11:30AM		☐Y ☐N
	12:00PM		☐Y ☐N
	12:30PM		☐Y ☐N
	1:00PM		☐Y ☐N
	1:30PM		☐Y ☐N
	2:00PM		☐Y ☐N
	2:30PM		☐Y ☐N
	3:00PM		☐Y ☐N
	3:30PM		☐Y ☐N
	4:00PM		☐Y ☐N
	4:30PM		☐Y ☐N
	5:00PM		☐Y ☐N
	5:30PM		☐Y ☐N
	6:00PM		☐Y ☐N
	6:30PM		☐Y ☐N
	7:00PM		☐Y ☐N
	7:30PM		☐Y ☐N
	8:00PM		☐Y ☐N
	8:30PM		☐Y ☐N
	9:00PM		☐Y ☐N
	9:30PM		☐Y ☐N

TAKE 5 MINUTES EACH MORNING TO PLAN YOUR DAY.

GET EIGHT HOURS OF SLEEP!

NOTE HIGH PRIORITY TASKS WITH A *

ANALYZE WHY A TASK WAS NOT COMPLETED, THEN MOVE TO NEXT DAY.

ONE POSITIVE

TODAY I GAVE

DAILY
GOAL SLAYERS
PLANNER

SETTING YOURSELF UP FOR SUCCESS DAILY!

DATE

_____ / _____ / _____

SCRIPTURE

MOTIVATIONAL QUOTE

ONE GOAL

ONE FUN THING

*	IMPORTANT TIME	SCHEDULE	SLAYED?
	5:00AM		☐Y ☐N
	5:30AM		☐Y ☐N
	6:00AM		☐Y ☐N
	6:30AM		☐Y ☐N
	7:00AM		☐Y ☐N
	7:30AM		☐Y ☐N
	8:00AM		☐Y ☐N
	8:30AM		☐Y ☐N
	9:00AM		☐Y ☐N
	9:30AM		☐Y ☐N
	10:00AM		☐Y ☐N
	10:30AM		☐Y ☐N
	11:00AM		☐Y ☐N
	11:30AM		☐Y ☐N
	12:00PM		☐Y ☐N
	12:30PM		☐Y ☐N
	1:00PM		☐Y ☐N
	1:30PM		☐Y ☐N
	2:00PM		☐Y ☐N
	2:30PM		☐Y ☐N
	3:00PM		☐Y ☐N
	3:30PM		☐Y ☐N
	4:00PM		☐Y ☐N
	4:30PM		☐Y ☐N
	5:00PM		☐Y ☐N
	5:30PM		☐Y ☐N
	6:00PM		☐Y ☐N
	6:30PM		☐Y ☐N
	7:00PM		☐Y ☐N
	7:30PM		☐Y ☐N
	8:00PM		☐Y ☐N
	8:30PM		☐Y ☐N
	9:00PM		☐Y ☐N
	9:30PM		☐Y ☐N

HEALTH • FITNESS

WATER INTAKE

OZ. OZ. OZ. OZ. OZ.

OZ. OZ. OZ. OZ. OZ.

TAKE 5 MINUTES EACH MORNING TO PLAN YOUR DAY.

GET EIGHT HOURS OF SLEEP!

NOTE HIGH PRIORITY TASKS WITH A *

ANALYZE WHY A TASK WAS NOT COMPLETED, THEN MOVE TO NEXT DAY.

ONE POSITIVE

TODAY I GAVE

DAILY
GOAL SLAYERS
PLANNER

SETTING YOURSELF UP FOR SUCCESS DAILY!

DATE

_____ / _____ / _____

SCRIPTURE

MOTIVATIONAL QUOTE

ONE GOAL

ONE FUN THING

*	IMPORTANT TIME	SCHEDULE	SLAYED?
	5:00AM		☐Y ☐N
	5:30AM		☐Y ☐N
	6:00AM		☐Y ☐N
	6:30AM		☐Y ☐N
	7:00AM		☐Y ☐N
	7:30AM		☐Y ☐N
	8:00AM		☐Y ☐N
	8:30AM		☐Y ☐N
	9:00AM		☐Y ☐N
	9:30AM		☐Y ☐N
	10:00AM		☐Y ☐N
	10:30AM		☐Y ☐N
	11:00AM		☐Y ☐N
	11:30AM		☐Y ☐N
	12:00PM		☐Y ☐N
	12:30PM		☐Y ☐N
	1:00PM		☐Y ☐N
	1:30PM		☐Y ☐N
	2:00PM		☐Y ☐N
	2:30PM		☐Y ☐N
	3:00PM		☐Y ☐N
	3:30PM		☐Y ☐N
	4:00PM		☐Y ☐N
	4:30PM		☐Y ☐N
	5:00PM		☐Y ☐N
	5:30PM		☐Y ☐N
	6:00PM		☐Y ☐N
	6:30PM		☐Y ☐N
	7:00PM		☐Y ☐N
	7:30PM		☐Y ☐N
	8:00PM		☐Y ☐N
	8:30PM		☐Y ☐N
	9:00PM		☐Y ☐N
	9:30PM		☐Y ☐N

HEALTH • FITNESS

WATER INTAKE

OZ. OZ. OZ. OZ. OZ.

OZ. OZ. OZ. OZ. OZ.

TAKE 5 MINUTES EACH MORNING TO PLAN YOUR DAY.

GET EIGHT HOURS OF SLEEP!

NOTE HIGH PRIORITY TASKS WITH A *

ANALYZE WHY A TASK WAS NOT COMPLETED. THEN MOVE TO NEXT DAY.

ONE POSITIVE

TODAY I GAVE

DAILY
GOAL SLAYERS
PLANNER

SETTING YOURSELF UP FOR SUCCESS DAILY!

DATE

_____ / _____ / _____

SCRIPTURE

MOTIVATIONAL QUOTE

ONE GOAL

ONE FUN THING

HEALTH + FITNESS

WATER INTAKE

*	IMPORTANT TIME	SCHEDULE	SLAYED?
	5:00AM		□Y □N
	5:30AM		□Y □N
	6:00AM		□Y □N
	6:30AM		□Y □N
	7:00AM		□Y □N
	7:30AM		□Y □N
	8:00AM		□Y □N
	8:30AM		□Y □N
	9:00AM		□Y □N
	9:30AM		□Y □N
	10:00AM		□Y □N
	10:30AM		□Y □N
	11:00AM		□Y □N
	11:30AM		□Y □N
	12:00PM		□Y □N
	12:30PM		□Y □N
	1:00PM		□Y □N
	1:30PM		□Y □N
	2:00PM		□Y □N
	2:30PM		□Y □N
	3:00PM		□Y □N
	3:30PM		□Y □N
	4:00PM		□Y □N
	4:30PM		□Y □N
	5:00PM		□Y □N
	5:30PM		□Y □N
	6:00PM		□Y □N
	6:30PM		□Y □N
	7:00PM		□Y □N
	7:30PM		□Y □N
	8:00PM		□Y □N
	8:30PM		□Y □N
	9:00PM		□Y □N
	9:30PM		□Y □N

TAKE 5 MINUTES EACH MORNING TO PLAN YOUR DAY.

GET EIGHT HOURS OF SLEEP!

NOTE HIGH PRIORITY TASKS WITH A *

ANALYZE WHY A TASK WAS NOT COMPLETED, THEN MOVE TO NEXT DAY.

ONE POSITIVE

TODAY I GAVE

DAILY
GOAL SLAYERS
PLANNER

SETTING YOURSELF UP FOR SUCCESS DAILY!

DATE

_____ / _____ / _____

SCRIPTURE

MOTIVATIONAL QUOTE

ONE GOAL

ONE FUN THING

HEALTH + FITNESS

✱	IMPORTANT TIME	SCHEDULE	SLAYED?
	5:00AM		☐Y ☐N
	5:30AM		☐Y ☐N
	6:00AM		☐Y ☐N
	6:30AM		☐Y ☐N
	7:00AM		☐Y ☐N
	7:30AM		☐Y ☐N
	8:00AM		☐Y ☐N
	8:30AM		☐Y ☐N
	9:00AM		☐Y ☐N
	9:30AM		☐Y ☐N
	10:00AM		☐Y ☐N
	10:30AM		☐Y ☐N
	11:00AM		☐Y ☐N
	11:30AM		☐Y ☐N
	12:00PM		☐Y ☐N
	12:30PM		☐Y ☐N
	1:00PM		☐Y ☐N
	1:30PM		☐Y ☐N
	2:00PM		☐Y ☐N
	2:30PM		☐Y ☐N
	3:00PM		☐Y ☐N
	3:30PM		☐Y ☐N
	4:00PM		☐Y ☐N
	4:30PM		☐Y ☐N
	5:00PM		☐Y ☐N
	5:30PM		☐Y ☐N
	6:00PM		☐Y ☐N
	6:30PM		☐Y ☐N
	7:00PM		☐Y ☐N
	7:30PM		☐Y ☐N
	8:00PM		☐Y ☐N
	8:30PM		☐Y ☐N
	9:00PM		☐Y ☐N
	9:30PM		☐Y ☐N

WATER INTAKE

OZ. OZ. OZ. OZ. OZ.
OZ. OZ. OZ. OZ. OZ.

TAKE 5 MINUTES EACH MORNING TO PLAN YOUR DAY.

GET EIGHT HOURS OF SLEEP!

NOTE HIGH PRIORITY TASKS WITH A ✱

ANALYZE WHY A TASK WAS NOT COMPLETED, THEN MOVE TO NEXT DAY.

ONE POSITIVE

TODAY I GAVE

DAILY
GOAL SLAYERS
PLANNER

SETTING YOURSELF UP FOR SUCCESS DAILY!

DATE

_____ / _____ / _____

SCRIPTURE

MOTIVATIONAL QUOTE

ONE GOAL

ONE FUN THING

HEALTH + FITNESS

WATER INTAKE

OZ. OZ. OZ. OZ. OZ.

OZ. OZ. OZ. OZ. OZ.

*	IMPORTANT TIME	SCHEDULE	SLAYED?
	5:00AM		☐Y ☐N
	5:30AM		☐Y ☐N
	6:00AM		☐Y ☐N
	6:30AM		☐Y ☐N
	7:00AM		☐Y ☐N
	7:30AM		☐Y ☐N
	8:00AM		☐Y ☐N
	8:30AM		☐Y ☐N
	9:00AM		☐Y ☐N
	9:30AM		☐Y ☐N
	10:00AM		☐Y ☐N
	10:30AM		☐Y ☐N
	11:00AM		☐Y ☐N
	11:30AM		☐Y ☐N
	12:00PM		☐Y ☐N
	12:30PM		☐Y ☐N
	1:00PM		☐Y ☐N
	1:30PM		☐Y ☐N
	2:00PM		☐Y ☐N
	2:30PM		☐Y ☐N
	3:00PM		☐Y ☐N
	3:30PM		☐Y ☐N
	4:00PM		☐Y ☐N
	4:30PM		☐Y ☐N
	5:00PM		☐Y ☐N
	5:30PM		☐Y ☐N
	6:00PM		☐Y ☐N
	6:30PM		☐Y ☐N
	7:00PM		☐Y ☐N
	7:30PM		☐Y ☐N
	8:00PM		☐Y ☐N
	8:30PM		☐Y ☐N
	9:00PM		☐Y ☐N
	9:30PM		☐Y ☐N

TAKE 5 MINUTES EACH MORNING TO PLAN YOUR DAY.

GET EIGHT HOURS OF SLEEP!

NOTE HIGH PRIORITY TASKS WITH A *

ANALYZE WHY A TASK WAS NOT COMPLETED, THEN MOVE TO NEXT DAY.

ONE POSITIVE

TODAY I GAVE

DAILY
GOAL SLAYERS
PLANNER

SETTING YOURSELF UP FOR SUCCESS DAILY!

DATE

_____ / _____ / _____

SCRIPTURE

MOTIVATIONAL QUOTE

ONE GOAL

ONE FUN THING

*	IMPORTANT TIME	SCHEDULE	SLAYED?
	5:00AM		☐Y ☐N
	5:30AM		☐Y ☐N
	6:00AM		☐Y ☐N
	6:30AM		☐Y ☐N
	7:00AM		☐Y ☐N
	7:30AM		☐Y ☐N
	8:00AM		☐Y ☐N
	8:30AM		☐Y ☐N
	9:00AM		☐Y ☐N
	9:30AM		☐Y ☐N
	10:00AM		☐Y ☐N
	10:30AM		☐Y ☐N
	11:00AM		☐Y ☐N
	11:30AM		☐Y ☐N
	12:00PM		☐Y ☐N
	12:30PM		☐Y ☐N
	1:00PM		☐Y ☐N
	1:30PM		☐Y ☐N
	2:00PM		☐Y ☐N
	2:30PM		☐Y ☐N
	3:00PM		☐Y ☐N
	3:30PM		☐Y ☐N
	4:00PM		☐Y ☐N
	4:30PM		☐Y ☐N
	5:00PM		☐Y ☐N
	5:30PM		☐Y ☐N
	6:00PM		☐Y ☐N
	6:30PM		☐Y ☐N
	7:00PM		☐Y ☐N
	7:30PM		☐Y ☐N
	8:00PM		☐Y ☐N
	8:30PM		☐Y ☐N
	9:00PM		☐Y ☐N
	9:30PM		☐Y ☐N

HEALTH • FITNESS

WATER INTAKE

OZ. OZ. OZ. OZ. OZ.

OZ. OZ. OZ. OZ. OZ.

TAKE 5 MINUTES EACH MORNING TO PLAN YOUR DAY.

GET EIGHT HOURS OF SLEEP!

NOTE HIGH PRIORITY TASKS WITH A *

ANALYZE WHY A TASK WAS NOT COMPLETED, THEN MOVE TO NEXT DAY.

ONE POSITIVE

TODAY I GAVE

DAILY
GOAL SLAYERS
PLANNER

SETTING YOURSELF UP FOR SUCCESS DAILY!

DATE

____ / ____ / ____

SCRIPTURE

MOTIVATIONAL QUOTE

ONE GOAL

ONE FUN THING

*	IMPORTANT TIME	SCHEDULE	SLAYED?
	5:00AM		☐Y ☐N
	5:30AM		☐Y ☐N
	6:00AM		☐Y ☐N
	6:30AM		☐Y ☐N
	7:00AM		☐Y ☐N
	7:30AM		☐Y ☐N
	8:00AM		☐Y ☐N
	8:30AM		☐Y ☐N
	9:00AM		☐Y ☐N
	9:30AM		☐Y ☐N
	10:00AM		☐Y ☐N
	10:30AM		☐Y ☐N
	11:00AM		☐Y ☐N
	11:30AM		☐Y ☐N
	12:00PM		☐Y ☐N
	12:30PM		☐Y ☐N
	1:00PM		☐Y ☐N
	1:30PM		☐Y ☐N
	2:00PM		☐Y ☐N
	2:30PM		☐Y ☐N
	3:00PM		☐Y ☐N
	3:30PM		☐Y ☐N
	4:00PM		☐Y ☐N
	4:30PM		☐Y ☐N
	5:00PM		☐Y ☐N
	5:30PM		☐Y ☐N
	6:00PM		☐Y ☐N
	6:30PM		☐Y ☐N
	7:00PM		☐Y ☐N
	7:30PM		☐Y ☐N
	8:00PM		☐Y ☐N
	8:30PM		☐Y ☐N
	9:00PM		☐Y ☐N
	9:30PM		☐Y ☐N

HEALTH + FITNESS

WATER INTAKE

OZ. OZ. OZ. OZ. OZ.
OZ. OZ. OZ. OZ. OZ.

TAKE 5 MINUTES EACH MORNING TO PLAN YOUR DAY.

GET EIGHT HOURS OF SLEEP!

NOTE HIGH PRIORITY TASKS WITH A *

ANALYZE WHY A TASK WAS NOT COMPLETED, THEN MOVE TO NEXT DAY.

ONE POSITIVE

TODAY I GAVE

DAILY
GOAL SLAYERS
PLANNER

SETTING YOURSELF UP FOR SUCCESS DAILY!

DATE

____ / ____ / ____

SCRIPTURE

MOTIVATIONAL QUOTE

ONE GOAL

ONE FUN THING

*	IMPORTANT TIME	SCHEDULE	SLAYED?
	5:00AM		☐Y ☐N
	5:30AM		☐Y ☐N
	6:00AM		☐Y ☐N
	6:30AM		☐Y ☐N
	7:00AM		☐Y ☐N
	7:30AM		☐Y ☐N
	8:00AM		☐Y ☐N
	8:30AM		☐Y ☐N
	9:00AM		☐Y ☐N
	9:30AM		☐Y ☐N
	10:00AM		☐Y ☐N
	10:30AM		☐Y ☐N
	11:00AM		☐Y ☐N
	11:30AM		☐Y ☐N
	12:00PM		☐Y ☐N
	12:30PM		☐Y ☐N
	1:00PM		☐Y ☐N
	1:30PM		☐Y ☐N
	2:00PM		☐Y ☐N
	2:30PM		☐Y ☐N
	3:00PM		☐Y ☐N
	3:30PM		☐Y ☐N
	4:00PM		☐Y ☐N
	4:30PM		☐Y ☐N
	5:00PM		☐Y ☐N
	5:30PM		☐Y ☐N
	6:00PM		☐Y ☐N
	6:30PM		☐Y ☐N
	7:00PM		☐Y ☐N
	7:30PM		☐Y ☐N
	8:00PM		☐Y ☐N
	8:30PM		☐Y ☐N
	9:00PM		☐Y ☐N
	9:30PM		☐Y ☐N

HEALTH • FITNESS

WATER INTAKE

OZ. OZ. OZ. OZ. OZ.

OZ. OZ. OZ. OZ. OZ.

TAKE 5 MINUTES EACH MORNING TO PLAN YOUR DAY.

GET EIGHT HOURS OF SLEEP!

NOTE HIGH PRIORITY TASKS WITH A *

ANALYZE WHY A TASK WAS NOT COMPLETED, THEN MOVE TO NEXT DAY.

ONE POSITIVE

TODAY I GAVE

DAILY
GOAL SLAYERS
PLANNER

SETTING YOURSELF UP FOR SUCCESS DAILY!

DATE

_____/_____/_____

SCRIPTURE

MOTIVATIONAL QUOTE

ONE GOAL

ONE FUN THING

*	IMPORTANT TIME	SCHEDULE	SLAYED?
	5:00AM		☐Y ☐N
	5:30AM		☐Y ☐N
	6:00AM		☐Y ☐N
	6:30AM		☐Y ☐N
	7:00AM		☐Y ☐N
	7:30AM		☐Y ☐N
	8:00AM		☐Y ☐N
	8:30AM		☐Y ☐N
	9:00AM		☐Y ☐N
	9:30AM		☐Y ☐N
	10:00AM		☐Y ☐N
	10:30AM		☐Y ☐N
	11:00AM		☐Y ☐N
	11:30AM		☐Y ☐N
	12:00PM		☐Y ☐N
	12:30PM		☐Y ☐N
	1:00PM		☐Y ☐N
	1:30PM		☐Y ☐N
	2:00PM		☐Y ☐N
	2:30PM		☐Y ☐N
	3:00PM		☐Y ☐N
	3:30PM		☐Y ☐N
	4:00PM		☐Y ☐N
	4:30PM		☐Y ☐N
	5:00PM		☐Y ☐N
	5:30PM		☐Y ☐N
	6:00PM		☐Y ☐N
	6:30PM		☐Y ☐N
	7:00PM		☐Y ☐N
	7:30PM		☐Y ☐N
	8:00PM		☐Y ☐N
	8:30PM		☐Y ☐N
	9:00PM		☐Y ☐N
	9:30PM		☐Y ☐N

HEALTH • FITNESS

WATER INTAKE

OZ. OZ. OZ. OZ. OZ.

OZ. OZ. OZ. OZ. OZ.

TAKE 5 MINUTES EACH MORNING TO PLAN YOUR DAY.

GET EIGHT HOURS OF SLEEP!

NOTE HIGH PRIORITY TASKS WITH A *

ANALYZE WHY A TASK WAS NOT COMPLETED, THEN MOVE TO NEXT DAY.

ONE POSITIVE

TODAY I GAVE

DAILY
GOAL SLAYERS
PLANNER

SETTING YOURSELF UP FOR SUCCESS DAILY!

DATE

_____ / _____ / _____

SCRIPTURE

MOTIVATIONAL QUOTE

ONE GOAL

ONE FUN THING

HEALTH • FITNESS

WATER INTAKE

OZ. OZ. OZ. OZ. OZ.

OZ. OZ. OZ. OZ. OZ.

*	IMPORTANT TIME	SCHEDULE	SLAYED?
	5:00AM		☐Y ☐N
	5:30AM		☐Y ☐N
	6:00AM		☐Y ☐N
	6:30AM		☐Y ☐N
	7:00AM		☐Y ☐N
	7:30AM		☐Y ☐N
	8:00AM		☐Y ☐N
	8:30AM		☐Y ☐N
	9:00AM		☐Y ☐N
	9:30AM		☐Y ☐N
	10:00AM		☐Y ☐N
	10:30AM		☐Y ☐N
	11:00AM		☐Y ☐N
	11:30AM		☐Y ☐N
	12:00PM		☐Y ☐N
	12:30PM		☐Y ☐N
	1:00PM		☐Y ☐N
	1:30PM		☐Y ☐N
	2:00PM		☐Y ☐N
	2:30PM		☐Y ☐N
	3:00PM		☐Y ☐N
	3:30PM		☐Y ☐N
	4:00PM		☐Y ☐N
	4:30PM		☐Y ☐N
	5:00PM		☐Y ☐N
	5:30PM		☐Y ☐N
	6:00PM		☐Y ☐N
	6:30PM		☐Y ☐N
	7:00PM		☐Y ☐N
	7:30PM		☐Y ☐N
	8:00PM		☐Y ☐N
	8:30PM		☐Y ☐N
	9:00PM		☐Y ☐N
	9:30PM		☐Y ☐N

TAKE 5 MINUTES EACH MORNING TO PLAN YOUR DAY.

GET EIGHT HOURS OF SLEEP!

NOTE HIGH PRIORITY TASKS WITH A *

ANALYZE WHY A TASK WAS NOT COMPLETED, THEN MOVE TO NEXT DAY.

ONE POSITIVE

TODAY I GAVE

DAILY
GOAL SLAYERS
PLANNER

SETTING YOURSELF UP FOR SUCCESS DAILY!

DATE

_____ / _____ / _____

SCRIPTURE

MOTIVATIONAL QUOTE

ONE GOAL

ONE FUN THING

HEALTH + FITNESS

*	IMPORTANT TIME	SCHEDULE	SLAYED?
	5:00AM		☐Y ☐N
	5:30AM		☐Y ☐N
	6:00AM		☐Y ☐N
	6:30AM		☐Y ☐N
	7:00AM		☐Y ☐N
	7:30AM		☐Y ☐N
	8:00AM		☐Y ☐N
	8:30AM		☐Y ☐N
	9:00AM		☐Y ☐N
	9:30AM		☐Y ☐N
	10:00AM		☐Y ☐N
	10:30AM		☐Y ☐N
	11:00AM		☐Y ☐N
	11:30AM		☐Y ☐N
	12:00PM		☐Y ☐N
	12:30PM		☐Y ☐N
	1:00PM		☐Y ☐N
	1:30PM		☐Y ☐N
	2:00PM		☐Y ☐N
	2:30PM		☐Y ☐N
	3:00PM		☐Y ☐N
	3:30PM		☐Y ☐N
	4:00PM		☐Y ☐N
	4:30PM		☐Y ☐N
	5:00PM		☐Y ☐N
	5:30PM		☐Y ☐N
	6:00PM		☐Y ☐N
	6:30PM		☐Y ☐N
	7:00PM		☐Y ☐N
	7:30PM		☐Y ☐N
	8:00PM		☐Y ☐N
	8:30PM		☐Y ☐N
	9:00PM		☐Y ☐N
	9:30PM		☐Y ☐N

WATER INTAKE

OZ. OZ. OZ. OZ. OZ.

OZ. OZ. OZ. OZ. OZ.

TAKE 5 MINUTES EACH MORNING TO PLAN YOUR DAY.

GET EIGHT HOURS OF SLEEP!

NOTE HIGH PRIORITY TASKS WITH A *

ANALYZE WHY A TASK WAS NOT COMPLETED, THEN MOVE TO NEXT DAY.

ONE POSITIVE

TODAY I GAVE

DAILY
GOAL SLAYERS
PLANNER

SETTING YOURSELF UP FOR SUCCESS DAILY!

DATE

_____ / _____ / _____

SCRIPTURE

MOTIVATIONAL QUOTE

ONE GOAL

ONE FUN THING

HEALTH + FITNESS

WATER INTAKE

✱	IMPORTANT TIME	SCHEDULE	SLAYED?
	5:00AM		☐Y ☐N
	5:30AM		☐Y ☐N
	6:00AM		☐Y ☐N
	6:30AM		☐Y ☐N
	7:00AM		☐Y ☐N
	7:30AM		☐Y ☐N
	8:00AM		☐Y ☐N
	8:30AM		☐Y ☐N
	9:00AM		☐Y ☐N
	9:30AM		☐Y ☐N
	10:00AM		☐Y ☐N
	10:30AM		☐Y ☐N
	11:00AM		☐Y ☐N
	11:30AM		☐Y ☐N
	12:00PM		☐Y ☐N
	12:30PM		☐Y ☐N
	1:00PM		☐Y ☐N
	1:30PM		☐Y ☐N
	2:00PM		☐Y ☐N
	2:30PM		☐Y ☐N
	3:00PM		☐Y ☐N
	3:30PM		☐Y ☐N
	4:00PM		☐Y ☐N
	4:30PM		☐Y ☐N
	5:00PM		☐Y ☐N
	5:30PM		☐Y ☐N
	6:00PM		☐Y ☐N
	6:30PM		☐Y ☐N
	7:00PM		☐Y ☐N
	7:30PM		☐Y ☐N
	8:00PM		☐Y ☐N
	8:30PM		☐Y ☐N
	9:00PM		☐Y ☐N
	9:30PM		☐Y ☐N

TAKE 5 MINUTES EACH MORNING TO PLAN YOUR DAY.

GET EIGHT HOURS OF SLEEP!

NOTE HIGH PRIORITY TASKS WITH A ✱

ANALYZE WHY A TASK WAS NOT COMPLETED, THEN MOVE TO NEXT DAY.

ONE POSITIVE

TODAY I GAVE

DAILY
GOAL SLAYERS
PLANNER

SETTING YOURSELF UP FOR SUCCESS DAILY!

DATE
____ / ____ / _____

SCRIPTURE

MOTIVATIONAL QUOTE

ONE GOAL

ONE FUN THING

*	IMPORTANT TIME	SCHEDULE	SLAYED?
	5:00AM		☐Y ☐N
	5:30AM		☐Y ☐N
	6:00AM		☐Y ☐N
	6:30AM		☐Y ☐N
	7:00AM		☐Y ☐N
	7:30AM		☐Y ☐N
	8:00AM		☐Y ☐N
	8:30AM		☐Y ☐N
	9:00AM		☐Y ☐N
	9:30AM		☐Y ☐N
	10:00AM		☐Y ☐N
	10:30AM		☐Y ☐N
	11:00AM		☐Y ☐N
	11:30AM		☐Y ☐N
	12:00PM		☐Y ☐N
	12:30PM		☐Y ☐N
	1:00PM		☐Y ☐N
	1:30PM		☐Y ☐N
	2:00PM		☐Y ☐N
	2:30PM		☐Y ☐N
	3:00PM		☐Y ☐N
	3:30PM		☐Y ☐N
	4:00PM		☐Y ☐N
	4:30PM		☐Y ☐N
	5:00PM		☐Y ☐N
	5:30PM		☐Y ☐N
	6:00PM		☐Y ☐N
	6:30PM		☐Y ☐N
	7:00PM		☐Y ☐N
	7:30PM		☐Y ☐N
	8:00PM		☐Y ☐N
	8:30PM		☐Y ☐N
	9:00PM		☐Y ☐N
	9:30PM		☐Y ☐N

HEALTH + FITNESS

WATER INTAKE

OZ. OZ. OZ. OZ. OZ.
OZ. OZ. OZ. OZ. OZ.

TAKE 5 MINUTES EACH MORNING TO PLAN YOUR DAY.

GET EIGHT HOURS OF SLEEP!

NOTE HIGH PRIORITY TASKS WITH A *

ANALYZE WHY A TASK WAS NOT COMPLETED, THEN MOVE TO NEXT DAY.

ONE POSITIVE

TODAY I GAVE

DAILY
GOAL SLAYERS
PLANNER

SETTING YOURSELF UP FOR SUCCESS DAILY!

DATE

_____ / _____ / _____

SCRIPTURE

MOTIVATIONAL QUOTE

ONE GOAL

ONE FUN THING

HEALTH • FITNESS

WATER INTAKE

*	IMPORTANT TIME	SCHEDULE	SLAYED?
	5:00AM		☐Y ☐N
	5:30AM		☐Y ☐N
	6:00AM		☐Y ☐N
	6:30AM		☐Y ☐N
	7:00AM		☐Y ☐N
	7:30AM		☐Y ☐N
	8:00AM		☐Y ☐N
	8:30AM		☐Y ☐N
	9:00AM		☐Y ☐N
	9:30AM		☐Y ☐N
	10:00AM		☐Y ☐N
	10:30AM		☐Y ☐N
	11:00AM		☐Y ☐N
	11:30AM		☐Y ☐N
	12:00PM		☐Y ☐N
	12:30PM		☐Y ☐N
	1:00PM		☐Y ☐N
	1:30PM		☐Y ☐N
	2:00PM		☐Y ☐N
	2:30PM		☐Y ☐N
	3:00PM		☐Y ☐N
	3:30PM		☐Y ☐N
	4:00PM		☐Y ☐N
	4:30PM		☐Y ☐N
	5:00PM		☐Y ☐N
	5:30PM		☐Y ☐N
	6:00PM		☐Y ☐N
	6:30PM		☐Y ☐N
	7:00PM		☐Y ☐N
	7:30PM		☐Y ☐N
	8:00PM		☐Y ☐N
	8:30PM		☐Y ☐N
	9:00PM		☐Y ☐N
	9:30PM		☐Y ☐N

TAKE 5 MINUTES EACH MORNING TO PLAN YOUR DAY.

GET EIGHT HOURS OF SLEEP!

NOTE HIGH PRIORITY TASKS WITH A *

ANALYZE WHY A TASK WAS NOT COMPLETED, THEN MOVE TO NEXT DAY.

ONE POSITIVE

TODAY I GAVE

DAILY
GOAL SLAYERS
PLANNER

SETTING YOURSELF UP FOR SUCCESS DAILY!

DATE

_____ / _____ / _____

SCRIPTURE

MOTIVATIONAL QUOTE

ONE GOAL

ONE FUN THING

HEALTH • FITNESS

✱	IMPORTANT TIME	SCHEDULE	SLAYED?
	5:00AM		☐Y ☐N
	5:30AM		☐Y ☐N
	6:00AM		☐Y ☐N
	6:30AM		☐Y ☐N
	7:00AM		☐Y ☐N
	7:30AM		☐Y ☐N
	8:00AM		☐Y ☐N
	8:30AM		☐Y ☐N
	9:00AM		☐Y ☐N
	9:30AM		☐Y ☐N
	10:00AM		☐Y ☐N
	10:30AM		☐Y ☐N
	11:00AM		☐Y ☐N
	11:30AM		☐Y ☐N
	12:00PM		☐Y ☐N
	12:30PM		☐Y ☐N
	1:00PM		☐Y ☐N
	1:30PM		☐Y ☐N
	2:00PM		☐Y ☐N
	2:30PM		☐Y ☐N
	3:00PM		☐Y ☐N
	3:30PM		☐Y ☐N
	4:00PM		☐Y ☐N
	4:30PM		☐Y ☐N
	5:00PM		☐Y ☐N
	5:30PM		☐Y ☐N
	6:00PM		☐Y ☐N
	6:30PM		☐Y ☐N
	7:00PM		☐Y ☐N
	7:30PM		☐Y ☐N
	8:00PM		☐Y ☐N
	8:30PM		☐Y ☐N
	9:00PM		☐Y ☐N
	9:30PM		☐Y ☐N

WATER INTAKE

OZ. OZ. OZ. OZ. OZ.
OZ. OZ. OZ. OZ. OZ.

TAKE 5 MINUTES EACH MORNING TO PLAN YOUR DAY.

GET EIGHT HOURS OF SLEEP!

NOTE HIGH PRIORITY TASKS WITH A ✱

ANALYZE WHY A TASK WAS NOT COMPLETED, THEN MOVE TO NEXT DAY.

ONE POSITIVE

TODAY I GAVE

DAILY
GOAL SLAYERS
PLANNER

SETTING YOURSELF UP FOR SUCCESS DAILY!

DATE

_____ / _____ / _____

SCRIPTURE

MOTIVATIONAL QUOTE

ONE GOAL

ONE FUN THING

✱	IMPORTANT TIME	SCHEDULE	SLAYED?
	5:00AM		☐Y ☐N
	5:30AM		☐Y ☐N
	6:00AM		☐Y ☐N
	6:30AM		☐Y ☐N
	7:00AM		☐Y ☐N
	7:30AM		☐Y ☐N
	8:00AM		☐Y ☐N
	8:30AM		☐Y ☐N
	9:00AM		☐Y ☐N
	9:30AM		☐Y ☐N
	10:00AM		☐Y ☐N
	10:30AM		☐Y ☐N
	11:00AM		☐Y ☐N
	11:30AM		☐Y ☐N
	12:00PM		☐Y ☐N
	12:30PM		☐Y ☐N
	1:00PM		☐Y ☐N
	1:30PM		☐Y ☐N
	2:00PM		☐Y ☐N
	2:30PM		☐Y ☐N
	3:00PM		☐Y ☐N
	3:30PM		☐Y ☐N
	4:00PM		☐Y ☐N
	4:30PM		☐Y ☐N
	5:00PM		☐Y ☐N
	5:30PM		☐Y ☐N
	6:00PM		☐Y ☐N
	6:30PM		☐Y ☐N
	7:00PM		☐Y ☐N
	7:30PM		☐Y ☐N
	8:00PM		☐Y ☐N
	8:30PM		☐Y ☐N
	9:00PM		☐Y ☐N
	9:30PM		☐Y ☐N

HEALTH • FITNESS

WATER INTAKE

OZ OZ OZ OZ OZ
OZ OZ OZ OZ OZ

TAKE 5 MINUTES EACH MORNING TO PLAN YOUR DAY.

GET EIGHT HOURS OF SLEEP!

NOTE HIGH PRIORITY TASKS WITH A ✱

ANALYZE WHY A TASK WAS NOT COMPLETED, THEN MOVE TO NEXT DAY.

ONE POSITIVE

TODAY I GAVE

DAILY
GOAL SLAYERS
PLANNER

SETTING YOURSELF UP FOR SUCCESS DAILY!

DATE

_____ / _____ / _____

SCRIPTURE

MOTIVATIONAL QUOTE

ONE GOAL

ONE FUN THING

HEALTH + FITNESS

WATER INTAKE

OZ. OZ. OZ. OZ. OZ.

OZ. OZ. OZ. OZ. OZ.

✱	IMPORTANT TIME	SCHEDULE	SLAYED?
	5:00AM		☐Y ☐N
	5:30AM		☐Y ☐N
	6:00AM		☐Y ☐N
	6:30AM		☐Y ☐N
	7:00AM		☐Y ☐N
	7:30AM		☐Y ☐N
	8:00AM		☐Y ☐N
	8:30AM		☐Y ☐N
	9:00AM		☐Y ☐N
	9:30AM		☐Y ☐N
	10:00AM		☐Y ☐N
	10:30AM		☐Y ☐N
	11:00AM		☐Y ☐N
	11:30AM		☐Y ☐N
	12:00PM		☐Y ☐N
	12:30PM		☐Y ☐N
	1:00PM		☐Y ☐N
	1:30PM		☐Y ☐N
	2:00PM		☐Y ☐N
	2:30PM		☐Y ☐N
	3:00PM		☐Y ☐N
	3:30PM		☐Y ☐N
	4:00PM		☐Y ☐N
	4:30PM		☐Y ☐N
	5:00PM		☐Y ☐N
	5:30PM		☐Y ☐N
	6:00PM		☐Y ☐N
	6:30PM		☐Y ☐N
	7:00PM		☐Y ☐N
	7:30PM		☐Y ☐N
	8:00PM		☐Y ☐N
	8:30PM		☐Y ☐N
	9:00PM		☐Y ☐N
	9:30PM		☐Y ☐N

TAKE 5 MINUTES EACH MORNING TO PLAN YOUR DAY.

GET EIGHT HOURS OF SLEEP!

NOTE HIGH PRIORITY TASKS WITH A ✱

ANALYZE WHY A TASK WAS NOT COMPLETED, THEN MOVE TO NEXT DAY.

ONE POSITIVE

TODAY I GAVE

DAILY
GOAL SLAYERS
PLANNER

SETTING YOURSELF UP FOR SUCCESS DAILY!

DATE

____ / ____ / ____

SCRIPTURE

MOTIVATIONAL QUOTE

ONE GOAL

ONE FUN THING

HEALTH · FITNESS

*	IMPORTANT TIME	SCHEDULE	SLAYED?
	5:00AM		☐Y ☐N
	5:30AM		☐Y ☐N
	6:00AM		☐Y ☐N
	6:30AM		☐Y ☐N
	7:00AM		☐Y ☐N
	7:30AM		☐Y ☐N
	8:00AM		☐Y ☐N
	8:30AM		☐Y ☐N
	9:00AM		☐Y ☐N
	9:30AM		☐Y ☐N
	10:00AM		☐Y ☐N
	10:30AM		☐Y ☐N
	11:00AM		☐Y ☐N
	11:30AM		☐Y ☐N
	12:00PM		☐Y ☐N
	12:30PM		☐Y ☐N
	1:00PM		☐Y ☐N
	1:30PM		☐Y ☐N
	2:00PM		☐Y ☐N
	2:30PM		☐Y ☐N
	3:00PM		☐Y ☐N
	3:30PM		☐Y ☐N
	4:00PM		☐Y ☐N
	4:30PM		☐Y ☐N
	5:00PM		☐Y ☐N
	5:30PM		☐Y ☐N
	6:00PM		☐Y ☐N
	6:30PM		☐Y ☐N
	7:00PM		☐Y ☐N
	7:30PM		☐Y ☐N
	8:00PM		☐Y ☐N
	8:30PM		☐Y ☐N
	9:00PM		☐Y ☐N
	9:30PM		☐Y ☐N

WATER INTAKE

OZ. OZ. OZ. OZ. OZ.

OZ. OZ. OZ. OZ. OZ.

TAKE 5 MINUTES EACH MORNING TO PLAN YOUR DAY.

GET EIGHT HOURS OF SLEEP!

NOTE HIGH PRIORITY TASKS WITH A *

ANALYZE WHY A TASK WAS NOT COMPLETED, THEN MOVE TO NEXT DAY.

ONE POSITIVE

TODAY I GAVE

DAILY
GOAL SLAYERS
PLANNER

SETTING YOURSELF UP FOR SUCCESS DAILY!

DATE

_____ / _____ / _____

SCRIPTURE

MOTIVATIONAL QUOTE

ONE GOAL

ONE FUN THING

HEALTH • FITNESS

WATER INTAKE

OZ OZ OZ OZ OZ

OZ OZ OZ OZ OZ

*	IMPORTANT TIME	SCHEDULE	SLAYED?
	5:00AM		☐Y ☐N
	5:30AM		☐Y ☐N
	6:00AM		☐Y ☐N
	6:30AM		☐Y ☐N
	7:00AM		☐Y ☐N
	7:30AM		☐Y ☐N
	8:00AM		☐Y ☐N
	8:30AM		☐Y ☐N
	9:00AM		☐Y ☐N
	9:30AM		☐Y ☐N
	10:00AM		☐Y ☐N
	10:30AM		☐Y ☐N
	11:00AM		☐Y ☐N
	11:30AM		☐Y ☐N
	12:00PM		☐Y ☐N
	12:30PM		☐Y ☐N
	1:00PM		☐Y ☐N
	1:30PM		☐Y ☐N
	2:00PM		☐Y ☐N
	2:30PM		☐Y ☐N
	3:00PM		☐Y ☐N
	3:30PM		☐Y ☐N
	4:00PM		☐Y ☐N
	4:30PM		☐Y ☐N
	5:00PM		☐Y ☐N
	5:30PM		☐Y ☐N
	6:00PM		☐Y ☐N
	6:30PM		☐Y ☐N
	7:00PM		☐Y ☐N
	7:30PM		☐Y ☐N
	8:00PM		☐Y ☐N
	8:30PM		☐Y ☐N
	9:00PM		☐Y ☐N
	9:30PM		☐Y ☐N

TAKE 5 MINUTES EACH MORNING TO PLAN YOUR DAY.

GET EIGHT HOURS OF SLEEP!

NOTE HIGH PRIORITY TASKS WITH A *

ANALYZE WHY A TASK WAS NOT COMPLETED, THEN MOVE TO NEXT DAY.

ONE POSITIVE

TODAY I GAVE

DAILY
GOAL SLAYERS
PLANNER

SETTING YOURSELF UP FOR SUCCESS DAILY!

DATE

____ / ____ / ____

SCRIPTURE

MOTIVATIONAL QUOTE

ONE GOAL

ONE FUN THING

*	IMPORTANT TIME	SCHEDULE	SLAYED?
	5:00AM		☐Y ☐N
	5:30AM		☐Y ☐N
	6:00AM		☐Y ☐N
	6:30AM		☐Y ☐N
	7:00AM		☐Y ☐N
	7:30AM		☐Y ☐N
	8:00AM		☐Y ☐N
	8:30AM		☐Y ☐N
	9:00AM		☐Y ☐N
	9:30AM		☐Y ☐N
	10:00AM		☐Y ☐N
	10:30AM		☐Y ☐N
	11:00AM		☐Y ☐N
	11:30AM		☐Y ☐N
	12:00PM		☐Y ☐N
	12:30PM		☐Y ☐N
	1:00PM		☐Y ☐N
	1:30PM		☐Y ☐N
	2:00PM		☐Y ☐N
	2:30PM		☐Y ☐N
	3:00PM		☐Y ☐N
	3:30PM		☐Y ☐N
	4:00PM		☐Y ☐N
	4:30PM		☐Y ☐N
	5:00PM		☐Y ☐N
	5:30PM		☐Y ☐N
	6:00PM		☐Y ☐N
	6:30PM		☐Y ☐N
	7:00PM		☐Y ☐N
	7:30PM		☐Y ☐N
	8:00PM		☐Y ☐N
	8:30PM		☐Y ☐N
	9:00PM		☐Y ☐N
	9:30PM		☐Y ☐N

HEALTH + FITNESS

WATER INTAKE

OZ. OZ. OZ. OZ. OZ.
OZ. OZ. OZ. OZ. OZ.

TAKE 5 MINUTES EACH MORNING TO PLAN YOUR DAY.

GET EIGHT HOURS OF SLEEP!

NOTE HIGH PRIORITY TASKS WITH A *

ANALYZE WHY A TASK WAS NOT COMPLETED, THEN MOVE TO NEXT DAY.

ONE POSITIVE

TODAY I GAVE

DAILY
GOAL SLAYERS
PLANNER

SETTING YOURSELF UP FOR SUCCESS DAILY!

DATE

_____ / _____ / _____

SCRIPTURE

MOTIVATIONAL QUOTE

ONE GOAL

ONE FUN THING

HEALTH • FITNESS

*	IMPORTANT TIME	SCHEDULE	SLAYED?
	5:00AM		☐Y ☐N
	5:30AM		☐Y ☐N
	6:00AM		☐Y ☐N
	6:30AM		☐Y ☐N
	7:00AM		☐Y ☐N
	7:30AM		☐Y ☐N
	8:00AM		☐Y ☐N
	8:30AM		☐Y ☐N
	9:00AM		☐Y ☐N
	9:30AM		☐Y ☐N
	10:00AM		☐Y ☐N
	10:30AM		☐Y ☐N
	11:00AM		☐Y ☐N
	11:30AM		☐Y ☐N
	12:00PM		☐Y ☐N
	12:30PM		☐Y ☐N
	1:00PM		☐Y ☐N
	1:30PM		☐Y ☐N
	2:00PM		☐Y ☐N
	2:30PM		☐Y ☐N
	3:00PM		☐Y ☐N
	3:30PM		☐Y ☐N
	4:00PM		☐Y ☐N
	4:30PM		☐Y ☐N
	5:00PM		☐Y ☐N
	5:30PM		☐Y ☐N
	6:00PM		☐Y ☐N
	6:30PM		☐Y ☐N
	7:00PM		☐Y ☐N
	7:30PM		☐Y ☐N
	8:00PM		☐Y ☐N
	8:30PM		☐Y ☐N
	9:00PM		☐Y ☐N
	9:30PM		☐Y ☐N

WATER INTAKE

OZ. OZ. OZ. OZ. OZ.
OZ. OZ. OZ. OZ. OZ.

TAKE 5 MINUTES EACH MORNING TO PLAN YOUR DAY.

GET EIGHT HOURS OF SLEEP!

NOTE HIGH PRIORITY TASKS WITH A *

ANALYZE WHY A TASK WAS NOT COMPLETED, THEN MOVE TO NEXT DAY.

ONE POSITIVE

TODAY I GAVE

DAILY
GOAL SLAYERS
PLANNER

SETTING YOURSELF UP FOR SUCCESS DAILY!

DATE

_____ / _____ / _____

SCRIPTURE

MOTIVATIONAL QUOTE

ONE GOAL

ONE FUN THING

HEALTH • FITNESS

WATER INTAKE

OZ. OZ. OZ. OZ. OZ.

OZ. OZ. OZ. OZ. OZ.

✱	IMPORTANT TIME	SCHEDULE	SLAYED?
	5:00AM		☐Y ☐N
	5:30AM		☐Y ☐N
	6:00AM		☐Y ☐N
	6:30AM		☐Y ☐N
	7:00AM		☐Y ☐N
	7:30AM		☐Y ☐N
	8:00AM		☐Y ☐N
	8:30AM		☐Y ☐N
	9:00AM		☐Y ☐N
	9:30AM		☐Y ☐N
	10:00AM		☐Y ☐N
	10:30AM		☐Y ☐N
	11:00AM		☐Y ☐N
	11:30AM		☐Y ☐N
	12:00PM		☐Y ☐N
	12:30PM		☐Y ☐N
	1:00PM		☐Y ☐N
	1:30PM		☐Y ☐N
	2:00PM		☐Y ☐N
	2:30PM		☐Y ☐N
	3:00PM		☐Y ☐N
	3:30PM		☐Y ☐N
	4:00PM		☐Y ☐N
	4:30PM		☐Y ☐N
	5:00PM		☐Y ☐N
	5:30PM		☐Y ☐N
	6:00PM		☐Y ☐N
	6:30PM		☐Y ☐N
	7:00PM		☐Y ☐N
	7:30PM		☐Y ☐N
	8:00PM		☐Y ☐N
	8:30PM		☐Y ☐N
	9:00PM		☐Y ☐N
	9:30PM		☐Y ☐N

TAKE 5 MINUTES EACH MORNING TO PLAN YOUR DAY.

GET EIGHT HOURS OF SLEEP!

NOTE HIGH PRIORITY TASKS WITH A ✱

ANALYZE WHY A TASK WAS NOT COMPLETED, THEN MOVE TO NEXT DAY.

ONE POSITIVE

TODAY I GAVE

DAILY
GOAL SLAYERS
PLANNER

SETTING YOURSELF UP FOR SUCCESS DAILY!

DATE

_____ / _____ / _____

SCRIPTURE

MOTIVATIONAL QUOTE

ONE GOAL

ONE FUN THING

*	IMPORTANT TIME	SCHEDULE	SLAYED?
	5:00AM		☐Y ☐N
	5:30AM		☐Y ☐N
	6:00AM		☐Y ☐N
	6:30AM		☐Y ☐N
	7:00AM		☐Y ☐N
	7:30AM		☐Y ☐N
	8:00AM		☐Y ☐N
	8:30AM		☐Y ☐N
	9:00AM		☐Y ☐N
	9:30AM		☐Y ☐N
	10:00AM		☐Y ☐N
	10:30AM		☐Y ☐N
	11:00AM		☐Y ☐N
	11:30AM		☐Y ☐N
	12:00PM		☐Y ☐N
	12:30PM		☐Y ☐N
	1:00PM		☐Y ☐N
	1:30PM		☐Y ☐N
	2:00PM		☐Y ☐N
	2:30PM		☐Y ☐N
	3:00PM		☐Y ☐N
	3:30PM		☐Y ☐N
	4:00PM		☐Y ☐N
	4:30PM		☐Y ☐N
	5:00PM		☐Y ☐N
	5:30PM		☐Y ☐N
	6:00PM		☐Y ☐N
	6:30PM		☐Y ☐N
	7:00PM		☐Y ☐N
	7:30PM		☐Y ☐N
	8:00PM		☐Y ☐N
	8:30PM		☐Y ☐N
	9:00PM		☐Y ☐N
	9:30PM		☐Y ☐N

HEALTH • FITNESS

WATER INTAKE

OZ. OZ. OZ. OZ. OZ.
OZ. OZ. OZ. OZ. OZ.

TAKE 5 MINUTES EACH MORNING TO PLAN YOUR DAY.

GET EIGHT HOURS OF SLEEP!

NOTE HIGH PRIORITY TASKS WITH A *

ANALYZE WHY A TASK WAS NOT COMPLETED, THEN MOVE TO NEXT DAY.

ONE POSITIVE

TODAY I GAVE

DAILY
GOAL SLAYERS
PLANNER

SETTING YOURSELF UP FOR SUCCESS DAILY!

DATE

_____ / _____ / _____

SCRIPTURE

MOTIVATIONAL QUOTE

ONE GOAL

ONE FUN THING

HEALTH • FITNESS

WATER INTAKE

*	IMPORTANT TIME	SCHEDULE	SLAYED?
	5:00AM		☐Y ☐N
	5:30AM		☐Y ☐N
	6:00AM		☐Y ☐N
	6:30AM		☐Y ☐N
	7:00AM		☐Y ☐N
	7:30AM		☐Y ☐N
	8:00AM		☐Y ☐N
	8:30AM		☐Y ☐N
	9:00AM		☐Y ☐N
	9:30AM		☐Y ☐N
	10:00AM		☐Y ☐N
	10:30AM		☐Y ☐N
	11:00AM		☐Y ☐N
	11:30AM		☐Y ☐N
	12:00PM		☐Y ☐N
	12:30PM		☐Y ☐N
	1:00PM		☐Y ☐N
	1:30PM		☐Y ☐N
	2:00PM		☐Y ☐N
	2:30PM		☐Y ☐N
	3:00PM		☐Y ☐N
	3:30PM		☐Y ☐N
	4:00PM		☐Y ☐N
	4:30PM		☐Y ☐N
	5:00PM		☐Y ☐N
	5:30PM		☐Y ☐N
	6:00PM		☐Y ☐N
	6:30PM		☐Y ☐N
	7:00PM		☐Y ☐N
	7:30PM		☐Y ☐N
	8:00PM		☐Y ☐N
	8:30PM		☐Y ☐N
	9:00PM		☐Y ☐N
	9:30PM		☐Y ☐N

TAKE 5 MINUTES EACH MORNING TO PLAN YOUR DAY.

GET EIGHT HOURS OF SLEEP!

NOTE HIGH PRIORITY TASKS WITH A *

ANALYZE WHY A TASK WAS NOT COMPLETED, THEN MOVE TO NEXT DAY.

ONE POSITIVE

TODAY I GAVE

DAILY
GOAL SLAYERS
PLANNER

SETTING YOURSELF UP FOR SUCCESS DAILY!

DATE

_____ / _____ / _____

SCRIPTURE

MOTIVATIONAL QUOTE

ONE GOAL

ONE FUN THING

HEALTH • FITNESS

WATER INTAKE

OZ. OZ. OZ. OZ. OZ.

OZ. OZ. OZ. OZ. OZ.

*	IMPORTANT TIME	SCHEDULE	SLAYED?
	5:00AM		☐Y ☐N
	5:30AM		☐Y ☐N
	6:00AM		☐Y ☐N
	6:30AM		☐Y ☐N
	7:00AM		☐Y ☐N
	7:30AM		☐Y ☐N
	8:00AM		☐Y ☐N
	8:30AM		☐Y ☐N
	9:00AM		☐Y ☐N
	9:30AM		☐Y ☐N
	10:00AM		☐Y ☐N
	10:30AM		☐Y ☐N
	11:00AM		☐Y ☐N
	11:30AM		☐Y ☐N
	12:00PM		☐Y ☐N
	12:30PM		☐Y ☐N
	1:00PM		☐Y ☐N
	1:30PM		☐Y ☐N
	2:00PM		☐Y ☐N
	2:30PM		☐Y ☐N
	3:00PM		☐Y ☐N
	3:30PM		☐Y ☐N
	4:00PM		☐Y ☐N
	4:30PM		☐Y ☐N
	5:00PM		☐Y ☐N
	5:30PM		☐Y ☐N
	6:00PM		☐Y ☐N
	6:30PM		☐Y ☐N
	7:00PM		☐Y ☐N
	7:30PM		☐Y ☐N
	8:00PM		☐Y ☐N
	8:30PM		☐Y ☐N
	9:00PM		☐Y ☐N
	9:30PM		☐Y ☐N

TAKE 5 MINUTES EACH MORNING TO PLAN YOUR DAY.

GET EIGHT HOURS OF SLEEP!

NOTE HIGH PRIORITY TASKS WITH A *

ANALYZE WHY A TASK WAS NOT COMPLETED, THEN MOVE TO NEXT DAY.

ONE POSITIVE

TODAY I GAVE

DAILY
GOAL SLAYERS
PLANNER

SETTING YOURSELF UP FOR SUCCESS DAILY!

DATE

_____ / _____ / _____

SCRIPTURE

MOTIVATIONAL QUOTE

ONE GOAL

ONE FUN THING

HEALTH + FITNESS

WATER INTAKE

*	IMPORTANT TIME	SCHEDULE	SLAYED?
	5:00AM		□Y □N
	5:30AM		□Y □N
	6:00AM		□Y □N
	6:30AM		□Y □N
	7:00AM		□Y □N
	7:30AM		□Y □N
	8:00AM		□Y □N
	8:30AM		□Y □N
	9:00AM		□Y □N
	9:30AM		□Y □N
	10:00AM		□Y □N
	10:30AM		□Y □N
	11:00AM		□Y □N
	11:30AM		□Y □N
	12:00PM		□Y □N
	12:30PM		□Y □N
	1:00PM		□Y □N
	1:30PM		□Y □N
	2:00PM		□Y □N
	2:30PM		□Y □N
	3:00PM		□Y □N
	3:30PM		□Y □N
	4:00PM		□Y □N
	4:30PM		□Y □N
	5:00PM		□Y □N
	5:30PM		□Y □N
	6:00PM		□Y □N
	6:30PM		□Y □N
	7:00PM		□Y □N
	7:30PM		□Y □N
	8:00PM		□Y □N
	8:30PM		□Y □N
	9:00PM		□Y □N
	9:30PM		□Y □N

TAKE 5 MINUTES EACH MORNING TO PLAN YOUR DAY.

GET EIGHT HOURS OF SLEEP!

NOTE HIGH PRIORITY TASKS WITH A *

ANALYZE WHY A TASK WAS NOT COMPLETED, THEN MOVE TO NEXT DAY.

ONE POSITIVE

TODAY I GAVE

DAILY
GOAL SLAYERS
PLANNER

SETTING YOURSELF UP FOR SUCCESS DAILY!

DATE

_____/_____/_____

SCRIPTURE

MOTIVATIONAL QUOTE

ONE GOAL

ONE FUN THING

HEALTH • FITNESS

WATER INTAKE

*	IMPORTANT TIME	SCHEDULE	SLAYED?
	5:00AM		☐Y ☐N
	5:30AM		☐Y ☐N
	6:00AM		☐Y ☐N
	6:30AM		☐Y ☐N
	7:00AM		☐Y ☐N
	7:30AM		☐Y ☐N
	8:00AM		☐Y ☐N
	8:30AM		☐Y ☐N
	9:00AM		☐Y ☐N
	9:30AM		☐Y ☐N
	10:00AM		☐Y ☐N
	10:30AM		☐Y ☐N
	11:00AM		☐Y ☐N
	11:30AM		☐Y ☐N
	12:00PM		☐Y ☐N
	12:30PM		☐Y ☐N
	1:00PM		☐Y ☐N
	1:30PM		☐Y ☐N
	2:00PM		☐Y ☐N
	2:30PM		☐Y ☐N
	3:00PM		☐Y ☐N
	3:30PM		☐Y ☐N
	4:00PM		☐Y ☐N
	4:30PM		☐Y ☐N
	5:00PM		☐Y ☐N
	5:30PM		☐Y ☐N
	6:00PM		☐Y ☐N
	6:30PM		☐Y ☐N
	7:00PM		☐Y ☐N
	7:30PM		☐Y ☐N
	8:00PM		☐Y ☐N
	8:30PM		☐Y ☐N
	9:00PM		☐Y ☐N
	9:30PM		☐Y ☐N

TAKE 5 MINUTES EACH MORNING TO PLAN YOUR DAY.

GET EIGHT HOURS OF SLEEP!

NOTE HIGH PRIORITY TASKS WITH A *

ANALYZE WHY A TASK WAS NOT COMPLETED, THEN MOVE TO NEXT DAY.

ONE POSITIVE

TODAY I GAVE

DAILY
GOAL SLAYERS
PLANNER

SETTING YOURSELF UP FOR SUCCESS DAILY!

DATE

____/____/____

SCRIPTURE

MOTIVATIONAL QUOTE

ONE GOAL

ONE FUN THING

HEALTH + FITNESS

WATER INTAKE

✱	IMPORTANT TIME	SCHEDULE	SLAYED?
	5:00AM		☐Y ☐N
	5:30AM		☐Y ☐N
	6:00AM		☐Y ☐N
	6:30AM		☐Y ☐N
	7:00AM		☐Y ☐N
	7:30AM		☐Y ☐N
	8:00AM		☐Y ☐N
	8:30AM		☐Y ☐N
	9:00AM		☐Y ☐N
	9:30AM		☐Y ☐N
	10:00AM		☐Y ☐N
	10:30AM		☐Y ☐N
	11:00AM		☐Y ☐N
	11:30AM		☐Y ☐N
	12:00PM		☐Y ☐N
	12:30PM		☐Y ☐N
	1:00PM		☐Y ☐N
	1:30PM		☐Y ☐N
	2:00PM		☐Y ☐N
	2:30PM		☐Y ☐N
	3:00PM		☐Y ☐N
	3:30PM		☐Y ☐N
	4:00PM		☐Y ☐N
	4:30PM		☐Y ☐N
	5:00PM		☐Y ☐N
	5:30PM		☐Y ☐N
	6:00PM		☐Y ☐N
	6:30PM		☐Y ☐N
	7:00PM		☐Y ☐N
	7:30PM		☐Y ☐N
	8:00PM		☐Y ☐N
	8:30PM		☐Y ☐N
	9:00PM		☐Y ☐N
	9:30PM		☐Y ☐N

TAKE 5 MINUTES EACH MORNING TO PLAN YOUR DAY.

GET EIGHT HOURS OF SLEEP!

NOTE HIGH PRIORITY TASKS WITH A ✱

ANALYZE WHY A TASK WAS NOT COMPLETED, THEN MOVE TO NEXT DAY.

ONE POSITIVE

TODAY I GAVE

DAILY
GOAL SLAYERS
PLANNER

SETTING YOURSELF UP FOR SUCCESS DAILY!

DATE

_____ / _____ / _____

SCRIPTURE

MOTIVATIONAL QUOTE

ONE GOAL

ONE FUN THING

*	IMPORTANT TIME	SCHEDULE	SLAYED?
	5:00AM		☐Y ☐N
	5:30AM		☐Y ☐N
	6:00AM		☐Y ☐N
	6:30AM		☐Y ☐N
	7:00AM		☐Y ☐N
	7:30AM		☐Y ☐N
	8:00AM		☐Y ☐N
	8:30AM		☐Y ☐N
	9:00AM		☐Y ☐N
	9:30AM		☐Y ☐N
	10:00AM		☐Y ☐N
	10:30AM		☐Y ☐N
	11:00AM		☐Y ☐N
	11:30AM		☐Y ☐N
	12:00PM		☐Y ☐N
	12:30PM		☐Y ☐N
	1:00PM		☐Y ☐N
	1:30PM		☐Y ☐N
	2:00PM		☐Y ☐N
	2:30PM		☐Y ☐N
	3:00PM		☐Y ☐N
	3:30PM		☐Y ☐N
	4:00PM		☐Y ☐N
	4:30PM		☐Y ☐N
	5:00PM		☐Y ☐N
	5:30PM		☐Y ☐N
	6:00PM		☐Y ☐N
	6:30PM		☐Y ☐N
	7:00PM		☐Y ☐N
	7:30PM		☐Y ☐N
	8:00PM		☐Y ☐N
	8:30PM		☐Y ☐N
	9:00PM		☐Y ☐N
	9:30PM		☐Y ☐N

HEALTH + FITNESS

WATER INTAKE

OZ. OZ. OZ. OZ. OZ.
OZ. OZ. OZ. OZ. OZ.

TAKE 5 MINUTES EACH MORNING TO PLAN YOUR DAY.

GET EIGHT HOURS OF SLEEP!

NOTE HIGH PRIORITY TASKS WITH A *

ANALYZE WHY A TASK WAS NOT COMPLETED, THEN MOVE TO NEXT DAY.

ONE POSITIVE

TODAY I GAVE

DAILY
GOAL SLAYERS
PLANNER

SETTING YOURSELF UP FOR SUCCESS DAILY!

DATE

_____ / _____ / _____

SCRIPTURE

MOTIVATIONAL QUOTE

ONE GOAL

ONE FUN THING

HEALTH • FITNESS

WATER INTAKE

OZ. OZ. OZ. OZ. OZ.

OZ. OZ. OZ. OZ. OZ.

*	IMPORTANT TIME	SCHEDULE	SLAYED?
	5:00AM		☐Y ☐N
	5:30AM		☐Y ☐N
	6:00AM		☐Y ☐N
	6:30AM		☐Y ☐N
	7:00AM		☐Y ☐N
	7:30AM		☐Y ☐N
	8:00AM		☐Y ☐N
	8:30AM		☐Y ☐N
	9:00AM		☐Y ☐N
	9:30AM		☐Y ☐N
	10:00AM		☐Y ☐N
	10:30AM		☐Y ☐N
	11:00AM		☐Y ☐N
	11:30AM		☐Y ☐N
	12:00PM		☐Y ☐N
	12:30PM		☐Y ☐N
	1:00PM		☐Y ☐N
	1:30PM		☐Y ☐N
	2:00PM		☐Y ☐N
	2:30PM		☐Y ☐N
	3:00PM		☐Y ☐N
	3:30PM		☐Y ☐N
	4:00PM		☐Y ☐N
	4:30PM		☐Y ☐N
	5:00PM		☐Y ☐N
	5:30PM		☐Y ☐N
	6:00PM		☐Y ☐N
	6:30PM		☐Y ☐N
	7:00PM		☐Y ☐N
	7:30PM		☐Y ☐N
	8:00PM		☐Y ☐N
	8:30PM		☐Y ☐N
	9:00PM		☐Y ☐N
	9:30PM		☐Y ☐N

TAKE 5 MINUTES EACH MORNING TO PLAN YOUR DAY.

GET EIGHT HOURS OF SLEEP!

NOTE HIGH PRIORITY TASKS WITH A *

ANALYZE WHY A TASK WAS NOT COMPLETED, THEN MOVE TO NEXT DAY.

ONE POSITIVE

TODAY I GAVE

DAILY
GOAL SLAYERS
PLANNER

SETTING YOURSELF UP FOR SUCCESS DAILY!

DATE

_____ / _____ / _____

SCRIPTURE

MOTIVATIONAL QUOTE

ONE GOAL

ONE FUN THING

HEALTH • FITNESS

WATER INTAKE

*	IMPORTANT TIME	SCHEDULE	SLAYED?
	5:00AM		☐Y ☐N
	5:30AM		☐Y ☐N
	6:00AM		☐Y ☐N
	6:30AM		☐Y ☐N
	7:00AM		☐Y ☐N
	7:30AM		☐Y ☐N
	8:00AM		☐Y ☐N
	8:30AM		☐Y ☐N
	9:00AM		☐Y ☐N
	9:30AM		☐Y ☐N
	10:00AM		☐Y ☐N
	10:30AM		☐Y ☐N
	11:00AM		☐Y ☐N
	11:30AM		☐Y ☐N
	12:00PM		☐Y ☐N
	12:30PM		☐Y ☐N
	1:00PM		☐Y ☐N
	1:30PM		☐Y ☐N
	2:00PM		☐Y ☐N
	2:30PM		☐Y ☐N
	3:00PM		☐Y ☐N
	3:30PM		☐Y ☐N
	4:00PM		☐Y ☐N
	4:30PM		☐Y ☐N
	5:00PM		☐Y ☐N
	5:30PM		☐Y ☐N
	6:00PM		☐Y ☐N
	6:30PM		☐Y ☐N
	7:00PM		☐Y ☐N
	7:30PM		☐Y ☐N
	8:00PM		☐Y ☐N
	8:30PM		☐Y ☐N
	9:00PM		☐Y ☐N
	9:30PM		☐Y ☐N

TAKE 5 MINUTES EACH MORNING TO PLAN YOUR DAY.

GET EIGHT HOURS OF SLEEP!

NOTE HIGH PRIORITY TASKS WITH A *

ANALYZE WHY A TASK WAS NOT COMPLETED, THEN MOVE TO NEXT DAY.

ONE POSITIVE

TODAY I GAVE

DAILY
GOAL SLAYERS
PLANNER

SETTING YOURSELF UP FOR SUCCESS DAILY!

DATE

_____ / _____ / _____

SCRIPTURE

MOTIVATIONAL QUOTE

ONE GOAL

ONE FUN THING

✱	IMPORTANT TIME	SCHEDULE	SLAYED?
	5:00AM		☐Y ☐N
	5:30AM		☐Y ☐N
	6:00AM		☐Y ☐N
	6:30AM		☐Y ☐N
	7:00AM		☐Y ☐N
	7:30AM		☐Y ☐N
	8:00AM		☐Y ☐N
	8:30AM		☐Y ☐N
	9:00AM		☐Y ☐N
	9:30AM		☐Y ☐N
	10:00AM		☐Y ☐N
	10:30AM		☐Y ☐N
	11:00AM		☐Y ☐N
	11:30AM		☐Y ☐N
	12:00PM		☐Y ☐N
	12:30PM		☐Y ☐N
	1:00PM		☐Y ☐N
	1:30PM		☐Y ☐N
	2:00PM		☐Y ☐N
	2:30PM		☐Y ☐N
	3:00PM		☐Y ☐N
	3:30PM		☐Y ☐N
	4:00PM		☐Y ☐N
	4:30PM		☐Y ☐N
	5:00PM		☐Y ☐N
	5:30PM		☐Y ☐N
	6:00PM		☐Y ☐N
	6:30PM		☐Y ☐N
	7:00PM		☐Y ☐N
	7:30PM		☐Y ☐N
	8:00PM		☐Y ☐N
	8:30PM		☐Y ☐N
	9:00PM		☐Y ☐N
	9:30PM		☐Y ☐N

HEALTH · FITNESS

WATER INTAKE

OZ. OZ. OZ. OZ. OZ.
OZ. OZ. OZ. OZ. OZ.

TAKE 5 MINUTES EACH MORNING TO PLAN YOUR DAY.

GET EIGHT HOURS OF SLEEP!

NOTE HIGH PRIORITY TASKS WITH A ✱

ANALYZE WHY A TASK WAS NOT COMPLETED, THEN MOVE TO NEXT DAY.

ONE POSITIVE

TODAY I GAVE

DAILY
GOAL SLAYERS
PLANNER

SETTING YOURSELF UP FOR SUCCESS DAILY!

DATE

_____ / _____ / _____

SCRIPTURE

MOTIVATIONAL QUOTE

ONE GOAL

ONE FUN THING

*	IMPORTANT TIME	SCHEDULE	SLAYED?
	5:00AM		☐Y ☐N
	5:30AM		☐Y ☐N
	6:00AM		☐Y ☐N
	6:30AM		☐Y ☐N
	7:00AM		☐Y ☐N
	7:30AM		☐Y ☐N
	8:00AM		☐Y ☐N
	8:30AM		☐Y ☐N
	9:00AM		☐Y ☐N
	9:30AM		☐Y ☐N
	10:00AM		☐Y ☐N
	10:30AM		☐Y ☐N
	11:00AM		☐Y ☐N
	11:30AM		☐Y ☐N
	12:00PM		☐Y ☐N
	12:30PM		☐Y ☐N
	1:00PM		☐Y ☐N
	1:30PM		☐Y ☐N
	2:00PM		☐Y ☐N
	2:30PM		☐Y ☐N
	3:00PM		☐Y ☐N
	3:30PM		☐Y ☐N
	4:00PM		☐Y ☐N
	4:30PM		☐Y ☐N
	5:00PM		☐Y ☐N
	5:30PM		☐Y ☐N
	6:00PM		☐Y ☐N
	6:30PM		☐Y ☐N
	7:00PM		☐Y ☐N
	7:30PM		☐Y ☐N
	8:00PM		☐Y ☐N
	8:30PM		☐Y ☐N
	9:00PM		☐Y ☐N
	9:30PM		☐Y ☐N

HEALTH • FITNESS

WATER INTAKE

OZ. OZ. OZ. OZ. OZ.
OZ. OZ. OZ. OZ. OZ.

TAKE 5 MINUTES EACH MORNING TO PLAN YOUR DAY.

GET EIGHT HOURS OF SLEEP!

NOTE HIGH PRIORITY TASKS WITH A *

ANALYZE WHY A TASK WAS NOT COMPLETED, THEN MOVE TO NEXT DAY.

ONE POSITIVE

TODAY I GAVE

DAILY
GOAL SLAYERS
PLANNER

SETTING YOURSELF UP FOR SUCCESS DAILY!

DATE

____ / ____ / ____

SCRIPTURE

MOTIVATIONAL QUOTE

ONE GOAL

ONE FUN THING

HEALTH • FITNESS

WATER INTAKE

*	IMPORTANT TIME	SCHEDULE	SLAYED?
	5:00AM		□Y □N
	5:30AM		□Y □N
	6:00AM		□Y □N
	6:30AM		□Y □N
	7:00AM		□Y □N
	7:30AM		□Y □N
	8:00AM		□Y □N
	8:30AM		□Y □N
	9:00AM		□Y □N
	9:30AM		□Y □N
	10:00AM		□Y □N
	10:30AM		□Y □N
	11:00AM		□Y □N
	11:30AM		□Y □N
	12:00PM		□Y □N
	12:30PM		□Y □N
	1:00PM		□Y □N
	1:30PM		□Y □N
	2:00PM		□Y □N
	2:30PM		□Y □N
	3:00PM		□Y □N
	3:30PM		□Y □N
	4:00PM		□Y □N
	4:30PM		□Y □N
	5:00PM		□Y □N
	5:30PM		□Y □N
	6:00PM		□Y □N
	6:30PM		□Y □N
	7:00PM		□Y □N
	7:30PM		□Y □N
	8:00PM		□Y □N
	8:30PM		□Y □N
	9:00PM		□Y □N
	9:30PM		□Y □N

TAKE 5 MINUTES EACH MORNING TO PLAN YOUR DAY.

GET EIGHT HOURS OF SLEEP!

NOTE HIGH PRIORITY TASKS WITH A *

ANALYZE WHY A TASK WAS NOT COMPLETED, THEN MOVE TO NEXT DAY.

ONE POSITIVE

TODAY I GAVE

DAILY
GOAL SLAYERS
PLANNER

SETTING YOURSELF UP FOR SUCCESS DAILY!

DATE

____/____/____

SCRIPTURE

MOTIVATIONAL QUOTE

ONE GOAL

ONE FUN THING

HEALTH + FITNESS

WATER INTAKE

OZ OZ OZ OZ OZ

OZ OZ OZ OZ OZ

*	IMPORTANT TIME	SCHEDULE	SLAYED?
	5:00AM		☐Y ☐N
	5:30AM		☐Y ☐N
	6:00AM		☐Y ☐N
	6:30AM		☐Y ☐N
	7:00AM		☐Y ☐N
	7:30AM		☐Y ☐N
	8:00AM		☐Y ☐N
	8:30AM		☐Y ☐N
	9:00AM		☐Y ☐N
	9:30AM		☐Y ☐N
	10:00AM		☐Y ☐N
	10:30AM		☐Y ☐N
	11:00AM		☐Y ☐N
	11:30AM		☐Y ☐N
	12:00PM		☐Y ☐N
	12:30PM		☐Y ☐N
	1:00PM		☐Y ☐N
	1:30PM		☐Y ☐N
	2:00PM		☐Y ☐N
	2:30PM		☐Y ☐N
	3:00PM		☐Y ☐N
	3:30PM		☐Y ☐N
	4:00PM		☐Y ☐N
	4:30PM		☐Y ☐N
	5:00PM		☐Y ☐N
	5:30PM		☐Y ☐N
	6:00PM		☐Y ☐N
	6:30PM		☐Y ☐N
	7:00PM		☐Y ☐N
	7:30PM		☐Y ☐N
	8:00PM		☐Y ☐N
	8:30PM		☐Y ☐N
	9:00PM		☐Y ☐N
	9:30PM		☐Y ☐N

TAKE 5 MINUTES EACH MORNING TO PLAN YOUR DAY.

GET EIGHT HOURS OF SLEEP!

NOTE HIGH PRIORITY TASKS WITH A *

ANALYZE WHY A TASK WAS NOT COMPLETED, THEN MOVE TO NEXT DAY.

ONE POSITIVE

TODAY I GAVE

DAILY
GOAL SLAYERS
PLANNER

SETTING YOURSELF UP FOR SUCCESS DAILY!

DATE

_____ / _____ / _____

SCRIPTURE

MOTIVATIONAL QUOTE

ONE GOAL

ONE FUN THING

HEALTH • FITNESS

WATER INTAKE

OZ. OZ. OZ. OZ. OZ.

OZ. OZ. OZ. OZ. OZ.

✱	IMPORTANT TIME	SCHEDULE	SLAYED?
	5:00AM		☐Y ☐N
	5:30AM		☐Y ☐N
	6:00AM		☐Y ☐N
	6:30AM		☐Y ☐N
	7:00AM		☐Y ☐N
	7:30AM		☐Y ☐N
	8:00AM		☐Y ☐N
	8:30AM		☐Y ☐N
	9:00AM		☐Y ☐N
	9:30AM		☐Y ☐N
	10:00AM		☐Y ☐N
	10:30AM		☐Y ☐N
	11:00AM		☐Y ☐N
	11:30AM		☐Y ☐N
	12:00PM		☐Y ☐N
	12:30PM		☐Y ☐N
	1:00PM		☐Y ☐N
	1:30PM		☐Y ☐N
	2:00PM		☐Y ☐N
	2:30PM		☐Y ☐N
	3:00PM		☐Y ☐N
	3:30PM		☐Y ☐N
	4:00PM		☐Y ☐N
	4:30PM		☐Y ☐N
	5:00PM		☐Y ☐N
	5:30PM		☐Y ☐N
	6:00PM		☐Y ☐N
	6:30PM		☐Y ☐N
	7:00PM		☐Y ☐N
	7:30PM		☐Y ☐N
	8:00PM		☐Y ☐N
	8:30PM		☐Y ☐N
	9:00PM		☐Y ☐N
	9:30PM		☐Y ☐N

TAKE 5 MINUTES EACH MORNING TO PLAN YOUR DAY.

GET EIGHT HOURS OF SLEEP!

NOTE HIGH PRIORITY TASKS WITH A ✱

ANALYZE WHY A TASK WAS NOT COMPLETED, THEN MOVE TO NEXT DAY.

ONE POSITIVE

TODAY I GAVE

DAILY
GOAL SLAYERS
PLANNER

SETTING YOURSELF UP FOR SUCCESS DAILY!

DATE

_____ / _____ / _____

SCRIPTURE

MOTIVATIONAL QUOTE

ONE GOAL

ONE FUN THING

HEALTH + FITNESS

WATER INTAKE

OZ. OZ. OZ. OZ. OZ.

OZ. OZ. OZ. OZ. OZ.

✱	IMPORTANT TIME	SCHEDULE	SLAYED?
	5:00AM		☐Y ☐N
	5:30AM		☐Y ☐N
	6:00AM		☐Y ☐N
	6:30AM		☐Y ☐N
	7:00AM		☐Y ☐N
	7:30AM		☐Y ☐N
	8:00AM		☐Y ☐N
	8:30AM		☐Y ☐N
	9:00AM		☐Y ☐N
	9:30AM		☐Y ☐N
	10:00AM		☐Y ☐N
	10:30AM		☐Y ☐N
	11:00AM		☐Y ☐N
	11:30AM		☐Y ☐N
	12:00PM		☐Y ☐N
	12:30PM		☐Y ☐N
	1:00PM		☐Y ☐N
	1:30PM		☐Y ☐N
	2:00PM		☐Y ☐N
	2:30PM		☐Y ☐N
	3:00PM		☐Y ☐N
	3:30PM		☐Y ☐N
	4:00PM		☐Y ☐N
	4:30PM		☐Y ☐N
	5:00PM		☐Y ☐N
	5:30PM		☐Y ☐N
	6:00PM		☐Y ☐N
	6:30PM		☐Y ☐N
	7:00PM		☐Y ☐N
	7:30PM		☐Y ☐N
	8:00PM		☐Y ☐N
	8:30PM		☐Y ☐N
	9:00PM		☐Y ☐N
	9:30PM		☐Y ☐N

TAKE 5 MINUTES EACH MORNING TO PLAN YOUR DAY.

GET EIGHT HOURS OF SLEEP!

NOTE HIGH PRIORITY TASKS WITH A ✱

ANALYZE WHY A TASK WAS NOT COMPLETED, THEN MOVE TO NEXT DAY.

ONE POSITIVE

TODAY I GAVE

DAILY
GOAL SLAYERS
PLANNER

SETTING YOURSELF UP FOR SUCCESS DAILY!

DATE

_____ / _____ / _____

SCRIPTURE

MOTIVATIONAL QUOTE

ONE GOAL

ONE FUN THING

HEALTH • FITNESS

WATER INTAKE

OZ. OZ. OZ. OZ. OZ.

OZ. OZ. OZ. OZ. OZ.

✱	IMPORTANT TIME	SCHEDULE	SLAYED?
	5:00AM		☐Y ☐N
	5:30AM		☐Y ☐N
	6:00AM		☐Y ☐N
	6:30AM		☐Y ☐N
	7:00AM		☐Y ☐N
	7:30AM		☐Y ☐N
	8:00AM		☐Y ☐N
	8:30AM		☐Y ☐N
	9:00AM		☐Y ☐N
	9:30AM		☐Y ☐N
	10:00AM		☐Y ☐N
	10:30AM		☐Y ☐N
	11:00AM		☐Y ☐N
	11:30AM		☐Y ☐N
	12:00PM		☐Y ☐N
	12:30PM		☐Y ☐N
	1:00PM		☐Y ☐N
	1:30PM		☐Y ☐N
	2:00PM		☐Y ☐N
	2:30PM		☐Y ☐N
	3:00PM		☐Y ☐N
	3:30PM		☐Y ☐N
	4:00PM		☐Y ☐N
	4:30PM		☐Y ☐N
	5:00PM		☐Y ☐N
	5:30PM		☐Y ☐N
	6:00PM		☐Y ☐N
	6:30PM		☐Y ☐N
	7:00PM		☐Y ☐N
	7:30PM		☐Y ☐N
	8:00PM		☐Y ☐N
	8:30PM		☐Y ☐N
	9:00PM		☐Y ☐N
	9:30PM		☐Y ☐N

TAKE 5 MINUTES EACH MORNING TO PLAN YOUR DAY.

GET EIGHT HOURS OF SLEEP!

NOTE HIGH PRIORITY TASKS WITH A ✱

ANALYZE WHY A TASK WAS NOT COMPLETED, THEN MOVE TO NEXT DAY.

ONE POSITIVE

TODAY I GAVE

DAILY
GOAL SLAYERS
PLANNER

SETTING YOURSELF UP FOR SUCCESS DAILY!

DATE

_____/_____/_____

SCRIPTURE

MOTIVATIONAL QUOTE

ONE GOAL

ONE FUN THING

HEALTH • FITNESS

WATER INTAKE

OZ. OZ. OZ. OZ. OZ.

OZ. OZ. OZ. OZ. OZ.

*	IMPORTANT TIME	SCHEDULE	SLAYED?
	5:00AM		☐Y ☐N
	5:30AM		☐Y ☐N
	6:00AM		☐Y ☐N
	6:30AM		☐Y ☐N
	7:00AM		☐Y ☐N
	7:30AM		☐Y ☐N
	8:00AM		☐Y ☐N
	8:30AM		☐Y ☐N
	9:00AM		☐Y ☐N
	9:30AM		☐Y ☐N
	10:00AM		☐Y ☐N
	10:30AM		☐Y ☐N
	11:00AM		☐Y ☐N
	11:30AM		☐Y ☐N
	12:00PM		☐Y ☐N
	12:30PM		☐Y ☐N
	1:00PM		☐Y ☐N
	1:30PM		☐Y ☐N
	2:00PM		☐Y ☐N
	2:30PM		☐Y ☐N
	3:00PM		☐Y ☐N
	3:30PM		☐Y ☐N
	4:00PM		☐Y ☐N
	4:30PM		☐Y ☐N
	5:00PM		☐Y ☐N
	5:30PM		☐Y ☐N
	6:00PM		☐Y ☐N
	6:30PM		☐Y ☐N
	7:00PM		☐Y ☐N
	7:30PM		☐Y ☐N
	8:00PM		☐Y ☐N
	8:30PM		☐Y ☐N
	9:00PM		☐Y ☐N
	9:30PM		☐Y ☐N

TAKE 5 MINUTES EACH MORNING TO PLAN YOUR DAY.

GET EIGHT HOURS OF SLEEP!

NOTE HIGH PRIORITY TASKS WITH A *

ANALYZE WHY A TASK WAS NOT COMPLETED, THEN MOVE TO NEXT DAY.

ONE POSITIVE

TODAY I GAVE

DAILY
GOAL SLAYERS
PLANNER

SETTING YOURSELF UP FOR SUCCESS DAILY!

DATE

____ / ____ / ____

SCRIPTURE

MOTIVATIONAL QUOTE

ONE GOAL

ONE FUN THING

HEALTH • FITNESS

WATER INTAKE

*	IMPORTANT TIME	SCHEDULE	SLAYED?
	5:00AM		☐Y ☐N
	5:30AM		☐Y ☐N
	6:00AM		☐Y ☐N
	6:30AM		☐Y ☐N
	7:00AM		☐Y ☐N
	7:30AM		☐Y ☐N
	8:00AM		☐Y ☐N
	8:30AM		☐Y ☐N
	9:00AM		☐Y ☐N
	9:30AM		☐Y ☐N
	10:00AM		☐Y ☐N
	10:30AM		☐Y ☐N
	11:00AM		☐Y ☐N
	11:30AM		☐Y ☐N
	12:00PM		☐Y ☐N
	12:30PM		☐Y ☐N
	1:00PM		☐Y ☐N
	1:30PM		☐Y ☐N
	2:00PM		☐Y ☐N
	2:30PM		☐Y ☐N
	3:00PM		☐Y ☐N
	3:30PM		☐Y ☐N
	4:00PM		☐Y ☐N
	4:30PM		☐Y ☐N
	5:00PM		☐Y ☐N
	5:30PM		☐Y ☐N
	6:00PM		☐Y ☐N
	6:30PM		☐Y ☐N
	7:00PM		☐Y ☐N
	7:30PM		☐Y ☐N
	8:00PM		☐Y ☐N
	8:30PM		☐Y ☐N
	9:00PM		☐Y ☐N
	9:30PM		☐Y ☐N

TAKE 5 MINUTES EACH MORNING TO PLAN YOUR DAY.

GET EIGHT HOURS OF SLEEP!

NOTE HIGH PRIORITY TASKS WITH A ✳

ANALYZE WHY A TASK WAS NOT COMPLETED, THEN MOVE TO NEXT DAY.

ONE POSITIVE

TODAY I GAVE

DAILY
GOAL SLAYERS
PLANNER

SETTING YOURSELF UP FOR SUCCESS DAILY!

DATE

_____ / _____ / _____

SCRIPTURE

MOTIVATIONAL QUOTE

ONE GOAL

ONE FUN THING

*	IMPORTANT TIME	SCHEDULE	SLAYED?
	5:00AM		☐Y ☐N
	5:30AM		☐Y ☐N
	6:00AM		☐Y ☐N
	6:30AM		☐Y ☐N
	7:00AM		☐Y ☐N
	7:30AM		☐Y ☐N
	8:00AM		☐Y ☐N
	8:30AM		☐Y ☐N
	9:00AM		☐Y ☐N
	9:30AM		☐Y ☐N
	10:00AM		☐Y ☐N
	10:30AM		☐Y ☐N
	11:00AM		☐Y ☐N
	11:30AM		☐Y ☐N
	12:00PM		☐Y ☐N
	12:30PM		☐Y ☐N
	1:00PM		☐Y ☐N
	1:30PM		☐Y ☐N
	2:00PM		☐Y ☐N
	2:30PM		☐Y ☐N
	3:00PM		☐Y ☐N
	3:30PM		☐Y ☐N
	4:00PM		☐Y ☐N
	4:30PM		☐Y ☐N
	5:00PM		☐Y ☐N
	5:30PM		☐Y ☐N
	6:00PM		☐Y ☐N
	6:30PM		☐Y ☐N
	7:00PM		☐Y ☐N
	7:30PM		☐Y ☐N
	8:00PM		☐Y ☐N
	8:30PM		☐Y ☐N
	9:00PM		☐Y ☐N
	9:30PM		☐Y ☐N

HEALTH + FITNESS

WATER INTAKE

OZ. OZ. OZ. OZ. OZ.
OZ. OZ. OZ. OZ. OZ.

TAKE 5 MINUTES EACH MORNING TO PLAN YOUR DAY.

GET EIGHT HOURS OF SLEEP!

NOTE HIGH PRIORITY TASKS WITH A *

ANALYZE WHY A TASK WAS NOT COMPLETED, THEN MOVE TO NEXT DAY.

ONE POSITIVE

TODAY I GAVE

DAILY
GOAL SLAYERS
PLANNER

SETTING YOURSELF UP FOR SUCCESS DAILY!

DATE
_____ / _____ / _____

SCRIPTURE

MOTIVATIONAL QUOTE

ONE GOAL

ONE FUN THING

HEALTH + FITNESS

WATER INTAKE

OZ. OZ. OZ. OZ. OZ.

OZ. OZ. OZ. OZ. OZ.

*	IMPORTANT TIME	SCHEDULE	SLAYED?
	5:00AM		☐Y ☐N
	5:30AM		☐Y ☐N
	6:00AM		☐Y ☐N
	6:30AM		☐Y ☐N
	7:00AM		☐Y ☐N
	7:30AM		☐Y ☐N
	8:00AM		☐Y ☐N
	8:30AM		☐Y ☐N
	9:00AM		☐Y ☐N
	9:30AM		☐Y ☐N
	10:00AM		☐Y ☐N
	10:30AM		☐Y ☐N
	11:00AM		☐Y ☐N
	11:30AM		☐Y ☐N
	12:00PM		☐Y ☐N
	12:30PM		☐Y ☐N
	1:00PM		☐Y ☐N
	1:30PM		☐Y ☐N
	2:00PM		☐Y ☐N
	2:30PM		☐Y ☐N
	3:00PM		☐Y ☐N
	3:30PM		☐Y ☐N
	4:00PM		☐Y ☐N
	4:30PM		☐Y ☐N
	5:00PM		☐Y ☐N
	5:30PM		☐Y ☐N
	6:00PM		☐Y ☐N
	6:30PM		☐Y ☐N
	7:00PM		☐Y ☐N
	7:30PM		☐Y ☐N
	8:00PM		☐Y ☐N
	8:30PM		☐Y ☐N
	9:00PM		☐Y ☐N
	9:30PM		☐Y ☐N

TAKE 5 MINUTES EACH MORNING TO PLAN YOUR DAY.

GET EIGHT HOURS OF SLEEP!

NOTE HIGH PRIORITY TASKS WITH A *

ANALYZE WHY A TASK WAS NOT COMPLETED, THEN MOVE TO NEXT DAY.

ONE POSITIVE

TODAY I GAVE

DAILY
GOAL SLAYERS
PLANNER

SETTING YOURSELF UP FOR SUCCESS DAILY!

DATE

_____ / _____ / _____

SCRIPTURE

MOTIVATIONAL QUOTE

ONE GOAL

ONE FUN THING

*	IMPORTANT TIME	SCHEDULE	SLAYED?
	5:00AM		☐Y ☐N
	5:30AM		☐Y ☐N
	6:00AM		☐Y ☐N
	6:30AM		☐Y ☐N
	7:00AM		☐Y ☐N
	7:30AM		☐Y ☐N
	8:00AM		☐Y ☐N
	8:30AM		☐Y ☐N
	9:00AM		☐Y ☐N
	9:30AM		☐Y ☐N
	10:00AM		☐Y ☐N
	10:30AM		☐Y ☐N
	11:00AM		☐Y ☐N
	11:30AM		☐Y ☐N
	12:00PM		☐Y ☐N
	12:30PM		☐Y ☐N
	1:00PM		☐Y ☐N
	1:30PM		☐Y ☐N
	2:00PM		☐Y ☐N
	2:30PM		☐Y ☐N
	3:00PM		☐Y ☐N
	3:30PM		☐Y ☐N
	4:00PM		☐Y ☐N
	4:30PM		☐Y ☐N
	5:00PM		☐Y ☐N
	5:30PM		☐Y ☐N
	6:00PM		☐Y ☐N
	6:30PM		☐Y ☐N
	7:00PM		☐Y ☐N
	7:30PM		☐Y ☐N
	8:00PM		☐Y ☐N
	8:30PM		☐Y ☐N
	9:00PM		☐Y ☐N
	9:30PM		☐Y ☐N

HEALTH • FITNESS

WATER INTAKE

OZ. OZ. OZ. OZ. OZ.
OZ. OZ. OZ. OZ. OZ.

TAKE 5 MINUTES EACH MORNING TO PLAN YOUR DAY.

GET EIGHT HOURS OF SLEEP!

NOTE HIGH PRIORITY TASKS WITH A *

ANALYZE WHY A TASK WAS NOT COMPLETED, THEN MOVE TO NEXT DAY.

ONE POSITIVE

TODAY I GAVE

DAILY
GOAL SLAYERS
PLANNER

SETTING YOURSELF UP FOR SUCCESS DAILY!

DATE

_____ / _____ / _____

SCRIPTURE

MOTIVATIONAL QUOTE

ONE GOAL

ONE FUN THING

HEALTH • FITNESS

WATER INTAKE

OZ. OZ. OZ. OZ. OZ.
OZ. OZ. OZ. OZ. OZ.

✱	IMPORTANT TIME	SCHEDULE	SLAYED?
	5:00AM		☐Y ☐N
	5:30AM		☐Y ☐N
	6:00AM		☐Y ☐N
	6:30AM		☐Y ☐N
	7:00AM		☐Y ☐N
	7:30AM		☐Y ☐N
	8:00AM		☐Y ☐N
	8:30AM		☐Y ☐N
	9:00AM		☐Y ☐N
	9:30AM		☐Y ☐N
	10:00AM		☐Y ☐N
	10:30AM		☐Y ☐N
	11:00AM		☐Y ☐N
	11:30AM		☐Y ☐N
	12:00PM		☐Y ☐N
	12:30PM		☐Y ☐N
	1:00PM		☐Y ☐N
	1:30PM		☐Y ☐N
	2:00PM		☐Y ☐N
	2:30PM		☐Y ☐N
	3:00PM		☐Y ☐N
	3:30PM		☐Y ☐N
	4:00PM		☐Y ☐N
	4:30PM		☐Y ☐N
	5:00PM		☐Y ☐N
	5:30PM		☐Y ☐N
	6:00PM		☐Y ☐N
	6:30PM		☐Y ☐N
	7:00PM		☐Y ☐N
	7:30PM		☐Y ☐N
	8:00PM		☐Y ☐N
	8:30PM		☐Y ☐N
	9:00PM		☐Y ☐N
	9:30PM		☐Y ☐N

TAKE 5 MINUTES EACH MORNING TO PLAN YOUR DAY.

GET EIGHT HOURS OF SLEEP!

NOTE HIGH PRIORITY TASKS WITH A ✱

ANALYZE WHY A TASK WAS NOT COMPLETED, THEN MOVE TO NEXT DAY.

ONE POSITIVE

TODAY I GAVE

DAILY
GOAL SLAYERS
PLANNER

SETTING YOURSELF UP FOR SUCCESS DAILY!

DATE

_____ / _____ / _____

SCRIPTURE

MOTIVATIONAL QUOTE

ONE GOAL

ONE FUN THING

✱	IMPORTANT TIME	SCHEDULE	SLAYED?
	5:00AM		☐Y ☐N
	5:30AM		☐Y ☐N
	6:00AM		☐Y ☐N
	6:30AM		☐Y ☐N
	7:00AM		☐Y ☐N
	7:30AM		☐Y ☐N
	8:00AM		☐Y ☐N
	8:30AM		☐Y ☐N
	9:00AM		☐Y ☐N
	9:30AM		☐Y ☐N
	10:00AM		☐Y ☐N
	10:30AM		☐Y ☐N
	11:00AM		☐Y ☐N
	11:30AM		☐Y ☐N
	12:00PM		☐Y ☐N
	12:30PM		☐Y ☐N
	1:00PM		☐Y ☐N
	1:30PM		☐Y ☐N
	2:00PM		☐Y ☐N
	2:30PM		☐Y ☐N
	3:00PM		☐Y ☐N
	3:30PM		☐Y ☐N
	4:00PM		☐Y ☐N
	4:30PM		☐Y ☐N
	5:00PM		☐Y ☐N
	5:30PM		☐Y ☐N
	6:00PM		☐Y ☐N
	6:30PM		☐Y ☐N
	7:00PM		☐Y ☐N
	7:30PM		☐Y ☐N
	8:00PM		☐Y ☐N
	8:30PM		☐Y ☐N
	9:00PM		☐Y ☐N
	9:30PM		☐Y ☐N

HEALTH • FITNESS

WATER INTAKE

OZ. OZ. OZ. OZ. OZ.

OZ. OZ. OZ. OZ. OZ.

TAKE 5 MINUTES EACH MORNING TO PLAN YOUR DAY.

GET EIGHT HOURS OF SLEEP!

NOTE HIGH PRIORITY TASKS WITH A ✱

ANALYZE WHY A TASK WAS NOT COMPLETED, THEN MOVE TO NEXT DAY.

ONE POSITIVE

TODAY I GAVE

DAILY
GOAL SLAYERS
PLANNER

SETTING YOURSELF UP FOR SUCCESS DAILY!

DATE

_____ / _____ / _____

SCRIPTURE

MOTIVATIONAL QUOTE

ONE GOAL

ONE FUN THING

HEALTH • FITNESS

WATER INTAKE

*	IMPORTANT TIME	SCHEDULE	SLAYED?
	5:00AM		☐Y ☐N
	5:30AM		☐Y ☐N
	6:00AM		☐Y ☐N
	6:30AM		☐Y ☐N
	7:00AM		☐Y ☐N
	7:30AM		☐Y ☐N
	8:00AM		☐Y ☐N
	8:30AM		☐Y ☐N
	9:00AM		☐Y ☐N
	9:30AM		☐Y ☐N
	10:00AM		☐Y ☐N
	10:30AM		☐Y ☐N
	11:00AM		☐Y ☐N
	11:30AM		☐Y ☐N
	12:00PM		☐Y ☐N
	12:30PM		☐Y ☐N
	1:00PM		☐Y ☐N
	1:30PM		☐Y ☐N
	2:00PM		☐Y ☐N
	2:30PM		☐Y ☐N
	3:00PM		☐Y ☐N
	3:30PM		☐Y ☐N
	4:00PM		☐Y ☐N
	4:30PM		☐Y ☐N
	5:00PM		☐Y ☐N
	5:30PM		☐Y ☐N
	6:00PM		☐Y ☐N
	6:30PM		☐Y ☐N
	7:00PM		☐Y ☐N
	7:30PM		☐Y ☐N
	8:00PM		☐Y ☐N
	8:30PM		☐Y ☐N
	9:00PM		☐Y ☐N
	9:30PM		☐Y ☐N

TAKE 5 MINUTES EACH MORNING TO PLAN YOUR DAY.

GET EIGHT HOURS OF SLEEP!

NOTE HIGH PRIORITY TASKS WITH A *

ANALYZE WHY A TASK WAS NOT COMPLETED, THEN MOVE TO NEXT DAY.

ONE POSITIVE

TODAY I GAVE

DAILY
GOAL SLAYERS
PLANNER

SETTING YOURSELF UP FOR SUCCESS DAILY!

DATE

____/____/____

SCRIPTURE

MOTIVATIONAL QUOTE

ONE GOAL

ONE FUN THING

HEALTH • FITNESS

WATER INTAKE

OZ. OZ. OZ. OZ. OZ.

OZ. OZ. OZ. OZ. OZ.

✱	IMPORTANT TIME	SCHEDULE	SLAYED?
	5:00AM		☐Y ☐N
	5:30AM		☐Y ☐N
	6:00AM		☐Y ☐N
	6:30AM		☐Y ☐N
	7:00AM		☐Y ☐N
	7:30AM		☐Y ☐N
	8:00AM		☐Y ☐N
	8:30AM		☐Y ☐N
	9:00AM		☐Y ☐N
	9:30AM		☐Y ☐N
	10:00AM		☐Y ☐N
	10:30AM		☐Y ☐N
	11:00AM		☐Y ☐N
	11:30AM		☐Y ☐N
	12:00PM		☐Y ☐N
	12:30PM		☐Y ☐N
	1:00PM		☐Y ☐N
	1:30PM		☐Y ☐N
	2:00PM		☐Y ☐N
	2:30PM		☐Y ☐N
	3:00PM		☐Y ☐N
	3:30PM		☐Y ☐N
	4:00PM		☐Y ☐N
	4:30PM		☐Y ☐N
	5:00PM		☐Y ☐N
	5:30PM		☐Y ☐N
	6:00PM		☐Y ☐N
	6:30PM		☐Y ☐N
	7:00PM		☐Y ☐N
	7:30PM		☐Y ☐N
	8:00PM		☐Y ☐N
	8:30PM		☐Y ☐N
	9:00PM		☐Y ☐N
	9:30PM		☐Y ☐N

TAKE 5 MINUTES EACH MORNING TO PLAN YOUR DAY.

GET EIGHT HOURS OF SLEEP!

NOTE HIGH PRIORITY TASKS WITH A ✱

ANALYZE WHY A TASK WAS NOT COMPLETED, THEN MOVE TO NEXT DAY.

ONE POSITIVE

TODAY I GAVE

DAILY
GOAL SLAYERS
PLANNER

SETTING YOURSELF UP FOR SUCCESS DAILY!

DATE

____ / ____ / ____

SCRIPTURE

MOTIVATIONAL QUOTE

ONE GOAL

ONE FUN THING

HEALTH • FITNESS

WATER INTAKE

*	IMPORTANT TIME	SCHEDULE	SLAYED?
	5:00AM		☐Y ☐N
	5:30AM		☐Y ☐N
	6:00AM		☐Y ☐N
	6:30AM		☐Y ☐N
	7:00AM		☐Y ☐N
	7:30AM		☐Y ☐N
	8:00AM		☐Y ☐N
	8:30AM		☐Y ☐N
	9:00AM		☐Y ☐N
	9:30AM		☐Y ☐N
	10:00AM		☐Y ☐N
	10:30AM		☐Y ☐N
	11:00AM		☐Y ☐N
	11:30AM		☐Y ☐N
	12:00PM		☐Y ☐N
	12:30PM		☐Y ☐N
	1:00PM		☐Y ☐N
	1:30PM		☐Y ☐N
	2:00PM		☐Y ☐N
	2:30PM		☐Y ☐N
	3:00PM		☐Y ☐N
	3:30PM		☐Y ☐N
	4:00PM		☐Y ☐N
	4:30PM		☐Y ☐N
	5:00PM		☐Y ☐N
	5:30PM		☐Y ☐N
	6:00PM		☐Y ☐N
	6:30PM		☐Y ☐N
	7:00PM		☐Y ☐N
	7:30PM		☐Y ☐N
	8:00PM		☐Y ☐N
	8:30PM		☐Y ☐N
	9:00PM		☐Y ☐N
	9:30PM		☐Y ☐N

TAKE 5 MINUTES EACH MORNING TO PLAN YOUR DAY.

GET EIGHT HOURS OF SLEEP!

NOTE HIGH PRIORITY TASKS WITH A *

ANALYZE WHY A TASK WAS NOT COMPLETED, THEN MOVE TO NEXT DAY.

ONE POSITIVE

TODAY I GAVE

DAILY
GOAL SLAYERS
PLANNER

SETTING YOURSELF UP FOR SUCCESS DAILY!

DATE

_____ / _____ / _____

SCRIPTURE

MOTIVATIONAL QUOTE

ONE GOAL

ONE FUN THING

HEALTH • FITNESS

WATER INTAKE

OZ. OZ. OZ. OZ. OZ.
OZ. OZ. OZ. OZ. OZ.

✱	IMPORTANT TIME	SCHEDULE	SLAYED?
	5:00AM		☐Y ☐N
	5:30AM		☐Y ☐N
	6:00AM		☐Y ☐N
	6:30AM		☐Y ☐N
	7:00AM		☐Y ☐N
	7:30AM		☐Y ☐N
	8:00AM		☐Y ☐N
	8:30AM		☐Y ☐N
	9:00AM		☐Y ☐N
	9:30AM		☐Y ☐N
	10:00AM		☐Y ☐N
	10:30AM		☐Y ☐N
	11:00AM		☐Y ☐N
	11:30AM		☐Y ☐N
	12:00PM		☐Y ☐N
	12:30PM		☐Y ☐N
	1:00PM		☐Y ☐N
	1:30PM		☐Y ☐N
	2:00PM		☐Y ☐N
	2:30PM		☐Y ☐N
	3:00PM		☐Y ☐N
	3:30PM		☐Y ☐N
	4:00PM		☐Y ☐N
	4:30PM		☐Y ☐N
	5:00PM		☐Y ☐N
	5:30PM		☐Y ☐N
	6:00PM		☐Y ☐N
	6:30PM		☐Y ☐N
	7:00PM		☐Y ☐N
	7:30PM		☐Y ☐N
	8:00PM		☐Y ☐N
	8:30PM		☐Y ☐N
	9:00PM		☐Y ☐N
	9:30PM		☐Y ☐N

TAKE 5 MINUTES EACH MORNING TO PLAN YOUR DAY.

GET EIGHT HOURS OF SLEEP!

NOTE HIGH PRIORITY TASKS WITH A ✱

ANALYZE WHY A TASK WAS NOT COMPLETED, THEN MOVE TO NEXT DAY.

ONE POSITIVE

TODAY I GAVE

DAILY
GOAL SLAYERS
PLANNER

SETTING YOURSELF UP FOR SUCCESS DAILY!

DATE

_____ / _____ / _____

SCRIPTURE

MOTIVATIONAL QUOTE

ONE GOAL

ONE FUN THING

HEALTH • FITNESS

WATER INTAKE

*	IMPORTANT TIME	SCHEDULE	SLAYED?
	5:00AM		☐Y ☐N
	5:30AM		☐Y ☐N
	6:00AM		☐Y ☐N
	6:30AM		☐Y ☐N
	7:00AM		☐Y ☐N
	7:30AM		☐Y ☐N
	8:00AM		☐Y ☐N
	8:30AM		☐Y ☐N
	9:00AM		☐Y ☐N
	9:30AM		☐Y ☐N
	10:00AM		☐Y ☐N
	10:30AM		☐Y ☐N
	11:00AM		☐Y ☐N
	11:30AM		☐Y ☐N
	12:00PM		☐Y ☐N
	12:30PM		☐Y ☐N
	1:00PM		☐Y ☐N
	1:30PM		☐Y ☐N
	2:00PM		☐Y ☐N
	2:30PM		☐Y ☐N
	3:00PM		☐Y ☐N
	3:30PM		☐Y ☐N
	4:00PM		☐Y ☐N
	4:30PM		☐Y ☐N
	5:00PM		☐Y ☐N
	5:30PM		☐Y ☐N
	6:00PM		☐Y ☐N
	6:30PM		☐Y ☐N
	7:00PM		☐Y ☐N
	7:30PM		☐Y ☐N
	8:00PM		☐Y ☐N
	8:30PM		☐Y ☐N
	9:00PM		☐Y ☐N
	9:30PM		☐Y ☐N

TAKE 5 MINUTES EACH MORNING TO PLAN YOUR DAY.

GET EIGHT HOURS OF SLEEP!

NOTE HIGH PRIORITY TASKS WITH A *

ANALYZE WHY A TASK WAS NOT COMPLETED, THEN MOVE TO NEXT DAY.

ONE POSITIVE

TODAY I GAVE

DAILY
GOAL SLAYERS
PLANNER

SETTING YOURSELF UP FOR SUCCESS DAILY!

DATE

____/____/____

SCRIPTURE

MOTIVATIONAL QUOTE

ONE GOAL

ONE FUN THING

*	IMPORTANT TIME	SCHEDULE	SLAYED?
	5:00AM		☐Y ☐N
	5:30AM		☐Y ☐N
	6:00AM		☐Y ☐N
	6:30AM		☐Y ☐N
	7:00AM		☐Y ☐N
	7:30AM		☐Y ☐N
	8:00AM		☐Y ☐N
	8:30AM		☐Y ☐N
	9:00AM		☐Y ☐N
	9:30AM		☐Y ☐N
	10:00AM		☐Y ☐N
	10:30AM		☐Y ☐N
	11:00AM		☐Y ☐N
	11:30AM		☐Y ☐N
	12:00PM		☐Y ☐N
	12:30PM		☐Y ☐N
	1:00PM		☐Y ☐N
	1:30PM		☐Y ☐N
	2:00PM		☐Y ☐N
	2:30PM		☐Y ☐N
	3:00PM		☐Y ☐N
	3:30PM		☐Y ☐N
	4:00PM		☐Y ☐N
	4:30PM		☐Y ☐N
	5:00PM		☐Y ☐N
	5:30PM		☐Y ☐N
	6:00PM		☐Y ☐N
	6:30PM		☐Y ☐N
	7:00PM		☐Y ☐N
	7:30PM		☐Y ☐N
	8:00PM		☐Y ☐N
	8:30PM		☐Y ☐N
	9:00PM		☐Y ☐N
	9:30PM		☐Y ☐N

HEALTH • FITNESS

WATER INTAKE

OZ. OZ. OZ. OZ. OZ.

OZ. OZ. OZ. OZ. OZ.

TAKE 5 MINUTES EACH MORNING TO PLAN YOUR DAY.

GET EIGHT HOURS OF SLEEP!

NOTE HIGH PRIORITY TASKS WITH A *

ANALYZE WHY A TASK WAS NOT COMPLETED, THEN MOVE TO NEXT DAY.

ONE POSITIVE

TODAY I GAVE

DAILY
GOAL SLAYERS
PLANNER

SETTING YOURSELF UP FOR SUCCESS DAILY!

DATE

____ / ____ / ____

SCRIPTURE

MOTIVATIONAL QUOTE

ONE GOAL

ONE FUN THING

HEALTH • FITNESS

WATER INTAKE

| OZ. | OZ. | OZ. | OZ. | OZ. |
| OZ. | OZ. | OZ. | OZ. | OZ. |

*	IMPORTANT TIME	SCHEDULE	SLAYED?
	5:00AM		☐Y ☐N
	5:30AM		☐Y ☐N
	6:00AM		☐Y ☐N
	6:30AM		☐Y ☐N
	7:00AM		☐Y ☐N
	7:30AM		☐Y ☐N
	8:00AM		☐Y ☐N
	8:30AM		☐Y ☐N
	9:00AM		☐Y ☐N
	9:30AM		☐Y ☐N
	10:00AM		☐Y ☐N
	10:30AM		☐Y ☐N
	11:00AM		☐Y ☐N
	11:30AM		☐Y ☐N
	12:00PM		☐Y ☐N
	12:30PM		☐Y ☐N
	1:00PM		☐Y ☐N
	1:30PM		☐Y ☐N
	2:00PM		☐Y ☐N
	2:30PM		☐Y ☐N
	3:00PM		☐Y ☐N
	3:30PM		☐Y ☐N
	4:00PM		☐Y ☐N
	4:30PM		☐Y ☐N
	5:00PM		☐Y ☐N
	5:30PM		☐Y ☐N
	6:00PM		☐Y ☐N
	6:30PM		☐Y ☐N
	7:00PM		☐Y ☐N
	7:30PM		☐Y ☐N
	8:00PM		☐Y ☐N
	8:30PM		☐Y ☐N
	9:00PM		☐Y ☐N
	9:30PM		☐Y ☐N

TAKE 5 MINUTES EACH MORNING TO PLAN YOUR DAY.

GET EIGHT HOURS OF SLEEP!

NOTE HIGH PRIORITY TASKS WITH A *

ANALYZE WHY A TASK WAS NOT COMPLETED, THEN MOVE TO NEXT DAY.

ONE POSITIVE

TODAY I GAVE

DAILY
GOAL SLAYERS
PLANNER

SETTING YOURSELF UP FOR SUCCESS DAILY!

DATE

_____ / _____ / _____

SCRIPTURE

MOTIVATIONAL QUOTE

ONE GOAL

ONE FUN THING

HEALTH • FITNESS

WATER INTAKE

OZ. OZ. OZ. OZ. OZ.

OZ. OZ. OZ. OZ. OZ.

✱	IMPORTANT TIME	SCHEDULE	SLAYED?
	5:00AM		☐Y ☐N
	5:30AM		☐Y ☐N
	6:00AM		☐Y ☐N
	6:30AM		☐Y ☐N
	7:00AM		☐Y ☐N
	7:30AM		☐Y ☐N
	8:00AM		☐Y ☐N
	8:30AM		☐Y ☐N
	9:00AM		☐Y ☐N
	9:30AM		☐Y ☐N
	10:00AM		☐Y ☐N
	10:30AM		☐Y ☐N
	11:00AM		☐Y ☐N
	11:30AM		☐Y ☐N
	12:00PM		☐Y ☐N
	12:30PM		☐Y ☐N
	1:00PM		☐Y ☐N
	1:30PM		☐Y ☐N
	2:00PM		☐Y ☐N
	2:30PM		☐Y ☐N
	3:00PM		☐Y ☐N
	3:30PM		☐Y ☐N
	4:00PM		☐Y ☐N
	4:30PM		☐Y ☐N
	5:00PM		☐Y ☐N
	5:30PM		☐Y ☐N
	6:00PM		☐Y ☐N
	6:30PM		☐Y ☐N
	7:00PM		☐Y ☐N
	7:30PM		☐Y ☐N
	8:00PM		☐Y ☐N
	8:30PM		☐Y ☐N
	9:00PM		☐Y ☐N
	9:30PM		☐Y ☐N

TAKE 5 MINUTES EACH MORNING TO PLAN YOUR DAY.

GET EIGHT HOURS OF SLEEP!

NOTE HIGH PRIORITY TASKS WITH A ✱

ANALYZE WHY A TASK WAS NOT COMPLETED, THEN MOVE TO NEXT DAY.

ONE POSITIVE

TODAY I GAVE

DAILY
GOAL SLAYERS
PLANNER

SETTING YOURSELF UP FOR SUCCESS DAILY!

DATE

_____ / _____ / _____

SCRIPTURE

MOTIVATIONAL QUOTE

ONE GOAL

ONE FUN THING

HEALTH • FITNESS

WATER INTAKE

*	IMPORTANT TIME	SCHEDULE	SLAYED?
	5:00AM		☐Y ☐N
	5:30AM		☐Y ☐N
	6:00AM		☐Y ☐N
	6:30AM		☐Y ☐N
	7:00AM		☐Y ☐N
	7:30AM		☐Y ☐N
	8:00AM		☐Y ☐N
	8:30AM		☐Y ☐N
	9:00AM		☐Y ☐N
	9:30AM		☐Y ☐N
	10:00AM		☐Y ☐N
	10:30AM		☐Y ☐N
	11:00AM		☐Y ☐N
	11:30AM		☐Y ☐N
	12:00PM		☐Y ☐N
	12:30PM		☐Y ☐N
	1:00PM		☐Y ☐N
	1:30PM		☐Y ☐N
	2:00PM		☐Y ☐N
	2:30PM		☐Y ☐N
	3:00PM		☐Y ☐N
	3:30PM		☐Y ☐N
	4:00PM		☐Y ☐N
	4:30PM		☐Y ☐N
	5:00PM		☐Y ☐N
	5:30PM		☐Y ☐N
	6:00PM		☐Y ☐N
	6:30PM		☐Y ☐N
	7:00PM		☐Y ☐N
	7:30PM		☐Y ☐N
	8:00PM		☐Y ☐N
	8:30PM		☐Y ☐N
	9:00PM		☐Y ☐N
	9:30PM		☐Y ☐N

TAKE 5 MINUTES EACH MORNING TO PLAN YOUR DAY.

GET EIGHT HOURS OF SLEEP!

NOTE HIGH PRIORITY TASKS WITH A *

ANALYZE WHY A TASK WAS NOT COMPLETED, THEN MOVE TO NEXT DAY.

ONE POSITIVE

TODAY I GAVE

DAILY
GOAL SLAYERS
PLANNER

SETTING YOURSELF UP FOR SUCCESS DAILY!

DATE

_____/_____/_____

SCRIPTURE

MOTIVATIONAL QUOTE

ONE GOAL

ONE FUN THING

HEALTH + FITNESS

WATER INTAKE

*	IMPORTANT TIME	SCHEDULE	SLAYED?
	5:00AM		☐Y ☐N
	5:30AM		☐Y ☐N
	6:00AM		☐Y ☐N
	6:30AM		☐Y ☐N
	7:00AM		☐Y ☐N
	7:30AM		☐Y ☐N
	8:00AM		☐Y ☐N
	8:30AM		☐Y ☐N
	9:00AM		☐Y ☐N
	9:30AM		☐Y ☐N
	10:00AM		☐Y ☐N
	10:30AM		☐Y ☐N
	11:00AM		☐Y ☐N
	11:30AM		☐Y ☐N
	12:00PM		☐Y ☐N
	12:30PM		☐Y ☐N
	1:00PM		☐Y ☐N
	1:30PM		☐Y ☐N
	2:00PM		☐Y ☐N
	2:30PM		☐Y ☐N
	3:00PM		☐Y ☐N
	3:30PM		☐Y ☐N
	4:00PM		☐Y ☐N
	4:30PM		☐Y ☐N
	5:00PM		☐Y ☐N
	5:30PM		☐Y ☐N
	6:00PM		☐Y ☐N
	6:30PM		☐Y ☐N
	7:00PM		☐Y ☐N
	7:30PM		☐Y ☐N
	8:00PM		☐Y ☐N
	8:30PM		☐Y ☐N
	9:00PM		☐Y ☐N
	9:30PM		☐Y ☐N

OZ. OZ. OZ. OZ. OZ.
OZ. OZ. OZ. OZ. OZ.

TAKE 5 MINUTES EACH MORNING TO PLAN YOUR DAY.

GET EIGHT HOURS OF SLEEP!

NOTE HIGH PRIORITY TASKS WITH A *

ANALYZE WHY A TASK WAS NOT COMPLETED, THEN MOVE TO NEXT DAY.

ONE POSITIVE

TODAY I GAVE

DAILY
GOAL SLAYERS
PLANNER

SETTING YOURSELF UP FOR SUCCESS DAILY!

DATE

_____ / _____ / _____

SCRIPTURE

MOTIVATIONAL QUOTE

ONE GOAL

ONE FUN THING

HEALTH · FITNESS

WATER INTAKE

*	IMPORTANT TIME	SCHEDULE	SLAYED?
	5:00AM		☐Y ☐N
	5:30AM		☐Y ☐N
	6:00AM		☐Y ☐N
	6:30AM		☐Y ☐N
	7:00AM		☐Y ☐N
	7:30AM		☐Y ☐N
	8:00AM		☐Y ☐N
	8:30AM		☐Y ☐N
	9:00AM		☐Y ☐N
	9:30AM		☐Y ☐N
	10:00AM		☐Y ☐N
	10:30AM		☐Y ☐N
	11:00AM		☐Y ☐N
	11:30AM		☐Y ☐N
	12:00PM		☐Y ☐N
	12:30PM		☐Y ☐N
	1:00PM		☐Y ☐N
	1:30PM		☐Y ☐N
	2:00PM		☐Y ☐N
	2:30PM		☐Y ☐N
	3:00PM		☐Y ☐N
	3:30PM		☐Y ☐N
	4:00PM		☐Y ☐N
	4:30PM		☐Y ☐N
	5:00PM		☐Y ☐N
	5:30PM		☐Y ☐N
	6:00PM		☐Y ☐N
	6:30PM		☐Y ☐N
	7:00PM		☐Y ☐N
	7:30PM		☐Y ☐N
	8:00PM		☐Y ☐N
	8:30PM		☐Y ☐N
	9:00PM		☐Y ☐N
	9:30PM		☐Y ☐N

TAKE 5 MINUTES EACH MORNING TO PLAN YOUR DAY.

GET EIGHT HOURS OF SLEEP!

NOTE HIGH PRIORITY TASKS WITH A *

ANALYZE WHY A TASK WAS NOT COMPLETED, THEN MOVE TO NEXT DAY.

ONE POSITIVE

TODAY I GAVE

DAILY
GOAL SLAYERS
PLANNER

SETTING YOURSELF UP FOR SUCCESS DAILY!

DATE

_____ / _____ / _____

SCRIPTURE

MOTIVATIONAL QUOTE

ONE GOAL

ONE FUN THING

*	IMPORTANT TIME	SCHEDULE	SLAYED?
	5:00AM		☐Y ☐N
	5:30AM		☐Y ☐N
	6:00AM		☐Y ☐N
	6:30AM		☐Y ☐N
	7:00AM		☐Y ☐N
	7:30AM		☐Y ☐N
	8:00AM		☐Y ☐N
	8:30AM		☐Y ☐N
	9:00AM		☐Y ☐N
	9:30AM		☐Y ☐N
	10:00AM		☐Y ☐N
	10:30AM		☐Y ☐N
	11:00AM		☐Y ☐N
	11:30AM		☐Y ☐N
	12:00PM		☐Y ☐N
	12:30PM		☐Y ☐N
	1:00PM		☐Y ☐N
	1:30PM		☐Y ☐N
	2:00PM		☐Y ☐N
	2:30PM		☐Y ☐N
	3:00PM		☐Y ☐N
	3:30PM		☐Y ☐N
	4:00PM		☐Y ☐N
	4:30PM		☐Y ☐N
	5:00PM		☐Y ☐N
	5:30PM		☐Y ☐N
	6:00PM		☐Y ☐N
	6:30PM		☐Y ☐N
	7:00PM		☐Y ☐N
	7:30PM		☐Y ☐N
	8:00PM		☐Y ☐N
	8:30PM		☐Y ☐N
	9:00PM		☐Y ☐N
	9:30PM		☐Y ☐N

HEALTH + FITNESS

WATER INTAKE

OZ. OZ. OZ. OZ. OZ.

OZ. OZ. OZ. OZ. OZ.

TAKE 5 MINUTES EACH MORNING TO PLAN YOUR DAY.

GET EIGHT HOURS OF SLEEP!

NOTE HIGH PRIORITY TASKS WITH A *

ANALYZE WHY A TASK WAS NOT COMPLETED, THEN MOVE TO NEXT DAY.

ONE POSITIVE

TODAY I GAVE

DAILY
GOAL SLAYERS
PLANNER

SETTING YOURSELF UP FOR SUCCESS DAILY!

DATE

_____ / _____ / _____

SCRIPTURE

MOTIVATIONAL QUOTE

ONE GOAL

ONE FUN THING

HEALTH • FITNESS

WATER INTAKE

✱	IMPORTANT TIME	SCHEDULE	SLAYED?
	5:00AM		☐Y ☐N
	5:30AM		☐Y ☐N
	6:00AM		☐Y ☐N
	6:30AM		☐Y ☐N
	7:00AM		☐Y ☐N
	7:30AM		☐Y ☐N
	8:00AM		☐Y ☐N
	8:30AM		☐Y ☐N
	9:00AM		☐Y ☐N
	9:30AM		☐Y ☐N
	10:00AM		☐Y ☐N
	10:30AM		☐Y ☐N
	11:00AM		☐Y ☐N
	11:30AM		☐Y ☐N
	12:00PM		☐Y ☐N
	12:30PM		☐Y ☐N
	1:00PM		☐Y ☐N
	1:30PM		☐Y ☐N
	2:00PM		☐Y ☐N
	2:30PM		☐Y ☐N
	3:00PM		☐Y ☐N
	3:30PM		☐Y ☐N
	4:00PM		☐Y ☐N
	4:30PM		☐Y ☐N
	5:00PM		☐Y ☐N
	5:30PM		☐Y ☐N
	6:00PM		☐Y ☐N
	6:30PM		☐Y ☐N
	7:00PM		☐Y ☐N
	7:30PM		☐Y ☐N
	8:00PM		☐Y ☐N
	8:30PM		☐Y ☐N
	9:00PM		☐Y ☐N
	9:30PM		☐Y ☐N

TAKE 5 MINUTES EACH MORNING TO PLAN YOUR DAY.

GET EIGHT HOURS OF SLEEP!

NOTE HIGH PRIORITY TASKS WITH A ✱

ANALYZE WHY A TASK WAS NOT COMPLETED, THEN MOVE TO NEXT DAY.

ONE POSITIVE

TODAY I GAVE

DAILY
GOAL SLAYERS
PLANNER

SETTING YOURSELF UP FOR SUCCESS DAILY!

DATE

_____ / _____ / _____

SCRIPTURE

MOTIVATIONAL QUOTE

ONE GOAL

ONE FUN THING

✱	IMPORTANT TIME	SCHEDULE	SLAYED?
	5:00AM		☐Y ☐N
	5:30AM		☐Y ☐N
	6:00AM		☐Y ☐N
	6:30AM		☐Y ☐N
	7:00AM		☐Y ☐N
	7:30AM		☐Y ☐N
	8:00AM		☐Y ☐N
	8:30AM		☐Y ☐N
	9:00AM		☐Y ☐N
	9:30AM		☐Y ☐N
	10:00AM		☐Y ☐N
	10:30AM		☐Y ☐N
	11:00AM		☐Y ☐N
	11:30AM		☐Y ☐N
	12:00PM		☐Y ☐N
	12:30PM		☐Y ☐N
	1:00PM		☐Y ☐N
	1:30PM		☐Y ☐N
	2:00PM		☐Y ☐N
	2:30PM		☐Y ☐N
	3:00PM		☐Y ☐N
	3:30PM		☐Y ☐N
	4:00PM		☐Y ☐N
	4:30PM		☐Y ☐N
	5:00PM		☐Y ☐N
	5:30PM		☐Y ☐N
	6:00PM		☐Y ☐N
	6:30PM		☐Y ☐N
	7:00PM		☐Y ☐N
	7:30PM		☐Y ☐N
	8:00PM		☐Y ☐N
	8:30PM		☐Y ☐N
	9:00PM		☐Y ☐N
	9:30PM		☐Y ☐N

HEALTH + FITNESS

WATER INTAKE

OZ. OZ. OZ. OZ. OZ.

OZ. OZ. OZ. OZ. OZ.

TAKE 5 MINUTES EACH MORNING TO PLAN YOUR DAY.

GET EIGHT HOURS OF SLEEP!

NOTE HIGH PRIORITY TASKS WITH A ✱

ANALYZE WHY A TASK WAS NOT COMPLETED, THEN MOVE TO NEXT DAY.

ONE POSITIVE

TODAY I GAVE

Made in the USA
Monee, IL
12 December 2021